Decolonial Communism, Democracy & the Commons

Decolonial Communism, Democracy & the Commons

Edited by
CATHERINE SAMARY & FRED LEPLAT

Resistance Books
IIRE
MERLIN PRESS

First published in 2019 by
The Merlin Press
Central Books Building
Freshwater Road
Dagenham
RM8 1RX
www.merlinpress.co.uk

Published in association with Resistance Books (www.resistancebooks.org)
and the International Institute for Research and Education (www.iire.org)

© this collection Merlin Press, Resistance Books and the IIRE, 2019

ISBN. 978-0-85036-747-8

Decolonial Communism, Democracy and the Commons
is issue number 62 of IIRE Notebooks for Study and Research

A CIP record of this book is available from The British Library

Printed in the UK by Imprint Digital, Exeter

Contents

Author's note	x
Introduction, *Catherine Samary*	1

GENERAL OUTLOOK 13

October 1917-2017: From a decolonial communism to the democracy of the commons, *Catherine Samary*	15
From the October Revolution to Stalinisation	18
Pursuit of the permanent revolution after Stalin	28
From the 'great debate' in Cuba to a self-managed system	37
Towards a 'society of the commons'?	45
Bibliography	53

THE YUGOSLAV EXPERIENCE 61

Yugoslavia since the revolution: a few key dates	63
Yugoslav self-management: a balance sheet, *Catherine Samary*	66
Socialism and humanism, *Zagorka Pešić-Golubović*	85
The June student movement and social revolution in Yugoslavia, *Svetozar Stojanović*	96
From post-revolutionary dictatorship to socialist democracy, *Svetozar Stojanović*	106
Workers' councils in Yugoslavia: successes and failures, *Goran Marković*	131
Historical background of the creation of workers' councils	131
Legal solutions	134
Workers' councils and reforms of the system	137
Successes	139
Failures	143
Conclusions	144

OTHER POST-CAPITALIST EXPERIENCES   151

Plan, Market and Democracy: the experience of the so-called
socialist countries, *Catherine Samary*   153

    Introduction: theoretical, political and
methodological questions   153

    Social relations and the plan   167

    Yugoslav 'market socialism' with self-management   169

    Updating the Soviet debate on the 'law of value'   176

    Conclusion   191

    Bibliography   203

The law of value in relation to self-management and investment
in the economy of the workers states, *Ernest Mandel*   206

Building socialism in Cuba, *Samuel Farber*   218

SUMMING UP AND FURTHER DEBATES   229

Chile and Portugal in the 1970s: the left, nationalisations
and 'workers' control' in the revolutionary processes,
Franck Gaudichaud & Raquel Varela   231

    Introduction   231

    The debate about 'workers' control', nationalisations
and 'people's power'   234

    Chile 1970-1973: Allende's government
and the nationalisations   239

    Portugal 1974-1975: nationalisations against workers' control   243

    Co-administration and 'battle for production' versus
cordones industriales and people's power?   245

    The struggle for political power: workers' control
in the Portuguese Revolution   251

    Conclusions   258

Latin America: state, popular power and class struggle,
Franck Gaudichaud   262

Eastern Europe: revisiting the ambiguous revolutions of 1989,
Catherine Samary   279

    Ideological bias of Cold War concepts   280

    Democratic revolutions or opaque 'refolutions'?   289

'Transition to democracy'? The German symbol:
what about 'Ostalgia'? ... 298

The repressed 'third way' ... 301

From the Prague Autumn of workers councils (1968)
to the Velvet Revolution (1989): continuity or antipodes? ... 306

The struggles for the commons in the Balkans,
The Balkan Forum Commons Working Group ... 310

   Concepts, history and evolution ... 310

   A radical critical conception of the commons ... 313

   Balkans as the European periphery ... 314

   Existing commons struggles in the Balkans ... 317

   Commoning the struggle ... 323

   Bibliography ... 326

Feminism and the politics of the Commons, *Silvia Federici* ... 328

EPILOGUE ... 339

Decolonial communism: Analytical, political and
democratic dimensions, *Catherine Samary* ... 341

About the Authors ... 348

Notes ... 351

About Resistance Books and the IIRE ... 385

Acknowledgements

The editors would like to thank Bernard Gibbons and Bill McKeith for translating and 'knocking into shape' much of this book. We would also like to thank Tony and Adrian at Merlin Press for their patience and advice. Finally, we would like to thank all those who have allowed us to republish their work in this book.

Dedication

This book is dedicated to Marielle Franco, a black, LGBT, feminist member of the PSOL (Party of Socialism and Liberty) in Brazil and a city councillor in Rio de Janeiro. She was assassinated on the 14 March 2018. Marielle was killed because she symbolised the collective struggle for human rights against all violence, inequality, and intersectional discriminations (of class, gender, race and homophobia), and for a concrete 'pluriversalism', which is essential for a 'decolonial communism' that has yet to be constructed.

It is also dedicated to Sonja, Rada, Predrag, Faïk, Rastko, Maja, Marko, Darko and to so many other 'ex' who have been dispossessed of a country, of a history, and of the Yugoslav system whose richness should not be buried. I thank you for having helped me feel it, understand it, and defend it against all its internal and external predators and any fatalism of failure. Moreover, thank you for having helped me 'commonise' what can be learnt from its progressive character and from its failures.

To my comrades of the Fourth International who have helped me detect the connections between the multitudes of resistances against the system we are fighting. Thank you for having maintained, against the current, a critical analysis that incorporates what we have learnt from what is 'ours' and from 'others', and for building a pluralist 'collective intellectual' working towards its own transcendence. Thank you for being open to the 'unforeseen' events of history, as was the case of the Yugoslav Revolution with its experience of self-management, and for having encouraged me to study this experience.

And to Hubert, at a political and personal level, for the major role you played in my discovery of the Fourth International. Thank you for having encouraged and helped me to get involved and study the Yugoslav experience – and to endure the consequences of this commitment to this day.

Catherine Samary

Author's note

The concept of 'decolonialism' that I use in this book does not come from those used by decolonial studies of Latin-American origin or those focused on migration. However, I fully share a decolonial approach, that is, analysing and fighting against any form or remnant of (neo)colonialism within former or present dependent and/or dominant countries and in their international relations an anti-imperialist Marxist framework. I use the term 'decolonial communism' to describe a non-linear process of understanding and resistance to the existing relations of dominations as articulated at the national and world level, and which raises not only socio-economic and political issues but also complex cultural and epistemic ones. This includes rejecting the idea that socialist and communist currents in the (semi)-periphery of the capitalist world-system should wait for socio-economic preconditions and for models of development from more 'developed' countries.

In this book, I stress the 'decolonial' features and orientations of the Russian Revolution which are also to be found in the Yugoslav Revolution. Both Revolutions occurred in the periphery of Europe, and both are organically linked to all the other decolonial revolutions of the 20th century. They changed the extent and the control of the capitalist world-system up to the 1980s, in spite of their bureaucratic features and the socio-political confrontations within the Communist movement. Dependant and world-system theories, like those of the non-aligned movements or of post-colonial and decolonial studies (whether or not they are Marxist), are all confronted with the ambivalent legacy of these revolutions and with the post-1989 globalized capitalist system.

My aim with this book is to contribute a decolonial communist interpretation of this past and an analysis of the challenges we face today. This decolonial communism needs to be rooted in all the struggles against relations of domination and to be open to criticism from all those who are oppressed, ignored and discriminated. This is the thread of the book.

Catherine Samary, November 2018

Introduction*

Catherine Samary

I've always treated neoliberalism as a political project carried out by the corporate capitalist class as they felt intensely threatened both politically and economically towards the end of the 1960s into the 1970s. They desperately wanted to launch a political project that would curb the power of labour. In many respects the project was a counterrevolutionary project.
David Harvey[1]

'Starting again from the middle'

The so-called neoliberal turn had many aspects including, as David Harvey puts it, 'counter-revolutionary' traits, and organising multiple 'dispossessions' and destructions of collective gains from the past that challenged the domination of commodity relations. To identify fully what is at stake, it is useful to 'start again from the middle', as Daniel Bensaïd used to say. The middle was the major, multidimensional crisis of the world order in the 1960s and 1970s. This book, which is around the theme of 'a decolonial communism and towards a democracy of the commons', finds its centre of gravity in this period which is seen through the prism of struggles and debates on the construction of socialism during the 'Soviet century',[2] but concentrates on that which is largely ignored.

Against the backdrop of deepening inequalities with the introduction of 'market socialism' in the mid-1960s, worker and student strikes spread in Yugoslavia to protest at the failure to respect socialist values and self-management rights. An autonomous movement of students culminated in June 1968 in the occupation of universities. It demanded 'self-management from below' and egalitarian measures, and displayed portraits of Che Guevara in the universities while denouncing the US intervention in Vietnam and debating the French May 1968.

The Yugoslav cauldron of 1968 was largely ignored around a world[3]

---

*   This 'Introduction' was translated by Bernard Gibbons and Bill McKeith.

smouldering in the shadow of two much more 'visible' dynamics. These had more weight at the international level and concerned 'actually existing socialism': the Chinese Cultural Revolution[4] on one hand, and the Prague 'Spring' on the other. The latter rallied young people throughout the 'Soviet camp' and well beyond for a 'socialism with a human face'. Its democratic dynamic was engulfed in the contradictions of the technocratic market reforms advocated from the USSR to Czechoslovakia since the first half of the 1960s. This book's chapter 'From decolonial communism to the democracy of the commons' presents what was the 'great debate' in Cuba at the beginning of the decade, between Charles Bettelheim, Che Guevara and Ernest Mandel about market stimulant versus moral or non-market stimulant.[5] In the same period, from Poland to Hungary via the German Democratic Republic, other Marxist analyses emanating from the countries of 'actually existing socialism' without the experience of self-management, were better known within far left circles than the Yugoslav debates.[6] The Prague Spring of 1968 is better known than the autumn of 1968 with its workers councils opposing Soviet tanks with the support of the trade unions and the self-management wing of the Czechoslovak Communist Party.

The democratic scope of these debates and movements did not stop at the doors of the workplace. It expressed the subversive search for a socialist political economy, based on the rights of the population (in all its diversity) to manage it, and allowing a democratic social appropriation of the big choices facing society. We would find an ultimate expression of this in the 'self-managed republic of Poland' emanating from the Solidarnosć trade union in the early 1980s.[7] Repressed or channelled by the parties ruling in the name of these workers and populations, such aspirations were to be eradicated by generalised privatisation[8] and capitalist market competition. This book aims to establish some bridges between these past aspirations, debates and struggles, and those of today that are going in the same direction and which seek to build 'another world that is possible'.

From self-management to the commons: with what 'powers' and social status?

Nobody knows if words which became unintelligible with the bureaucratic degeneration of revolutions will be re-appropriated and redefined, or if they will be replaced by others. Nor do we know if these new words will place at the centre of our objectives everything which a century of setbacks now makes us value: 'wellbeing', democratic practices which are respectful of egalitarian rights, opposition to all relations of domination and support for defence of the environment. The appropriation of 'the commons' will be perhaps the way of reformulating the debates on self-management – but that is why we wish to stress in what ways the experiences and debates respectively associated with each of these notions are possible mutual enrichments. Yet no word to describe the struggles for emancipation is destined to have one single meaning and to be protected from conflicting orientations on the ground. That is even the case for 'workers (or social) control'.[9]

Such risks become even greater when, while being against the stream in a context dominated by the logic of competition for profit, one aspires to illustrate other ways of organising the production of goods, services or territory, by taking responsibility for management of production supposedly based on solidarity and not the search for profit. However, such attempts at self-management or cooperatives in a hostile context are important to embody hope and stimulate imagination and resistance, providing that they do not remain isolated and/or rapidly emptied of their initial radical potential. Nevertheless, such projects for the management of the commons can, knowingly or not, facilitate the destruction of public services. That is why we specify in what sense and context we wish to carry out the debates on the commons, as Silvia Federici[10] or David Harvey[11] have done.

Globally, we support approaches which stress that no good can be 'by nature' protected from the privatisation or statisation dilemma: it is a question of choice. What is important is not the 'nature' of the good but the social relation which is connected with the good(s) in question. A good only becomes 'common' when the persons concerned establish themselves the rules and criteria that they will apply – with the possibility of modifying them in practice. Even if this approach is often presented as a third way between privatisation and statism (and even if it is true that this is in part what is interesting), we adopt an open approach as to the goods and forms of ownership which can be the subject of 'putting in common' (well expressed in English by 'commonising' as a process) rights and rules. As has often been stressed (in particular by David Harvey), the criteria adequate for the management of a 'local' common (a health clinic, a factory that has been taken over, a municipality and so on) are not the same if these goods become a component of a bigger set of rights which have to be rendered egalitarian and coherent. The adequate overall scale, whether it is local, national or indeed supranational, depends on the political context: what persons, what populations are ready to link up in a common project? We must resist sexist or homophobic behaviour and xenophobic logics which can seek to impose the exclusion of 'the Other' who is not a 'real' citizen, from the process of commonising, because of his/her ethnicity, religion, or country of origin.

Globally, experiences which are opposed to the criteria of capitalist management must sooner or later face, at a territorial scale which is first local then rapidly national, and indeed regional and international, the need for another 'power' of coherent decision-making at this scale. This raises the issues of relationship of forces and who decides the 'rules' and constitutional rights – what new 'power' needs to be built out of the new forms of self-organisation of the struggles? An increasing amount of scattered experiences is linked to this process of 'communising' knowledge, goods, and services, against dominant criteria.[12] The Zapatistas were, in the mid-1990s, the first to forcefully express the global and multidimensional character of their struggle, confronting simultaneously the dominant forces and logics in Mexico, in NAFTA (the North American Free Trade Agreement) and in globalised competition. From this they have drawn conclusions which are still relevant in their 'intergalactic' approach, and which have been developed further by the movement for global justice against a globalised capitalism. But the global justice movement has been confronted with strategic issues – shared up to now by all emancipatory movements.

In the critique and rejection of the statist and bureaucratic experience derived from the socialism of the 20th century, given the worsened relationship of forces, the dominant problematic was first the wish 'to change the world without taking power',[13] or to 'fissure' capitalism.[14] Without expecting comprehensive responses to strategic questions, networks of a great richness were deployed challenging the social and environmental destruction of a capitalism which penetrates all spheres of daily life and organises its decision-making power from the local to the planetary level.

Alternatives seek to create and mutually enrich one another: from free software to the networks of the 'rebel cities';[15] from the self-managed territories of Chiapas to the communalism inspired by Murray Bookchin[16] and the Commune of Rojava. Faced with the aggravation of the globalised social war, we have also seen the rebirth of the hope that progressive governments can re-appropriate power at the national scale and modify the situation. But the interpenetration, at least regional or continental, indeed global, of the big socio-economic, political and ecological issues, without in any way invalidating the need for national anchorages, obliges transnational responses and alliances. It also forces thinking and actions which articulate socio-economic and democratic rights with the self-determination of each people and which also redefine the nature of states and multinational spaces. It is at the international scale that a new architecture of fundamental rights is being sought which encompasses environmental justice and the big movements of emancipation, feminism, antiracism, and anti-colonialism.

Parallel to this, from Greece to Latin America there has been disillusionment and questioning on the respective role (or recomposition) of parties, social movements, and self-organisation. 'Politics', which does not only belong to parties,[17] enriches itself from the autonomous expression, individual and collective, of multiple struggles for equality and dignity. The new precariat or 'independent workers', dragooned at will, create cooperative movements[18] to protect themselves from this 19th century form of capitalism. Via Campesina[19] has become, with the World Women's March, the motor for international, multidimensional campaigns. The 'actors', male and female, of the social transformation are no longer without 'gender', without cultures, without roots, and (happily) no longer accept that others should speak for them. The 'proletariat' which has nothing to lose but its chains, and which Marx thought could defend the humanity of all the oppressed, cannot only be white, heterosexual, and employed in the big factories. Universalism can only be built on the multiplicity of struggles and pathways of the subaltern peoples towards a 'pluriversalism'. This will be against all intersecting oppressions and discriminations and against all barbaric violence of this globalised system, and also against those who claim to fight it, on racist and sexist lines, without challenging privilege and war.

From decolonial communism ...

I use here the term decolonial, sharing how it is used in decolonial studies (which can include a diversity of viewpoints), the idea that it is necessary to fight not only open colonialism but all the enduring traces of 'coloniality'[20] in the long term,[21] and in multiple domains – cultural, linguistic, socio-economic or military – in the dominant countries as well as in the former colonies.[22] The 'decolonial' position includes awareness that the relations of domination can involuntarily mark political or intellectual relations – including those identifying with Marxism. But we should distinguish organic coloniality (as a racist ideology legitimating international and national relationships of domination) from a cognitive fault. This fault can be overcome and can affect any research lacking a globalised space of elaboration allowing the intersection of viewpoints and rectification of major omissions. It is a cognitive and political issue. The recognition of such cognitive (collective and/or personal) faults means an explicit research of 'intersecting views' on an egalitarian basis, promoting the self-organisation of collective research, and taking into account material and social inequalities (languages, cultures, gender, means of publications). It should also include all efforts to build 'spaces' aimed at facilitating the exchanges of views on an equal cultural footing (including gender dimensions).

This is of course to be applied to Marxist approaches. As Kevin B.

Anderson has shown and as underlined by Glen Sean Coulthard,[23] Marx undertook a real decentring which can, albeit the term was not yet coined, be characterised as 'decolonial' in relation to the western-centric bias detectable in certain passages of the *Communist Manifesto,* which stressed the 'civilising' aspects of capitalist colonial expansion.[24] Because he was convinced (in contrast to 'utopian' schemas) that 'the emancipation of the workers will be the task of the workers themselves', it was uprisings in Ireland and India, and those of black people against slavery in the US, which made him evolve his thinking. Marx's discussions with Vera Zasulich on the peasant question in the Russian semi-periphery show that other subaltern social forces and their forms of self-organisation could capture his attention and reflection. He was far from an 'orthodoxy' attributed to him, claiming that only the working class is revolutionary and that the developed West 'showed the way' for development and emancipation.

After Marx came the possibility of analyses of new waves of (neo) colonisation. In the new world capitalist context, the drive for (neo) colonisation, for the powers of the industrialised 'centre' such as Britain, was a response to their crises of over-accumulation of capital or of overproduction of commodities which lay behind their conflicts over the division of the world. The 'international division of labour' inserted commercial relations in the globalised capitalist relations of production and domination. This was developed by Ricardo to respond to the crisis of profit in Britain and imposed on the dominated countries in the form of pseudo 'free' trade. The combination of capitalist industrial revolution and colonial relations was to deepen the 'development of under-development' and global inequalities like never before. This does not however in any way mean that pre-capitalist colonialism and the pillage of the Iberian powers were 'less serious' or less violent than the relations of domination inflicted by the British industrial power throughout its empire.

Marxist analyses of imperialism[25] have allowed a major political and analytical shift. At the analytical level, they generally imply approaching capitalism as a globalised system of relations of domination. The historic and concrete approach, combining economic and political dimensions, was strengthened by the possibility of long-term analyses, and of highlighting the structural crises of the system, without automatic, purely economic or technical conditions of exits from such crises.[26] Furthermore, the analyses evoked above of the 'uneven and combined development' of different 'social formations' dominated by capitalism permitted the highlighting of characteristics inherited from various phases and different modes of production. These analyses also allowed the countering of abstract economism, of a linear vision of 'development' on the model of the first industrial powers. But it was in the context of the First World War – analysed as inter-imperialist by some Marxists – and then under the dynamic of the Russian Revolution that the 'political' dimension of a 'decolonial' communism was to become concrete. It was, like any political and intellectual approach, not a homogeneous process and it was liable to advances and retreats that should be analysed concretely.

The decolonial approach is deeply present in the orientation advocated by Lenin, explicitly anti-colonial and anti-racist, in the highlighting of dominated and dominant nations of the Tsarist Empire, as opposed to an abstract (supposed proletarian) 'universalism', and in his different struggles against the 'Great Russian' heritage which left its marks in the behaviour of too many Bolsheviks.[27] Language policy, cancellation of the debts of colonised countries, recognition of the right to self-determination of dominated nations were concrete examples of this. There were many disagreements and conceptions that were not clarified, notably on the manner in which the national question is entwined with social and political issues. Genuine political dilemmas emerged, like the Brest-Litovsk treaty which was to profoundly divide Bolsheviks and their allies.

But the general orientation was there. It was concretised in the creation of a Third International (the Communist International/CI or Comintern), expressing a line of major rupture inside Marxism, against the line of many social democratic parties of the Second International, on the imperialist war and its ideology. This theoretical practical engagement against colonialism was at the heart of the organisation of the 1920 Congress of the Peoples of the East in Baku, encouraging anti-colonial revolutions,[28] notably in China. It was also strongly expressed by the 21 conditions of membership of the CI which required that the CPs of the western world denounce colonialist policies and the racism which accompanied them. The Marxism which inspired them had begun to 'deprovincialise Europe' (western and imperialist) and to recognise the global scope of the revolutionary uprisings against the Tsarist Empire, in a Euro-Asiatic 'semi-periphery'.

... to world-systems,[29] before and after 1989

The dominant ideology and vocabulary evoke 'Europe' when what is meant is the power of Western Europe, or more recently of the European Union (EU), in the same way that the United States has claimed to be America. The 'uncivilised' who disappear from these narratives have obviously been first and foremost the non-white racialised people subject to slavery and then neo-colonised. But the weak links of the imperialist chain were broken first through the First World War, on a European continent where the major issue for the 'core countries' was the dismantling of the big empires (Austro-Hungarian, Ottoman and Tsarist). In what remained under the control of capitalist Europe, the subaltern and the 'uncivilised' were also the populations of the Eastern European 'semi-peripheries'. These populations were implicated in various ways from the Yugoslav Revolution to the initial direct domination of the USSR over the 'buffer zone' which was recognised at Yalta. But there was no doubt for them that it amounted to a rupture with the capitalist 'world-system' and its character of 'civilisation'. This rupture occurred whether it was perceived positively or negatively when communism was associated with the fight against Nazism, or for radical and progressive social transformations with all the variants open to aspirations for 'socialism with a human face'.

We are not interested here in wearisome 'semantic' debates. The analysis proposed in this book of the contradictions of the system identified with socialism puts a concrete stress on their 'impurities'. But our conviction is that they are the 'rule' of any logic of rupture with capitalism: bureaucratism and relations of domination (with their 'intersectionality') do not disappear with the challenging of the domination of capital.

But we must also realise at what point during the 'Soviet century' the reality of two conflictual systems, with their own mechanisms and relations of domination, has radically modified the relationship of forces – in an exceptional manner – both in an 'impure' way at the heart of the countries of the capitalist centre, and in the semi-peripheries. This has been highlighted by the deterioration of the relationship of forces after 1989 which occurred in difficult conditions. For the first time, the capitalist world-system has effectively become planetary and 'global' in many of its mechanisms of functioning – including the transnational organisation of 'value chains' and of the process of distribution. And instead of the illusion of capitalist development leading to reduced inequalities and more democratic and social rights, we are confronted by the opposite. Even technological transformations and increases in productivity, which could permit the reduction of labour time and of the most arduous work, are turned against human rights, worsening conditions of work and unemployment.

The world is now confronted with an extremely complex and unstable recomposition. The transformations of the 'Soviet century' leave multiple traces, with radical dispossessions and marketisation affecting the subaltern classes at the level of the whole planet. Global relations of domination continue to exist, but the imperialist and neo-colonial modalities of domination have become differentiated in wars and rivalries of highly different appearances.

There is a 'South' in the 'North' and a 'North' in the 'South', as well as different ways for the former countries of the 'world system' identifying with socialism to insert themselves within capitalist globalisation. The military-industrial complexes of China and Russia, which allowed these countries to have significant weight at the court of the Great Powers, are a heritage and transformation of the former bureaucratic and anti-capitalist 'world-system' of the 'short 20th century'. But none of these new capitalist powers offers a progressive alternative to the populations they exploit – and thus to those of the whole world. They have, on the contrary, contributed to the universal dismantling of social gains won in the previous century and to the generalised competition within the labour force, combined with increasing xenophobia. It is necessary to continue to track the neo-colonial relations of domination (in the behaviour of the leading bodies of the EU towards the Greek people, for example[30]), challenging the destructive competition between subaltern classes, which undermines their potential for transnational alliances. The neoliberal destruction began at the 'centre'. Racism and xenophobia divide and rule on the basis of destructive capitalist exploitation and discriminations, whether 'national-neoliberal' or multinational, using 'civilised war' against terrorism to spread Islamophobia and destroy liberties.

Finally, the reality, although opaque, of a past confrontation between two systems was also manifest at their 'margins'. This is why, while very much sharing the criticisms formulated by Peter Worsley[31] of Wallerstein's approach, which places the countries of 'actually existing socialism' inside the capitalist world system, I do not think that we should speak of this 'Soviet century' as being of 'Three world systems'. Titoist Yugoslavia could not, inside an eclectic movement of the 'non-aligned', make a coherent 'third way' emerge (which Worsley recognises despite speaking of 'three worlds'). Radically egalitarian self-managed relations could only become consistently anti-capitalist if they were at the heart of a real socialist system,[32] not in an isolated country, which is where this battle was waged – and lost. But we can learn from it. That is why, despite all attempts to bury such a unique experience, we put its study at the heart of our contribution.

Bibliography

Anderson K. B., *Marx at the Margins, on nationalism, ethnicity and non-Western Societies,* Chicago: Chicago University Press, 2010, <http://abahlali.org/files/Anderson%20-%20Marx%20at%20the%20Margins.pdf>
David Bollier and Silke Helfrich, *Wealth of the Commons: A World Beyond Market and State,* Amherst, Mass.: Levellers Press, 2012.
Bahro R., *The Alternative in Eastern Europe,* London: Verso, 2017.

Biehl J., 'Bookchin Breaks with Anarchism', *Communalism*, no.12, 2007, <https://theanarchistlibrary.org/library/janet-biehl-bookchin-breaks-with-anarchism>
Bookchin M., *The Third Revolution: Popular Movements in the Revolutionary Era*, London/New York: Cassell and Bloomsbury, 1996.
Bookchin M., *Social Ecology and Communalism*, Chico California: AK Press, 2004.
Bouamama S., *La Tricontinentale. Les peuples du tiers-monde à l'assaut du ciel*. Genève/Paris; Ed du Cetim/Syllepse, 2016.
Commons websites: <https://www.stirtoaction.com/issues/issue-21 and http://patternsofcommoning.org/>
Harvey D., *A brief history of Neoliberalism*, Oxford: Oxford University Press, 2007.
Harvey D., interview 'Neoliberalism is a political project', *Jacobin*, 23 July 2016, <https://www.jacobinmag.com/2016/07/david-harvey-neoliberalism-capitalism-labor-crisis-resistance>
Harvey D., 'The future of the Commons', *Radical History Review*, issue 109, winter 2011.
Fanon F., *Black Skin, White Masks*, New York: Grove Press, 1967.
Farber S. 'Building Socialism in Cuba', *Jacobin*, 10 December 2016. <https://www.jacobinmag.com/2016/10/alternative-cuba-socialism-left-opposition-worker-control>
Federici S., 'Feminism and the Politics of Commons', *The Commoner*, 2011, <http://www.thecommoner.org/>
Gaudichaud F., 'Amérique Latine, Etat, pouvoir populaire et luttes sociales', *Contretemps*, 25 April 2015, <https://www.contretemps.eu/amerique-latine-etat-pouvoir-populaire-et-luttes-sociales-22/>
Grosfoguel R., 'Vers une décolonisation des 'uni-versalismes' occidentaux: le 'pluri-versalisme décolonial', d'Aimé Césaire aux zapatistes', in *Ruptures Postcoloniales*, Paris: La Découverte, 2010.
Haraszti M., *A Worker in a Worker-State. Piece-Rates in Hungary*, London: Pelican Books/Penguin, 1977.
Holloway J., *Change the World Without Taking Power: The Meaning of Revolution Today*, London: Pluto Press, 2010.
Holloway J., *Crack Capitalism*, London: Pluto Press, 2010.
Hurtado López F., 'Universalisme ou pluriversalisme? Les apports de la philosophie latino-américaine', in *Tumultes,* no. 48, 2017/1, < https://www.cairn.info/revue-tumultes-2017-1.htm>.
Katz C., *Bajo el Imperio del Capital,* Buenos Aires: Ed. Luxemburg, 2011.
Kowalevski Z., *Rendez nous nos usines: Solidarność dans le combat pour l'autogestion ouvrière*, Paris: La Brèche, 1985.
Kuron J. & Modzelevski K., 'Open Letter to the Polish Workers Party'*, New Politics,* Spring 1966, pp. 5-46, <http://www.unz.org/Pub/NewPolitics-1966q2-00005>.
Lebowitz M., *Beyond Capital: Marx's Political Economy of the Working Class*, Palgrave Macmillan, 2003.
Lewin M., *The Soviet Century*, London: Verso, 2016.
Mandel E., *Long waves of capitalist development, a Marxist interpretation*, London: Verso, 1995.
Goran Marković, 'Workers' Councils in Yugoslavia: Successes and Failures', *Socialism and Democracy Online*, 29 December 2012, <http://sdonline.org/57/workers-councils-in-yugoslavia-successes-and-failures/>.
Renault M., *L'Empire de la Révolution: Lénine et les musulmans de l'empire russe*, Paris: Syllepse, 2017.
Samary C., 'The social stakes of the great transformation in Eastern Europe', *Debatte*, vol. 17, 2009, <https://www.tandfonline.com/doi/abs/10.1080/09651560902778345>
Samary C., 'Europe: No 'LEXIT' without 'Another Europe Possible' – based on struggles in/outside/against the EU, CADTM, 22 September 2016, <http://www.cadtm.org/Europe-

No-LEXIT-without-Another>
Saïd E., *Orientalism,* New York: Pantheon Books, 1978.
Sean Coulthard G., *Red Skin, White Masks*, Mineapolis: University of Minnesota Press, 2018
Scholz T., *Platform cooperativism: challenging the corporate sharing economy*, New York: Rosa Luxemburg Stiftung, 2016, <http://www.rosalux-nyc.org/wp-content/files_mf/scholz_platformcoop_5.9.2016.pdf>
Trotsky L., *The Permanent Revolution*, London: Resistance Books, 2011, and <http://www.marxists.org/archives/trotsky/index.htm>
Uhl P., *Le Socialisme Emprisonné*, Paris: Stock2/la Brèche, 1980.
Via Campesina, <https://viacampesina.org/en/who-are-we/>
Wallerstein I., 'The Itinerary of World-system Analysis: How to resist becoming a Theory', in *New Directions in Contemporary Socialogical Theory*, J. Berger & M. Zelditch (eds.) New York: Rowman and Littlefield, 2002, <https://www.iwallerstein.com/wp-content/uploads/docs/THEORY.pdf>
Worsley P., 'One or three: A Critique of the World-System of Immanuel Wallerstein', *Socialist Register*, 1980, <http://www.socialistregister.com/index.php/srv/article/view/5456>

GENERAL OUTLOOK

October 1917-2017: From a decolonial communism to the democracy of the commons*

The 'Soviet century' in the turmoil of the 'permanent revolution'

Catherine Samary

> *But when it comes to the nature of the thousand concrete, practical measures, large and small, necessary to introduce socialist principles into economy, law and all social relationships, there is no key in any socialist party program or textbook ... Only experience is capable of correcting and opening new ways. Only unobstructed, effervescing life falls into a thousand new forms and improvisations, brings to light creative new force, itself corrects all mistaken attempts.*
> Rosa Luxemburg, The Russian Revolution, 1918.

We no longer live in the 'Soviet century'[33] and we can witness various forms of organisation that transcend those of the workers' movement anchored in that era. Yet, as the political polarisations and crisis of civilisation (ecological, socio-economic, political) associated with globalised capitalism unfold, the 'classic' strategic questions of the 20th century – reformulated in complex fashion under radically new conditions – confront all who remain convinced of the urgent need to 'change this world'.[34] 'Pure capitalism' in the 21st century,[35] based on globalised firms and institutions, both financial and military, tends to revert to the 19th century, viewing all the movements of resistance in what Eric Hobsbawn called the 'short 20th century' as simply aberrant interludes, reducing those revolutions which wanted to change the world to the creation of the gulag. Capitalism's social war is accompanied by ideological operations worthy of George Orwell's formulation (in a work which should have been called 1989!): 'He who controls the present controls

* This 'General Outlook' was translated by Bill McKeith.

the past. He who controls the past, controls the future.'

It is not possible to resist this without carrying out a plural and systematic inventory of the advances, setbacks and defeats of the 'permanent revolution' in the 'Soviet century' – around key issues which are still current and deepening the democratic and egalitarian dimensions of a decolonial communism born in October 1917.[36]

Putting the task of inventory in perspective

The new social and geopolitical era opened by the so-called 'neoliberal' turn of the 1980s is that of a radicalised and globalised social war, and of new overt 'wars of civilisation' since the events of 1989/1991. Its starting point was a class response, within a 'neoliberal' ideology, to the profound challenge to the 'capitalist world system'[37] which marked the 1960s and 1970s. This was experienced by the ruling elites as the internal/external threat of 'communism' – as can be seen in the secret police reports on the Conference of Solidarity with the Peoples of Asia, Africa and Latin America, 'the Tricontinental' conference, held in Havana in 1966.[38] This threat, beginning from the events of October 1917, was uninterrupted despite the bureaucratisation of the soviets and the totalitarian Stalinisation of the USSR, and despite the behaviour of this new 'great power' seeking to subordinate the Communist Parties (CPs) of the world to its diplomacy, in the worst of ideological interferences.

We must then return to the 'impure' scenario (in relation to Trotsky's predictions in particular) of the Second World War, of the new revolutions that were engulfed in a structural crisis of capitalism marked by the rise of fascism and of the revolutionary ruptures at the heart of two world wars and in the post-Stalinist phase of the 'Soviet century'.[39] There were various forms of 'defeating communism in its victory'[40] – preventing socialist transformations by the bureaucratism and 'substitutionism' of the ruling parties (speaking in the name of the workers) which would later facilitate capitalist restoration – but also some revolutionary advances in the world. What is required is a concrete analysis of the unexpected, of the hybrid, and notably of the orientations of the different CPs according to whether they bent or not (and how) to the 'defence of socialism in one country'.

A detailed examination is also needed of the defeats in that century which were due neither to class enemies, nor to the reformism of adaptation to capitalism, nor to Stalinism – but to all those who, sincere revolutionaries, made errors and mutually 'excommunicated' each other without criticising, in their own ranks, the methods they denounced in others.

The task of inventory is necessary, as Daniel Bensaïd[41] puts it, inside each political family and on egalitarian basis with views from all sides. This task has begun and should be continued in a pluralistic fashion in the name of a communism which is, as Bensaïd said in a continuity with Marx and Engels, 'neither a pure idea, nor a doctrinaire model of society', but 'the name of a movement which permanently transcends/suppresses the established order' and contests all relations of domination.

It is also necessary to analyse how this communism worked in the 'Soviet world system', including all revolutions against and despite Stalinisation: the emergence of workers' councils against the occupation by Soviet tanks in Czechoslovakia in 1968; or in the same year in Yugoslavia with the movements demanding 'self-management from below' against the 'red bourgeoisie';[42] and, in spite of an increasingly muddled ideological context, Polish workers' demand 'Give us back our factories'[43] and the project of the self-managed republic of their autonomous trade union Solidarność in 1980 – the polar opposite of the neoliberal shock therapy and privatisations a decade later. More generally, a feature that is 'communist' in that sense can be analysed in all movements aspiring to reduce the gap between proclaimed Communist ideals and the reality, revealing the real contradictions of these regimes.

The inventory should then integrate several requirements and objectives, enriching and updating the problematic of a decolonial communism of 'permanent revolution' at work in the October revolution, towards a 'decolonial pluriversalism'.[44]

The present contribution can be only a partial insight in this necessary plural inventory. It proposes an interpretation of the 'permanent revolution' within the 'Soviet century', from an international angle and with the 'impurities', advances and setbacks of a socialist project not interrupted by Stalinism. The objective is also to go beyond old debates on the 'construction of socialism' by avoiding false dilemmas in the light of elaborations of a self-managed society born from experience – that of the contradictions and crises of the Yugoslavia of the 1960s, and those which concern land and goods 'held in common'[45] in the world. Extensive reflection on the latter can help to understand what was lacking in Yugoslav self-management; nevertheless, the Yugoslav experience also allows us to raise issues of power and of system in the current debates and experiences on the 'commons' in such a way as to reflect on the conditions of emergence of a 'society of commons' that contradicts the logic of capitalism – a concrete utopia?

From the October Revolution to Stalinisation
The conception of the socialist transformation and the beginning of a decolonial communism

Was Stalinism the price of a 'premature' revolution? In The Lessons of October, Trotsky criticises those who argue that 'the country that is more developed industrially only shows, to the less developed, the image of its own future'.[46] The formulation synthesises the rupture between Bolsheviks and Mensheviks[47] – but also an evolution of Marxist thought. Before the October revolution, the dominant scenario supposed that the socialist revolution would take place in the most developed capitalist societies which 'would show the way' – not without 'civilising' visions penetrating the earliest Marxist formulations, which K.B. Anderson has analysed.[48] It needed the popular uprisings in (neo)colonised countries and in Russia to modify this perception. This is at the heart of many current debates against western-centric visions of the struggles and transformations today.

The revolutions of February and October 1917 emerged from the specific contradictions of a Russian society that was linked to the 'capitalist world system', then in crisis. In April 1917 Lenin vigorously identified an anti-capitalist rupture beginning in Russia in the context of the inter-imperialist world war.[49] This approach was anchored in his analysis of imperialism,[50] marking an inflection of Marxist thought that Stalinisation would hide: capitalism was understood as a system, articulated and hierarchical, and not as a sum of states which would all experience the same scenario of industrialisation. The approach also updated and extended the initial recognition by Marx of emerging resistance in 'the margins' of the British Empire, stressed by K.B. Anderson[51] – from Ireland to India – as well as in Russia. In his letters about Russia to Vera Zasulich from 1881, Marx raised the strategic importance of the peasantry in this type of social formation. And he also raised the hypothesis of a Russian Revolution which would become 'the signal for proletarian revolution in the West, so that the two complement each other'.

In his *History of the Russian Revolution,* Trotsky writes:

> To realise the Soviet state, what was required was a drawing together and mutual penetration of two factors belonging to completely different historic species: a peasant war – that is, a movement characteristic of the dawn of bourgeois development – and a proletarian insurrection, the movement signalizing its decline. That is the essence of 1917.

Rosa Luxemburg,[52] based on her own research on imperialism, shared this viewpoint. She criticised the Menshevik analysis of a Russian Revolution which 'should have' remained simply 'bourgeois' and anti-Tsarist (the February revolution): 'The problems of the Russian Revolution, moreover – since it is a product of international developments plus the agrarian question – cannot possibly be solved within the limits of bourgeois society.'

Trotsky's analysis of 'permanent revolution' (caricatured by Stalin) rests on a notion which remains essential to current analyses. It starts from the 'combined and uneven development' of a social formation of the capitalist semi-periphery, like Russia, combining in its structures traits of pre-capitalist phases and industrialisation, closely dependent on the imperialist centres.[53] Socialist transformation in such a society depended on three articulated processes which Trotsky called the 'permanent revolution': the evolution of the bourgeois democratic revolution (the February Revolution against Tsarism) into an anti-capitalist rupture (October) anchored in the dynamic of class struggle;[54] the radical transformation of the old society to the benefit of the dominated classes, workers and peasants, towards a classless socialist society – without recipes on how this might be attained; and the global extension of the revolution against a capitalist system in structural crisis.

It was, then, in an internal/external revolutionary perspective, laden with uncertainties and tensions, that the Bolshevik leaders in the early 1920s had to tackle strategically combined tasks as they confronted the existing world order. The construction of the Communist International (CI) led to big splits in the Second International: these differentiated the new Communist Parties from social democracy both in opposition to imperialist war and proposing the extension of the world socialist revolution in the aftermath of October. The cleavages imposed by the '21 conditions' for adhesion to the CI took place in the European imperialist heartland and in the colonised countries, notably in the East,[55] – and in the relations with the dominated populations of the Russian Empire.[56]

Simultaneously, the practical tasks of organising the new society in 'transition to socialism' were posed concretely for the first time.

What permanent revolution at the societal level?

The Bolsheviks assumed that the first revolutionary rupture could take place in a 'weak link' of the imperialist chain. This introduced a phase of 'transition to socialism' handicapped by the 'under-development' of the productive forces and with a peasant majority population – with a dominant view that extension of the revolution to Europe was vital, to Germany in particular.

But, with hindsight, we can see several weaknesses here: an absence of clear consensus on national questions,[57] in particular that of the oppressed nations of the Russian empire; the distrust shown towards the peasantry; an economist vision of the 'primacy' of the growth of the 'productive forces' favouring the postponement of the transformation of social relations of production to a subsequent stage. These are significant dimensions of the 'permanent revolution' opened up by October 1917: a challenge to the relations of domination between nations; the alliance of workers and poor peasantry; the self-organisation of the subaltern populations in the soviets and factory committees.

The difficulties encountered on the road to 'direct management' of the economy by the producers themselves, the absence of experience and presence of a massively illiterate population, were often stressed. The breadth of the educational tasks undertaken by the Bolsheviks[58] underlines the political will to overcome this handicap to the realisation of socialist objectives. But this 'backwardness' did not prevent the impressive emergence of the soviets and of 'workers' control' in the factories and the self-organisation of the councils (or 'soviets') of workers, peasants and soldiers in the revolution of 1917. All this convinced the Bolsheviks of the overall revolutionary dynamic and of these forms of organisation as 'schools of communism'. In this period, the Bolsheviks practiced real political pluralism (internal and external), polarised around the complex issues of peace against imperialist war and patriotic orientations – not without major conflicts of orientation between the various internationalist currents, indeed inside the Bolshevik party – and of the relevance of demanding 'all power to the soviets!'

Moving from struggle against to struggle for [59] would trigger a change of issues at stake and reveal considerable unpreparedness. The complexity of the issues is tangible for anybody who re-examines the precise scenarios that indicate a rapid evolution of viewpoints and crossovers on various questions during 1918-27 which cannot be seriously dealt with here.

Simply recognising that a course of action is erroneous is easier than analysing it – in the former case, distinctions are blurred between 'counter-revolutionary' action or treason, on the one hand, and divergences between revolutionaries (Marxist and/or libertarian) sharing the same defence of October, on the other. It is better to go beyond invective and focus on the analysis and fact: that of a hyper-centralist course advocated by Lenin, as minutely described by Jean-Jacques Marie.[60] We won't describe here his swings, from the 'iron hand' to the 'steel corset' imposed not only on enemies (real or presumed) of the revolution, but also on layers of the proletariat and peasantry 'who do not act in the state interest' – in practice, an interest interpreted by the party, if not the Bolshevik leadership, and indeed Lenin with all his prestige. This radical substitutionism and the worst violence in the actions of the Cheka (supposedly in defence of the revolution and often hasty and arbitrary) accompanied the militarisation of the economy and measures that increasingly reduced political pluralism inside and outside the party – although opposition and public debate continued until 1926.

In Lenin's *State and Revolution*,[61] the new Soviet state, based on the dominated classes of the old regime, is intended to 'wither away' and become 'accessible for all'. This thesis of the necessary withering away of the state was contested the following year by Lenin himself, faced with the decay of the economy and the explosive character of the situation. The enormous gap between Lenin's thesis and the actual form taken by the 'dictatorship of the proletariat' has been analysed and criticised,[62] notably by (apart from libertarians) 'left Communists' and other oppositions inside Bolshevism.[63] The members of the 'Democratic Centralism' current regrouped in 1919 to defend democratic party life against bureaucratic centralism. They also advocated revitalisation of the councils, and workers' control over 'specialists' placed at the head of enterprises – contrary to Lenin's advocacy of a 'single' leadership under the control of the Bolshevik party alone. This opposition also expressed itself against the militarisation of labour advocated by Trotsky.[64] For its part, the Workers' Opposition[65] stressed collective management of factories through the activity of the Bolsheviks inside the industrial trade unions.[66]

These positions evolved in the face of the breakup of the economy and then the war, but they were shaped by certain initial theoretical approaches. A year before their introduction, Lenin had been somewhat unfavourable towards over-radical measures of nationalisation. In a context where he perceived individualist peasant and commodity decentralisation as a key problem, he had advocated a certain 'state capitalism' combining some nationalisations and a recourse to Russian or foreign capital – under the control of the 'proletarian state'. Bukharin was rather opposed to this, supporting the radical nationalisations of what was called 'War Communism' and opposed to having recourse to qualified specialists, positions very different from those he later defended in the context of the NEP in favour of 'tortoise-paced planning' to placate the peasantry. The *ABC of Communism* written by Bukharin in 1919 (and widely circulated in the Communist International) reflected an initial radicalism close to that of Lenin in its analysis of advanced capitalism as 'paving the way for communism' by its destruction of petty commodity production and by monopolist concentration. From this was developed a critique of capitalism from the point of view of the anarchy of its crises, associated with commodity mechanisms, while obviously being critical of the appropriation by private profit of the surplus value produced by the workers.

In a certain way, War Communism was perceived, through its radical nationalisations and the suppression of any money (no central bank, as Jean-Jacques Marie reminds us), as the means of brutally suppressing this 'capitalist anarchy' and the anarchy of petty commodity production (supposedly nourishing capitalism) at the same time as the private appropriation of the surplus. The praising by Lenin of 'the scientific organisation of labour' associated with piecework, or the proposals for militarisation of trade unions integrated in the 'proletarian' state which Trotsky supported, reflected these 'economist' illusions and errors. This orientation increased the bureaucratisation of the state. Lenin's concerns about that led him to oppose Trotsky on the trade union question, arguing that the autonomy of the unions should be preserved so they could defend the workers against 'their' state.

But the *ABC of Communism* did not emphasise 'the political economy of the workers',[67] in conflict with the political economy criteria of *Capital*. The 'despotism of the enterprise' was not challenged – and the approach dominant among Marxists of the 'primacy' of growth of the productive forces[68] as a condition for a socialist transformation undoubtedly marked, beyond the pragmatism of the emergency, a form of economist stagism. The notion of 'transition to socialism' undoubtedly partially reflected – it may be argued – this stagism. The anarchists and 'left Communists' criticised it, correctly advocating democracy at the heart of the enterprises. This implied no simple and obvious response to the question of how to organise the economy and 'power'.

For the time being, the self-managed logic of workers' control was blocked, either because it was perceived as contradictory to the state of development of the economy, or because the mistrust as regards then ability of inexperienced workers to overcome a certain localism in a 'workers' control' or enterprise management faced with the urgent tasks of coordination of the economy. Statism imposed itself against the transformation of social relations expressed in embryonic fashion in the factory committees and soviets – and this was later to facilitate the crystallisation of the Stalinist apparatus. Twenty years on, the Yugoslav Communists would challenge this statist logic, against Stalin. Permanent revolution would once again take its winding course. But for the time being, the regressive dynamic was to continue amidst debates and major confrontations.

The tragic error of the repression of Kronstadt

The increasing awareness among Bolshevik leaders of the bureaucratisation of the state and of the party – which now contained many members of the old Tsarist apparatus, and of the counter-productive effect of suppressing of any market in agricultural production, was the result of pressure from growing popular revolts. But the awareness came too late, and with insufficient clarity, to avoid the 'tragic error' of the repression of the Kronstadt uprising (which was not, as widely believed at the time by all internal opposition to the Bolsheviks including Victor Serge, a 'tragic necessity' against the threat of the Whites).

In his chapter on 'the crisis of the revolution' Pierre Broué[69] relies notably on the historian Paul Avrich's work on this subject.[70] While confirming the reality of counter-revolutionary components inside the rebellion, he concludes clearly:

> Do these significant discoveries support the caricature of the insurrection-conspiracy, a conspiracy theory version of history according to which the insurgents were in some way simply the instruments of manipulation by 'agents'? Such an interpretation is unsustainable. The sailors of Kronstadt undoubtedly reflected, in their demands and their programme, the popular anger, and the will to put an end to the oppression which War Communism signified for them, of a unanimous peasant mass and a significant fraction of the working class.[71]

Paul Avrich also stresses the preponderant influence of anarchists 'in tune with the feelings of the sailors', which were 'disgust at privilege and authority, hatred of regimentation, the dream of local autonomy and self-administration' – in a context of great 'distress in the country'.

This tends to confirm the similar viewpoint expressed by Victor Serge in 1947. This is significant, because it was still located in a framework of support for the October Revolution, and explicit refutation of the lies concerning Bolshevik policies (supposedly putschist or refusing to work with other currents in the revolution).[72] But he subsequently clearly denounced a fatal chain of errors, notably the establishment of the Cheka with all its arbitrariness, and the repression at Kronstadt. One can support his conclusion:

> Lenin, by proclaiming the end of 'War Communism' and the introduction of the 'New Economic Policy', satisfied the economic demands of Kronstadt after the battle and the massacre. He thus recognised that the

Party and he himself had been wrong to maintain an untenable regime whose perils had been denounced by Trotsky, who had proposed a change a year earlier. The New Economic Policy abolished requisitions in the countryside, which were replaced by a tax in kind, re-established freedom of trade and small enterprise, and in a word dismantled the deadly framework of complete state ownership of production and exchange. But (he adds), it would have been natural to dismantle at the same time the framework of government, through a policy of tolerance and reconciliation towards socialist and libertarian elements disposed to place themselves on the terrain of the Soviet constitution.[73]

Such was not Lenin's choice. On the contrary, the repression of pluralism was extended with the ban on factions. However, the manner of understanding society and economy changed among Russian Marxists. It broke with the illusions of 'War Communism', which had been widely shared; it was now located on the more realistic level of a 'society in transition to socialism'. This concept dominated debates in the 1920s between Trotsky, Preobrazhensky, and Bukharin[74] – and was taken up, after Stalin, in Cuba and in Yugoslavia.[75] Its virtue is to make explicit (rather than hidden by Stalinism) the reality of a fragile, conflictual non-socialist society where questions of the relations between planned industrialisation and market agriculture were concretely posed. But these 'economic' debates did not explicitly integrate the questions of the bureaucratisation of the state (and the party) and the 'despotism' of the factory that only an explicit approach of self-management could hope to challenge.

Objective difficulties in democratic issues at the heart of the permanent revolution

Victor Serge in 'Thirty Years After',[76] like Rosa Luxemburg[77] when expressing her criticisms of the Bolsheviks, began by 'situating' himself. Whatever their criticisms, both remained faithful to an impressive revolution whose profundity had been confirmed by the work of historians,[78] as had the links subtly forged between a Bolshevik party (that was far from homogeneous and disciplined, with Lenin often in a minority) and the democratic self-organisation of the popular masses inventing the soviets and factory committees. It was the attractive character of such a party that allowed it to be present on numerous battle fronts, and to rally to its ranks libertarians like Serge,[79] inasmuch as the Bolsheviks defended fundamental popular aspirations – bread, peace, workers' control in the factories, the land to those who worked it and 'all power to the soviets'. But what kind of Soviet was to be constructed?

After October 1917, did opposition to the logic of the single party and its power in the Soviet state imply 'soviets without parties' or 'without Bolsheviks', as some libertarian currents proposed? Was it necessary to leave it to the members of the soviets themselves whether or not to accept different parties (or their members) according to their behaviour in practice, their respect for the democracy of the soviets, and to the rules to be drawn up in a congress or a 'constituent assembly' on pluralistic bases?

The dissolution of the Constituent Assembly by the Bolsheviks was questioned by Rosa Luxemburg.[80] But she considered that they were right inasmuch as 'They did not want to entrust, nor should they have entrusted, the fate of the revolution to an assemblage which reflected the Kerenskyan Russia of yesterday, of the period of vacillations and coalition with the bourgeoisie.' Her differences with Lenin and Trotsky concerned their arguments rejecting any project for a new constituent assembly. Even if it was not convincing to say, as she wrote from prison, that it was necessary to 'immediately convene' a new assembly, her arguments against the democratic restrictions, from the viewpoint of the consolidation of the revolution, are essential.

Did the difficulties of the situation justify repressive measures? Luxemburg explicitly raised this difficult question, without contesting the need for repressive measures 'to protect the collectivity'. But her dominant logic was, rather, that the difficulties were, on the contrary, an argument against a general attack on liberties: 'The giant tasks which the Bolsheviks have undertaken with courage and determination demand the most intensive political training of the masses and the accumulation of experience, which is not possible without political liberty', she said. That went for the soviets and the party, and not just for the convening of a constituent assembly.

Far from turning away from the tasks of socialist transformation, Luxemburg said she wanted to combat the illusion of 'regarding the social revolution as a thing for which there is a recipe ready in the pocket of the revolutionary party'. And she added:

> This is, unfortunately – or perhaps fortunately – not the case. Far from being a sum of ready-made prescriptions which have only to be applied, the practical realisation of socialism as an economic, social and juridical system is something which lies completely hidden in the mists of the future ... Only experience is capable of correcting and opening new ways. Only unobstructed, effervescing life falls into a thousand new forms and improvisations, brings to light creative new force, itself corrects all mistaken attempts.[81]

In 1923, while stressing the need for debate on the urgency of the struggle against the bureaucratisation of the apparatus and of the party, Trotsky[82] confronted the rise of 'factionalism' and its destructive polemics, which also greatly concerned Luxemburg. He added that this had begun to affect the freedom to express political divergences:

> There should be no oversimplification and vulgarisation in understanding the thought that party differences, and all the more so groupings, are nothing but a struggle for influence between antagonistic classes. In 1920, the question of the invasion of Poland stirred up two currents of opinion, one advocating a more audacious policy, the other preaching prudence. Were there different class tendencies there? I do not believe that anyone would risk such an assertion. There were only divergences in the appreciation of the situation, of the forces available, and of the means. But the essential criterion of the appreciation was the same with both parties.

Soon, the entire Bolshevik old guard would be eliminated – politically and physically – by Stalin. The various 'factional groupings' and critical positions, whatever they were, from Bukharin to Trotsky, would be likened to those of an infiltrating 'class enemy'.

Internal and international Stalinisation, and the political-social bureaucratisation at the heart of the revolutions

It was in a context of a hungry and exhausted population, of major tensions inside society and the Bolshevik party in which the 'succession' to Lenin was being prepared, and of the isolation of the Russian revolution[83] notably with the setback in Germany, that Stalin put the concept of 'socialism in one country' (as opposed to the weary 'permanent revolution'!) on the agenda.

At the end of the 1920s, the forced collectivisation of agriculture (with all its dimensions of Great Russian national oppression, notably in Ukraine) consolidated the apparatus of the state/party. State and party had become one after a radicalisation of the repressive measures taken by the Bolsheviks when Lenin was alive. The waves of major trials and purges, aimed particularly at the old Bolsheviks, and the physical liquidation of real or supposed opponents, was combined with the installation of hyper-centralised and detailed planning, radicalising the approach of Preobrazhensky in a repressive fashion.

Accelerated industrialisation also favoured a massive vertical social and political promotion of peasants in the working class, and of workers in the state/party apparatus up to the very top. Despite Lenin's last struggles[84] against the bureaucratisation of the 'workers' state' and Stalin's 'Great Russian' orientations, a totalitarian Stalinist system crystallised out. At the end of the 1930s, Stalin proclaimed that the USSR had become socialist. His model of planning henceforth became the basic 'criterion' of 'socialism' in the Stalinised CPs. Certainly, socialism was also supposed to be free of conflict. The regime was henceforth to suppress any expression of conflict – of classes or otherwise. A 'Stakhanovite' dragooning of the workers accompanied very rapid industrial growth and an immediate priority given to heavy industry.

However, the rise of fascism and the Second World War were to produce bloody and opaque polarisations. After the collapse of the Soviet-German pact, the involvement of the CPs and the USSR in the anti-fascist camp and its victories gave a new impetus and international prestige to the Stalinist regime. This would not, however, conceal the forced annexation of the Baltic states or the deportation of the Crimean Tartars, accused of collective complicity with the Nazis.

But the CPs would now popularise, albeit in somewhat apologetic fashion, the Soviet successes and avoid any anti-capitalist excesses for fear that they would be attributed to the USSR. This, it was believed, would hinder it in negotiations, as at Yalta, for the division of the world between the great powers, on the backs of the peoples. If aid was provided by the USSR to those fighting Francoism, the latter were repressed and killed by the Kremlin if they went beyond anti-fascist struggle – as Ken Loach highlighted in his film *Land and Freedom*.

Faced with the rise of fascism and the behaviour of the CPs, Trotsky judged that the Stalinised CI was dead and decided with his comrades to create the Fourth International at the end of the 1930s. This was before Stalin decided to replace the Comintern with a simple Bureau of information, an act that confirmed a strategic turn: henceforth the world socialist transformation was subordinated to 'the construction of socialism in one country'.

The reformism of the Communist parties was, then, distinguished from that of social democracy by its long-maintained reference to a socialist project – incarnated by the USSR. This was credible in the context of the reconstruction of the countries of the capitalist centre after the war. But it was different in the semi-peripheries of capitalism characterised by dictatorship and extreme class polarisation. This is where new revolutionary crises would emerge following the Second World War.

Pursuit of the permanent revolution after Stalin

Yugoslav Communists rejected the Marshall Plan and did not bend to the Yalta agreements. Chinese revolutionaries also did not respect the limits of a stagism that the radicalism of social and political confrontations rendered impractical. These revolutions were, with their different chronologies and scenarios, sources of a major crisis of Stalinist hegemony in the Communist world, without however ending to the substitutionism of the single party speaking in the name of the workers, or to bureaucratism – both evils affecting the whole workers' movement, even its revolutionary component.[85]

The Chinese and Yugoslav revolutions endangered the control of the Communist Party of the Soviet Union (CPSU) over other CPs and the anti-capitalist struggles of the entire world. But it was the Yugoslav Revolution that was in direct conflict with the diplomatic deals at Yalta and had a direct and immediate continental impact on the Kremlin's sphere of influence (as witnessed by the popularity of projects of a Balkan confederation). That is why Stalin decided to hail the victory of Communist China but to 'excommunicate' 'Titoism' in 1948 by slandering it – and imposing a purge in the CP.

In the context of Khrushchev's excuses to the Yugoslav Communists and the denunciation of 'Stalin's crimes' at the 20th Congress in 1956 – without warning the CPs that had identified with Stalin – relations with China would become tense. Mao sided with Stalin against Khrushchev, but at the same time radicalised its support for anti-imperialist resistance, as opposed to the 'peaceful coexistence' advocated by Moscow. The Yugoslav Communists identified with Marx and the Paris Commune as opposed to with Stalin – by introducing self-management in 1950. This decision opened the floodgates to an experience and debates of huge value, without equivalent elsewhere, which we will return to later.[86]

In other words, the revolution continued to spread – but at the same time incorporated conflicts both with the imperialist world and internal to the Communist movement. The defeat of 'construction of socialism in one country' did not mean the end of the single party and relations of domination between fraternal countries. However, it did modify the world relationship of forces, marking a decisive stage of decolonisation.

The impact of the Communist movement in the colonial world accentuated the shift of the United States. It had presented itself initially as anti-colonialist, through its rivalry with the old European powers, but it would henceforth adopt the warlike profile of 'defender of the free world'. Their fear of communism was a self-fulfilling prophecy in Cuba, where US interventionism radicalised the revolutionary process, leading to an anti-capitalist rupture and a rapprochement with the USSR in 1962. The fight against communism was also the explicit motive for the US intervention in Vietnam after the French defeat. From now on, in that century, it was the 'axis of evil' legitimating supposedly civilising imperialist wars, and reinforcing in turn the transition of anti-colonial struggles to anti-imperialism.

Mehdi Ben Barka, the Moroccan leader who chaired the 1965 preparatory committee of the Tricontinental conference (he was assassinated before it was held in Havana in 1966), summed up the conference's historic importance.[87] For him, what would be represented there the next year was 'the current that emerged with the October Revolution and the current of the revolution of national liberation'. The Cuban Revolution was at the crossover of these two currents. This conference was certainly more important and politically radical than that of Bandung, which is valued more by postcolonial studies, as Robert J. C. Young analyses.[88]

Che's appeal at the Tricontinental, the following year – 'Create one, two, three Vietnams' – would stress its dynamic: seeking to vanquish imperialist aggression and extend the revolution, which was the polar opposite of the 'peaceful coexistence' between systems sought by the Kremlin. Saïd Bouamama recalls the impact of this conference against colonialism, neo-colonialism and imperialism both in the third world and at the very heart of the imperialist powers. The latter were confronted with the rise of the anti-war movement and the radicalisation of all components of the US black movement, and with the revolutionary fringes of May 1968 in France.

But this impact was also felt in Belgrade in June 1968 in the rise of strikes and faculty occupations where the texts of the French May 1968 circulated, along with photos of Che Guevara and slogans for the victory of the Vietnamese NLF. The demands raised against 'market socialism', such as 'self-management from below!' and against the 'red bourgeoisie', were influenced by the criticisms of Marxist academics around the review *Praxis*. After the Prague Spring calling for 'socialism with a human face', workers' councils in Czechoslovakia resisted Soviet tanks with the support of the pro-self-management wing of the CP and the trade unions. On a world scale, 1968 was marked by this 'dialectic of world revolution'[89] and the radicalism of the confrontations.[90]

The post-Stalinist USSR confirmed its weight in a contradictory fashion. 'Pro-Soviet' rallying to the Cuban regime expressed for the latter the search for an essential counterweight to US imperialism at its door; such a rallying was a source of prestige on which the Kremlin could lean in an anti-imperialist world. However, this did not put an end to its bureaucratic reality and its behaviour as a great power. Its policy of 'coexistence' was that of a rival with capitalism, in the context of a strong growth, higher than the average in developed capitalist countries, with Khrushchev's prediction of overtaking capitalism by 1980! But this was not a rivalry free of tensions, as the Cuban 'missile crisis' confirmed. More than ever it was accompanied by the demand of the post-Stalinist regime to control the 'fraternal countries': Soviet aid required alignment on 'the model', in a manner that could not be contested by the temptation of other orientations. The Soviet intervention in Hungary in 1956, against the revolution of the workers' councils, put an end to the illusions of the Yugoslav Communists of a 'post-Stalinism' which would be egalitarian and respectful of the diversity of choices. This was the reason for convening a congress of self-management to proclaim the 'self-managed road to socialism' and for the insertion of Yugoslavia in the 'Non-Aligned Movement' (with all its ambiguities).

Post-capitalist societies after Stalinisation: the new dialectic between socio-economic conflicts and politics

The history of the USSR did not end with Stalinisation, which would be challenged in a spectacular and unexpected – although partial – fashion with the global shock of the 20th congress of the CPSU. After the death of Stalin, it was necessary for the bureaucratic apparatus to stabilise its power by other means. From inside the apparatus itself, the need to break with the arbitrariness of totalitarianism was then expressed, along with the need to render planning more effective – without challenging the reign (and the privileges) of the single party. This was necessary from the viewpoint of the ruling nomenklatura, for the protection of the lives and jobs of the bureaucrats themselves, but also to legitimise their power, which they exercised 'in the name of the workers' and 'of socialism' (something that repression would not allow for very long). This involved official repudiation of the gulag and at least some of Stalin's crimes – and so the rehabilitation of some of his victims: the apologies expressed in Belgrade to the Yugoslav Communists were part of this.

But it was also about changing the priorities of planning to satisfy the needs of consumption by society. The role of the trade unions was modified, although they would remain a transmission belt for the party's choices: this was necessary to render the planned distribution of material resources compatible with a henceforth free choice of employment for workers. It was thus necessary to stabilise the labour force in the plan's priority sectors by means other than imperative assignation: the unions would ensure distribution to workers of benefits in kind associated with employment (housing, crèches, medical centres, consumer goods and so on) in priority sectors. The stabilisation of the system would increasingly require the development of these hybrid forms of non-commodity 'socialisation' at the heart of the big enterprises, expressing the pressure of the workers in an alienated but often effective fashion.

Real democratic workers power (in the broadest sense) as producers and citizens remained absent. That is why anti-Stalinist Marxists refused to characterise the USSR and similar regimes as 'socialist'. This was not changed by Khrushchev's reforms. But as Moshe Lewin pointed out, this did not mean the USSR was capitalist. But it could become so again, and how could this be judged?

Seeing alienation of labour as only a 'capitalist' feature does not allow analysis of the unforeseen in particular the bureaucratic relations inside the workers' movement and revolutions. This was anticipated by the anarchists, but they had no convincing responses. In the same way, it is not convincing to reduce the specific forms of socialist legitimisation of one-party regimes to simple 'scraps of paper', without qualifications. Concrete analysis of the actual relations of production is necessary to see through the opacity and the lies of speeches and constitutions. But the capitalist restoration clarifies the 'essence' of what distinguishes this system from a system of capitalist exploitation.

Karl Polanyi stressed the contours of the 'Great capitalist transformation' in his work[91] of 1945: labour power, land, and money become specific commodities. The market of goods pre-existed capitalism, and was 'built into' societies and social relations not dominated by commodity production. And such a market has also existed in post-capitalist societies, built into their non-commodity social-political relations. Concrete analysis of real property relations involves the examination of the 'active' role of the money and the market.[92]

The 'targets' of capitalist restoration since 1989 have in fact been similar to those analysed by Polanyi, but in a profoundly different context. Concrete analysis of the scenario of the privatisations of the 1990s allows us to measure up to what point – above all in the USSR – capitalist restoration means a structural change in the role of the money and the state, a privatisation of natural resources and means of production (covering a whole non-market industry that has become dominant), and a commodification of labour power which lost its previous legal status and protections. Indeed, in the 'Soviet' system, money did not function as capital able to be accumulated and invested. There was no market for capital or private banks; the 'accounting' rouble used to express the administrative prices in industry was distinct from the currency-rouble distributed as change having the purchasing power of consumer goods. Economic imbalances (shortages, queues) expressed a poor production of use values, without any market sanction of enterprises (no bankruptcies) or workers (no lay-offs), without even any real accounting of costs, and without market mechanisms of adjustment and investment choices.

The party/state political system was related to both the ideological 'superstructure' and the economic 'infrastructure' of these societies – creating contradictions, rational behaviour (of managers and workers), and specific imbalances. Gérard Roland[93] has produced an interesting conceptualisation concerning the manner in which this 'political economy of the Soviet system' tried very hard to 'measure' and fix (via various non-monetary indices) the production of use values and not of commodity values – in spite of the use of 'prices' and a currency. Also, international exchanges between these countries illustrate a logic combining relations of 'barter' and political choice, taking world prices partially into account – very distant from both commodity relations and real, efficacious egalitarian socialist cooperation.[94]

The absence of domination of commodity relations and the impossibility of a capitalist accumulation of monetary surplus value did not prevent pro-capitalist pressures and social forces from becoming manifest. Nor did it prevent workers being subject to specific, bureaucratic relations, which in many cases were no better than those of actually existing capitalism. This was what the concept of 'state capitalism' was partly intended to explain.[95] But the expansion of the revolutions and the specificity of the CPs in relation to social democracy, were better accounted for by the partisans of 'new class' theses.[96] However, during the 'Soviet century', the different phases, experiences, contradictions and crises of countries identifying themselves with socialism cannot be fully understood with 'pure' concepts. It is necessary to take 'the best' from each approach, retaining what allows integration of the diversity of phases and countries and the real and global new development of what was the 'great capitalist transformation' of these countries.[97]

The approach proposed by Michaël Lebowitz[98] of the 'contradictions of actually existing socialism' (in the sense of actual countries which identified themselves as socialist) is useful in that it both stresses the main contradiction in the absence of real power of the workers in whose name the party governs, and fully integrates the political-economic dimension of governing 'in the name of the workers' and of socialism. Lebowitz also stresses that all 'real socialist' regimes tried to establish a stability reflected – apart from phases of totalitarian repression[99] – in a de facto 'contract' between the party (the so-called 'vanguard'), seeking a form of legitimisation of its power in the name of the workers and society. But society and the party-state are 'worked' by contradictory logics, including pro-capitalist pressures.[100]

These conflicts were dependent on open social and political struggles (in several historic phases) with variants that included capitalist restoration. However, it is possible to arrive at wrong judgements. Comparative analysis of crises and socio-economic dynamics over a longer period helps rectification. Globally, the characterisation of these societies as 'transitional between capitalism and socialism' makes sense, provided this formula is not associated with any hypothesis of an assured socialist transformation. This inclusive concept in no way prevents analysis of the contradictory tendencies evoked by Lebowitz. We can add here analysis of tendencies of the bureaucracy to crystallise as a non-bourgeois 'class'[101] (which has always sought to transmit its privileges to its offspring!). Castoriadis was right to say that the ruling CPs did not behave as 'defenders of capitalism', even those in capitalist countries. We can analyse the final defeat of this tendency: before the 1980s-90s, the specific constraints of governing in the name of the workers had never allowed the emergence of a coherent new autonomous class. The 'Bonapartist' semi-class bureaucracy then oscillated between the fundamental classes, depending on the context. A good part of the nomenklatura sought to consolidate its privileges of power in the 1990s in the direction of capitalism. This amounted to a political-social choice that took into account the political repression of anti-bureaucratic aspirations and struggles to reduce the gap between reality and socialist promises.

Socialist ideology was contradicted by everything that prevented the workers themselves from controlling their labour. But the system, which forbade the self-organisation of workers, including at the trade union level, had a wide range of social protections. It was antagonistic to commodity relations and to full powers of bureaucratic ownership because of alienated 'political-social dimensions' penetrating the relations of production and hybrid ownership: the bureaucrats were 'nominated' and without stability in property relations. They were not 'real' proprietors (they could not transmit any ownership to their descendants, or close and sell enterprises) – they were only managers, 'in the name of the workers'.

Numerous strikes (which took place despite being forbidden as 'against the workers' state'!) rapidly affected a management apparatus that was politically 'appointed', in the name of the workers. This expressed a structural but very alienated form of 'veto' by the workers (lacking as it did any capacity of coherent control), which blocked both market mechanisms[102] and unchecked bureaucratic power. The final example from the 'Soviet century' considered here is the autonomous trade union Solidarność in Poland in the early 1980s. It arose out of opposition to the introduction of market prices for consumer goods – a decision perceived, correctly, as 'political' (coming 'from above') and contrary to the egalitarian principles of the system. In spite of the ideological confusion that affects the meaning of the words, it was certainly a 'self-managed republic' that emerged from the programme of Solidarnośc, and the polar opposite of the neoliberal shock therapy of privatisation ten years later. In each of these phases many Communist Party members supported the workers' demands, while the ruling layers hesitated between recourse to Soviet intervention or to a Polish 'Communist' general.

Overall, the very fact of not being subject to the 'blind' laws of the capitalist market when identifying with socialism always gave, as has been stressed, political content to the social-economic issues – and vice versa.[103] It opened up specific contradictions whose outcome was unpredictable. It placed (until the shift to capitalist restoration) all countries of 'actually existing socialism' in the same 'conceptual basket' – the category adopted by the Bolsheviks from the 1920s: 'societies of transition between capitalism and socialism' – without any assurance as to the direction of their evolution, without suppressing the internal critique on the great gap between reality and socialist/communist finalities, and rejecting any stagism. It would be wrong to include the USSR of 'War Communism' in the 1920s (before Stalinisation) in the category of 'society of transition between capitalism and socialism' but not the Yugoslavia of self-management. But it is still necessary to understand why self-management could be (and was) introduced by a Communist Party when Stalin dominated the USSR.

Self-management introduced because of the break with Stalin: Why?

The 'development of productive forces' in the Yugoslavia which emerged from the war was in no way more advanced than it was in the USSR in the 1920s. Self-management was not the product of a spontaneous movement from below, unlike the introduction of soviets. It was very much a political choice. It was and remains both an asset of the leadership of the Yugoslav Communist party and a weakness. But what was the character of that leadership? Tito declared himself 'the biggest Stalinist in the world', while the Fourth International (FI) had been built on the basis of the revolution being betrayed by Stalin. The FI was opposed to the subordination of CPs to the 'construction of socialism in one country', and after the sectarian then rightist 'zigzags' of the CI, then denounced the CI's inability to orient the CPs against fascism. The launching of the Fourth International registered the effective end of the communism of the Comintern, not long before it was explicitly dissolved by Stalin to give credibility to his policies. The diagnosis by the FI was clear. The CPs linked to Moscow were variants of reformism. That meant for sincere anti-Stalinists (who were called 'Trotskyists' by Stalin and the Stalinists in order to associate with the worst of insults and to liquidate them) there could no longer be a revolution led by the Stalinist CPs. The assassination of Trotsky and of numerous real or presumed Trotskyists and their repression could not, for the FI, be deeds of revolutionaries. This was why, with sadness, Natalia Sedova-Trotsky distanced herself from the Fourth International when it supported the Yugoslav Revolution against Stalin.[104]

But in the repressive Stalinised world, it was necessary to see the underlying conflicts well before the 1948 break with Stalin – this also helps to understand both what this party was and why self-management was introduced. The causes are to be found in the reality of a revolution led by the Yugoslav Communists during the Second World War (still alive in the popular memory in 1950) – a party which was protected from the pure dissolution suffered by the Polish fraternal party and had become independent from Moscow since the 1930s, even at the financial level. The revolution itself was in contradiction with the orientation advocated by Stalin, arising from the strategy of 'construction of socialism in one country' within the framework of the Yalta agreements. According to the 'spheres of influence' decided between the great allied powers, Yugoslavia was to remain within the western sphere under the domination of a Serbian dynasty which had sought refuge in London. The rule of the latter had been both a social dictatorship (the Communist Party was banned, as were trade unions) and Great Serbian nationalist (with the oppression of non-Serbian nationalities). This ideology and the project of the king's return were supported by the Chetnik resistance, whose radical anti-communism tempered their anti-fascism.

What the Yugoslav Communists rejected was both this past, the subordination to the resistance of the Chetniks (who were supported initially by the Allies), and Stalin's demand that they renounce the hammer and sickle so as to carry out the Yalta agreements. While the Yugoslav CP had barely more than 5,000 members before the war, its great strength was to organise the struggle of the partisans, on the basis of a People's Army of several hundred thousand peasants, workers and intellectuals in arms and the Liberation Committees (inspired by the soviets) formed against the fascist invaders and on social and national federal bases. But all that also explains why and how the Yugoslav Communists could face down Stalin and his allies for whom what was essential was victory against the Axis forces led by Germany. To say, as some Trotskyist currents do, that there was only a 'political' or 'petty bourgeois' revolution, or that it was the pressure of the masses which pushed the CP, is a failure to recognise all historical evidence.

Yet it is true that, until 1948, any public critique of the Soviet 'big brother' was forbidden, and aid from the latter was (legitimately) hoped for. But the conflicts with Stalin were major, as was revealed in particular in the writings of Milovan Djilas[105] and Dedijer.[106] Tito, who had organised the international brigades in Spain, had noticed the disappearance of many of their members in the Stalinist trials and purges – and he had protected himself. Above all, the strategic orientation was autonomous: beyond the line argued by the Partisans, there were numerous meetings between the Communist parties of the region to advance a projected Balkan federation escaping Stalin's control (stretching from Bulgaria to Greece) – so illustrating the dynamic of permanent revolution in the 'Soviet century'. This was the real cause (behind the lies and pretexts from Moscow) for the 'excommunication' of Titoism decreed by Stalin in 1948. We cannot analyse all its consequences here, notably for Albania and Greece, but it was accompanied by purges throughout the region, with 'Titoism' becoming a new insult like 'Trotskyism'. For all those who had joined the struggle of the Partisans, and joined a Communist Party which identified with October 1917 and 'therefore' with Stalin, the rupture was a profound shock. Kosturica's film *When Father Was Away on Business* highlights with humour how overnight the pro-Soviet 'Cominternists' were repressed in Stalinist fashion.

As has been said, self-management did not emerge 'from below' or in continuity with revolutionary mobilisations but from above, not to 'restore capitalism' (as some Trotskyist currents continue to argue!) but to resist on two fronts. The choice of a self-managed system in 1950 met several objectives. In identifying with Marx's praise for the Paris Commune as opposed to the Kremlin leader, the Titoist leaders claimed legitimacy inside the world Communist movement and sought support there. But it was also about consolidating the social base of the regime, by ensuring the industrialisation of the country despite the end of all Soviet aid and, in this phase of isolation, by mobilising the population in a concrete and popular programme of 'construction' of the country (infrastructure, factories) associated with the proclamation of self-managed status. The latter would also provide a counterweight to the pressures of imperialist 'aid' – even if concessions were made in this regard, in the context of the Korean war. Finally, it was also necessary to explain (and compensate for) a traumatic break with the 'Fatherland of socialism', which until then had been glorified (and with which the hope of reconciliation remained). The critique of statism, notably expressed by Milovan Djilas, allowed an explanation of the bureaucratic consolidation of a revolutionary party which had become a state apparatus, acting like a 'great power'. So it was necessary to protect against that and dissociate from Stalin through a popular mobilisation, while seeking support on the left, among those who valued the reference to the Paris Commune against Soviet statism.

As was the case from the USSR to Cuba and indeed all other revolutions, the same 'substitutionist' tendencies of a vanguard party which had led a revolutionary armed mass struggle were manifested, on a broadly state-directed basis. But self-management was a reality experienced by hundreds of thousands of workers, in all spheres of society (except the army!), with constitutional recognition of a 'status' which was to be very popular, even if it struggled to become efficient according to its socialist aims. Three great combinations of plan, market and self-management would be tested – not just the 'market socialism' variant (1965-71). All reforms were introduced and wound up from above – taking account of the contradictions and struggles which emerged, after repression of any autonomous movement. But until the death of Tito (and other historic leaders) at the turn of the 1980s, every reform strengthened the rights of self-management and national rights – the two bases 'legitimising' the revolutionary regime at the constitutional level. After 1989, it was on the contrary a matter of dismantling this system and its bases, in the logic of capitalist restoration. 1968 would be the high point of struggles and proposals in the direction of overcoming the alienation of self-management of the workers by statism and by the market.

From the 'great debate' in Cuba to a self-managed system

Soviet planning suffered from a slowdown in growth, the damaging impact of bureaucratism on both on the quality of the products and their cost, internal pressures (popular and from the apparatus) in favour of the consumption of western products, and the need to improve exports to countries with strong currencies. It was under these pressures that the debate on planning reform took place. It was initiated in the first half of the 1960s from within an apparatus which, in the USSR, had put an end to the 'chaos' of Khrushchev's 'thaw' and undertaken Soviet intervention against the Hungarian workers' councils. That is to say that, in the main, the reformist economists discussing 'economic laws' and productivity avoided any issues of democratisation and workers' self-management – except in Yugoslavia and, inside the Czech CP, the self-management wing linked to Jaroslav Sabata.

The 'great debate' in Cuba was situated within the Soviet or Maoist orbit, in which the Yugoslav debates, by contrast, were ignored. But it was similar to the debate among Bolshevik Marxists in the USSR in the 1920s:

socialist democracy was excluded from it, either because of a belief that the 'level of development of the productive forces' and of the education of the workers did not allow its introduction, or through a desire for protection from repression. As a result, the issue of an effective workers' and popular self-management system was absent from the Cuban debate.

Return to the use of the concept of 'transition between capitalism and socialism' in the post-Stalinist phase reintroduced continuities with the debates of the 1920s in the USSR. It marked a positive break with Stalinist apologetic concepts proclaiming a 'socialism' realised solely on the basis of centralised planning. All Marxist thinkers who have used this concept to analyse countries of 'actually existing socialism' stress that the corresponding social formations were both conflictual and fragile, subject to internal and external capitalist pressures, behind different forms of legal ownership, without uncertain outcomes. We find this approach in the writings of Che Guevara,[107] Ernest Mandel,[108] Charles Bettelheim,[109] Edvard Kardelj[110] and Marxist intellectuals of the Praxis current in Yugoslavia – and earlier in Bukharin or Preobrazhensky. This is the case whatever the evolutions of their thought and their divergences on the place of the market in the post-capitalist transition. They affirmed their adhesion to Communist objectives but diverged on the means to attain them. However, the bureaucratisation of revolutions was mostly absent from these approaches – apart from that of Ernest Mandel.

Finally, history has shown that this was not a 'higher level' of development which 'legitimised' the historic introduction of rights of self-management in a post-capitalist society, but, as we have seen, the Yugoslav Communists' break with Stalin. This audacity modified the conception of the transition to socialism in an important part of the anti-Stalinist Marxist currents[111] – notably those who debated with Yugoslav Marxists. The irreplaceable and precious character of this example is to have contested the idea of the 'primacy' of the productive forces, or 'material preconditions', in order to introduce self-management, which was to open the way to the anarcho-communist debate on practice. Such debates did not take place in the USSR or Cuba.

The 'great debate' in Cuba[112]

This occurred in 1963-64 in the context of the market reforms advocated by the reformist communists presenting their analyses inside the party/state in the USSR (Liberman) and Czechoslovakia (Ota Sik). Alberto Mora in Cuba shared their viewpoint, which was supported by Charles Bettelheim.[113] The accent was on economic 'efficiency', which in their view was related to 'laws' independent of consciousness and ideology. Relying on Marx's Introduction to the critique of political economy, Bettelheim argued that the level of development of the productive forces did not (yet) allow the application of socialist relations of production, whatever the legal appearances. From this he deduced that, in practice, informal relations between Soviet enterprises in planning depended on market exchanges and an (incorrect) application of the law of value. He criticised the voluntarism of ineffective 'moral' incentives and advocated efficiency. Thus, like the Soviet or Czechoslovak reformers, he recommended accounting autonomy for enterprises. This allowed, beyond the calculation of costs, the extension of market determination of prices and an increase in wages according to results in the context of greater responsibility for directors, linked to bonuses if they reduced production costs (thus generating 'profits'). The debate recalled that of the early 1920s in the USSR on the 'law of value' (Bukharin at the time believed that the plan should apply it), as against the viewpoint of Preobrazhensky, for whom the advantage of planning was to make its own criteria or 'law of socialist accumulation' emerge).

Che Guevara did not share the analysis of planned relations as 'commodities' subject to the law of value. He also opposed what he considered a recourse to capitalist methods, contradictory to the quest for the emergence of a socialist 'new man'. In the concrete case of Cuba, he also believed that the country was small enough for centralised planning to be efficient. While he opposed individual monetary incentives, which he believed undermined solidarity and to be contrary to socialist objectives, he favoured 'moral' and possibly material incentives, providing the latter were collective and not commodities.

Ernest Mandel did not deny that the law of value was manifest in the pressures of the world market or relations within the internal commodity sector. But he supported Guevara, on both incentives and the interpretation of the law of value under planning. He stressed that economic planning (whatever its bureaucratic waste) rightly did not respect the 'law of value', notably by investing in sectors which were 'non-profitable' from a market point of view (especially on a world market basis). Also, the imbalances, errors, and wastage of planning were not reflected in any enterprise closures or automation. He stressed the need to distinguish the domination of a 'market regulator' (or a 'law of value' which orients investment) from the partial use of market categories inserted in non-market choices. Money and prices would remain necessary, in his view, until abundance permitted their disappearance through the extension of the free satisfaction of needs.

In a text written under the name of Ernest Germain,[114] he thus specified, against Bettelheim's thesis, that the obstacle to effective socialisation did not lie 'in centralism in itself'; it stemmed from the 'absence of workers' democracy on the national political level'. He continued:

> This means that a genuine guarantee against bureaucratisation depends on workers' management at the enterprise level and workers' democracy at the state level. Without this combination, even enterprise autonomy will fail to eliminate any of the authoritarian, bureaucratic and (often) erroneous character of economic decisions made at the government level of the plan. With this combination, centralisation of investment – priorities being democratically established, for example through a national congress of workers councils – would not encourage bureaucratisation but, on the contrary, suppress one of its principle sources.[115]

Nonetheless it remains true, as Samuel Farber[116] has said, that none of the public positions in the Cuba debate raised the democratic question in Cuba up front. It is in this context that we should judge a specific aspect of the debate: Mandel shared with Che a certain 'New Man' humanism (as did the Marxists of the Praxis current in Yugoslavia), against Bettelheim and the Althusserian currents.[117] Indeed, the absence of socialist democracy was reflected, in Cuba as in Lenin's USSR, by 'substitutionism' on the part of Che (and Castro). This was the reason for the ineffectiveness of the appeal to the 'New Man'. The Althusserian or Mao-Stalinist currents could hardly raise this question, given their support for Mao's China, which criticised Khrushchev's USSR while defending Stalin and his excommunications. It was true that 'moral' appeals to mobilisation and revolutionary consciousness in order to 'increase productivity' without socialist democracy – that is, without workers, of all kinds and categories, taking direct responsibility in the management of the economy at the level of the enterprise and of the country – could not but be ineffective. But the appeal to productivity increases stimulated by market relations, and the renunciation of the 'New Man' in the name of insufficient development of the productive forces, were nonetheless worthy of criticism.

Samuel Farber attempts to transcend this false choice:

> Che Guevara advocated what in effect was the 'sweating of labour.' But better organisation, technology, and – most importantly – worker control would have the same effect.
>
> Control in itself represents a powerful motivator. The current low productivity comes from a bureaucratic system that systematically creates

disorganisation and chaos and does not provide workers either with political incentives – allowing them to have a say and control over what they do – or with material incentives – typical of the developed capitalist world – to motivate them. Guevara's moral incentives failed: they were a method to get workers to take responsibility without power and to work harder without control or pay.[118]

This critique is at the heart of the issue – and close to what Ernest Germain was saying in 1963. It should be added, as Farber reminds us, that market reforms interrupted in Czechoslovakia, but applied in Yugoslavia in the context of a system of decentralised self-management rights, very quickly showed their disruptive effect. But what he does not know (and what is not widely known) is that in the second half of the 1960s a third way was elaborated in practice in both Yugoslavia and Czechoslovakia (in the self-management wing of the CP and the trade unions, inspired by the Yugoslav debates) that was at the same time critical of both bureaucratic statism and market reforms.

Self-management alienated by statism and/or the market

Fidel Castro and Tito remained presidents of regimes that arose from revolutions, until their deaths – Tito in 1980 at age 88, Fidel in 2016 at 90.

We will not analyse here the different phases and reforms of Yugoslav self-management: this we have done elsewhere.[119] But it is important to stress that the 1965 reforms introducing 'market socialism' in Yugoslavia stemmed from several rationales. First, that of Marxist or non-Marxist reformist economists in the USSR and Czechoslovakia discussing 'efficiency' as defined by the market. There were also libertarian or Marxist currents favourable to workers' rights to self-management who wished these to be extended to the control of social 'surplus income'[120] as opposed to statist (or para-statist in the 1950s) planning.[121] Finally, representatives of the richest republics opposed the redistributionist logic of the plan which, in their view, reduced the efficacy of those republics and undermined the system as a whole. Such critiques were sensitive in a multi-national federation whose revolution had only gained victory by recognising the plurality of the Yugoslav nations. The Slovene leader Edvard Kardelj was notably attentive to these questions while nonetheless opposing nationalism.

The stakes were, therefore, much bigger (and more current) than debates on the 'law of value'. It is an error to reduce them to the threat (real, but not dominant in that phase) of capitalist restoration or worse, to interpret the dominant pro-reform currents as a pro-capitalist orientation of the Titoist leadership (as argued by Maoist currents and some Trotskyist groupings). Such a reductionist approach displays historical and theoretical blindness and prevents serious debate about the place of the market in a post-capitalist society. The philosophical current expressed in the review Praxis put the emphasis of its criticism on the different sources of 'alienation' of human labour, not only in the capitalist system but also in the different experiences claiming socialist goals, including Yugoslavia itself. In the 1960s it developed a theory of radical humanist Marxism, explicitly anti-Stalinist and linked to a new international left outside the pro-Soviet CPs or the Maoist groups, which met every summer on the island of Korčula. Without being involved in the Cuban debate, the intellectuals of Praxis shared de facto the critique of the market reforms, though they considered the latter a substitute for the introduction of an effective self-managed socialist, which should urgently be put on the agenda.

Indeed, the rapid effect of the 'socialist market' in destroying the self-managed coherence that it was supposed to establish proved them right. Yugoslavia was confronted with a crisis where, certainly, many roads remained open. But society was polarised by contradictory tendencies in a system which remained dominated by a legal framework and ideology identified with self-managed socialism. The historic Titoist leadership, which had held back during the economists' debate, was soon to intervene in its own way to try to stem the explosive dynamic unleashed by a combination of repression of autonomous movements and of constitutional changes. The latter were introduced without clarification of the economic debate and pragmatically according to the needs of the 'contract' binding the regime to its social base: increased rights for self-managing workers and national rights,[122] not without contradictions.

Indeed, it was on these two fronts that the crisis became clear. On the one hand, thousands of strikes erupted against the growing inequalities of the market and disrespect of self-management rights by the technocratic heads of enterprises and of banks. Also against increasing inequalities, the student movement, especially in Serbia around the Praxis current, denounced the 'red bourgeoisie' and privilege, demanding 'self-management from below'[123] against both statism and the market reforms – and other precise demands to which we shall return below. Meanwhile, the Albanians of Kosovo, a very poor province of Serbia, mobilised in favour of equal status as a republic. In the 'Croat spring' of 1971, in one of the two richest republics, the demand for increasing 'national rights', besides its linguistic dimensions, went hand in hand with a radicalisation of market reforms, notably in the faculties of law and economics. That movement was favourable to a more confederal decentralisation, with the demand for control over foreign trade (and hence currency) at the level of the republics. In Slovenia, some of the Marxist youth turned towards Althusser and Charles Bettelheim.[124] Others considered the battle for self-management as 'premature' because world capitalism did not create the preconditions for socialist success – a consequence of the 'primacy of the productive forces' thesis?

All this did not facilitate the emergence of a pan-Yugoslav political current in defence of self-management. There was no real politico-social 'space' where all defenders of the Yugoslav multi-national and self-managed system could come together to analyse the roots of the conflicts and the means of surmounting them on the basis of jointly established rights and rules. That precisely is what is at the centre of debates on the 'commons'.

In the absence of such a 'context', a response was imposed from above

The Titoist leadership presented its response to the crisis, after listening carefully listening to all sides of the conflicts, by introducing what could have been a democratic 'space' sufficient to manage the crisis: a congress of self-managers which met in Sarajevo in 1971.[125] In practice that congress was managed in the Titoist manner: the critiques expressed by the Praxis current and the youth movement, demanding a self-managed system, and by those who demanded the rights of Yugoslav national communities and peoples, were adopted (without acknowledging their authors) and 'processed' in the form of draft constitutional amendments put forward by Edvard Kardelj, after a clampdown on the main protagonists. In 1968, Tito had congratulated the students of Belgrade for their commitment to socialism and self-management, but at the same time the young libertarian or Marxist leaders of the autonomous movement (which was dissolved) were sentenced to several months in prison, and the Praxis intellectuals were subjected to repressive measures.[126]

The Titoist leadership exploited the Soviet intervention in Czechoslovakia during the summer of this same year of 1968 on three levels. First, by launching a citizens' 'national mobilisation' to create, alongside the national army, a decentralised popular army against an alleged risk of Soviet intervention in Yugoslavia. Secondly, the oppositional left was excluded from military preparation exercises, and so were categorised as unreliable to defend the system. Thirdly, the establishment of links with neighbouring Albania, which had also condemned the Soviet intervention, allowed the creation of an Albanian language university in Kosovo. This encouraged the Albanianisation of the province and its status as a 'quasi-republic' in the Constitution of 1974 – which was unsatisfactory to both Serbian and Albanian nationalists. The Constitution also conceded a more confederal system, notably in the management of foreign trade, in response to pressure from the richer republics.

The second congress of self-management in 1971 in Sarajevo denounced the technocratic powers at the head of the banks and big enterprises, which were dismantled. The banks were reinserted into the self-managed system and the big enterprises were dismantled by the introduction of the 'base organisations of associated labour' – smaller units equivalent to the workplaces, to bring them closer to the workers, and with basic rights in the new system.

The concrete proposals which emerged from the critiques of the Marxist left were nearly all introduced by Kardelj (the last survivor of the historic leadership) as amendments to the new Constitution of 1974, but without a consistent system:

- The creation of 'self-managing communities of interest' of producers, consumers and state functionaries concerned with specified goods or services (schools, crèches, hospitals, roads and so on). They were to manage jointly the overall production and use of goods or services on the basis of funds allocated at the appropriate territorial level, provided by social contributions. This challenged a vision of self-management perceived solely from the point of view of the producers.
- The introduction of 'self-managed planning' at various territorial levels on the basis of cooperation between 'base organisations of associated labour', dismantling the big enterprises. This was rooted in the workplaces and enterprises, at the same time broadening the horizon of the management of social ownership against both statism and the limited horizon of the enterprise or of group. But there was no global procedure of choices, priorities and criteria.
- The establishment of 'chambers of self-management' at the communal and republican levels, but not at the federal level because of the looser confederalisation of the system requested by the richest republics. This could have given the various self-managing socio-political communities a political space for elaboration and control of the major planned objectives.

The role of the single party and the army was strengthened at the constitutional level, in order to try to contain centrifugal tendencies. The new, extremely complex, system of rights was explicitly intended to protect social ownership against statism and 'group ownership'. But it allowed no overall control of foreign trade and favoured internal growth based on high rates of borrowing. There was, then, no overall 'regulator'; no plan was established and controlled democratically at the macro-economic level, nor was there a socio-political framework to render coherent a system of self-managed planning from below. The League of Communists of Yugoslavia was increasingly penetrated by corruption and the rise in the republics' state apparatus of aspiring bourgeois elements who were to use nationalism to consolidate their privileges, while the system remained vulnerable to external shocks of the world market. This would enable the Yugoslav experience to be forgotten in a context of people (including former defenders of self-management) teetering between (or combining) nationalisms and widespread privatisation.

Towards a 'society of the commons'?

The search for an alternative to both generalised privatisation and the statism of the old Soviet system explains the interest in theorising on the question of the 'commons'.[127] There is no single and unequivocal approach to this subject. We are not talking here about the 'nature', as such, of various goods – from which, according to these naturalist theses, adequate forms of governance would be 'deduced' – but on the collective actions of people who decide to put in common goods of various kinds (in a space which can be very diverse) and together establish the rules they will apply.[128]

However, these debates ignore the wealth of the discussions and proposals raised about 'social ownership' in the self-managed Yugoslavia of the 1960s on the basis of an unprecedented experience. Such ignorance has obviously been reinforced either by contempt for rights introduced 'from above' (in what remained a single party system, even if more flexible), or by the conviction that it amounted to a utopia – two postures reinforced by the dramatic end of the federation and the Yugoslav system. But, even if unintentionally, this ignorance of the past conforms to the ideological operation which in various ways has accompanied the neoliberal counter-revolution, 'demonstrating' the impossibility of effective 'collective' management.

From 'The Tragedy of Commons' to the 'Commonwealth'

During the international 'turning point' of the 1960s, when Yugoslavia was experiencing self-managed 'market socialism' and its conflicts, the review *Science* published 'The Tragedy of the Commons' by Garett Hardin.[129] This did not deal with the Yugoslav experience, but rather with natural goods (parcels of land, ponds) put in common, as was the case in England before the 16th century. The 'enclosures' (forms of privatisation of these lands, which marked the emergence of capitalist agriculture) were supposed to respond to a perverse effect analysed by Hardin: that the rationale of the individual led to the exhaustion of collective resources. The response was either state ownership or privatisation.

This type of reflection has been extended since then by neoliberal theoreticians opposed to anything that was not private ownership, as stressed by David Harvey,[130] who indicated the narrowness of the dilemma within which recent debates have been confined: privatisation or state ownership. The usual proposition of the neoliberal school, supported in part by actual events, is that the absence of private ownership can only lead to inefficient behaviour. This stems from either the logic of the 'clandestine passenger' (everybody expects someone else, hence nobody in practice, to take care of the common good, which deteriorates) or the 'rationality' attributed to self-managing workers of necessarily sacrificing long-term investment (and recruitment) to an immediate increase in incomes.

Except that, where such behaviour did indeed exist, it was in the context of a management (micro-economic) and market imposed on the self-managers, which was inadequate for a rationale of management of social ownership of the means of production to form a 'system'. The critique obviously ignored the existence of other responses, based on solidarity and consistent with self-management rights, which had not had the time and the context to be applied and become broadly known. On the contrary, an open crisis and then a globalised ideological and social counter-revolution were imposed in the 1980s and 1990s.

This was the context in which a breath of fresh air pervaded the academic world through the work of Elinor Östrom on the 'commons'.[131] She rejected the thesis of the ineluctable 'tragedy of the commons'. Her main research was anchored above all (like that of Hardin) on the management of common natural goods – land, water and so on. Studying the experience of indigenous communities, she shows that such a management has been efficient, through rules adopted by the populations directly concerned.

The academic recognition of this work through the award of a 'Nobel prize' has broadened the limits of ideological resistance to privatisation, although, as with many other ideas, neoliberal appropriation of these themes has also been manifest. This has been analysed in particular by Silvia Federici: the neoliberal state can very well adjust, indeed satisfy its needs, using the energy deployed by generous volunteers in an attempt to compensate for the destruction of the social state. This is even integrated into World Bank 'anti-poverty' programmes. But it can also be seen in measures that subvert the existing order, notably if one is conscious of such traps and has access to international networks.

What goods lend themselves to becoming 'common' and what precisely do we understand by this? Views on this have been and remain very diverse and ambiguous, as has been stressed notably by Sébastien Broca,[132] although we cannot deal with the subject here. We will note only the tendency of several approaches to rely on supposedly objective, indeed 'scientific' criteria to 'legitimise' either privatisation or the commons. Indeed, there is no serious theoretical disquisition on this terrain. Experience proves that there are no goods that 'by their very nature' would be absolutely 'non-appropriable', and thus fated to be either put in common or in public ownership. When the relationship of forces allows it, as is the case at certain periods, capitalism privatises everything, sparing nothing – from the human body (and being) to public services, nature and knowledge.

The real question is then who decides and to do what, on the basis of which criteria – on which territorial scale? We must rehabilitate choices against all the slogans which deny them, like Margaret Thatcher's TINA (there is no alternative), consolidated by the intellectual dogmatism of neoliberal economists seeking to impose pseudo-scientific criteria. On the other hand, it is true that choices face constraints: of resources, but also (conditioning the use of resources) systems of property rights and relations protected by dominant institutions, camouflaging private interests. It is therefore necessary to explain the existence of 'systemic' constraints and issues of relationships of forces, social and intellectual. This is necessary, notably to create an ideological and socio-political 'counter-hegemony' that works towards a coherent alternative to neo-liberalism as a system. But can we change the world 'without taking power'[133] or by multiplying the 'fissures' and cracks[134] – or again by the 'power of the common'? And if not, according to what logic, from above and below, what new type of 'power' breaking with the existing or the rejected past? It is also a matter of the power of decision-making and control over recognised rights as a whole, from the local to the planetary. Such issues concern the movement for global justice.[135]

Instead of an approach based on the nature of the goods, we should support one focused on explicit finalities, on rights, and a plural, democratic approach in the clarification of these objectives. It should be without preconditions as to which goods and political spaces are concerned. It should be decided freely, in the context of searches for an alternative to financialisation, commodification, and privatisation of the planet, of its resources, and of human beings.

What rights?

Pierre Dardot and Christian Laval[136] have favoured an approach to the commons as linked to 'rights of use' which, according to them, can reinvigorate a revolutionary approach in the 21st century. Their study and approach is very stimulating, inasmuch as it is true that rights of use, and sharing, appear more essential than the right of ownership. Yet it is not easy to dismiss the Yugoslav reflections on social appropriation,[137] which are more all-encompassing than the right of use alone, and allow statism and nationalism to be transcended.

Benjamin Coriat[138] proposes approaches in addition to 'right of use'. In an interview in 2016, he summarised his viewpoint:

> A common only exists under three conditions. A shared resource, rights and obligations in relation to this resource attributed to commoners, and a structure of governance which assures of long-term reproduction of the resource and the collective entity which governs it.

If the third attribute, in particular, is lacking, we possibly have, he says, a 'common good' – such as the climate – which is not (yet) a 'common'. Therefore: 'the key issue of the negotiations underway, like the huge mobilisations around the climate issue, is precisely to transform this common good into a common by assuring its governance.'

As Coriat says:

> We understand ... that when the size of the resource increases (notably if it is a global public good like the climate), conceiving the structure of governance and implementation becomes very complicated. We need to be able to link regulation and local monitoring and vigilance structures to have this regulation respected. Whatever the difficulty, the establishment of this structure of governance is an indispensable moment.

However, a criterion which works at one scale may not do so at another, as stressed by David Harvey.[139]

The 'putting in common' of fundamental goods must resist the ravages of the destruction of the very notion of public service by neoliberal policies which have closed off many horizons of resistance, at the local level. Should a hospital or a university be 'self- financed', possibly on the basis of unequal resources according to region or locality? Should we fix the price of transport or other services according to their real local cost, abandoning the regions most disadvantaged by nature? Struggles over rights, in an unfavourable context, can be concentrated on a local health centre, a school or public transport, on the basis of a local population. But we should highlight the fact that the responses provided in such cases are restricted by the environment, and leave a growing number of people without homes, schools or health services. However, the criteria of management, organisation of work, and satisfaction of needs are considerably enlarged if we transcend the rules and constraints of competition and capitalist financing. We must simultaneously take over local possibilities of resistance and continue our reflections and solidarity-based links at the territorial levels – national, continental (notably European), indeed transnational – wherever they could become effective and just.

In the countries of 'actual existing socialism', as under capitalism, accounting autonomy and competition did not allow the emergence of a 'political economy of the workers' with its own indicators of development. These indicators would have integrated concrete criteria of access to essential goods and services and environmental protection, elaborating 'in common' rules of social justice and egalitarian relations, against all relations of exploitation and discrimination. This is certainly on the agenda to counter an increasingly barbarous world which treats human beings and the planet as commodities whose 'cost' must be minimised – in reality, exploitation for profit. And this also poses the strategic question of a challenge to the dominant logic of market privatisation and the institutions of globalisation – from the privatised state to financial and military institutions.

Neither 'big bang' nor stalemate

It is often around issues of the survival or protection of jobs sacrificed by the logic of profit that experiences of management of commons emerge. As has been said, these are sometimes welcomed by neoliberal currents if they allow acceptance of the destruction of the social state. This is also true for xenophobic nationalisms, selecting for access the 'true Greeks', 'true French', 'true Hungarians', or Americans.

In such a context, resistance faces two impasses. The first is to believe that it is possible democratically to deepen and extend the management of commons – and their financing – without major confrontations with the privatised states under the control of a minority of property owners and financial markets. The dictatorial imposition of neoliberalism and its criteria, initiated with Pinochet, has continued up to the Greece of Syriza – and there are many other experiences. The second impasse is, through fear of stalemate or corruption by the system (dangers which are very real), to reject the self-organised experiences of survival and the search for self-managed alternatives, appealing instead to the 'big bang' of social revolution. But this is to remain on the margins, failing concretely to outline perceptions of other criteria and possible worlds, not waiting for the response to 'strategic' questions; it is to believe wrongly that one can invent other possibilities after a hypothetical seizure of power without preparation and without relapsing into past setbacks. It is another form of illusion and paralysis.

The Yugoslav self-management experience can be rethought in the light of these debates – and in turn, enrich them. Why limit oneself to a 'right of use', or on the contrary to a 'private' or group appropriation? The notion of self-management is often perceived as relevant only to 'small enterprises' or cooperatives or it is assimilated into the management of an enterprise or service by its own working community, in a solely 'autonomous' fashion. If we fight regional inequalities (or inequalities between cities), this raises the question of financing. Self-management, or the management of 'commons', becomes ineffective and very unjust if its financing and choices made lead to a logic of market competition, or if it is atomised according to an autonomous egotistical approach of 'everybody for themselves'.

The anchoring of self-management in 'base units' at 'human scale' – workshops, enterprises, land – should not prevent cooperative and concerted collective construction, 'networking' of local experiences, and 'territorialisation' that allows consumers and producers to link up in 'self-managing communities of interest'. The possibility of decentralised choices, under constraints of mutualised resources and rules elaborated at scale that ensure the coherence and justice of the system, is greatly facilitated today by the use of computers. Far from confining ourselves to atomised responses, it is necessary to integrate into struggles the need for self-managed planning of choices that express solidarity (at various territorial levels), against the market and statist logic. Debates are also needed about adequate institutions, including judicial ones, that regulate the process of political debates, decision-making and of making choices. In such a process we need to discover the 'principles of subsidiarity' according to which one only elects delegates to a broader territorial level matters that are best decided there (such as environmental questions, the coherence of criteria, joint financing and so on) with regular corrections and adjustments.

As Benjamin Coriat said in one discussion, the emergence of a 'Common of commons', that is, a state of commoners, is one of the strategic issues. Such a 'Common of the commons' could include: chambers of self-management, 'self-managed planning', multiple 'communities of self-managed interest', and congresses of self-management, to elaborate its rules – 'socialisation' of the state by self-managers?

Today, several sources today facilitate the networking and mutualisation of resistance to generalised privatisation, from the local to the planetary. One of these is the multidimensional rise of the 'shared tool' (shared notably by the younger generation) that is the Internet. The Internet also helps the creation of communities managing 'non-rival' goods (whose use by one person does not prevent, indeed favours, their use by others on the basis of cooperation). There are many domains which can help combat the legitimisation of market relations of profit and privatisation as 'efficient'.

But, going more to the heart of the system, a wave of indignation is arising in the face of social and ecological disasters linked to the transformation of natural wealth, goods, services and human beings into 'market values'. There are many examples of mobilisations of peasant and indigenous populations of Latin America, Africa, and Asia, and the global justice networks, notably Via Campesina, rooted in demands for the re-appropriation of commons against the destruction of agricultural crops by agro-export firms and the neo-colonisation of resources by multinationals. 'Everything can change,' Naomi Klein[140] asserts forcefully, notably when dispossessed populations rise up and organise to produce and to live in another manner.

The re-appropriation and collective management of enterprises, lands, services, territories, and towns where fundamental rights are suppressed by privatisation is (and will continue to be) an essential component of relationships of forces which are becoming transformed, along several axes.

The appropriation of the cities and networking between 'rebel cities'[141] is undoubtedly ones of these grand axes. This was witnessed notably in Barcelona[142] where a programme was launched including anti-racism and the welcoming of refugees as well as the management of public spaces. In June 2017, the city organised 'The alliance of cities against the new political monsters', a meeting of 'cities without fear'. The young mayor of Valparaiso, Chile, Jorge Sharp,[143] expressed a new internationalist radicalism issuing from the social movements, in a vibrant plea for 'municipalism' – one unrestricted by localism. Joan Subirats, one of the inspirers of the Spanish citizens' platforms, argued that 'the agenda of the municipalities proves that they are capable of raising hope, in the face of the financialisation of our everyday life'.

Everywhere, in enterprises laying off workers, in the fight against the privatisation of services, and against the pressures of creditors on municipal or national public debt, counter-powers – notably those stimulated by the network CADTM[144] network – contest the criteria of management, financing and efficiency linked to the dominant policies. Pluralist 'social control' must be established everywhere, taking up the slogan of 'workers' control', which was an essential phase during the October Revolution. It is in this logic that the CADTM has begun to denounce 'odious' and 'illegitimate' debts which contradict basic human rights, relying on mobilisations for pluralist 'citizens' audits' which transform the question of debt into a political issue.

The demand for opening the books should be raised when enterprises lay off workers or relocate to boost dividends, and also when discussing municipal or state budgets. This will highlight the hidden criteria of modes of financing which favour rentiers and increase debt, while public expenditure is reduced. It is necessary to put in the public arena other criteria and other concrete choices, starting with the mobilisation of the populations concerned. A 'workers' economy' is thus elaborated, based on the networks[145] and the experiences of enterprises that have been taken over, of cooperatives, of resistance, and of people imagining other possibilities.

In all cases, this rests on the defence of rights for all – against racism and against the reign of financial oligarchies, against rights which are de facto dependent on income, which affects especially women, the old, youth, and immigrants, who form the great mass of 'the working poor'. The 'pluriversalism' of rights defended should be concrete and be opposed to xenophobia, Islamophobia, racism and discrimination on the basis of gender. This involves the explicit recognition of inequalities (of class, gender, or racialised populations). The sole guarantee of not hiding discrimination is to recognise and encourage the self-organisation of the populations concerned and to create meeting places and networks of common struggle.[146]

The defence and re-appropriation of commons concerning everyday life and basic rights (health, education, transport, housing, water, land and so on) also raises the democratic issue of their management. This is at the heart of mobilisations rejecting the false alternatives of privatisation or statism. They bring out the perception of other possibilities of human conditions: the protection of ancient rights could be combined with the struggles for new ones that will be not only legitimised but legalised through powerful revolutionary democratic movements at the national, continental, even planetary level. A new international structure of rights is being drawn up, resisting the powers of multinationals and denouncing the submission of states to the institutions of global finance, and the markets and their values. These are the values of so-called 'free and unbridled competition' which destroys human rights and the environment, and the imposition of free trade treaties. These have been denounced by massive mobilisations and networks of popular education 'focused on action'.[147]

The fact that these actions are rooted among the poorest and most dispossessed populations on the planet places them at the crossroads of social, cultural, and environmental issues, where women often play a major role. Such actions today are built on the basis of an accumulation of experience notably since the 1990s around Via Campesina and peasant and indigenous resistance. A seventh international meeting of this network took place in the Basque country, on 16-24 July 2017. The Declaration of Euskal Herria made there proclaimed that 'the capitalist and patriarchal system is not capable of responding to the crisis in which humanity finds itself plunged, which destroys our peoples and heats up Mother Earth. The Earth is living but capitalism is a sickness which is killing it.'[148]

The World Social Forum in Bahia in Brazil in 2018 had for its central theme 'peoples, territories, and movements in resistance', seeking a 'collective, creative, and transformative construction in the face of a grave and uncertain Brazilian, Latin American, and planetary context'.[149] It faced strategic debates which the 'capitalist tragedy' raises everywhere, and the emergence of a 'society of commons' which must find the means to impose itself against the law, institutions, and dominant relations of ownership.

The new phase of structural crisis of capitalism is located within a profoundly different world from that of the 20th century. But the crisis is nonetheless profound and global. More than ever, movements of resistance cannot win and find coherence 'in one country' but must be anchored at local, national, and transnational levels. The challenge to the system will go through other scenarios than those of the 20th century – but we can already see its contours. From the local to the planetary, the same targets emerge – financial oligarchies with their political, institutional, economic, and repressive powers – as well as the same drivers of resistance: the aspiration to social justice and dignity, for the defence of rights for all, for the protection and management of the commons, and to imagine democracy which does not stop at the door of enterprises and popular neighbourhoods. These movements of resistance should deploy a 'counter-hegemony' from the local to the planetary, by re-appropriating the lessons of all past resistances and revolutions.

Bibliography

Achcar G., Bensaid D. et al., *A quels saints se vouer? Espaces publics et religions*, Contretemps, no. 12, 2005, <https://www.contretemps.eu/gauche-marxisme-laicite-religions>.

Ali Z. & Dayan-Herzbrun S. (eds.), 'Un pluriversalisme décolonial', *Tumultes*, no. 48, Paris: Editions Kimé, 2017.

Marty C., Rome D., et al., *Etat des lieux sur le revenu d'existence universel*, Paris: ATTAC, 2017, <https://france.attac.org/actus-et-medias/le-flux/article/revenu-d-existence-universel-un-etat-des-lieux>.

Anderson K.B., *Marx at the Margins, on nationalism, ethnicity and non-Western Societies*, Chicago: University Press Chicago, 2010.
Andreff W. (ed.), *Réforme et Echanges extérieurs dans les Pays de l'Est*, Paris: l'Harmattan, 1992.
Andreff W., *Economie de la transition – La transformation des économies planifiés en économies de marché*, Lyon: Persee/Bréal, 2007.
Artous A., Maler H., & Texier J., 'Marx et l'appropriation sociale', *Cahiers de Critiques Communistes*, Paris: Syllepse, 2003.
Artous A., *Marx – l'Etat et la politique*, Paris: Syllepse, 1999.
Artous A., *Démocratie, Citoyenneté, Emancipation. Marx, Lefort, Balibar, Rancière, Rosanvallon, Negri*, Paris: Syllepse, 2010.
Artous A., Ducange J., et al., *Mai 2008 – 1968, Un monde en révoltes, Contretemps*, no. 22, 2008, <http://www.contretemps.eu/revolte-mai68-ranciere>.
Artous A., Tran hau Hac, J. Gonzalès & P. Salama, *Nature et forme de l'Etat capitaliste*, Paris: Syllepse, 2015.
Au Long Yu et al., *China's rise: strength and fragility*, London: Resistance Books and Merlin Press, 2012.
Avrich P., *Kronstadt 1921*, Princeton, New Jersey: Princeton University Press, 1970.
Bensaïd D., 'Puissances du communisme', *Contretemps*, January 2010, <http://www.contretemps.eu/puissances-communisme>.
Besancenot O. & Löwy M., *Affinités révolutionnaires. Nos étoiles rouges et noires. Pour une solidarité entre marxistes et libertaires*, Paris: Milles-et-une-nuits, 2014.
Bettelheim C., *Transition to socialist economy*, Hemel Hempstead: The Harvester Press, 1975, <http://marx2mao.com/Other/TSE68NB.html>.
Bettelheim C., *Calcul économique et formes de propriété*, Paris: Maspero, 1970.
Bettelheim, C., *'On socialist planning and the level of the development of the productive forces', Man and Socialism in Cuba: The Great Debate*, New York: Atheneum. 1971.
Bettelheim C., *Class Struggles in the USSR*, New York: Monthly Review Press, 1976, <http://www.marx2mao.com/Other/CSSUi76NB.html>.
Bettelheim C., *Cultural Revolution and Industrial Organization in China: Changes in Management and the Division of Labour*, New York: Monthly Review Press, 1974,
Bettelheim C., *Question sur la Chine: après la révolution culturelle*, Paris: Maspero, 1978, <http://chinepop.chez-alice.fr/chinepop/bettelheim1.pdf>.
Bouamama S., *La Tricontinentale. Les peuples du tiers-monde à l'assaut du ciel*, Geneva/Paris: Ed. du Cetim/Syllepse, 2016.
Boukharin N. & Preobrazhensky E., *The ABC of Communsim*, 1920 <https://www.marxists.org/archive/bukharin/works/1920/abc>.
Boukharine N., Preobrajensky E., Trotski L., *Le débat soviétique sur la loi de la valeur*, Critiques de l'Economie politique, Paris: Maspero, 1972.
Brenner R., 'La Théorie du système-monde et la transition au capitalisme', *Revue Période*, November 2014, < http://revueperiode.net/la-theorie-du-systeme-monde-et-la-transition-au-capitalisme-perspectives-historique-et-theorique/>.
Briton M., *The Bolsheviks and Workers' Control, The State and Counter-Revolution*, London: Solidarity, 1970, <https://www.marxists.org/archive/brinton/1970/workers-control>.
Brana S. et al., *La transition monétaire russe. Avatars de la monnaie, crises de la finance (1990-2000)*, Paris: L'Harmattan, 2002.

Broca S., 'Les Communs, un projet ambigu', *Monde Diplomatique,* December 2016, <http://www.monde-diplomatique.fr/2016/12/BROCA/56916>.
Broué P., *Le parti bolchevik,* Paris: Minuit, 1963, <https://www.marxists.org/francais/broue/works/1963/00/broue_pbolch.htm>.
Broué P., *Trotski,* Paris: Fayard, 1988, in particular chapter XVIII:'Communisme de guerre et terreur' <https://www.marxists.org/francais/broue/works/1988/00/PB_tky_17.htm#_edn8> and chapter XIX 'La crise de la révolution' <https://www.marxists.org/francais/broue/works/1988/00/PB_tky_18.htm#_ednref3>.
Bürbaumer B., 'Retour vers le future: les origines du capitalisme', *Revue Periode,* November 2016, <http://revueperiode.net/retour-vers-le-futur-les-origines-du-capitalisme>.
Brus W., *The General Problems of the Functioning of the Socialist Economy,* 1961.
Brus W., *Socialist ownership and political systems,* London/Boston: Routledge & Kegan Paul, 1975.
Caldarovic M., *'Dissolutionary processes in the system of self-management',* Praxis 1965/4, Zagreb, <https://www.marxists.org/subject/praxis/>.
Cliff T., *State Capitalism in Russia,* London: Pluto Press, 1974, <https://www.marxists.org/archive/cliff/works/1955/statecap/index.htm>.
Congress of the Peoples of the East, Baku, September 1920, London: New Park, 1977, <https://www.marxists.org/history/international/comintern/baku/index.htm>.
Congrès (2ème) des autogestionnaires yougoslaves 1972, 'Discours et analyses', Beograd, *Mejdunarodna Politika,* 1972.
Corcuff P., Löwy M., et al., *Changer le monde sans prendre le pouvoir? Contretemps,* no. 6, 2003, <http://www.contretemps.eu/numero-6-fevrier-2003-changer-le-monde-sans-prendre-le-pouvoir-nouveaux-libertaires-nouveaux-communistes>.
Coriat B., (ed.), *Le Retour des communs. La crise de l'idéologie propriétaire,* Paris: Les Liens qui libèrent, 2015.
Coriat B., 'Ne lisons pas les communs avec les clés du passé', *Contretemps,* January 2016, <https://www.contretemps.eu/ne-lisons-pas-les-communs-avec-les-cles-du-passe-entretien-avec-benjamin-coriat>.
Coutrot T., *Jalons vers un monde possible: redonner des racines à la démocratie,* Lormont: Editions Le Bord de l'eau, 2010.
Dardot P. & Laval C., *Commun. Essai sur la révolution au XXIè siècle,* Paris: La Découverte, 2014.
Dedijer V., *The Battle Stalin Lost; Memoirs of Yugoslavia 1948-1953.* New York: Viking, 1970.
Djilas M., *Wartime: With Tito and the Partisans,* London: Martin Secker & Warburg Ltd, 1980.
Draper H., 'The Two Souls of Socialism', *Socialism from Below,* Atlantic Highlands NJ: Humanities Press, 1992.
Elson D., 'Market socialism or socialisation of the market?', *New Left Review* I/172, 1988, <https://newleftreview.org/I/172/diane-elson-market-socialism-or-socialization-of-the-market>.
Fanon F.,_*The Wretched of the Earth,* New York: Grove Press, 1963, <http://abahlali.org/wp-content/uploads/2011/04/Frantz-Fanon-The-Wretched-of-the-Earth-1965.pdf>.

Farber S., *Before Stalinism: The Rise and Fall of Soviet Democracy*, London/New York: Verso, 1990.
Farber, S., 'Building Socialism in Cuba, *The Jacobin*, October 2016 <https://www.jacobinmag.com/2016/10/alternative-cuba-socialism-left-opposition-worker-control>.
Farber S., *The Politics of Che Guevara: Theory and Practice*, Chicago: Haymarket Books, 2016.
Federici S., 'Feminism And the Politics of the Commons', *The Commoner*, 2011, <http://www.commoner.org.uk/wp-content/uploads/2011/01/federici-feminism-and-the-politics-of-commons.pdf>.
Ferro M., *The Russian Revolution of 1917*, New Jersey: Prentice-Hall, 1972
Flaherty P.,'Perestroika and the Soviet Working-Class', *Studies in Political Economy*, No. 29, Summer 1989, <spe.library.utoronto.ca/index.php/spe/article/view/13170>.
Gallissot R., 'Mehdi Ben Barka et la Tricontinentale', *Le Monde Diplomatique*, October 2005, <https://www.monde-diplomatique.fr/2005/10/GALLISSOT/12827>.
Gaudichaud F. 'Amérique latine, Etat, pouvoir populaire et luttes sociales', *Contretemps*, April 2015, <https://www.contretemps.eu/amerique-latine-etat-pouvoir-populaire-et-luttes-sociales-22>.
Germain/Mandel E.,'The Law of Value in Relation to Self-Management and Investment in the Economy of the Workers' States', *World Outlook*, no.14, 1963, <https://www.marxists.org/archive/mandel/1963/xx/value-self-man.html>.
Guevara, Che, *Socialism and Man in Cuba*, 1965, <https://www.marxists.org/archive/guevara/1965/03/man-socialism.htm>.
Hardin G., 'The Tragedy of the Commons', *Science*, vol. 162, no 3859, Washington DC, 1968, <http://science.sciencemag.org/content/162/3859/1243.full>.
Harribey J-M., *La richesse, la valeur et l'inestimable*, Paris: Les Liens qui Libèrent, 2013.
Hardt, M. and Negri, A., *Commonwealth*, Cambridge MA: Harvard University Press, 2009.
Harvey D., *Spaces of global capitalism*, London: Verso, 2006.
Harvey D., 'The future of the Commons', *Radical Historic Review*, issue 109, Winter 2011.
Harvey D., *Rebel Cities, From the Right to the City to the Urban Revolution*, London: Verso, 2013.
Holloway J., *Change the world without taking power*, London: Pluto Press, 2003.
Holloway J., *Crack Capitalism*, London: Pluto Press, 2010.
Haupt G., Löwy M. et Weill C., *Les marxistes et la question nationale – 1848-1914*, Paris: L'Harmattan, 1976.
Hobsbawm E., *The age of extremes 1914-1991*, London: Vintage, 1994.
Husson M., *Un pur capitalisme*, Lausanne: Cahiers libres/Editions Page deux, 2008
Johsua I., *La Face cachée du Moyen-Âge, Les premiers pas du Capital*, Paris: La Brêche, 1988.
Johsua I., *La Révolution selon Karl Marx*, Lausanne: Cahiers libres/Editions Page deux, 2012.
Johsua S., 'Ils ont osé ! L'expérience de l'école soviétique des années 1920',

Contretemps, June 2017, <https://www.contretemps.eu/ils-ont-ose-ecole-sovietique-1920>.
Kardelj E., *Contradictions of Social Property in a Socialist Society*, Belgrade: Socialist Thought And Practice, 1981.
Kay J.-M. (ed), *L'épreuve du pouvoir, Russie 1917*, Collectif Smolny, 2005, <http://www.collectif-smolny.org/article.php3?id_article=1301>
Katz C., 'La théorie classique de l'impérialisme', Avanti, 2014, <http://www.avanti4.be/debats-theorie-histoire/article/la-theorie-classique-de-l-imperialisme>.
Klein N., *This Changes Everything: Capitalism vs. the Climate*, London: Penguin, 2015.
Kollontaï A, *The Workers' Opposition, 1921*, <https://www.marxists.org/archive/kollonta/1921/workers-opposition/index.htm>.
Kornaï J., *Economics of shortage*, New York: North-Holland, 1980.
Kowalewski Z., *Rendez nous nos usines: Solidarność dans le combat pour l'autogestion ouvrière*, Paris: La Brèche, 1985
Kowalewski Z., 'L'indépendance de l'Ukraine: préhistoire d'un mot d'ordre de Trotski', *Inprecor*, no. 611, January 2015, <http://www.inprecor.fr/article-Ukraine-L'indépendance de l'Ukraine : préhistoire d'un mot d'ordre de Trotski ?id=1706>.
Lavigne M., 'Les relations intra-CAEM dans les années 1990: un marché unique est-il concevable ?', *Réforme et échanges extérieurs dans les Pays de l'Est*, Wladimir Andreff (ed.), Paris: L'Harmattan, 1990.
Lebowitz M., *Beyond Capital: Marx's Political Economy of Workers*, London: Palgrave Macmillan, 2003.
Lebowitz A. M., *The Contradictions of 'Real Socialism': The Conductor and the Conducted*, New York: Monthly Review Press, 2012.
Lenin V.I., *The Tasks of the Proletariat in the Present Revolution (The April Theses)*, Pravda, 7 April 1917. <https://www.marxists.org/archive/lenin/works/1917/apr/04.htm>
Lenin V.I., *State and Revolution*, 1918 <https://www.marxists.org/archive/lenin/works/1917/staterev/index.htm>.
Lewin M., *The Gorbatchev Phenomenon*, Oakland CA: University of California Press, 1991.
Lewin M., *The Soviet century*, London: Verso, 2016.
Lewin M., *Lenin's last struggle*, Ann Arbor MI: University of Michigan Press, 2005.
Löwy M., 'L'humanisme historiciste de Marx, ou relire le Capital', *L'Homme et la société*, volume 17, no.1, 1970, <http://www.persee.fr/doc/homso_0018-4306_1970_num_17_1_1321>.
Löwy M., 'L'actualité de la révolution permanente', *Inprecor*, no. 449-450, July 2000.
Löwy M., *Fire Alarm. Reading Walter Benjamin's 'On the Concept of History'*, London: Verso, 2005.
Luxemburg R., *The Russian revolution*, 1918, <https://www.marxists.org/archive/luxemburg/1918/russian-revolution/index.htm>.
Makhno N., <http://www.nestormakhno.info/index.htm>.
Maler H., *Convoiter l'impossible*, Paris: Albin Michel, 1995.
Maler H., 'Marx, le communisme, l'utopie', *Revue des Deux Mondes*, April 2000, <http://www.homme-moderne.org/societe/philo/hmaler/textes/marx.html>.

Maler H., 'Communisme sans Etat ou démocratie sans domination ? Retour critique sur le dépérissement de l'Etat', *Contretemps*, 13 May 2016, <https://www.contretemps.eu/communisme-sans-etat-ou-democratie-sans-domination-retour-critique-sur-le-deperissement-de-letat>.
Mandel D., 'Economic Reform and in the Soviet Union', *Socialist Register 1988*, <http://socialistregister.com/index.php/srv/article/viewFile/5915/2811>.
Mandel D., 'Révolution, contre-révolution et classe ouvrière en Russie', *Inprecor*, November 1997.
Mandel D., 'Economic power and factory committees in the Russian Revolution', *October 1917, Workers in power*, London: Resistance Book/Merlin Press, 2016.
Mandel E., 'Du nouveau sur la question de la nature de l'URSS. 'Lutte entre la 'loi de la valeur' et la logique du plan', *Quatrième Internationale,* no. 45, Septembre 1970.
Mandel E., *De la bureaucratie,* Paris: La Brèche, 1978, <http://www.ernestmandel.org/new/ecrits/article/de-la-bureaucratie>.
Mandel E., 'Le grand débat économique à Cuba 1963-1964', Lowy M. (ed.), *Ernesto Che Guevara: Ecrits d'un révolutionnaire,* Montreuil: La Brèche-PEC, 1987, <http://www.ernestmandel.org/new/ecrits/article/le-grand-debat-economique-cuba>.
Mandel E., 'In defence of socialist planning', *New Left Review,* no.159, September-October 1986, < https://www.marxists.org/archive/mandel/1986/09/planning.html>.
Marie J-J., *Lénine. La révolution permanente,* Paris: Payot, 2011.
Marty C., Rome D., et al., *Etat des lieux sur le revenu d'existence universel,* Paris: ATTAC, 2017, <https://france.attac.org/actus-et-medias/le-flux/article/revenu-d-existence-universel-un-etat-des-lieux>.
Marx K., *The Communist Manifesto,* 1847, <https://www.marxists.org/archive/marx/works/1848/communist-manifesto/>.
Marx K., *Preface and Introduction to a Contribution to the Critique of Political Economy,* 1859, < https://www.marxists.org/archive/marx/works/1859/critique-pol-economy/preface.htm>.
Marx K., *The International Workingmen's Association 1864 General Rules,* 1864, <https://www.marxists.org/history/international/iwma/documents/1864/rules.htm>.
Massiah G., *La stratégie altermondialiste,* Paris: La Découverte, 2011.
Mesa-Lago C., 'Le débat socialiste sur les stimulants économiques et moraux à Cuba', *Annales, Economies, Sociétés, Civilisations,* vol. 26, no.2, 1971, <http://www.persee.fr/doc/ahess_0395-2649_1971_num_26_2_422368>.
Miliband R., *'Lenin's The State and Revolution', Socialist Register,* 1970, <http://www.socialistregister.com/index.php/srv/article/viewFile/5303/2204>.
Myant M. & Drahokoupil J., *Transition Economies: Political Economy in Russia, Eastern Europe, and Central Asia,* USA, Hoboken NJ: John Wiley & Sons, 2011.
Nove A., 'Markets and socialism', *New Left Review,* I/161, January-February 1987, <https://newleftreview.org/I/161/alec-nove-markets-and-socialism>.
Olivier M., *La Gauche bolchevik et le pouvoir ouvrier: 1920-1927,* <http://www.leftcommunism.org/IMG/pdf/GR_-_Decistes_-_presentation.pdf>.
Ostrom Elinor, *Governing the Commons: The Evolution of Institutions for Collective Action*, Cambridge: Cambridge University Press, 1990.

Palmier J.M., 'Les difficultés de 'Praxis' et de l'école d'été de Korčula ', *L'Homme et la société*, vol. 27, no.1, 1973, <http://www.persee.fr/doc/homso_0018-4306_1973_num_27_1_1797>.
Polanyi K., *The great transformation*, London: Victor Gollancz, 1945.
Poulantzas N., *State, Power, Socialism*, London: New Left Books, 1978
Praxis (1965-1973) – archives <https://www.marxists.org/subject/praxis/>.
Quatrième Internationale (QI), Textes du congrès mondial de janvier 1961, in particular the 'Bilan, problemes et perspectives de la revolution coloniale', <http://association-radar.org/IMG/pdf/16-014-00092.pdf>.
Quatrième Internationale (1963)– Textes du Congrès mondial de 1963, in particular 'la dialectique de la révolution mondiale', <http://asmsfqi.org/IMG/pdf/16-014-00099.pdf>.
Rabinowitch A., *The Bolsheviks Come To Power: The Revolution of 1917 in Petrograd*, Chicago IL: Haymarket, 2017.
Roland G., *Economie politique du système soviétique*, Paris: L'Harmattan, 1989.
Rosdolsky R., *Engels and the 'Non-historic' Peoples: the National Question in the of 1848*, Glasgow: Critique books, 1987.
Samary C., 'Les conceptions d'Ernest Mandel sur le socialisme', 1997, <https://www.ernestmandel.org/fr/surlavie/txt/samary.htm>.
Samary C., 'Les deux âmes du socialisme ou la dialectique des fins et des moyens', 2007, <http://www.europe-solidaire.org/spip.php?article7509#nh17>.
Samary C., 'La centralité du statut autogestionnaire contre tout rapport de domination salarial', *Y-a-t-il un avenir après le capitalisme ?* Paris: Le Temps des Cerises, 2008, <http://www.europe-solidaire.org/spip.php?article11871>.
Samary C., 'La grande transformation capitaliste en Europe de l'Est', 2008, <http://revista-theomai.unq.edu.ar/NUMERO17/Samary.pdf>.
Samary C., 'Lutter à la fois contre l'islamophobie et contre tous les intégrismes', 2010, <http://quefaire.lautre.net/spip.php?page=article&id_article=253>.
Samary C., 'From the dictatorship of the party to the dictatorship of the market', *Communism of the 21st century*, vol. 2, Santa Barbara CA: Praeger, 2014.
Samary C., 'Russie: du court siècle soviétique à la Russie de Poutine', *Contretemps*, 2015, <https://www.contretemps.eu/du-court-siecle-sovietique-a-la-russie-de-poutine-ruptures-et-reinsertions-dans-le-systeme-monde-capitaliste>.
Samary C., 'Quel internationalisme dans le contexte de la crise ukrainienne? Les yeux grands ouverts contre les 'campismes' borgnes', 2016, <http://www.europe-solidaire.org/spip.php?article37993>.
Samary C., 'Contribution au débat sur la situation mondiale et l'impérialisme aujourd'hui', 2016, <http://www.cadtm.org/Contribution-au-debat-sur-la>.
Samary C., 'Essor et crises du mouvement altermondialiste', *En quête d'alternatives. L'état du monde 2018*, Paris: La Découverte, 2017.
Serge V., 'Les anarchistes et l'expérience de la révolution russe', 1920, <https://www.marxists.org/francais/serge/works/1920/08/exprevrusse.htm>.
Serge V., 'Thirty years after the Russian Revolution', *Russia, Twenty Years After*, New Jersey: Humanities Press, 1996.
Shapiro L., *The Origin of the Communist Autocracy: Political Opposition in the Soviet State First Phase – 1917-1922*, London: Palgrave MacMillan, 1987.

Silverman B. (ed.), *Man and Socialism in Cuba: The Great Debate*, New York: Atheneum, 1971.

Stojanovic S., 'The June student movement and social in Yugoslavia', *Praxis 3/4-1970*, <https://www.marxists.org/subject/praxis>.

Supek R. (ed.), *Participation, Workers' Control and Self-management*, 1974.

Traverso E., *Left-Wing Melancholia: Marxism, History, and Memory*, Columbia NY: Columbia University Press, 2017.

Trotsky L., *The New Course*, 1923, <https://www.marxists.org/archive/trotsky/1923/newcourse/index.htm>.

Trotsky L., *Recueil de la Révolution,* Paris: Editions de Minuit, 1963, <https://www.marxists.org/archive/trotsky/index.htm>.

Trotsky L., *Lessons of October*, 1924, <https://www.marxist.com/classics-old/trotsky/lessonsoct.html>.

Toussaint E., *Lénine et Trotski face à la Bureaucratie. Révolution Russe et Société deTtransition,* 2017, <http://www.europe-solidaire.org/spip.php?article37007>.

Varela N. G., 'Le Marxisme et l'Ukraine: contre la 'real politik' infantile', 2004, <http://www.avanti4.be/debats-theorie-histoire/article/le-marxisme-et-l-ukraine-contre-la-realpolitik>.

Wallerstein I., *World-Systems Analysis: An Introduction,* Durham NC: Duke University Press, 2004.

The International Bank for Reconstruction and Development/The World Bank, *Transition: the first ten years, Analysis and Lessons for Eastern Europe and the Former Soviet Union*, Washington DC, 2002.

Young J.C.R., 'Postcolonialism: From Bandung to the Tricontinental', *Historein Vol 5*, 2005, <http://ejournals.epublishing.ekt.gr/index.php/historein/article/view/2160>.

THE YUGOSLAV EXPERIENCE

Yugoslavia since the revolution: a few key dates

1945, March 8: A compromise between the Yugoslav Communist Party (YCP) and the government-in-exile officially establishes a coalition cabinet, but the YCP maintains its army of 800,000 partisans and its people liberation committees.

1945, October: The last two bourgeois ministers leave the cabinet. The new state apparatus consolidates its gains: the means of production and banks are nationalized, a land reform implemented and a de facto monopoly of foreign trade imposed.

1945-1950: Period of completely centralised planning and collectivization of agriculture on the Soviet model.

1945, November 29: Following a referendum on the issue, the People's Federative Republic of Yugoslavia is proclaimed.

1948: The Kremlin denounces the 'Titoite clique' and publicly calls on 'the healthy forces within the YCP' to impose a new course. In retaliation, Kominform supporters are brutally purged from the YCP; the overwhelming majority of the party supports the Yugoslav leadership. The Kominform then launches a vast purge of 'Titoites' in many Communist Parties, in particular in Hungary (the 'Rajk trial') and Poland (arrest of Gomulka).

1950: The law on workers' self-management is adopted; private property is restored over 80% of cultivable land, but the size of private land as the number of possible workers employed by private owners is strictly limited, while cooperation is encouraged.

1950/1952-1965: In this period, self-management is introduced and extended to all public factories and communes, and after 1965 to services and the cultural sector, but the state retains control over 70% of investments; the private sector is confined to agriculture and the small crafts. Instead of detailed and administrative planning like in USSR, strategic choices and priorities are implemented through investment funds; the share of the 'surplus' (value produced above productive costs) kept within the factories and controlled by self-management organs at the factory and commune level is about 30 per cent.

1953: Death of Stalin.

1954: Milovan Djilas is purged.

1955: Soviet Premier Khrushchev comes to Yugoslavia to seal the reconciliation of the two regimes.

1956: Hungarian anti-bureaucratic revolution. Tito hopes for a compromise. After the intervention of Soviet tanks, and the arrest of Imre Nagy, the majority of the Yugoslav leaders behind Tito radically turn towards 'The Non-aligned Movement'.

1958: The Seventh Congress of the League of Yugoslav Communists, after the organisation of the first congress of self-management (October 1957), asserts that self-management is a universal goal of the socialist revolution, not just a particular 'Yugoslav road to socialism'.

1965-1971: In this period, the market-oriented economic reform is implemented most fully: profitability is sought through competition between firms and on the world market, prices are deregulated and the Central Investment Fund is abolished.

1965: The decentralized economic reform is introduced. Self-management rights at the level of each factory are legally strengthened (the surplus which was channelled through the Central Investment Fund is shared between self-management funds and market-oriented banks. But de facto, the latter, in alliance with part of the factory's managers increase their power of decision-making and accumulation.

1968: Student revolts against increasing inequalities, workers' strikes, holding of a very critical congress of the trade unions. In June, many universities are occupied and an autonomous youth socialist movement is launched. It denounces the 'red bourgeoisie' and is in favour of 'self-management from bottom to top' and against US's intervention in Vietnam. Tito denounces the development of capitalist relations and condemns (like Albania) the Soviet intervention in Czechoslovakia. A popular armed defence is organized, consolidating a patriotic front and isolating opponents. Albanians in Kosovo demonstrate in favour of an independent republic.

1971: Rise of a Croatian nationalist movement. This 'Croatian spring' combines cultural democratic demands and market-oriented ones in favour of the Republican control of Foreign exchange.

1971-1980: This period combines repression, legal consolidation of the 'leading role of the party' and of the army, but more confederalisation (on foreign trade, in particular) while the banking system is dismantled and submitted to self-management organs. Self-management rights and social ownership are strengthened in Constitutional amendments; 'self-managed planning' is instituted through negotiated agreements. The effects of market decentralisation and of repression prevent any consistent system to be established.

1972: Repression and purges in Croatia; Tito denounces millionaires.

1973-1974: Repression is unleashed against the left-wing review, *Praxis*, considered to be responsible of the youth revolts.

1976: The law on associated labour formally extends the powers of self-management in the framework of a division of firms into small units.

1980-1988: Increasing inequalities and nationalism, three-digit inflation. This is the period of growth of the foreign debt, economic crisis, political standstill and growing pressure from the International Monetary Fund.

1990s: this is the decade of disintegration of the Federation (1991: the first declarations of independence from Croatia and Slovenia); open conflict with the Serbian minority in Croatia; Kosovo crisis (peaceful self-organisation of the Albanian in a separate way after Belgrade's suppression of the Province autonomy); war of ethnic cleansings in Bosnia (1993-1995) ending with the Dayton agreements; armed struggle in Kosovo and NATO intervention (1999).

Yugoslav self-management: a balance sheet*

Catherine Samary

The violent dismantling of the Yugoslav system and Federation during the 1990s, with no international and self-managed alternative, has given strength to reactionary forces, at the local or world level, willing to impose their monopoly of interpretation of failures. Through their denial of any progressive aspects of past revolutions and initial experiences of rupture with capitalism, they want to break any attempt at criticism of the existing order.

That is why mastering the balance sheet of the past, against fatalist and linear views, is a key political task for on-going resistance. That can be done only through a process of pluralist internal and external points of views about experiences and interpretations of key periods of the past when alternative orientations were possible.

As a contribution to those necessary debates, three parts are presented here.

A discussion about the meaning of 'self-management' as a notion expressing the fundamental ends and aspirations of emancipatory movements. The issue is to distinguish ends from means, and clarify 'words', finding criteria to judge the gaps between concrete experiences and ends, and means to reduce them.

With such a methodology, the different phases of the Yugoslav self-management system are analysed; the tensions and contradictions of each phase, but also the internal and external causes of the crises are stressed.

The third part analyses how the Yugoslav system and Federation were

---

* This text is based on a contribution by Catherine Samary at the 'Days of Debate on Alternatives to Capitalism' to commemorate the centenary of the CNT (1910-2010), Barcelona, April 16, 2010. It has been translated from the French by Bernard Gibbons. It was first published online in 2010 in French as 'Pour une appropriation plurielle des bilans', at *Europe-Solidaire-Sans Frontières,* 2010, <http://www.europe-solidaire.org/spip.php?article21299>, and in Spanish as 'Por una apropiación plural de los balances. Contra un entierro programado' at *Viento Sur,* <http://vientosur.info/spip.php?article1048>.

dismantled, i.e. how the new nation-states 'territorialized' and ethnicised the rights of ownership and the national rights.

The crisis and bloody break-up of the Yugoslav system and Federation have (outside of Yugoslavia) given credence to the idea that there was nothing to lose, keep or learn from this past, either because self-management was only a scrap of bureaucratic paper, without any reality, or because the system was basically inefficient, whatever its generous intentions. This perception contrasts with the significance of 'Yugonostalgia' today often noted among the population of the former Federation faced with the arrogant denigrations of any positive aspects of this past.

But words are muddied, as much as balance sheets which have not had the political space and time to be drawn, and this forms part of the deep-seated causes of the defeat. The ethnic cleansing of territories and the dismantling of the Federation in the 1990s, without the emergence of an internationalist and self-managed alternative, gave weight to reactionary forces which, at the global or local level, wished to break any link with past revolts and revolutions. They wished to impose their monopoly of interpretation of the defeats to kill off the still living roots with the past and any notion of opposition to the existing order.

And that is why drawing balance sheets from the past is a major political task for the current resistance. This can only be assured by the coming together of internal and external viewpoints on the former Yugoslavia, implying a certain plurality of experiences and viewpoints. These encounters between different generations, notably, are essential in the 'Yugoslav space' with what is immediately at issue being not only preserving a 'memory' of past struggles and experiences, but also of allowing their analysis by young people who have only experienced the dismantling and social disintegration of the old system and those less young, who were participants during certain historic 'forks in the road' where everything was still possible.[150]

The necessary debates should first concern the principles of self-management and its goals, independently of the words used to designate the systems. In order to avoid dogmatism or sectarianism, these goals should be made explicit and can, of course, be contested. They are then liable to be enriched and updated, but are in some way the inter-generational – if not in some way, universal – 'link' of profound and durable aspirations, both past and present, expressed in mass democratic struggles and movements. This work of explanation of goals can lead to a critical understanding of experiences and 'models', and it is in the light of the conflicts associated with these aspirations that the history of Yugoslav self-management and its dismantling can be re-examined.

Self-management and the Yugoslav experience are often assimilated with 'market socialism', that is a system where self-management was atomised enterprise by enterprise, with the market as coordination, thus without planning. In fact this model was only a phase, and an extremely conflictual one, in the story of Yugoslav self-management. It was introduced and modified over three decades of reforms, according to the outcome of major conflicts. Apart from the conflict with the Stalinized USSR which existed from the beginning, there were internal contradictions involving the 'actors' of the system, which produced tensions and reforms. These conflicts and contradictions should be understood not as 'anomalies' but as embryonic forms of the democracy to be invented. The study of the Yugoslav conflicts is not then that of a defeat, but of a real experience confronted with what any movement of emancipation must resolve. The actors in this were the self-managing workers, in their complexity and diversity of education, training, culture, religion and language, nationality, gender and so on. But they were also the peoples of a multinational federation, with evolving subjective identities which were influenced by the relations of tension or of closeness which were created. And all of this was linked by the evolving relationship of plan and market, as well as, obviously, by the political, trade union or other organizations which 'represented' these actors.

The question of the scope of management, rights and institutions allowing decision-making, solidarity without ignoring diversity, is obviously at the heart of the complex questions to be debated and resolved, by approximation, in the evolving contexts. This can be done by distinguishing the general principles liable to be taken up in various contexts from the concrete responses, that is the 'resources' necessary to resolve the problems which where posed, taking into account the contexts, dominant values, levels of development, tensions and so on.

Hence it is necessary to clarify what we are talking about and the concepts employed. We cannot progress without distinguishing the self-managing goals and the means or 'systems' proposed to meet them, so as to take into account the unforeseen.

Ends and means: how to express them?

If the notion of self-management keeps or rediscovers a meaning, it is according to its capacity to express simple and transparent goals, which can be easily explained. The future should show whether the term is used again, or if others are found to better express what is sought, but 'self-management' has the advantage of saying something essential simply: management by oneself, by each individual.

That does not mean individualism and egoism, but individual responsibility, free personal decision-making. Cooperation, 'the free association of the producers', can be enriched by the vast array of the diversity of multiple-faceted individuals: one can be a producer in various areas and with different qualifications but at the same time a consumer and, also a citizen in the broadest political sense. One can have multiple identities: male, female, parent, young, old, as well as cultural, religious, professional and so on. Associations can freely express specific viewpoints of communities which are not homogenous so that hidden questions, such as discrimination, can be taken into account without the resolution of these being the task of each community alone. It is the broadening of the horizons of all which is key in this rich process of combining struggles and autonomous forms of organisations as well as political plurarity. The individual must remain free to manage the evolving articulation of their own facets: what dominates depends in one way or another on the question posed to them at the time.

Management of what? We should not be restrictive on this level either. There is no reason, for example, why a worker should only be responsible for the management of the product corresponding to their factory in which they are, often by chance. Why, moreover, should such a responsibility relate exclusively to their job or sector? Why should the organisation of the post office and the price of stamps be solely the responsibility of postal workers? Why should the conditions of production in mines only be an issue for miners? Why leave to public transport workers or car workers alone the choice of what should be produced? And why should income distribution and acceptable differentials, organization of working time and leisure only be dealt with by each specific category? Broadly speaking, 'self-management' should be thought of as the right and/or the responsibility of all to participate in the management of everything that is of concern to them in the production and reproduction of the means of existence. This is about dealing with education or work, whether it is manual or intellectual, industrial, agricultural or service-related, paid or unpaid, as well as domestic labour, or dealing with what is necessary to live in general. So it is about each individual being responsible for everything which concerns them.

Such a goal expresses a radical emancipatory project, even when its 'anti-capitalist' dynamic is not explicit. We can fight for such a general human right involving full responsibility and with the resources to assume it, within or against capitalist systems, which proclaim 'liberty, equality, fraternity'. It is a formidable political, social and moral tool for highlighting the great discrepancy between these proclaimed rights and reality. And in doing so, one can indeed lay bare the reality of the capitalist system, its relations of exploitation and all the class inequalities that it generates behind these established rights that are basic obstacles designed to reduce the gap between reality and these rights. The process of revealing gaps between rights and reality has been and can be implemented, in past or future countries claiming to be socialist. In the context where relations of exploitation and domination are supposed to have been eradicated, the recognized right to be responsible for the management of 'social or public property' has been and can be used to criticise bureaucracy and any tendency towards a monopoly of power by self-proclaimed parties and states. This process can be implemented in any self-managed society against bureaucratic tendencies even where there are no official parties.

Self-management as a principle or general right is by its essence, in contradiction with relations of domination and exploitation, whether they are capitalist or not. That is why self-management can also, in its goals, be associated with 'socialism' or 'communism', but on condition that we have the same attitude towards words and concepts which may be clouded by experience. We have to be able to explain the goals that these words can express, today more than ever – beyond a mere critique of 'models'. Is it not the goal of socialism/communism for human beings to be fully and universally responsible, both individually and collectively, for their work, the manner in which to satisfy their needs, and for challenging all relations of exploitation and domination?

It is necessary to integrate into the balance sheet the unforeseen or the underestimated from the past: the male/female relations of domination, which are far from having disappeared by the challenging of capitalist private property, or the relations of domination between nations. But we also need to integrate the new social stratifications that subsist, and indeed expand including when the bourgeoisie is challenged as a specific class associated with capitalism. To reduce all contemporary relations of domination or exploitation to bourgeois versus proletarian relations or to capitalism is an impoverishment of thought. It is ignoring what should be thought of as an issue unforeseen by Marx, a 'normal' difficulty of any revolution, and not of one exception, that is Stalinism, – even if the historic circumstances specific to the isolation of the October have given it a monstrous form. The analysis of new revolutions emerging in conflict with the USSR should help us to understand and consciously fight against such bureaucratic and repressive developments. They are present as germs in parties, including the radical left which denounces Stalinism yet forbids internal tendencies, or ignores bureaucratic and dominating behaviour in the social movements. Any movement with an emancipatory project must analyse and critique the substitutionism of the party, the inequalities of power relationships linked to qualification, gender, origin and so on. The movement must also analyse passive behaviour, which crystallises on the basis of initial relations of confidence, to become the basis of emotional blackmail and 'party' loyalty where individuals must submit themselves to a 'general interest' defined and imposed by others.

The reflexion on the practical, legal or institutional means to fight bureaucratism and 'substitutionism' before they are crystallized into the power of an élite or a party/state is an essential component of the reflection on self-management. It is far from being proven that the logic of the anarchists (who were sensitive to these issues sooner than the Marxists) for the disappearance of institutions, parties or associations is the response to this question. These experiences should be systematically examined, with an analytical to-and-fro between ends and means as they have been implemented in the great variety of circumstances.[151]

If democracy is the issue which is generally recognised as essential, we are for the moment very far from having satisfactory responses (because insufficiently tested by experience) as to the forms of organisation of the economy and to the use of money, planning and market, let alone on the different possible forms of ownership and, generally, on the institutions adequate to achieve the goals. But we do not start from nothing, if we really want to study what has existed, including the Yugoslav experience, but also all the cooperative and associative experiences of past and present.

In the collective discussion of 'models' and historic experiences, the study of Tito's Yugoslavia is exceptional in its breadth and innovatory audacity, especially as it took place in a difficult context, a 'detail' which is often forgotten. For the first time, a political regime of the 20th century that emerged from a victorious revolution after bloody anti-fascist struggles, in a harsh capitalist and imperialist environment, was confronted with the experience of bureaucratic degeneration of a revolution – that of the USSR.[152] And to resist it, it decided to abolish the wage earning class, identifying itself with Marx against Stalin.

It is first necessary to highlight the origins, strength and limits of this audacity, and then the different systems in which the development of management rights was recognised to workers from 1950 onwards in response to struggles.

Yugoslav self-management – resisting Stalin

Yugoslav Communist cadres, of all nationalities around Josip Broz (Tito), were influenced in their education by the study of the soviets which had emerged in the Russian revolutions. This education often took place in the debates they organized in the jails of the interwar Yugoslav dictatorship, which banned the CP. If they had not been formed in the crucible of internationalist struggle, they would not have had the breath to allow them to lead the struggle for to the seizure of power by a powerful multinational and revolutionary popular mobilisation, and they would not have been able to resist the Kremlin.[153] This resistance did not emerge in 1948 out of a blue sky, without the storms of the ambiguous relationship with Moscow.

In the division of the world decided between the great powers (Roosevelt, Churchill and Stalin) allied against fascism during the war, Yugoslavia did not form part of the 'Soviet bloc' (the zone of influence reserved to the USSR). It should have remained a monarchy anchored in the 'western' part of the world. The Communist Party, whose membership went from around 5,000 members to several hundred thousand armed partisans in the resistance, was in a position to reject the monarchy and the parliamentary seats which were promised to it. This is in contrast to it being banned and repressed by the dictatorship in the first Yugoslavia of the interwar period, which was dominated by the Serbian dynasty.

Tito was not 'Stalin's man'. Having organised the International Brigades in Spain and noted the disappearance of its former members and their comrades in the jails of Moscow, he was wary of the Kremlin. Furthermore, many Yugoslav communist cadres, including Tito, had experienced the prisons of the dictatorship under the reign of the Serbian royalty, which had fled to London during the war following the invasion of Yugoslavia by the troops of the German and Italian Axis. This first Yugoslav regime had moreover been perceived as a 'prison of peoples' because of its unitary aspect which did not recognise the full national diversity of the peoples of the region, while remaining dependent on external capitalist financing as it was incapable of ensuring the industrialization of most of the country.

The Partisans, at the head of a popular Army of liberation of some 500,000 combatants whose leadership was communist, established organs of power in all the liberated territories which prefigured the future federation. This gave the resistance a profound legitimacy and strength against the Croat 'Ustaše' (fascists) and the other Serbian nationalist resistance, the pro-royalist and anti-communist 'Chetnik' forces which were initially recognized by the Allies. The National Liberation Committees, established in the liberated territories by the Partisans, distributed land to the peasants. These peasants, in a country which was still 80% agricultural, represented the immense majority of the rank and file members of the Communist Party, although its cadres were intellectuals and workers. The National Liberation Committees were established as organs of local power. They cancelled the debts of the pauperised populations and structured the army and territories on a federal basis to recognize the diversity of the Yugoslav nations. Despite the protests of Stalin, who demanded 'respect' for diplomatic deals, the Yugoslav communists did not hide the 'hammer and sickle' which symbolized their goals.

The establishment of the second Yugoslavia took place in the midst of war, on revolutionary and democratic footings, which ensured its popularity and the victory against fascism, as well as the defeat of the nationalist currents and royalist projects. The delegates from the National Liberation Committees of all the territories, met in 1943 at the conference of the Anti-Fascist Council of National Liberation of Yugoslavia (AVNOJ according to its Serbo-Croat acronym) to proclaim the new Yugoslavia on a federal basis, explicitly rejecting the monarchy, against the choices of the Allies. The representatives of Great Britain, who had come to assess the balance of forces on the ground, had to recognise the Partisans as the broadly dominant and popular rank-and-file anti-fascist resistance rather than the Chetnik royalists.

Parallel to this, the meetings of the Communist leaders of the region as a whole (Bulgaria, Hungary, Rumania, Albania and Greece) with those of the Yugoslav Communist Party prepared projects for a Balkan confederation which would not be subordinated to the views and the control of the Kremlin.

It was basically this, and this alone, that Stalin sought to break in 1948 by 'excommunicating' Tito's Yugoslavia. It was accused in an obviously dishonest fashion of having fallen into the 'enemy' (i.e. imperialist) camp. This rupture was not desired by the Yugoslav leaders who had repressed any internal criticism of the USSR and had reproduced its centralised 'model' up until the time of the break. By organising the Yugoslav resistance independently of Moscow, (especially at the military level, the basis of their power) they had combined two political choices. First, they did not in practice recognise any of the limits imposed by Stalin and his Allies. The anti-fascist struggle that they had led had succeeded because it was profoundly popular and effective in its ability to beat fascism and its allies on the ground. Nevertheless they expected Soviet aid in the international relationship of forces and in post-war reconstruction. They had not publicly expressed criticisms of Moscow and accepted its choice to establish the post-war Bureau of the Comintern in Belgrade, despite being aware that this would place them 'under high surveillance'.

The Stalin/Tito schism was unexpected in the entire world: Moscow has sung the praises of Tito who in turn had declared himself 'the first Stalinist'. Behind the brutal cessation of all Soviet aid and the lies to legitimise this move to the Communist movement, Moscow's intention was to isolate a regime whose independence could make it capable of opposing Soviet hegemony over the CPs and first and foremost those of the region.

Tito's regime was accused (in continuity with the Moscow trials) of 'pro-imperialist' espionage, with the refusal to collectivise the lands of small peasants being cited as 'proof' of this accusation. A wave of Stalinist trials spread in the region, together with purges, hanging or imprisonments impelled by the Kremlin against real or presumed 'Titoists' in the CPs of Eastern Europe and beyond between 1948 and 1954.[154] All the western CPs – including the French one – aligned themselves with Moscow.

Milovan Djilas, a leader of the Yugoslav CP in 1948, explained the Kremlin's behaviour by substantially taking up the thesis of bureaucratic degeneration of the Russian advanced by Trotsky in 'The Revolution Betrayed'. He stressed how the situation of a 'besieged fortress' and the isolation of the October had favoured the regime's fusion with the state and its transformation into a great power trying to impose its hegemony on its sister parties. But he would be himself punished some years later for also criticizing in Yugoslavia the tendencies to bureaucratism and the emergence of a 'new class'.

The introduction of self-management from the 1950s sought, in a coherent manner, to radically distinguish itself from the Soviet model – but without challenging the single party system. It was the autonomy, the deep popularity of the Yugoslav revolution, the reality of the Communist convictions of its leaders which allows us to understand this audacity. But its limits would be marked by the absence of real socialist democracy, and the ambiguity of relations with the post-Stalinist USSR.[155]

This was the first great schism of the Soviet camp, officially proclaiming the end of the wage relaationship in the socialist project, at the same times as a first critique of the USSR. It would open the internal sluice gates to a genuinely critical and innovative Marxist thought, of which the regime's theorist, Edvard Kardelj, was undoubtedly a symbol without any equivalent in the other ruling Communist parties.[156] But it was above all in the fringes which opened up inside the League of Yugoslav Communists and in its periphery where various currents of Marxist analysis would be expressed, notably in the review Praxis which for several years organised meetings with the new international left on the island of Korčula. But these fringes of free expression would be perceived as dangerous 'excesses' from when movements autonomous of the party (among youth, the intelligentsia or the trade unions) began to take root at the end of the 1960s in the context of the tensions produced by 'market socialism'.

The tensions between goals of self-management and rights: the various Yugoslav reforms.

The balance sheet of three decades of Yugoslav self-management is far from being unilaterally a failure, but it combines two contradictory aspects:

1. A deepening of the rights of self-management which expressed the deep popularity of these rights as a factor of dignity, and was one of the major sources of growth and increased living standards until the late 1970s;

2. The absence of an adequate democratic and institutional political framework for the self-managers themselves to resolve emerging tensions and difficulties.

Its failure then its destruction was the result of a combination of internal and external political-economic factors. The main factor was the bureaucracy of the different parties and states becoming autonomous in the 1970s both from the activists and leaders associated with the revolutionary past and from the federal institutions. This was increasing the confederalisation of the system which would be the crucible – as elsewhere – for a shift of a substantial part of these apparatuses towards capitalist globalization, under the external pressure of the debt in the early 1980s.[157]

But we should review the important stages of this non-linear process.

The first phase (1953-1965) experienced the highest growth rates and was based on the introduction of workers' councils. Their ability to manage at a local level was confronted by a planning system whose criteria and choices escaped them. The plan was however adapted: it concentrated on the big priorities, and was backed by investment funds distinct from the state budget.

The first congress of self-management organized in 1957 was convened to resist the new Soviet interventionism manifested in Hungary (in 1956). Out of some 1,700 delegates, more than 60% were workers in a job, while 80% were low or unskilled. In the 1960s, self-management, which was proclaimed as the universal road to socialism (not only in Yugoslavia), was henceforth perceived as a right and an ideal to be attained for individuals to have full responsibility in all spheres of society. But the maintenance of the planning system, even adapted, under the control of the federal bodies of the party/state was a source of conflicts with the organs of self-management and between the republics. It could have been possible then to socialize, through self-management forms of representation, both the plan and the state by democratizing the procedures of decision-making and management of public funds – which would suppose also renouncing the political monopoly of the single party. But this was not the orientation of the Titoist leaders.

Their privilege of political power was preserved, by enlarging the scope of the market.

The second phase (1965-1971) is the only one which could be characterized as market socialism. It was very short, because of the tensions produced by the reforms.

These dismantled the investment funds and all planning, thus enlarging the mechanisms of formation of prices by the market, including the international market, by the lowering of protections on foreign trade. The banking system itself was transformed, being turned towards criteria of allocation of resources on the bases of profitability.

But we should understand the underlying issue, not reduced to those of the single party, which could be reproduced elsewhere. These reforms were occurring in a context of strong growth and popularity of the regime. They responded on the one hand to the pressures of the rich republics wishing to increase at the institutional level the confederalisation of the system (with increased rights for the republics over the federal centre), but above all, on the part of Slovenia and Croatia (the richest republics) which were challenging the policies of redistribution from the richer to the poorer regions. On the other hand, the market decentralization also responded to demands for increased rights of self-management to be recognized for workers (e.g. rights to hire and fire, of management over miscellaneous funds) inside enterprises. This was perceived as a move away from planning towards enterprise-by-enterprise management, linked by the market which was supposed to be neutral and effective – while the banks were ensuring the allocation of resources according to profitability.

This second phase rapidly led to the growth of discrepancies of income between enterprises and regions, the development of unemployment and the rise of inflation. It led to a rise of strikes by workers and students between 1968 and 1971 against these inequalities and the 'red bourgeoisie', for 'self-management from below upwards' (that is for a self-managed planning system containing and limiting commodity relations). Parallel to this, the erosion of solidarity between regions was expressed by demands from the leadership of the richest republics (Slovenia and Croatia) seeking to render decentralization yet more systematic. For them, it was about on the one hand keeping all the currency resources originating from their exchanges; and on the other challenging the financial aid to the less developed regions which still existed – in particular for the benefit of Kosovo, Serbia's poorest region.

The Marxist left denounced market socialism as an illusory and dangerous response to the stifling of self-management by the system of planning previously in force, instead of working for its real democratization. It criticized the loss of substance of self-management rights in the narrow horizon of enterprises placed into competition by the market, the pressure of criteria of profitability contrary to the principle of income according to work, as well as the rampant independence of management of the enterprises and the banks since the ending of planned funding. The rise in strikes illustrated these processes which were also reflected, as in Czechoslovakia in 1968-1969, by the radicalization of the official trade unions.

The legal and ideological legitimisation of the reforms had been that the self-managed social ownership was interpreted as de facto ownership by the enterprise collectives and coordinated by the banks. This also facilitated opposition in the name of self-management and a deepening of thinking on social ownership, which was critical of both statism and enterprise corporatism.

It was then under the influence of social resistance and analyses formulated by the Marxist left that the student movement in 1968 demanded 'self-management from below upwards!' This was seen as a self-managed planning and the political representation of the organs of self-management at the federal level in ad-hoc committees, which would widen the horizon of the management of society as a whole and politicize its stakes. The movement denounced the 'fraudulent privatizations' hiding behind 'enterprises of groups of citizens', the growth of inequalities and the independence of technical and financial management bodies.

Bureaucratism and the single party, including the cult of Tito, raised critical and caustic reactions among the young – as reported by the newspapers, notably in Slovenia. But socialist ideals were not discredited and solidarity with peoples in struggle against imperialism was real, notably amongst the young. Cultural freedoms gained thanks to the self-management practices in publishing, the university and in the media, were certainly much superior – in spite of the ban on political pluralism – than existed in many parliamentary 'democracies'.

Meanwhile, in the Serbian province of Kosovo, Albanians, who represented 80% of the population, took advantage of the first margins of economic and institutional decentralization of the system introduced in 1965 to demand, in 1968, legal equality with the Slav peoples constituting the Federation, linked to a status as a republic for the province.[158]

These movements would find little international support because they expressed an internal opposition to the Titoist regime, something which was exceptional within the Communist world: many of those who criticized the USSR from a socialist perspective turned towards an idealized Yugoslav regime and mistrusted its oppositionists.

The Prague Spring in 1968 had on the contrary a global impact, partly because it emerged at the heart of the Soviet camp but also because it was influenced by the reforms impelled by a reformist wing of the ruling party; the movement therefore had a real significance at the national and international level.

The Soviet intervention in Czechoslovakia eclipsed what happened in Yugoslavia in its significance, while, in a country which had already suffered Stalinist aggressions, Tito's regime took advantage of it to discreetly regain control.

The last phase (1971-1980), before the crisis of the 1980-1990s was typical of the Titoist responses to conflicts: a combination of selective repression and increased rights. Substantial constitutional changes to a great degree conceded the rights demanded, while the movements which had expressed them were repressed.

Tito praised the socialist aspirations expressed by the youth, but the leaders were imprisoned. The lecturers at Praxis, held responsible for the excesses of the young, were forbidden to teach only after the resistance which lasted several years by the self-managed universities. They kept their jobs as researchers, but the review Praxis and its international conferences were banned. As the Marxist left had proposed, the banking system was re-socialized and subordinated to the self-managed enterprises. Against the technocratic powers, the big enterprises were divided into base units ('basic organs of associated labour') with strengthened powers and given the right to link up in a contractual 'self-managed planning'. This, together with the transformation of funds from banks subordinated to the self-management of the enterprises, represented a halt to the march of market socialism. A system of delegation in the Chambers of self-management was instituted – but unfortunately it was limited to the level of communes, republics and provinces and so did not provide the multi-national (inter-republican) framework where the self-managing workplaces could transcend nationalist horizons at the federal level. 'Communities of self-managing interest' (SIZ, according to the Serbo-Croat acronym) linked users of and workers in services, in crèches, hospitals, or transport, which considerably extended the network of services in small municipalities.

The new Constitution of 1974 included all these changes, and the oppositional Marxist left was disarmed at two levels: by selective repression and by the institutionalization of some of its criticisms, strengthening the innovatory international image of the regime.

In a similar way, but on an incoherent basis, the Constitution incorporated a response to the Croat movement which in 1971 demanded, against the Marxist left, more market decentralization of foreign trade and the right to keep the resultant foreign currencies. These rights were institutionalized after the leaders of the 'Croat spring' had been repressed.

Meanwhile, the Titoist regime took advantage of the denunciation of the Soviet intervention in Czechoslovakia made by Enver Hoxha's Albania to establish cultural links with this neighbour and attempt to calm the situation with the Albanians in Kosovo. The new Constitution accentuated the confederal aspect of the system and gave Kosovo a status as quasi-republic which came close to meeting the demands of the Albanian demonstrations repressed in 1968. Kosovo was represented like the republics and with the same rights in the federal bodies. The 'ethnic key' instituting an annual rotation of the presidency to each nation was extended to the Albanians. However, the latter did not become a 'constituent people' with the right to self–determination and Kosovo remained formally a province of Serbia, although Belgrade had no oversight over its management.

Slobodan Milošević cut through these ambiguities in 1989 by reintroducing the subordination of the province to Belgrade, with the support of the federal bodies. But in the 1970s, the Albanianisation of the province strengthened and the rate of university attendance among young Albanians was one of the highest, leading to mass youth unemployment.

In order to control the eminently conflictual and fragile aspects of the Constitution, the leading role of the party was incorporated therein. The latter was emptied of its most militant and critical substance and in the 1980s it lost the cadres who had emerged from the and had played the roles of arbiters of conflict, notably the theorist of the regime Edvard Kardelj, and Tito. Plagued by corruption, the party increasingly differentiated itself on nationalist bases since the confederalisation of the system enlarged the privileges of power and economic management of each republic and province. There was no longer a federal framework giving weight to what brought the self-managed workers together since the ad-hoc Chambers only existed at the communal and republican or provincial levels, not at the national level. The combination of growing decentralized rights, such as the subordination of the banks to the organs of self-management of the enterprises, and of repression favoured the rise of a spirit of 'everybody for themselves' and a generalized indebtedness in a final phase of growth.

External shocks and endogenous factors of crisis: the absence of a political framework of self-managing resistance

The oil shocks and then, at the turn of the 1980s, the rise of external interest rates on foreign credits would add external factors to the growth of indebtedness to internal causes of the crisis.

The resistance, expressed by thousands of strikes, to the various plans for repayment of the debt fed the hyperinflation of the 1980s.[159] This gave weight to the neoliberal rules of the International Monetary Fund (IMF), in this country as elsewhere. The reforms of the last Yugoslav government of Ante Marković in 1989 implemented free market doctrine both concerning the so-called policy of stabilization (against inflation) and the structural changes concerning ownership. The austerity policy sought to put an end to self-management rights, that is to social ownership which was not state ownership. Therefore logic of privatization could not be realized directly, it had to be implemented via the reintroduction of state ownership and territorial conquest, simultaneously ethnicising conflicts, national rights and social rights.

Titoism was not then solely responsible for the failure: the recurrent Soviet pressure, then that of the IMF and of the new European and world order of the 1980s weighed heavily. But in 1956 as in the late 1960s, a real resistance by the Yugoslav regime to Soviet interventionism, supporting and seeking to extend, in an internationalist manner, aspirations to self-managed socialism, would have been popular among the neighbouring countries and elsewhere in the world.[160] The Yugoslav leaders did not make this choice. The repression meant the rise of the corruption and the discrediting of the regime, as well as the inability to offer a way out of the crisis on a socialist basis.

The essential issue was not the concrete measures but the process: there were no public debates, political in a rich sense, on what criteria of effectiveness (hence goals) would be adequate for a self-managed Yugoslav society. Thus there was never any debate on the means to achieve these goals and to mobilize those concerned to implement common decisions.

The turn towards the free market and nationalism in the 1980-1990s was the terrifying price of this absence of democracy: nationalist 'values' became central to the various bureaucracies who were transforming themselves into a new bourgeoisie seeking to control the appropriation of wealth by the formation of nation-states on ethnic bases.

In discussion with the participants involved in the organs of self-management in the 1980s, we can still find traces of a contradiction. On the one hand, self-management remained popular, indeed increasingly so among workers. This was because it had been necessary for two generations to go through a concrete apprenticeship linked to a 'status' of dignity, while the decentralization of the structures of self-management in the base units brought it closer to those affected. But on the other hand, they had no political or trade union framework to express their aspirations and provide responses to the crisis at the level of society as a whole. The popularity of self-management among workers was combined with its impotence as it was confronted with a system which was incoherent at the macro-economic level – expressed in hyperinflation and waste as well as the overall paralysis of the system. This crisis and the repression were together the cause for most intellectuals moving towards nationalism or the free market. The predominant place in the party/state apparatus of the 1980s of pragmatic cadres attached essentially to their privileges of power, who were under pressure from the overall tendencies at work at the international level, would mark the end of any progressive Yugoslav political project of any weight.

Capitalist restoration: the state-driven dismantling of social and national rights through privatization

The general changes of ownership in Yugoslavia from 1989 onwards were introduced as a response to the economic crisis and were seeking to re-establish a coherent market. Indeed, in Yugoslavia more than the other socialist countries, the workers enjoyed explicit rights of collective ownership. It was impossible to remove them directly and still less so after a democratic consultation, given the popularity of self-management among the workers.

The first federal law on privatization under the government of the Croat liberal Ante Marković (which was modified in some of the republics in 1990-1991) stripped social ownership of its supremacy by putting all forms of ownership on the same level.

The reforms of Ante Marković from 1989-1990 were drafted and accepted by all the representatives of the republics and provinces without any constitutional debate or popular consultation. These representatives sat in the federal bodies on an egalitarian basis and enjoyed the right of veto.

At this time, Slobodan Milošević was already in power in Serbia. Trained in banking management, he played an active role in the preparation of the reforms. According to Susan Woodward, 'the proposals advanced by the 'Milošević commission' in May 1988 were drawn up by free market economists and directly drawn from the IMF cookbook'.[161] They had the objectives of the removing the rights of self-management and the emergence, ultimately, of a capital/wage-earner property relationship. But in Yugoslavia, still less than elsewhere, such an objective was never made explicit. It was necessary to dismantle social ownership without saying so and to bypass the rights acquired, notably in the big workplaces.

The law dismantled the social aspect of ownership by giving the self-managed enterprises (in an atomized fashion) the status of the true owners, while associating with the right to privatize 'their' enterprise. The atomisation of the enterprises, necessary for market competition, also undermined self-managed planning. But the form of the process undertaken allowed the maintenance of self-management rights where they were most concrete, namely in the narrow horizon of the enterprise. Each enterprise collective was to begin by having estimated the value of 'its' share of capital, a stage that was opening the way to subsequent privatization.

The first phase of reform consisted then in returning, without saying so and without any popular consultation, towards *group* ownership, which had been explicitly excluded by the Constitution of 1974. The 'refolution' (combination of revolution in the system and reforms from above, without real mobilizations from below defining the objectives) was under way, bypassing the taboo of self-management.[162]

Which states would be the beneficiaries and guarantors of privatization? The overall socio-economic and political crisis of the 1980s affected the credibility of the federal state. Post-Yugoslav nationalism provided a double source of legitimacy to a transition with two aspects: change of ownership and break-up of the Federation. The previous advantages of socialist self-management would be replaced by nationalist communitarianism for the most fragile categories (workers and peasants expecting 'their' state to protect their jobs and land) and the proclamation of the right to leave the Federation (self-determination) consolidating the ethnicisation/statisation of ownership.

This right to self-determination was ambiguous. Was it a right of the peoples constituting Yugoslavia or a right of the republics, knowing that the latter generally included large minorities or several communities recognized as peoples? Without being able to discuss it at more length here, let us say that the right to self-determination was interpreted in a conflictual and developing way, in a sort of 'à la carte' manner. Sometimes it was the right of a state with frequent procedures of consultation of citizens by referendum where the community demanding self-determination was in the majority. At other times it was the right of peoples in the ethnic-national sense prevailing when the community concerned was in the minority and divided between several states, each refusing to others what it demanded for itself.

During the 1990s, the key issue in the breakup of the Federation was the establishment of borders by the emerging new nation states: who would be able to control privatisation in their interests, in a generally clientelist manner.[163]

They intended to appropriate the wealth (and foreign currencies derived from exports) corresponding to these territories and to ensure their insertion in dispersed order in European construction and globalization. The conflicts and wars in Yugoslavia, notably in Bosnia and Kosovo, reflected, at the internal level, this logic of control of territories, dependent on ethnic majorities.

However, not all the national communities of the former Yugoslavia enjoyed the same status or rights to self-determination mentioned above, or the same institutional tools to advance their cause.

The Albanians and Hungarians of Yugoslavia did not have the status of 'nation' (*narod* in the ethnic-national sense) but that of 'nationalities' (*narodni*), a term which sought to avoid that of minority and referred to communities whose state they related to was located outside Yugoslavia. These people did not enjoy the right to self-determination. On the other hand, the provinces of Vojvodina and Kosovo, which explicitly formed part of the Republic of Serbia (article 1 of the 1974 Constitution), benefited from rights which were progressively imposed in practice, notably a right of veto in the federal bodies and of representatives in those bodies. Slobodan Milošević 'resolved' the incoherence of this status in a strong-arm manner by re-establishing Belgrade's power over the provinces.

Bosnia-Herzegovina and Macedonia were also fragile entities – their status as republics and the national rights of the respective peoples had been consolidated by Titoism and the Yugoslav context, soon deemed 'artificial' and thus contested, internally and by their neighbours.[164] The representatives of these two republics tried desperately to maintain a Yugoslav context of compromise between the increasingly confederalist projects of Slovenia and Croatia and the recentralization of the Federation to the benefit of the Serbian majority, advocated by Belgrade. The secession of Slovenia and Croatia in June 1991 placed them before a dilemma: independence at the risk of confrontation or a tête-à-tête with Serbia in a truncated Yugoslavia.

Montenegro was pulled between several logics but it remained attached, in the absence of independence, to the Titoist consolidation of its autonomy and its economic prerogatives – which it really only exercised after 1997 (privatization laws, monetary system, specific customs regime) – as the basis of negotiation of its alliance with Serbia, resisting any variant of a unitary state, then shifting towards independence.

Slobodan Milošević tried to control the biggest territory possible by playing on all the ideological registers. He presented himself as a defender of Serbian minorities and interests in Kosovo, Croatia and Bosnia while negotiating with the Croat leader Franco Tudjman the break-up of Bosnia and playing on the 'Yugoslav' string. This was essential for preserving the integrity of a multi-ethnic Serbia, consolidating the alliance with Montenegro and not alienating the army, which wanted to see the Yugoslav state, the source of its privileges, survive.

Yet the abrogation of the provisions of the Constitution of 1974 on social ownership and the status of the provinces of Serbia marked the beginning of its break-up. In June 1991, Slovenia and Croatia, governed by pro-independence parties which had come to power in 1990, proclaimed their independence, which was ratified by the EU in autumn 1991 and, legally, in January 1992.

The transformation of the system henceforth concerned new independent states.[165] It was undoubtedly the success of Yugoslav self-management in Slovenia, the main beneficiary of the Titoist past, which explains the notable difference of Slovenia in relation to the other states emerging from the dismantling of the Federation and the system of self-management.[166] Even that difference, because it is the product of a still lively social resistance, remains intolerable and under pressure from the European institutions and globalization – and is thus worth being studied and supported.

Socialism and humanism*

Zagorka Pešić-Golubović

1

When discussing socialism today, in conditions that differ essentially from those in which the scientific theory of socialist society was created, we must ask the question: how should socialism be defined today in order to represent a more humanistic society in comparison with other social systems. In other words, there is a need to revise the principles and ideals on the basis of which socialist society is being developed, i.e. to find a reply to the question whether they are sufficiently broadly defined and humanistically founded to be able to form, even in the present changed conditions, the foundation of a new humanistic society. [...]

The socialist transformation of society becomes a much more complex and responsible task if the view is accepted that it is not enough to change external circumstances alone, but that it is necessary to change man's internal alienated nature and his system of values and ideals.

The explanation of man's alienation and de-alienation exclusively by external circumstances (socio-economic and political) is based on the still accepted sociologistic assumption that man is the 'absolute product of social circumstances', or, according to E. Fromm, 'a blank sheet of paper on which society and culture write their text'. The socialist theory, which insists that the humanisation of man and inter-human relations should be left to the spontaneous effect of socio-economic processes, means, in fact, a rejection of the fundaments of humanism based on Marxist conceptions. Because the realisation of socialism presupposes revolutionary action, whose champions cannot be the un-awakened masses but only developed and responsible personalities. And in order to bring about such action, people must experience other much more profound transformations, alongside the

---

* 'Socialism and Humanism' was first published in *Praxis international edition*, no.4, 1965, Zagreb. This is a slightly abridged version from the original. It is available online at <https://www.marxists.org/subject/praxis/praxis-international/Praxis,%20international%20edition,%201965,%20no.%204.pdf>.

transformation of social conditions. Therefore, socio-economic cannot be artificially set apart from the mental and moral as primary and secondary tasks; this means that economic and political liberation cannot be given priority in order to make possible the revaluation of the human personality on the basis of its achievements, for the one does not work without the other.

Marx's view that man is the 'totality of social relations' is often taken as confirmation of the sociologistic thesis in socialist theory. But Marx never vulgarised and simplified human nature in the way ascribed to him by some of his followers. The socialist theory of modem society must take the line that man is neither an automaton nor a passive biological organism which reacts to external stimuli in a stereotyped and instinctive manner. Man does not reflect his environment, he experiences it. It may, therefore, happen that he regards his alienation, as his subjective experience of external circumstances, as a natural state, and identifies himself with it. [...]

Marx understood man as a multi-dimensional being. As such he has the fundamental requirement to keep developing the totality of his being, which includes both 'generic' features and individual potentialities. [...] This does not mean, however, that socialism will be able here and now to carry out completely this task. For it should not be forgotten that socialist countries are still grappling with the problem of bringing about more highly developed material conditions and sufficient amounts of consumer goods. But if the socialist society fails at the present juncture to define its long-term goals more clearly and to show their relationship to immediate aims, there is a danger that what is condition may turn into purpose, and that the purpose – the liberation of man from all aspects of his alienation, restrictedness and partialisation – by being put off for some other and more suitable time, will not be achieved at all. The demand for such a comprehensive human emancipation implies the realisation of those social conditions that make such an emancipation possible, for: 'man is not an abstract being squatting somewhere outside the world. Man is man's world, the state, society.'[167]

Leaving on one side other specific human needs referred to by Marx, we shall draw attention to only one more, that one which is most alienated in our present-day civilisation: the need to evaluate man according to human standards. The drastic alienation of this need was dealt with by Marx in texts on the fetishisation of money by means of which everything, including human qualities, can be bought. This topic is also treated by the contemporary sociologist Erich Fromm, who instances advertisements from daily papers, where man is offered like goods whose value can be expressed in terms of money. But the alienation of this need is also reflected in the fact that man is identified with the position he occupies (not with the actual role he plays), and in thus evaluated according to his position rather than according to what he really is. What consequences have been drawn from Marx's anthropological conception in socialist theory as it is practiced?

Before trying to answer this question and examining our practice critically, we must consider two problems:

1. Until recent times socialist theory and practice developed independently of Marx's anthropological ideas. Socialist theory was characterised by outright sociologism, an exclusive orientation towards the problems of society, the belief that changed social conditions would automatically lead to the humanisation of human relationships. For a long time, socialist theory neglected to deal with human problems, and Marxism was reduced to a science of society. Much more progress has, therefore, been made in the sphere of socio-economic relations than in the sphere of building appropriate human personalities which could bear the burden of building a humanistic society. The consequences can be seen in the fact that conflicts are increasingly frequent and open; and

2. Not starting from Marx's anthropology but concentrating on political economy, theoreticians of socialism have developed a simplified image of human nature. The complexity of human nature, indicated in Marx's works, puts the obligation on the theoreticians of socialism to develop a much more comprehensive and penetrating theory of socialist society. Inspired above all by the practical necessity of overcoming the contradictions of capitalism in its primary phase, socialist theories chiefly formulated immediate aims, neglecting to outline more clearly a wider humanist perspective of long-term goals.[168]

The consequence of such theoretical patterns has been the separation of 'primary' from 'secondary' needs, i.e. a straight-line orientation and a temporal separation of the processes which only combined can bring about a result (this was also discussed by Danko Grlić in *Praxis* 2, 1964, who pointed out that the artificial separation of the aims and ideals of socialism as the first phase from the goals and ideals of communism as the second phase, which was putting off certain goals and ideals for the future, was bringing into question both the humanistic character of the first phase and the possibility of the realisation of the second). This is shown clearly by the fact that the entire available energy is concentrated on the development of the material basis of society and the political system (which is, certainly, an imperative need, without the realisation of which there can be no truly humanistic community, but can this need be separated from other needs?), while other, anthropological problems are not given systematic attention and they remain almost exclusively part of the private life of the individual. It might be stated that in many important spheres of human life there are no developed socialist (humanistic) conception. Such a sphere is the sphere of work and labour relations, where 'humanistic' ideas are borrowed from the West (Taylor and the theory of 'human engineering'), as though admitting that socialism is incapable of solving the problems of the alienation of work.[169] A particularly undefined sphere is that of interpersonal relations and socialist systems of values. Although certain generally formulated principles exist (in the Programme of the Yugoslav League of Communists), they often remain proclamations and declarations, because they have not become an organic, component part of practice.

In other words, it may be said, that there is a lack of synchronisation of the different spheres of human life (priority is given to the material basis at the expense of other spheres of social life, while, by analogy, material needs are raised above others in private life), and that a parallel development and satisfaction of different levels of need has not been achieved.[170]

Summing up the first part of the paper we may state that if modern socialist theory is to be a more adequate expression of its time and ensure the creation of a truly humanistic community of people, it must carry out the following corrections:

1. It should define the relationship between capitalism and socialism in the light of the changes that have taken place in capitalism and the modern world and in the light of the new problems faced by humanity and man, in order to bring out more clearly the advantages of the socialist system as a humanistic community; and

2. It should determine more clearly the principles and envisage the mechanisms which will make it possible for the process of political and economic liberation to be permanently accompanied by the creation of new interpersonal relations in the social sphere, and the realisation of new and higher human needs in the sphere of the personality itself. (Taking the view that political and economic liberation are the primary objectives, especially in such a backward country as is ours. socialist theory must keep it in mind that neither political nor economic liberation can take place in isolation from the struggle for the humanisation of man, which can only be partial if nothing more is aspired at beyond politico-economic liberation, however radical this may be, and must be supplemented by the humanisation of work and human needs).

2

Let us try and consider critically certain fundamental principles of our socialist system from the point of view of humanistic requirements which we must infer from Marx's philosophical anthropology. We shall examine only two fundamental principles proclaimed by the Constitution of the Socialist Federal Republic of Yugoslavia as the basic of our socialist system: (1) the system of workers' and social self-management, and (2) the principle of the liberation of work. These principles offer a basis for the realisation of Marx's anthropological ideas. The Programme of the League of Yugoslav Communists, therefore, lays down:

> Labour becomes free, and labour relationships lose the character of hired-labour relationships. At the same time such free creative labour becomes a factor both in the material progress of society and in the constant advancement of socialist relationships among the people ... Under conditions of social ownership of the means of production emancipated labour is the only factor promoting the reproduction both of the free individual and of socialist relationships and socialist society. That is why any restriction of the freedom of labour must necessarily lead to the deformation of socialist relationships.[171]

In another place, in linking these principles with the creation of new relations among people it is stated:

> It is inevitable that new humanistic qualities in relationships among people should gradually emerge from such social and political relationships. The new, basic, social role of the factories, co-operatives, communes, schools, social organisations and the family as well consists in the development of relationships of sincerity, trust, humaneness, understanding, tolerance, and mutual co-operation and help, in short: human sympathies and comradeship among people ... Man becomes his own master and increasingly free, the more he participates in various forms of the common struggle, co-operation and assistance which are based on the feeling and conviction that man is the highest value.[172]

The Constitution of the Socialist Federal Republic of Yugoslavia states that work thus freed will ensure the further development of self-management (and vice versa), and that these two principles, in their dialectical interdependence, form the basis of socialist relations.[173]

To what extent have humanistic ideas been developed in these principles (in view of the contents ascribed to them), and in what measure have they been realised in practice? We shall consider both the system of self-management and the process of the liberation of work as two component parts of the integrated process of the development of humanistic relations.

It is indisputable that the system of self-management provides the most suitable framework within which the liberation of the personality can be achieved through the liberation of work in modern conditions. This system contains the following elements for solving the problems of the alienation of man and work:

1. By the change of the position and role of the worker in the labour process through his participation in management and making decisions is being abolished one of the factors of the alienated work, – i.e. the separation of productive work from management;

2. By the system of distribution according to work, as a composite part of the consistently implemented principle of self-management, is being solved to a certain extent the problem of the alienation of the product of work (it must be kept in mind that in conditions of market production the de-alienating effect of distribution according to work is limited); and

3. Self-management can be effectively realised only if it encourages the worker to a more universal education so that he may be able to perform the complex functions of management. The need for the acquisition of a wider and more complete education as a manager offers compensation for the decrease of the importance of technical skill and qualifications in conditions of technical civilisation where the process of practical training in partial work operations has been reduced to a minimum.

But the system of self-management does not in itself mean a de-alienation of man and his work. It offers the *possibility* to solve the problems posed by our technical civilisation in the most suitable manner. This possibility should be used as a basis for developing further the principles of the much more comprehensive process of the liberation of work and the emancipation of personality. In our practice these ideas are not differentiated, and often what is in fact a *condition* is taken as a *solution*.

That the system of self-management cannot be consistently realised without the interlinked process of the liberation of work, i.e. that the humanistic character of either can be realised only on the basis of their dialectical inter-connection, has been shown by certain limitations in the orientation of self-managing bodies which have already emerged. They can also produce the opposite effects. Self-management has by now become established almost exclusively as a political and economic organisation, solving practical questions of the production process, the organisation of work, distribution, etc. and, in this way, developing the system of more direct democracy in the work organisation. Certain deformations in our socialist system and the system of workers' self-management indicate the lack of some other components which are outside the politico-economic sphere, and which would prevent socialist principles from turning into their opposites. It may be said that these other components have not been in the sphere of the work of self-managing bodies: for they have not been seriously concerned with the problems of the humanisation of work and human relations, i.e. they have failed to link their activity systematically with the process of the revaluation of work. I think that this tendency cannot be exclusively attributed to the weaknesses of the self-management organisations, but that it has resulted from the fact that these problems have not found their proper place in the theoretical conceptions and principles of the system of self-management.

We shall illustrate these reflections with instances which show that there is no bridge that would span the gap between the declaration in the Yugoslav Constitution and in the Programme of the League of Yugoslav Communists and the system as it should be realised in practice, so that the consequences are different, often even the opposite of what is expected in a humanistic society.

At a time when scientists and humanists in the West are worried at the appearance of increasing problems and difficulties, resulting from the partialisation of work and the increasing mechanisation of the labour process which, although opening up new prospects, also creates new difficulties in the sphere of the depersonalisation and dehumanisation of the personality, these problems seem as though they did not exist in this country. Any attempt to discuss them is labelled 'abstract humanism', for these processes have allegedly not yet become so drastic here as to make it necessary to worry about them (in other words, when the problems really become urgent, ways and means will be found to 'cure' them; for 'preventive treatment' we are still not rich enough – it is the usual reasoning). In practice, however, the actual attitude taken is that only political and economic causes form the source of difficulties in the sphere of productive relations, while it is neglected that even partialised, and depersonalised routine work can also be an important cause. Even when discussing the great number of injuries at work, the consideration of the self-managing bodies do not go beyond the terms of protective measures at work, omitting to consider whether the cause is perhaps mental fatigue which results from an inadequate organisation of work, which strictly links the workers to a single partial operation, or perhaps the fact that the abilities of a certain worker are not suited to a given operation, and the like. Attention is focused chiefly on the external conditions of work, while the worker-machine relationship is still treated along the lines of Taylor's 'scientific organisation of work', which has been proclaimed as inhuman even in the capitalist world, because in Taylor's system the basic question is not how to adapt the machine to man but the other way round, how to adapt man's gestures and rhythm to the machine, and thus, replace man's natural rhythm with a technical one, turning man himself into a robot. In this country there is no institute for the study of the problem of the scientific organisation of work (nor is any institution earnestly concerned with the study of this problem)[174] which would try to determine what forms of work organisation are best suited to the system of self-management and what can be done within the framework of the socialist system for the humanisation of work, that would constitute a more radical step towards abolishing alienation in the sphere of human activity. The problem of the scientific organisation of work cannot be exclusively a technical and economic question, but is also a sociological and anthropological one. Therefore, this problem cannot be dealt with exclusively by engineers and economists within a work organisation; sociologists and psychologists are equally required for the task. But it is also necessary that a more broadly conceived organisation of work should become the concern of the self-managing bodies as well, as concern with the provision of more suitable conditions of work, i.e. concern for man and his human affirmation.

All this indicates that although self-management is the most suitable way to ensure the liberation of man, it is not an end in itself, but only a *way* which can ensure the greatest possible measure of freedom. Lest the opposite should happen in practice (when self-management is regarded as an objective with the resulting absurd situations where man, in the name of the institution of self-management, tends to be forgotten), there must be a clearer definition of the humanistic aspect of the principle of self-management, in order to prevent self-management, as a form of political emancipation, from developing into a struggle for power and an encouragement to local bureaucracy.

In consistently implementing Marx's idea, the realisation of the principle of the liberation of work can be based on solving the problem of alienation in the process of work itself, and, in connection with this, in the system of distribution. Is it from this point of view justified to transfer the centre of gravity on to problems of distribution and to conclude that in more appropriate distribution lies the key for the revaluation of human work? Certainly, the abolition of hired-labour relationships (but this does not depend on the distribution system alone) and a consistently implemented principle of distribution according to work, form one of the ways of abolishing alienation in the sphere of work. But in this there is a tendency to forget: (1) that the system of production (i.e. the sphere of human work) and the system of distribution constitute two sides of one and the same production process, and that outstanding problems on the one side form an obstacle to the humanisation of the other (i.e. of the system of distribution); (2) that in the conditions of market production, work is a contradictory process (as revealed by Marx in *Das Kapital*) and that it has a double character: as the producer of use-values and as goods production (as producer of exchange values).

Therefore, in socialism (as long as the conditions of market production continue to prevail) work remains a means of subsistence, a means of the survival of individual existence; and thus a more just system of distribution can only 'correct' the fact of alienation, but not abolish it; and (3) as long as money remains the standard of the value of work it is impossible to change, exclusively by distribution according to work, man's attitude towards the activity he performs, and at the same time, to develop work as a need, because it is still through work that we primarily earn money for living.

It should, therefore, be determined through investigation whether the principle of distribution according to work achieves the desired effect if it is used as the only corrective to the alienation of work, or whether it leads to the opposite effect, reviving old values: the fetishisation of money and the monetary effect of work. It would be especially interesting to examine sociologically to what extent the conditions have been created in this country for the realisation of the principle of distribution according to work, in view of the low technical level of production and the uneven conditions of economic operation, as well as how far scientific methods have been developed for the application of this principle in other activities outside the production process. Since the indispensable conditions for the application of this principle have not been examined, it is difficult to envisage its effects. Failing to be included in a broader system of standards, designed to ensure a more comprehensive realisation of the humanisation of work, the principle of distribution according to work is a partial measure limited in results and scope, the more so as it is regarded exclusively as a system of distribution instead of also as a way to raise the value of work. The impression is thus gained that this principle is being fetishised and offered as a magic formula for solving all economic, social and interpersonal problems.

The priority of economic effect has often been emphasised in our practice even when economic measures have been realised at the expense of basic human needs and demands. Thus, it has happened that self-managing bodies have pushed on with the introduction of incentive payment, without a previous examination of the conditions in their respective work organisations. Thus, it would seem that the principle must be realised for the sake of the principle itself, even when such insistence may present a new form of exploitation; for in conditions of antiquated mechanical equipment and a poor technical basis, work according to norms or, for instance, work on several looms demands a maximum input of energy without any visible effects, since the realisation of the norm and the target does not depend on the worker alone, but also on the capacity of the machinery and on other conditions of work.

Naturally, in these conditions the effects of incentive payment are negligible and the purpose is not achieved, while at the same time dissatisfaction and resistance are caused among the workers.

The question to what extent hired-labour relationships have been removed is also a problem that has remained outside the work organisations' field of vision, although they operate on the system of self-management. The fact must be kept in mind that in Yugoslav enterprises there have often been instances of violations of rights arising from employment: arbitrary dismissals from work, application of sanctions against workers who criticise leaders and negative practices in the work organisation, infringements of rights when taking persons into employment, violations of rights in the case of industrial apprentices, etc.[175]

Do self-managing bodies act in such cases as factors of protection of the workers' rights, enabling the worker really to feel more like a free worker and not like a person who offers and sells labour like a commodity? It has not infrequently happened that workers had to realise their rights by way of court proceedings, often in dispute with self-managing bodies, if they emerged as victors from this dispute.

We do not intend to examine all the practice that could serve as an illustration of the thesis discussed above, i.e. that it is imperative from the humanistic point of view to carry out a re-assessment of the principles on which we are building our own variant of socialist society, in order to prevent socialist principles from leading to non-socialist practice. For a more thorough study we lack the results of concrete empirical investigations, because sociology has not so far been concerned with this sphere or, if it has done anything, in this respect, it has not been bold enough, and thus we are unable to support these reflections with scientific arguments. I believe, however, that these trends are very noticeable and that they should prompt existing institutes to a better organised and more systematic study of the above-mentioned problems. Only on this basis could a more confident reply be given to the question whether the principles we have chosen are producing the desired results, and what ought to be changed in them from the point of view of long-term humanistic ideals. More clearly defined socialist theory would make possible less painful socialist practice and help to prevent an unwelcome tendency, which is spreading in the system of self-management – i.e. that self-management is regarded as an end in itself, and that in work organisations the self-managing bodies are beginning to separate themselves as a political force, which is often opposed to the will of the workers instead of articulating it, unifying it and serving to it.

It has been the aim of this paper to direct attention to the fact that the existence of serious problems, both in theoretical formulations and in the realisation of the principles of our socialist society, indicate that science must not have an apologetic attitude towards socialist practice (and there have been such tendencies in it); Marxist science must be much more critical in order to advance both the theory and practice of socialism. Theoretical thought cannot be a mere comment on the existing situation and what is inferred from the present situation as the immediate future. Marx's philosophy was the vision of what man should bring about, and from the point of view of this 'should' (Sollen) it was able to assess the existing and indicate its limitations and narrow-mindedness. Only by comparing what exists with the ideal can reality be evaluated and critically dealt with. Due to this, Marx's philosophy was not a mere pragmatic tool for action, but a scientific and humanistic vision of the future, which lays on us the obligation to subject, in the name of humanism, all other principles to man and to assess, from this point of view, the value of what we have achieved in socialism. It is, therefore, indispensable to keep revising philosophical and socialist principles in the light of the new conditions and new human problems, as was realised by Lenin when he wrote: 'By no means do we regard Marx's theory as something completed and above criticism. On the contrary, we are convinced that it merely laid the foundation stone for that science which socialists must advance in all directions if they are not to lag behind life.'

It is therefore the task of the Marxist scientist to examine objectively and critically the reality in which he lives; he must be ready to discover the weaknesses of the socialist system which result from inconsistently defined or realised Marx's humanistic ideas, the more so since there have been cases when 'socialist' principles and 'socialist' practice have been built on non-Marxist ideas. Stalin had to die before Stalinism was proclaimed pseudo-Marxism. This is a tragic fact of socialist theory and practice. But we must draw consequences from it, and not allow Marxist science to become apologetic, but rather let it, as 'critical consciousness', continuously correct reality and prevent whole decades of human history from being proclaimed as errors in the future.

The June student movement and social revolution in Yugoslavia*

Svetozar Stojanović

1

Every revolution, relatively quickly after the assumption of power, is followed by signs of its own entropy.[176] A revolution awakens the masses from their lethargy – the question is how to stop them from becoming passive again? The daily train of events surreptitiously attempts to reduce revolution to a short-term event – what is to be done to stop *political* revolution from swallowing the *social* revolution?

The great revolutionary utopian, Ernst Bloch, asks the dramatic question: why has the bourgeois revolution succeeded so quickly whereas the socialist revolution is a succession of crises.[177] The answer, in my opinion, should be sought in the fact that the socialist revolution was conceived quite differently from all previous revolutions. It is the infant of the great Hope for the end class prehistory and the beginning of real history.

The light of an extinguishing long shines on the participants and witnesses, whilst concealing entropy within it. Those who have been the most *enchanted* by revolution[178] feel the most anguish at signs of its entropy. Not everyone, like Trotsky *(The Revolution Betrayed),* seeks a way out of disillusion through opposition to the entropy of revolution. Many retreat into an ironical passivity. Resignation is, of course, not only a consequence, but at the same time a cause of the entropy of revolution. The worst are those whom power makes incapable of seeing the symptoms of the waning of the revolution in those revolutionaries who try to open their eyes to the entropy. The original enthusiasm, the feeling of strength, youth and dynamism soon subsides in them. Tired out along the long and painful road to the revolutionary Rainbow, they gradually turn from revolutionaries

---
*   This article first appeared in *Praxis, international edition,* no. 3/4, 1970, Zagreb. It is available online at <https://www.marxists.org/subject/praxis/praxis-international/Praxis,%20international%20edition,%201970,%20no.%203-4.pdf>.

into evolutionaries, and rationalize this as being the realism of the matured mind. The trivial observation that no revolution ever realized everything it proclaimed, and that each one of them had its twilight as well as its dawn, also serves to save them from a schizoid split.

2

The assessment whether or not there is entropy in a revolution is not only a matter of knowledge. It inevitably has the nature of a value judgement because it is dependent on how *concretely* the basic aims and ideals of the revolution are imagined. Hence some forces in the mainstream of revolution may see entropy in precisely those manifestations which other forces in the same mainstream see as the quickening of the revolution. Just as there are opposing views in the assessment of the fate of a revolution, there are also various methods of struggle against its entropy. Here we shall deal with two of those ways. The first is the Maoist 'cultural revolutions'.

Maoists seek a remedy against entropy of the revolution in a romantic attitude towards primitive communism as the substance of their revolutionary tradition. They believe that this tradition will best be preserved if an all-out effort is made *not to change it*. This is a kind of a permanent fixation for the initial phase of the revolution.

The 'cultural revolution' is not the first attempt by the Maoists to consolidate, perpetuate and extend primitive communism. For the same reason Maoists once conducted the policy of the 'Great Leap Forward'. However, its difficulties only strengthened the Liu Shao Chi faction, which was in favour of certain modernization. Let us mention in passing that the difference between these two conceptions and orientations is very relative and hence hardly visible from the height of those countries that are far more developed than China. In order to suppress the opposing faction, Mao sought support outside the party apparatus, projecting, initiating and organizing the 'cultural revolutions'. It was not difficult to win the youth masses ('Red Guards') for the policy of continuity with the period of the 'Great Leap Forward', and, more generally, for the policy of the romantic return to 'the good old days' of the revolution.

The fundamental principle of primitive communism are: asceticism, collectivism and levelling egalitarianism. In other words, this type of communism is characterized by a kind of a collectivistic and egalitarian asceticism. I have already written about this type of communism at some length,[179] and have no intention of repeating it here. It is quite certain that no hedonism, even a very moderate one, could be a realistic solution for China. A very backward country would have no prospects at all unless its population resigned themselves to the need of selfless sacrifices in favour of the future generations. However, it is questionable whether the true solution for such a country lies in the *absolutisation* of ascetic communism: exhausting labour, exaggerated saving, a complete suppression of material incentives for the sake of moral-political stimulation.

In recent years Maoist ideology underwent an important internal change which is characterized by the absolutisation of asceticism. At first Maoists justified the sacrifice of the present generations by the happiness of the future generations: 'Ten years of suffering – ten thousand years of happiness!' This conception of sacrifice is sensible (*sacrifice for the sake of happiness* of future generations) but it conflicts with the principle of justice. The present generations, namely, are to live a life of sacrifice in order to secure happiness for the future generations, but could the burden of it not be distributed more justly among the generations? Furthermore, asceticism which has an exclusively instrumental value is not highly suitable for the ideological struggle against the USSR. The present generations in the Soviet Union want affluence, which has been made possible by the self-denials of the earlier generations. This is in accordance with the principle which was preached by Maoists themselves. Could they object to the USSR only that its population is unwilling to continue sacrificing themselves, this time for the sake of the happiness of the future Chinese generations and to relieve the burden now carried by the present Chinese generations?

In the 'cultural revolution' Maoists absolutise asceticism: a rich life is *in principle* unacceptable, because it supposedly inevitably leads back to capitalism.[180] Thus when pauperism is taken as a lasting model of living, then the mentioned difficulty with justice and the mentioned weakness in the ideological dispute with the USSR are done away with. However, another big problem arises: the crisis of the sense of sacrifices. An exemplary life implies a ceaseless sacrifice: the present generations sacrifice themselves 'for the sake of' future generations which must also sacrifice themselves and so on *ad infinitum*. Since all generations, both the present and the future ones, are expected to live according to the principle of sacrifice, then this sacrifice must turn around in circles trying to find its purpose within itself, because it is not supposed to seek it outside.

However, independently of all these, the question arises whether the 'cultural revolution' may constitute a sufficiently efficient way of fighting the entropy of the revolution. Sensing that aspirations for modernization will inevitably be renewed, Mao Tse-tung believes that some kind of a cultural revolution will be necessary in China once in about twenty years. In fact, in order to preserve collectivistic and egalitarian asceticism as a permanent social atmosphere, it will not be sufficient just to renew the campaigns; the trend for modernization, which will acquire its impetus, will demand ever stronger and more violent campaigns.

However, if the praetorians of the revolutions are to be ascribed this role, then they will gradually turn themselves into its gravediggers. A lasting curbing of human nature's desire for comforts can only be effected by more ruthlessness. But, being men themselves, the ruthless praetorians have the same desire for comforts. After a certain time, they are bound to start satisfying this impulse within themselves, while at the same time curbing it through violence in others. In this manner, in the name of preserving the revolution, there will be an ever-growing gulf in society between the oppressed masses and the oppressing apparatus. The latter will force the masses to live according the principle of collectivist and ascetic egalitarianism, they themselves will be living a vulgar-hedonist and selfish life of privilege. The participation of masses in renewed political campaigns will continue creating the illusion of democracy, because their 'spontaneity' will conceal the great string-pullers.

3

Now let us consider the Yugoslav June student movement. There has still been no serious analysis of it.[181] This is a good indicator of the state of social sciences in Yugoslavia. Not even the basic documents on the student movement have been published, which just goes to show the level of democracy in our society. In the more advanced countries not only documents are published immediately, but also entire libraries of books and discussions on the student movements.

The most popular view is that our student movement is a reaction against the difficulties of the socio-economic reform, the serious socio-political 'deformations', the monopoly over social and political positions held by older generations, etc. It cannot be denied that these and similar factors are relevant in explaining the student movement. However, the real significance of this phenomenon cannot be understood unless it is considered against the entire background of the social revolution in Yugoslavia. In my opinion the fundamental significance of the Yugoslav student movement should be seen in the resistance to the entropy of the social revolution.

Long before students appeared on a large scale on the political scene, our society had had experience with the entropy of the revolution. The first symptoms appeared very soon after the revolutionaries had taken power in 1945. The main cause of the entropy at that time was the copying of the Stalinist model of social organization. I purposely said the *Stalinist* and not the *Soviet* model, since a certain continuity with the latter was established only with the introduction of workers' councils. The turning point was the Communist Party's conflict with the Cominform in 1948. The most important consequence of this break was the introduction of the forms of self-management in the basic social groups. This was a kind of *revolution within the revolution*. As is always the case, the entropy of a revolution can only be combated by further revolutionalisation.

However, the golden age of revolution this within the revolution was a short one and had its ideological culmination in the adoption of the Programme of the League of Communists of Yugoslavia in 1958. It soon began to reveal its limitations. No matter how enthusiastically it was embraced by the working masses, the revolution within revolution was nevertheless initiated, directed and strictly controlled from above. Thus slowly but surely stagnation has set in. Social changes are still in evidence, but now they are more quantitative and do not extend to essential matters. The forms of self-government, established long ago, have still not been able to get out of the ghetto of small social groups and to develop into an *integral system* of self-management. This accounts for the hybrid system: self-management (such as it is) at the base and strong statism at all higher levels of social organization.

This statist structure is well accommodated by the obsolete system of political organization. Occasionally it is rightfully observed that the socio-political organizations are in a crisis and that they should be thoroughly reformed. No better illustration of this is needed than the fact that to this very day workers have not succeeded in democratically electing someone from their midst to the leadership of the trade unions. In the very best of cases they are still represented by people who were workers three decades ago, but even more so by the trade union apparatus that reproduces itself. Nevertheless, all the proclaimed *reforms* of the system of political organization end up as *reorganizations*.

To build up an integral system of self-government it is necessary to have a developed and democratic system of political organization and activities. But our socio-political organizations, despite declarations to the contrary, still are the transmissions of the League of Communists. And in the League of Communists itself, democracy is still in its infancy.

The common language of self-government and self-management, which even the statists use, creates an ideological screen around the real socio-economic system. Herein lies the special nature of statism in Yugoslavia. Everyday life, however, shows that the statists are fighting tooth and nail to retain control over the centres of decision-making power at all higher levels of social organization, since they have to tolerate the forms of self-management at the lowest level. When one group of statists carries off a political victory over another group, this is usually celebrated as the 'definitive victory over statist forces'. That is why we have so far had so many such successive 'definitive' victories. When the conflicts within the statist structure unexpectedly come to the surface, they create an illusion of revolutionary dynamism and cause serious political crises and shocks.

A *radically* conceived and implemented socio-economic reform could make an end to the present stagnation and entropy of the social revolution. However, of late less is being said about the socio-economic reform, and more just about the economic reform. During the implementation of the economic reform there was a significant differentiation and even polarization of forces advocating it. At first it looked as though there was only a conflict between the statists, who were obstructing the economic reform, and those who supported it. Further developments, however, revealed that there were two basically different conceptions of the reform: one was petty-bourgeois and the other was democratic-socialist. There was a very sharp conflict between these two lines, especially immediately before the student demonstrations.

In the petty-bourgeois conception, the economic reform justly threw out the centralist-distributive, statist economic model, but unjustifiably made a fetish of uncontrolled market forces. On the eve of the student demonstrations the adherents of this view had sent up trial balloons in the press and in other ways on the introduction of stocks. A certain number of shares would, they said, be distributed to the producers, so that they would have closer involvement with their self-managing collectives. After this, of course, stock markets for the buying and selling of shares would have to be opened. Only we were not told what would happen to that little socialism in practice when the short idyll of a universal owning of stocks was over, and society had been divided into those producers without shares and the 'producers' in whose hands shares would be concentrated. There had even been an ideological adjustment to the trend towards uncontrolled social differentiation as the essential feature of 'petty-bourgeois socialism'. The idea of social equality and solidarity had increasingly disappeared from theory and press. The illusion had spread that the revolution could survive even without a struggle to realize ideals.

The economic reform as conceived by the democratic-socialist forces should create a modern market economy controlled and planned by the self-governing society. This line advocates material incentives for professional work and distribution according to the results of work, but at the same time it resolutely opposes exaggerated social differentiation, since this would rapidly lead to a disintegration of the socialist society. According to this view, the finance from public funds, among them the finances of the Yugoslav community for the rapid development of undeveloped regions, should in the future be spent much more rationally, but should not be cut back. The burden of the economic reform should rightfully be distributed so that it would not be disproportionately borne by the working class, as has been the case so far.

The student action was directed against both lines – the statist and the petty bourgeois – which jeopardize the social revolution in Yugoslavia. For this reason both forces united to combat the students. The students extended support to democratic-socialist forces working to create an integral system of social self-government and self-management based on an economy that would be simultaneously planned and market-oriented. When the documentation on the student movement is published, this will be quite clear.

People behave differently when they see the symptoms of entropy of the revolution. Some are surprised, disillusioned, and resigned.

There are many who recognize all 'deformations' (which we refer to here as entropy), but because of their metaphysical conception of the social revolution still consider that there is still essentially a continuity of the revolution. The students joined those forces that are actively fighting to stop entropy and to revitalize the social revolution.

What was the *basic* reaction of the state and party leadership to the student demonstrations? Our politicians had previously met with numerous, albeit isolated, strikes. Now they were unexpectedly faced with mass demonstration and for this reason were nervous and frightened. They were particularly worried because they were aware that owing to the lack of democracy they did not have a proper idea of the forces at work beneath the social surface. They were particularly fearful of the possibility that the student movement would set off an eventual workers' movement. Therefore the first concern of the politicians was to isolate the students from the rest of the population, particularly from the workers, and gradually to reduce the student action to a political and cultural happening within the walls of the university. In this respect the misinformation that the students were only asking for an improvement in their material position (whereas 'the working class was consciously bearing the burden of the economic reform') came in handy. In other republics, the rumour was spread that the student movement in Belgrade had a nationalistic Serbian character.

It is well known that for an organization man a spontaneous social movement is a book with seven seals. Thus from the first moment the politicians feverishly tried to find the initiators and organizers of the student movement. One of the top politicians publicly stated immediately after the student demonstrations that it was backed by a 'reactionary political conspiracy'. Rumours about the *Stalinist-statist* background of the student movement were spread on all sides. Of the politicians that came forward during and after the student action, there were some honourable but very rare exceptions to this rule.

The allusions, and afterwards increasingly open assertions that the student movement essentially had a primitive-communist and even Maoist character stood much better chances of success. As we have seen, primitive communism, including the Chinese type, is characterized by collectivism, asceticism and levelling egalitarianism. In our student movement, however, there was not one slogan or idea tinted with collectivism or asceticism. And if there were any ingredients of primitive egalitarianism at all, they were completely secondary. But still this was made the main charge against the student movement. The struggle of the students against uncontrolled and exaggerated social differentiation was cleverly portrayed as a primitive communist crusade against small entrepreneurs (artisans, truck owners etc.) in the tertiary activities.

However, even if primitive communism were a salient feature of the movement, its origin certainly could not be found in the influence of Maoism. Primitive communism was the dominant conception of the Yugoslav communist movement during the armed revolution, war communism and reconstruction of the country. It should not be forgotten that between primitive communism and the modern communism that we advocate today there is not only a conflict, but also in a certain degree a continuity. Thus the critics of the student movement should have more respect for our common revolutionary, primitive-communist tradition.

It should emphatically be made clear that the programme and manner of entering the political scene of our student movement basically differ from the youth movement in the Chinese 'cultural revolution'. Our student movement is spontaneous and *democratic*-communist in character.

One of the common accusations has been deduced from the student slogan about a 'movement within a movement'. This slogan was meant to convey that the student movement was a movement within the communist and socialist movement, and not a movement *outside* it. This slogan is deliberately interpreted as a desire to set up a new political organization or even party. The organization man simply cannot understand that someone can carry on a political struggle and at the same time not wish to found a separate political organization.

The student movement is often criticized for not being able to cope with a modern economy. This is meant to reinforce the accusation of primitive communism. There is no doubt that a modern socialist society cannot be built without the development of an efficient and rational economy. But in respect to this excuse, it should be pointed out that the economy is the weak side not only of the student movement, but also of the state-party leadership in Yugoslavia. Some of them accuse the student movement of utopianism, targeting that before the war as young communist they were such great 'realists' that they promised the people they would not have to pay taxes when they came into power!

What have been the results of the student movement? My answer to this question might sound paradoxical: the results have been small, but important.

The student movement was in many ways responsible for shaking – and this for the first time so publicly and on such a large scale – the prevailing ideological (distorted) vision of 'our self-governing society'. The reaction to the student action indirectly revealed that in this country there is a degree of self-management exclusively in the social institutions at the base, but that above it, in spite of the theory of the 'withering away of the state', a state force is operating which has a *dominant* social position. The students have lost their political innocence; at first they were sincerely surprised to receive knocks on the head in answer to their revolutionary demands. The young revolutionaries also discovered the 'justness' of the state: in addition to being beaten, they were charged with using violence. Finding themselves up against the wall of solidarity of the state apparatus, the student movement could not bring about the replacement or even resignation of a single official, no matter how insignificant. One of its greatest successes nevertheless was that it forced some politicians to remove their democratic-socialist mask and to use brute force. Since such politicians always feel better behind a mask, it is no wonder that the student action has infuriated them so.

The student movement also forced some intellectuals to take off their leftist-democratic make-up. Some of them (e. g. D. Pejović in the journal *Kritika* 7/1969) revealed their true ideological-political face when they began to write about the world and the Yugoslav student movement in more pejorative terms than typically conservative intellectuals.

The student demonstrations levelled a significant ideological and political (although a less practical) blow against the petty-bourgeois conception of the economic reform. Among other things, under the influence of the students the 'Guidelines of the Central Committee of the League of Communists of Yugoslavia' were adopted.

It should be said that in the given conditions the student movement could not produce any very visible results in the struggle for the development of integral self-government in Yugoslav society. The radical change of the system which is necessary is not possible unless a revolution from above, which we have already discussed, grows into a revolution from below. This requires that the working class and the working masses in general come onto the political scene. The barriers to social revolution should be removed under pressure from below, since integral social self-government and socialist democracy cannot be dependent on someone's good will, least of all of those 'above'. It must be the result of the relationships of social forces. Entropy of the revolution can be effectively stopped only by conscious and large-scale revolutionary engagement. Indeed this was the basic significance of the student action.

However, in Yugoslavia, particularly at the higher levels of social organization, forces are still dominant which find it in their interest to maintain the present hybrid system: a degree of self-management in everyday life, and statism in all the higher and more important centres of decision-making. The democratic socialist forces in these centres have still not become strong enough to be able to take a more energetic action and to rely more openly on pressure from below, including student pressure. Since this shifting of power in the basic centres have still not taken place, the student movement could not give any large results. For this reason there has been a 'gentlemen's' agreement in the state-party hierarchy to avoid discussions of the student movement as much as possible. The entire 9th Congress of the League of Communists was held without a word being spoken about the student movement. The fateful showdown has ben postponed for later. Only then will the anticipatory significance of such a social movement as was Yugoslav student movement be quite clear.

From post-revolutionary dictatorship to socialist democracy*

Yugoslav socialism at the crossroads

Svetozar Stojanović

1

There is only one adequate word to describe the present social situation in Yugoslavia, and that word is *crisis*. For a long time now, the intellectuals of the Left, and, more recently, the leftist student movement, especially since 1968, have been dramatically drawing attention to the accumulating symptoms of the impending crisis. However, awareness of the crisis has become widespread only since the deterioration of the relationships between the Yugoslav nationalities (the most sensitive side of Yugoslav life) caused a kind of social neurosis.

It is no longer possible to conceal the true state of affairs by verbal evasions or by well-known intellectual acrobatics, using the notion of the 'transitional period'. This notion in itself does not say much, for *every* period is a transition between two others, one past and one future. The 'only' question is what will the period toward which the transition is heading be like. The fatalistic optimism of our officials, so clearly exposed by the satirist's aphorism 'The past is constantly changing, but the future is fully certain', has been discredited long ago.

In fact, even some officials speak of the seriousness of the situation, and even of crisis. However, this is done with an attitude of peculiar objectivism, as if the crisis were a natural catastrophe in which they have taken no part and for which they share no responsibility. Nearly all of them remain 'at the head' of the crisis, just as before they were 'at the head' of stagnation, and before that, 'at the head' of success. It is not difficult to foresee that most of

---

* This article first appeared in *Praxis*, international edition, no. 4, 1973, Zagreb. It is available online at <https://www.marxists.org/subject/praxis/praxis-international/Praxis%2C%20international%20edition%2C%201973%2C%20no.%204.pdff>

them will simply continue their attacks on radical Marxists who are resolute in exposing the sources of the crisis, rather than seek a genuine solution.

2

Stalinists also speak of the Yugoslav crisis. But in my opinion, the Yugoslav crisis is not the result of de-Stalinisation, but, on the contrary, its source lies in the unwillingness to be *radical* in this break with the past. The Stalinists have no reason to rejoice since their own system is in an even more hopeless predicament. One need not cite past examples to substantiate this point; there are more recent ones, e.g., Poland (1971), and Czechoslovakia (1968).

However, we must be on our guard against theoretical monomania which is quite common in Yugoslavia. It should be emphasized that the suspending of de-Stalinisation, although essential, is only one of several reasons for the crisis and cannot, therefore, provide a *complete* explanation. I should add that I am deliberately speaking of 'de-Stalinisation' avoiding as much as possible the official euphemism 'destatisation', because this latter term seems to lend itself to ideological mystifications, due to its abstract and non-historical character. Finally, I shall be speaking here only of the political dimension of the crisis; a full discussion would have to take into consideration the economic and moral dimensions as well.

Without an adequate historical consciousness it is not possible to develop a sufficiently sharp social consciousness with regard to the present. We are, unfortunately, still far from possessing an adequate knowledge of the history of the Yugoslav Communist Party and the Yugoslav revolution. This is not simply an accident nor the result of sheer intellectual inability. It is instead the case of the dominant interest in the society imposing a limit on historical knowledge. It is to be hoped, nevertheless, that historians will be resolute enough to undertake a revision of the official picture of the history of the Yugoslav Communist Party and the Yugoslav revolution.

The official version obscures the close connection between the Stalinist social organisation adopted at the time of the taking over power and the Stalinist dimension of the Yugoslav Communist Party before and during the revolution. It is therefore necessary to investigate immediately the process of 'Bolshevization' (the period expression for Stalinisation) of the Yugoslav Communist Party; sectarianism of the Party; the Party's attitude towards the leftist intellectuals; the suppression of internal opposition to the Stalinisation of the Party; the relationships between the Yugoslav Communists in the USSR, especially at the time of the Stalinist purges; the revolutionary terror during the war and after the victory.

Until now, the primary concern of Marxists, both in Yugoslavia and throughout the world, has been the *struggle* with Stalin's cult. There have been very few serious *studies* of the charismatic leaders and their role in socialist revolutions and in post-revolutionary developments. Since the need for an investigation of this kind is evident, we may conclude that the lack of it is due to the power of charisma, rather than to intellectual incompetence.

Stalin's cult represented an immense material power and not a few Yugoslav communists, who were torn apart by a painful dilemma between two charismatic giants, were broken by it in 1948 and chose to follow the hierarchic principle, betraying the domestic for the international charisma. It may be said that until now the socialist revolutions have not been able to summon up the strength to treat their leaders only as human, and therefore, as limited beings. They have, *in this respect* completely failed, since they have in fact allowed their leaders to achieve unrestricted power. As Sartre said: 'Human roles always have a reference to the future: to each of us they appear as tasks to be fulfilled, snares to be avoided, power to be exercised, etc.' ('The Question of Method') Revolutionary leaders should be no exception, since they too, as long as they live, are a potential source of evil as well as good. Nevertheless, even during their lifetime their historical role is given a 'definitive' assessment, monuments to them are raised, people are bound to them by 'unconditional loyalty', etc.

A most interesting theme for research would be the relationship between the spontaneous and deliberate elements in the creation of a leader's cult. It is, of course, a commonplace of social science that great leaders *spontaneously* acquire charismatic status in times of great social crisis and revolution. The cult of Lenin is the best example. After Lenin's death, however, the leaders of communist parties have more and more ceased to rely on spontaneity, making *deliberate efforts* through the party and state apparatus to create their cults.

The building of Stalin's cult is interesting to the social scientist in many ways. First of all, it is a rare example of one big cult following almost immediately after another. Stalin relied on the existing cult of Lenin, turning his grave into a sanctuary and making Lenin's word, naturally in his own interpretation, the final authority on all questions. Spontaneity was, in this way, replaced by design, in the development of both Lenin's and Stalin's cult. Stalin's case has shown how fatal a charismatic leader with great theoretical ambitions but little talent for theory can be to intellectual life.

Special attention should be given to the fabrication of leaders' cults in Eastern Europe, where Stalin allowed the local leaders to develop their own cults in his shadow. Unlike Stalin's cult, which was to *a certain extent* spontaneously based on the fact that he was a member of the leadership of the October revolution, these cults were fully fabricated.

The cult of the leader, fabricated or not, gradually becomes an immense material force. The leading members of the party and state apparatus as well, who have worked with so much faith and enthusiasm to create the cult, inevitably become its prisoners. Even if they wanted to, they would now be unable to fight successfully against their own creation. One finds here, not only historical irony, but a certain kind of historical justice as well.

Unfortunately, even when charisma has exhausted all the internal possibilities it had for coping with social problems, it can still remain a formidable source of power. I am referring to the extremely humiliating situations in which a society can find itself, for example as in the USSR, during the last years of Stalin's reign, when the members of the party and state hierarchy were concerned only with surviving the leaders' arbitrary whims, while together with the people, they both feared his death and desired it secretly. Can a socialist revolution, this real flight to freedom, degrade itself more than by surrendering to the determinism of chance and a chance of a *biological* character at that? This confirms splendidly a thesis about the positive social and moral functions of death.

These are some of the reasons why the transition from the charismatic to the post-charismatic period presents a particularly difficult problem. The only socialists to make this transition with ease were the Vietnamese, probably owing to the fact that they did so in the midst of armed struggle. On the other hand, it is well known how serious the repercussions in the party and state hierarchy of the USSR were after the death of Stalin.

A particular problem for the social scientist is the behaviour of the charismatic leader of the post-revolutionary dictatorship when it enters the process of liberalisation. If the decisive role of the charismatic leader is not made clear, it will be impossible to understand why the liberalisation of a post-revolutionary dictatorship as a rule follows a zigzagging pattern. It is true that liberalisation inevitably subverts the power of the charisma. Although this may seem paradoxical, it is also true that the charismatic leader can compensate for this loss precisely by acting as the initiator and champion of liberalisation. This, of course, can be his *genuine* role only to a very limited extent, for, the stronger the democratic institutions, the weaker the charisma, and conversely, the stronger the charisma, the smaller the chances are for creating and maintaining democratic institutions. This is why the tides of liberalisation regularly alternate with counter-attacks by the charismatic leader, who appeals to the principle of monolithic unity. To maintain his charisma at such times, the leader resorts, among other tactics to 'leftist' demagogy: although he lives in abundance, the leader nevertheless leads the egalitarian political campaign.

Social scientists since Weber have often drawn attention to social crises and the attempts to resolve them as the most favourable condition for the appearance of charismatic leaders. But they failed to note that the cause sometimes reverses direction, and that the charisma can play an important part in *creating* social crises. In this process, too, we should differentiate between *spontaneous* effects and *deliberate* efforts. Systematically obstructing the process of liberalisation in a post-revolutionary dictatorship, the charismatic leader inevitably leads the society into a crisis. Although this may again seem paradoxical, the charismatic character of the leader is renewed in times of crisis, owing to his monopolization of the saviour's role. One of the consequences of such a renewal of charisma is the widespread feeling of uncertainty and fear about a future in which the charismatic saviour and guide will no longer be present.

The charismatic leader is aware that democratisation would gradually deprive him of his power unless he secures for himself the saviour's role. He may, therefore, occasionally even instigate disagreements, tensions, as well as conflicts in the party and state hierarchy, and thus, in society as a whole. A crisis created in this way will then be energetically resolved by him, thus refreshing his charismatic prestige. However, the leader is also aware that too strong an attack on one part of the hierarchy will make him dependent on the other, thus preventing him from exercising his role as arbitrator. In other words, he will refrain from resolving too radically the disagreements, tensions and conflicts, i.e. the sources of eventual future crises within the hierarchy, since only in crisis can his charisma be renewed and refreshed.

3

After the taking of power, the Yugoslav Communist Party carried out a series of revolutionary measures (the nationalization of private capital, the land-reform, etc.); but the new social system introduced in Yugoslavia was to a great extent an application of the Stalinist model. I would like to emphasise that I am speaking of the *Stalinist* rather than the *Soviet* model. A certain measure of continuity with the latter was achieved only after the creation of the first workers' councils in 1950. But continuity was never complete because an essential difference remained from the beginning. The workers' councils in Russia emerged as the result of the spontaneous revolutionary self-activity of the working class; the Bolshevik Party had to make great efforts to gain a majority in the councils. In Yugoslavia, however, 'the party and state leadership *turned over* the management of the factories to the workers', (quotation from memorial tablets found in factories), so that, even today, the communist organisation is not *forced* to contest for influence

FROM POST-REVOLUTIONARY DICTATORSHIP TO SOCIALIST DEMOCRACY 111

within the worker's councils.

Fortunately, however, Stalinism was not the only dimension of the Yugoslav Communist movement. The Yugoslav Communist Party led an indigenous national liberation movement and succeeded in transforming it into a socialist revolution. The Yugoslav revolution of 1941-45 must be regarded as one of the important revolutions of our times, especially because since 1948 it has shown signs of being a revolution within a revolution. If a demystification of the and CPY failed to acknowledge this fact, it would itself become a new mystification.

The dualistic nature of the Yugoslav socialist (Stalinist vs. indigenous dimension) could not remain hidden for long. The latent contradiction had to become an actual conflict. One can detect here a certain regularity: there is no autonomous socialist which did not resist the hegemonistic pressures of the 'international revolutionary centre'. Cuban post-revolutionary development too would have been far more independent of the USSR if Cuba had not found itself so seriously threatened by the USA.

There is no need to insist today on the well-known facts concerning Stalin's attempts to quash the autonomy of the Yugoslav in order to subordinate it to the interests of the USSR as a great power. However, one should mention that during the war Stalin, *in fact,* though not explicitly, criticized the Yugoslav revolutionary leadership for 'leftist' tendencies. It is also interesting to note Stalin's perfidious suggestion to the same Yugoslav leaders which induced them to attack from the 'left' the French and Italian communist parties at the first meeting of the Cominform in 1947; this had, of course, contributed to the isolation of the Yugoslav party when it was itself attacked the next year. In 1948, however, Stalin reversed his tactics completely and attacked the Yugoslav leadership from the 'left' for alleged 'rightist deviations'. In these changes of tactics one can easily recognize an essential feature of the policy he had pursued with such success against the anti-Stalinist opposition in the Bolshevik party: first against the 'left' wing (in coalition with the 'right'), and then against the 'right' using the platform of the suppressed 'lefts'.

The Yugoslav leadership reacted with characteristic ambivalence in 1948 against Stalin's accusations. There is nothing surprising in this when one remembers the ingenious point made by William James, that nothing new can be accepted as a truth until it is received into the body of recognized truths with the *minimum of disturbance and the maximum of continuity*. On the one hand, the Yugoslav leadership indignantly rejected all the accusations, declaring that it would show by its actions that it had been slandered. On the other hand, these actions were gradually transformed into a series of 'ultra leftist' measures which the Yugoslav Communist Party would later regret: the nationalization of the last remnants of small, private retail businesses and crafts; the hardening of the policy toward the rich and the middle peasant as shown by the forced selling of agricultural products to the state and the attempts at forced collectivization; a series of purges of the 'bourgeois element' from the Popular Front, etc. Through this *practical* self-criticism the leaders of the Yugoslav Communist Party tried to be faithful Stalinists and at the same time to take the force out of Stalin's 'leftist' arguments.

Sartre has said in another connection: 'It is always time, of course, that to fight something one must change one self into it: in other words one must become its true opposite and not merely other than it' (interview published in *The New York Review of Books*, 26 March 1970). In the case of Yugoslavia in 1948, no special effort of this kind was required as the conflict was between two very similar social entities. It is not surprising, therefore, that for a long time the Yugoslav attitude was in fact a *Stalinist anti-Stalinism*. The evidence for this may be found in the markedly Stalinist *methods* of struggle against domestic Stalinists, although the struggle was and still remains justified. Since I have written at length on this topic in my book *Between Ideals and Reality* (1969, Beograd),[182] I shall merely add here that the *methods* used against the Stalinists may explain the willingness to easily resort to repression in later years.

Protagonists of great historical events generally cannot appreciate their full historical significance. For a long time the leaders of the Yugoslav Communist Party were unable to understand the full historical import of their decision to oppose Stalin. They entered the conflict without having any new social ideas. Theoretical elaboration and justification followed in the wake of political struggle. The first workers' councils, which were basic to the new position, were introduced two years later, in 1950. It is only an apparent paradox to say that only Stalinists, enjoying Stalin's confidence on the one hand and having an inside knowledge of Stalinism on the other, had a chance to resist Stalin successfully.

To say that the process of de-Stalinisation in Yugoslavia has always shown this essential internal limitation is, of course, not to cast doubt on the historical importance of it. If the Yugoslav Communist Party had capitulated to Stalin, the Yugoslav of 1941-45 would have been of purely local significance. The resistance to Stalin gave it a dimension within the framework of world history, as the first breaking away of a socialist from the 'socialist encirclement. As a result of this encirclement there came the suppression of the socialist revolutions in Hungary (1956) and Czechoslovakia (1968), the failure of socialist reforms in Poland (begun in 1956), and now the threat to the beginnings of socialist reform in Rumania. The Yugoslav victory in the conflict with Stalin has certainly been one of the most important events in the international communist movement since the October revolution.

This is undeniable even if one gives due weight to reasons which have influenced the Yugoslav New Left in its somewhat more moderate evaluation of 1948. The New Left rightly objects to the immodesty of the protagonists of 1948 for, in *the last resort,* they had only revised their own Stalinist choices and corrected their own Stalinist errors. I am not saying, of course, that conscious choice is the only real factor in history and that the principle of determinism has no application to it. But one should note an inconsistency in the attitude of the protagonists of 1948. They regard the break with Stalin as the result of their own *choice,* while their previous Stalinist policies are represented primarily as the outcome of *objective* factors. But, one can ask oneself, why was the *objective* situation more favourable to the introduction of the workers' councils in 1950 (at a time when Yugoslavia was completely isolated, from the political, economic and military points of view) than immediately after the taking of power?! It seems clear that the decisive factor in this case was the Stalinist attitude of the Yugoslav Communist Party at the time of the taking of power, and not an objective necessity independent of that attitude. The notions of 'objective necessity' and 'objective factors' line themselves up very easily to ideological mystification, once they are conceived as independent from the choices made by the principle figures in historical events.

There is another thing to be taken into account in the analysis of 1948, a brutal fact that a small country cannot achieve anything great in this world of immensely concentrated material and military power if it is not prepared to resist and sacrifice. The Vietnamese shows that, if they possess these qualities, their position is not hopeless. But Yugoslavia itself, since 1941 also provides a good example. This is something one needs to emphasize today, and for two apparently contradictory reasons.

The external Stalinist threat to Yugoslavia is still present and will be so for a long time to come. But the threat of foreign intervention is also used in internal politics, as an excuse for slowing down the process of de-Stalinisation. Sometimes this reaches such proportions that Yugoslavia's present position could be naively misinterpreted as worse than in 1948-53. According to this strange logic, it would seem that the safest defence against the external Stalinist threat is to slow down the process of de-Stalinisation. It is not difficult to see, however, that this attitude is, in fact, a rationalization which reveals a hostility to radical socialist democratisation. In fact, the best defence against Stalinism would be a system in which the most important positions would be held only by people who have *completely* broken away from Stalinism. Such a system, though, is impossible without a genuine socialist democratisation. I do not want to underestimate, of course, the seriousness of the problems – such as the need for transition from post-revolutionary dictatorship to socialist, particularly in a small country between two great blocks.

4

The fundamental principles of de-Stalinisation in Yugoslavia are: 1) workers' self-management and social self-government; 2) withering away of the state, and de-professionalization of politics; 3) transformation of the Communist Party into the League of Communists; and 4) gradual emancipation of mass political organisations from the Party in opposition to the Stalinist conception of 'transmission belts'.

Although these ideas were first formulated by the party and state leadership, it is impossible to deny their revolutionary character. What happened to them in actual social practice is an important question for revolutionary forces.

The fundamental achievement of de-Stalinisation in Yugoslavia was to introduce the *forms and institutions* of self-management into working collectives. At first self-management was introduced into the factories, and then, later, into other types of collectives (universities, schools, medical and cultural institutions etc.). This step was a logical consequence of the Marxist assumption that the working class is unable to liberate itself if it does not, at the same time, liberate the society as a whole.

Beyond the working collectives, however, there is neither real self-government, nor even real *participation* of the working class. The 'producers' chambers' in the representative bodies (parliaments and local assemblies) as a possible form of their participation, were from the very beginning the chambers of managers and intellectual ideologists of self-government. Although these 'representations of self-government, from the very base' are, as a rule, quite obedient, the professional politicians have, nevertheless, found it necessary to protect themselves even against *them:* the 'producers' chambers' were never given the same power as the chambers composed of professional politicians. One should add that the various supposedly self-governing associations and unions are also controlled by professional politicians with the help of technocrats. This is, of course, true, as well, of the important state bodies, such as the new Presidium of Yugoslavia, which is composed exclusively of professional politicians. Since the party and state leadership never took seriously the proposal that the Congress of Self-governing People become the supreme legislative body of the country, this congress turned out to be only a periodic manifestation at which politicians, managers, and ideologists of self-government expressed their unanimity.

This is reality. However, there is also the *ideological myth* concerning Yugoslavia as a *'society'* of self-management and self-government' which has grown together along with genuine forms and institutions of self-management and self-government in the working collectives. On the one hand, self-management and self-government provides a potentially revolutionary element in the existing system and they are rightly relied upon by socialist forces. On the other hand, it has become transformed into an ideology. Our radical Marxist intellectuals have a moral obligation towards the leftist movements throughout the world, which have introduced the notion of self-government into their programmes, and to point out the essential difference between the ideological pretensions and the social reality in Yugoslavia.

How did the revolutionary *idea* of self-management and self-government degenerate into an *ideology* of the *status quo* which is made up of forms and institutions of self-government in the working collectives, but statism at all higher levels of social organisation? I have already emphasized that de-Stalinisation in Yugoslavia had certain characteristics of a within the revolution. It was, nevertheless, a *from above,* even though it was wholeheartedly accepted by the majority of the people. De-Stalinisation was initiated and then carefully led and controlled by the party and state hierarchy. Its golden age was therefore quite brief: entropy followed after ten years, and this was followed by stagnation and crisis. The Yugoslav politocracy has never *in practice* abandoned the Stalinist model of the political system of socialism.

I have just said that self-management in Yugoslavia is to be found in the working collectives; but even there, it is restricted to the questions of production and distribution. All political questions *par excellence* are kept within the existing political organisations, i.e. within their leadership. Self-management, therefore, is strictly within the 'realm of necessity.' Yet, as Gramsci pointed out, the workers' self-management and self-government cannot work out and develop if it does not extend beyond the economic, to all other spheres of social life.

The politocracy is determined to use repression, if necessary, to protect its monopoly and prevent any breakthrough of self-government into political life. While the politocracy usually hesitates before intervening in economic life, no ideological scruples restrain it in politics.

Drawing a simple deduction from the myth of 'our self-governing society', the politocracy concludes that all Yugoslav institutions and organisations are genuine manifestations of self-government. According to this logic, any attempt to transcend them or even to submit them to radical criticism becomes, *by definition*, an attack on self-government. In this way, the struggle for genuine self-government can easily be stigmatized and suppressed as an attack on the 'system of self-government'. In this sense one can speak of *repressive 'self-government'* in Yugoslavia.[183]

There are politicians who are willing to concede that Yugoslavia is hardly a good example of developed political, but this is in their opinion compensated by economic. This, too, is a myth since economic democracy cannot be properly developed without political. That is why economic democracy is still in its infancy, and only within the working collectives. True, politicians admit that a new development of economic requires that a larger share of surplus value be left to the working collectives. Although this would certainly be a positive measure, it is far from being revolutionary, because the real centres of political power would remain unaffected.

In addition, the incomparably more radical idea that the entire surplus value should be under the control of the working class, does not have a real revolutionary character until it is combined with a thorough criticism and reform of the present politocratic-statist system. Without a reform of this kind, it is not realistic to hope for institutional arrangements that would enable the working class to exercise effective control over surplus value. The slogan *'factories to the workers'* once played a revolutionary role in Yugoslavia. It has ceased to do so for a long time now, not because the factories already in fact belong to the workers, but because it will remain impossible until the workers begin to play the decisive role in society as a whole. The only position which remains truly revolutionary today is the one which insists on the demand: *society to the workers.*[184]

5

When speaking of the withering away of the state and the de-professionalization of politics one should again clearly distinguish social reality from ideological myths. I do not think that there is any valid evidence to show that the historical process of the withering away of the state and the transcending of politics, as alienated social power dominated by a particular professional group, has begun in Yugoslavia.

Following the socialist in Yugoslavia, the privately owned means of production were expropriated by the state, all political power was concentrated in its hands, and an *immense* party and state apparatus was created at the same time. Since de-Stalinisation began in 1950, this apparatus has been diminished and its power has decreased; there have also been important decentralizing measures within it.

Stalin thought, as we know, that the socialist state must become increasingly stronger in the present in order for it to be able to wither away in the future. This sophistry was exposed in Yugoslavia in the early fifties. But, from the fact that the power of the state in Yugoslavia has been diminished *compared to* its power immediately after the armed revolution, it does not follow that we have a case of the withering away of the state in the Marxist sense. This point remains valid even if one takes into account that the dimensions and powers of the state apparatus in Yugoslavia are in fact *less than* they are in any other so-called socialist country. Besides, there are countries no one would call socialist, where the power of the state apparatus, even in the basic production units, is less than the power of the state apparatus in Yugoslavia. No Marxist would say, however, that in these societies the state has begun to wither away, and that its politics are being de-professionalized, and even less, that they, are ahead of Yugoslavia in that process.

6

To get to the roots of the situation in Yugoslavia one must deal with the ruling communist organisation. The Yugoslav society today remains a political society *par excellence*. The Party is the fundamental factor of power, legitimacy, continuity and change. In a situation of this kind, there is no possibility for a genuine democracy within the society as long as democracy is in its infancy within the ruling party.

De-statisation has been the object of great theoretical and practical concern in Yugoslavia. Yet, it has generally been overlooked that the Party is the core of the Yugoslav state. Until the parcel-concept of statism is opened, it is impossible to appreciate the fact that Yugoslav statism belongs to the party-politocratic type. It is naive to believe that the state has begun to wither away as long as the country is still ruled by a Party which predominantly follows the pattern of the Third International. To criticize statism without reference to the Party as its core is to turn attention from the roots of the problem to its peripheral aspects (state administration).

Also, the real problems concerning the nature and function of the LCY are ignored since the ideological struggle is often aimed at the idea of a multiparty system in Yugoslavia. I should like to say immediately that I do not believe in the possibility of a developed socialist society which would be politically monolithic. I am not concerned here, however, with developed socialism, but with socialism in Yugoslavia as it is at present and as it will be in the near future. I have argued against the multi-party system for present day Yugoslavia in my book *Between Ideals and Reality* and therefore think that it is not necessary to repeat that argument here. Even if the idea were acceptable for Yugoslavia, it would have no chance of being realized. It is well known that the *way* in which a political movement comes to power tends to determine its future behaviour. It is not realistic to expect that a ruling party will be willing to allow the organised entry into the political scene of those social forces which drove it underground in pre-war Yugoslavia and which later fought against it in the civil war and in the revolution. A multi-party system during the post-revolutionary dictatorship could arise only through spontaneous disintegration of the ruling party, if the balance of power between the contending groups would not allow for the political elimination of the one by the other.

Although it may appear paradoxical, the real question concerning the nature and function of the LCY is obscured not only through the attacks on the idea of the multi-party system, but also through the insistent dwelling upon the visionary ideal of a party-less system in the socialist future. However, I do not wish to discuss here the reality of this element of revolutionary utopia. I shall proceed on the assumption that Yugoslavia will be keeping its one-party system in the near future, and I shall therefore concentrate on its critical analysis. I shall be particularly interested in the possible 'checks and balances' within this system of political monopoly. It is a mistake to assume, as dogmatic advocates of the multi-party system do, that there is absolutely nothing that can be done against political monopoly within a one-party system. In admitting defeat on this point, the Marxists unintentionally surrender to the theoreticians of bourgeois democracy and thus reveal an inferiority complex before the developed political systems of capitalist societies.

I shall begin by pointing out that nothing essential has been achieved in the transformation of the Communist Party into the League of Communists. All attempts at a radical reform of the Party have ended up very modestly, as mere reorganisations. For this reason it is still justifiable to speak of the Party in spite of the fact that it has changed its name to the League of Communists.

The Party not only does not *in practice treat* the working class as a 'class for itself', but also within its own ranks there is a *de facto* division into a 'party for itself' (the leadership) and a 'party in itself' (the membership). True, it cannot be denied that the Party has been considerably liberalised and that in this respect no other Communist Party with a monopoly of power can be favourably compared to it. Nevertheless, there is no doubt, that the Party has achieved neither any form of new radical, nor even classical.

The group which dominates Party politics, and Yugoslav political life in general, was formed under the influence of the Stalinist conception of the

Party and has remained to a considerable degree faithful to it ever since. This is the reason why the Party still is, in fact, although not in theory, obsessed by monolithism, centralization and uniformity.

On the other hand, the Party is a heterogeneous mixture since its members belong to very different classes and strata. There are other factors as well that tend to undermine the monolithism of the Party: economic development, education, the openness of Yugoslavia to ideological influences from abroad, and so on. It follows that all attempts to save monolithism are ultimately doomed to failure, and that sooner or later it will have to give way to the diversity of the Party membership. Yet, Yugoslav practice has been consistently aimed at bringing reality into accord with the principle of monolithism. Because of this predominance of the principle of monolithism, all the groups and orientations within the Party tend to subscribe to *abstractly identical* platform. Thus, all declarations favouring open discussion of ideological differences must remain in vain, since they are, in fact, provocations.

The right to differ in certain important matters has implicitly been conferred only on the leadership of the republics which make up the Yugoslav federation; monolithically conceived democratic centralism is still insisted upon within each republic. In a country like Yugoslavia this is the most dangerous and undesirable way of creating pluralism within the Party since it may quickly lead to the emergence of nationalistic factions. This might eventually turn all social disputes into national conflicts, and find the revolutionary concept of the League of Communists degenerating in practice into a coalition of *monolithic national* communist parties.

There is still no possibility of finding out whether the majority of the Party membership supports the official platform since there are no real elections in the Party: the candidates neither offer a platform nor is there generally more than one candidate for each important post. If the absence of free elections in the society as a whole could perhaps be justified, there can be no valid justification for a similar situation in the Party. Under these circumstances the leading hierarchy is able if it so wishes, to secure perpetual renewal of its power. In other words, there exists monolithic, rather than democratic, rotation.

It should also be pointed out that the leading hierarchy will not be exposed to serious challenge and competition until the Party recognizes the legitimacy of an *active minority*. I have in mind the right of the minority to openly advocate changes in the officially adopted party policies. This idea is usually denounced as anarchistic by the ruling hierarchy and it is contended that if adopted, the activity of the Party would be paralyzed.

However, the idea is not anarchistic, nor can this practical argument against it be convincing, simply because acting upon the democratically adopted policies would be binding for everyone, until the minority might possibly turn into a majority.

There is another factor favouring the monopoly of the leading hierarchy: the members and the party cells are, to use Sartre's term, serialised. They are not allowed to communicate *directly,* and, even less, to cooperate *directly* in order to influence the policies of the Party. The present leadership is an *unavoidable* intermediary in this respect. One should not overlook the fact that the membership does not choose the mode of association within the Party; it merely complies with the organisation scheme, prescribed by the leadership. This is not all: as the power to exclude individual members and to disband entire party cells today still rests with the leadership, it therefore is in the position to exercise full control over the rest of the Party. This allows also for the theoretical possibility that the leadership may, in this way, fundamentally change the composition of the Party. The example of the Czechoslovak Communist Party since 1969 shows that this possibility can in fact be realized in exceptional cases.

This position of the party cells and the individual party members explains why even that part of the working class which belongs to the Party is nevertheless precluded from significantly influencing its policies. It has been argued by politicians and even certain theoreticians, that this situation in the Party is in sharp contrast with the present state of self-management and self-government in Yugoslavia. I am inclined to think, however, that this supposed asymmetry is an illusion. Both the working class and the institutions of self-management and self-government are no less fragmented and 'serialised' than the membership of the Party. It would otherwise be impossible to explain why the crucial decisions in the Party as well as in the society are still made by the professional politicians. One of the characteristics of our prevailing political culture, to which I shall return later, is the constant criticism of professionalized politics, even by the politicians themselves; while, at the same time, the professional political elite continues to retain full power. The de-professionalization of politics is proclaimed so loudly and so often that its monopolization *by* professional politicians is thus obscured and the significant qualitative differences among the latter are overlooked.

I have, so far, analysed and criticized the situation in the Party in terms of well-known imagination, one might require, for example, that the present composition of the Party membership be altered in favour of an obligatory working-class majority for the future. Why should not the Party statutes follow the practice of the workers' councils and require that all leading bodies should have a majority composed of democratically elected workers and other creators of material and spiritual values who live exclusively from the result of their labour? What serious arguments can there be against the proposal that in addition to the existing leading party organs in which there must be professional politicians, party organs composed of 'common' Party members should be elected as well. These latter organs could take part in all of the activities of the leading Party organs (except for the decision making), and would, before the Party congresses and conferences, give their own assessment of the work of the leading party organs and of the situation in the Party.

7

From what I have said above concerning the Party and its situation, it is not difficult to see what must follow in regard to the other political organisations and their relationship to the Party. If a communist party internally continues to follow the pattern set up by the Third International, it can hardly be expected that its external relationship will follow a different pattern.

It is time that the Party organs no longer simply overlap with the leading bodies of other political organisations and mass media; to a certain extent, a division of labour and competence has been carried out between the Party and other factors of the socio-political system. However, the Party continues to control them as its 'transmission belts' simply by appointing its disciplined members to all crucial positions. To this day the Party is not *obliged* to resort to argument in order to gain influence and to command respect in those institutions. In this sense, it has not become the internal avant-garde, but instead, has remained the predominantly external avant-garde. Without forgetting the sincere attempts to gain authority for the Party by the force of argument, mention can be made of the fact that whenever these arguments failed, they were abandoned in favour of the old authoritarian methods.

The real role of other political organisations in comparison to the Party can best be seen through a thought-experiment. What would be changed if all these organisations vanished and only the Party remained? Almost nothing! The remaining illusions of the political apparatus of these organisations would suffer the final blow. I do not want to draw from this any cynical conclusion, but merely wish to point out that political organisations in Yugoslavia still await radical reform.

8

It is time to change the theoretical perspective. We often argue in Yugoslavia about cultural politics, yet hardly ever speak of *political culture*. The political under-development of Yugoslavia is usually explained by its economic and cultural backwardness. Yet, in Yugoslavia today there is a higher level of economic and cultural development than political development.

In every society one can find a variety of different political cultures, but I shall speak here only of the prevailing political culture. As Yugoslav society is predominantly political, it is dominated by the political culture of its professional politocracy. This culture, as we shall see in a moment, is still closely related to Stalinism. It is, nevertheless, an error to see Yugoslav politocracy as a single homogeneous world which absolutely does not allow for any breakthrough towards democratic socialism. However, I shall not speak explicitly of this other side of Yugoslav politics. The reader will *per contradictionem* easily come to the conclusion what are its main features. How welcome are these new politicians and how foreign they appear in their surroundings!

The majority of politicians still *live in intermundias,* not, of course, in the sense of non-interference in public affairs. On the contrary, their interference is excessive. However, the yawning gap between their actual achievements and their own ideas concerning these achievements is hardly disputable. The engine idles in reservation often incapable of imparting movement to the 'transmission belts' inherited from the period of revolutionary enthusiasm. In mass political organisations, the professional apparatus has for a long time now remained its own principal preoccupation. The intellectuals, managers, workers, women and young people chosen by the professional politicians to represent the society, merely help them to live in the illusion that they are not cut away from it.

This isolation is connected with an *overbearing vanity*, which is another characteristic of the majority of Yugoslav politocracy. G. Lukacs once argued that the essential trait of Stalinism is that it treats tactical moves as strategic principles. This diagnosis applies *mutatis mutandis* to the Yugoslav situation as well. The difference is that Stalinism has been somewhat transformed: political meetings and measures are often declared to be of *historical significance*. Thus, we have more phases of the than the itself. This can be taken as a sure sign that the revolutionary and the ephemeral have been confused, and that the sense of what has genuine historical importance has been lost.

It is hardly surprising that this inflation of historical turning points has led to the loss of optimism and, therefore, to the contrary of what has been intended. Permanent cannot be identified with the constant escalation of historical pretensions. On the contrary, the more genuine historical achievements, there are, the less is the need for ideological-political noise. Already Greek philosophers knew that the fact of movement is proved by actual movement and not by statements about it.

It is interesting to observe that the majority of our politocracy remains bragging even in times of crisis. Yet, at such times, their self-confidence manifests itself in sharp criticisms of the existing situation, so that even their failures become pretentious. To be self-critical is undoubtedly a virtue, but it can hardly be considered proof of success. The least the Yugoslav politocracy could do in the present crisis would be to lower their tone and speak *pianissimo*.

The language of the politocracy is a story in itself. We are often concerned today about the pollution of our natural environment. Perhaps we should also pay more attention to the *pollution of the linguistic environment* and its prevention. I am not thinking of something like Orwell's 'double-speak', but of some kind of 'half-speak', 'quarter-speak', etc. It is not a language of straightforward lies, but of half-truths, and quarter-truths, to which people have become accustomed and, at the same time, numb. The language sometimes has such power that as Ovid says in *Metamorphosis*, 'By magic songs and powerful spells even the moon may be taken out of the sky'. The politicians I am speaking of are not deluded to such an extent. Their language has primarily an anaesthetic function.

The second basic function of this language is ritual. It is some kind of pass-talk of professional politicians. If they did not make use of certain words constantly, they would remain exposed to attack by their superiors or rivals. Politicians recognize each other by the use of this language which represents a guarantee that the uniform rules of the game will not be violated through a deviant personal attitude. Someone wanting to compile a dictionary of good political terminology would find very little material in Yugoslavia, but he could easily put together a rich collection of political nonsense.

A. Koestler once wrote about a young man who was discovered by his captors to be a communist because he repeatedly used the word 'concrete'. The majority of our politicians could likewise be discovered through their overused stereotypes, clichés, and euphemisms, e.g. 'structure', not to mention senseless expressions such as 'self-governing logic' (language, process, consistency).

The prevailing political language is also 'enriched' by giving new names to old things. There are two principal reasons for this practice. The first is that linguistic innovations create an illusion of political dynamics which has the effect of concealing the practical stagnation. The second is that new expressions such as 'self-governing agreement' and 'self-governing settlement' conceal the failure of previous policies, in this case the failure of the *laissez-faire* conception of distribution, according to which income is to be distributed by completely autonomous workers' collectives.

The prevailing political cultural is also characterized by a *specific variant of practicism*. The importance of theory is not denied, but in practice, no hypothesis is excluded in advance and so the expense of social experimentation is unnecessarily high. So it 'had' to be proved in practice that, e.g., the whole LCY or Yugoslavia cannot simply be the sum of its parts or that *laissez-faire* market economy necessarily leads to economic crisis.

At the end of this sketch I would like to say something on *the central role of the enemy* in Yugoslav political culture. It is very closely connected with the remnants of a specific pseudo-dialectical understanding of social conflict.

The original version of this pseudo-dialectical understanding is well-known: in pure Stalinist ideology the existence of conflicts in socialist societies is admitted, but only in the form of conflicts of the 'old' with the 'new.' However, when it comes to the polarization within the 'new', it is declared that one side of the conflict in fact belonged to the 'old' and was only disguising itself as the 'new'. So it seems that there has been no conflict within the 'new' since the other side is subsequently excommunicated.

There is another, somewhat milder, form of the same theory, particularly in the Chinese ideology manifested in the Cultural Revolution. According to this view, conflicts may appear even within the 'new', in the Party, and even in its leadership, e.g., the conflict between bureaucracy and communism. However, there is ultimately very little difference between this view and the original one. In both cases, only one side is completely untainted, completely socialist, and all others are finally seen as enemies and given 'appropriate' names such as 'revisionism', 'the restoration of capitalism', etc.

This pseudo-dialectical theory is explicitly and contemptuously rejected in Yugoslav ideology, but it constantly reappears in new and concealed forms. Apart from certain unimportant conflicts, *all fundamental* conflicts in Yugoslavia are renounced as being of a non-socialist character. *All* these conflicts are ultimately reduced to different pairs of contraries – e.g. unitarianism/nationalism, statism/anarcho-liberalism, state ownership/privatization of ownership – which are equally hostile to *pure* socialist orientations (internationalism, self-management and self-government, social ownership, etc.). Official Yugoslav ideology has never admitted that any important social conflict in *socialism* could be really *socialist in character*. This might serve to explain the tendency to suppress social conflicts rather than to allow for their solution through democratic process. Fear and near panic invariably accompany any serious disagreements or conflicts in the Party, i.e. in the organisation which should be socialist *by definition*.

It is well known that Stalin thought that class struggle becomes intensified with the development of socialism. Although it has been officially rejected, this thesis is constantly reappearing in concealed forms in Yugoslav political life. Judging by the frequency of the politicians' attacks on the enemies of 'self-governing socialism', their number must be constantly increasing. In more developed political cultures the more successful a politician is, the fewer enemies he has. However, listening to political speeches in Yugoslavia, one sometimes gets the impression that socialist forces are surrounded by the enemy, both from the inside as well as the outside. It would be naive to deny that socialism has dangerous enemies, but it is one thing to be aware of their existence, and quite another to be haunted by them. It is not incorrect to say even now that the struggle against the enemies of socialism is often disproportionate to the genuine struggle for socialism.

Following the principle that opposites coincide many politicians treat different 'enemies' as if ultimately there was no difference between them. The opposites coincide, but merely because they were forced to (A. Huxley). As the official politics believes itself to be the standard of socialism, any criticism of it becomes *by definition* an attack on socialism. At the same time it is always considered to be an insult to some 'Platonic socialist idea' which is felt to stand behind the official politics. Such ideas not only justify current politics, but every change of political course as well, since nothing can sully the purity of the 'Platonic idea'. The change in policy often entails the acceptance of the critique and ideas of radical Marxist intellectuals but the official propaganda continues to attack their authors as enemies of socialism. Woe to him who is shown to have been right before his time!

9

It can safely be said that the past thirty years since the beginning of the revolution, have in many respects, been an historical epoch' for Yugoslavia (as distinct from an historical period', to use for the moment Merleau-Ponty's distinction). Before the revolution one could say that Yugoslavia lived for the most part in the margins of history. The revolution of 1941-45 and the beginning of the revolution within the revolution in 1948, resulted in a great acceleration of the historical process in Yugoslavia, which brought it closer to the centre of the historical stage. This has, actually, happened disproportionately to its physical size and economic and political power. There is no need to dwell on the social progress that followed the revolution in Yugoslavia. It is well-known that under difficult conditions Yugoslavia made an industrial 'take-off' and almost caught up with the low middle developed countries; that urbanization proceeded at a staggering rate; that institutions of workers' self-management and social self-government are introduced at the local level; that the independence of the country was won and preserved under difficult geo-political conditions; that Yugoslavia is the first, and until now, the only socialist society which is in many respects open towards the world, etc.

There are three possible approaches to any social situation: 1) the historical, 2) the comparative, 3) the revolutionary. Although the internal development of Yugoslavia has come into a crisis, the *status quo* continues to be legitimized successfully by appealing to the first two criteria: by assessing that which has been accomplished in terms of the starting point, and the attendant difficulties, as well as by comparing Yugoslavia to closed societies, which nevertheless call themselves socialist.[185] The revolutionary approach has, of course, nothing in common with nihilism, but goes beyond the historical and the comparative perspective, without neglecting them.

Marxists have, in the past, paid more attention to the transformation of the revolutionary into a conservative (Stalinist) dictatorship than to its evolutionary potential for a socialist. Some Marxists have come to the conclusion, almost in agreement with certain bourgeois analysts of communism, that the corruption of revolutionary dictatorship is some kind of 'iron law' inevitability.

Political democracy is often appealed to in order to justify invidious comparisons between socialism and developed capitalism (standard of living is another criteria used for this same purpose). This practice has been so successful that it results in an unconscious sense of inferiority of socialism shown in the aping of the *most formal* elements of bourgeois democracy; and socialism therefore lags still further behind developed capitalism.

It is not accidental that the theory of permanent revolution has almost retained its original form in which it postulated a continuous development from the bourgeois to the socialist revolution. The need to more resolutely extend the theory of the permanent revolution is long overdue; it should also cover a continuous development from socialist political to socialist social revolution as well. The theory of permanent socialist revolution ought particularly to take into account recent historical experiences in Yugoslavia and Czechoslovakia. Yugoslav experiments are of fundamental importance in connection with the democratisation of the workers' collectives, and after the Prague Spring of 1968, the democratisation of political life in socialism is no longer a *terra incognita*. Are we to say that the majority of Yugoslav theoreticians and politicians do not really believe in the possibility of political democracy in contemporary socialism since they show no genuine analytical interest in the Czechoslovak political ideas and experiments of the Prague Spring? It seems that here again we in Yugoslavia are going about in circles. The times of the most important theoretical breakthroughs and innovations coming from the top of the political elite are inextricably past. The democratic conception of socialism can only be built with the participation of *all* the intellectual and progressive forces of society but this kind of mobilisation itself presupposes a certain measure of political democratisation.

I shall now return to my statement that social developments in Yugoslavia after 1948 had some characteristics of a revolution within the revolution. It might be objected that the processes of de-Stalinisation were initiated and controlled from *above* and that therefore they could not have been genuinely revolutionary. I have of course, no wish to deny the premise of the argument, but I do not believe that the conclusion follows. What I said earlier concerning the role of the party and state leadership was not meant to imply that there was no pressure from below. This pressure was partly responsible for certain fundamental structural reforms whose revolutionary nature it is very hard to deny. Finally, it should not be forgotten that Yugoslav Stalinism until 1948 was a part of the *international Stalinist system,* so that the revolutionary character of the break with it in 1948 and afterwards is due to both Yugoslav secession from that system and to internal structural reforms in Yugoslavia as well.

One cannot, of course, speak of a revolution within a revolution in *the full sense of the word* before the rise of a communist movement. Since this failed to happen in Yugoslavia, our revolution within the revolution proceeded from stagnation, through entropy, to crisis. I am afraid that we have thus passed from an historical epoch to an historical period, to use once again Merleau-Ponty's pair of terms.

It is increasingly evident that the Yugoslav political system has become petrified in the past few years and that it has found itself in opposition with its own previous results. The present distribution of economic and political power is incompatible with the mobilization for an *essential* breakthrough; the selection of people for important posts is controlled by basic centres of social power and is not made according to satisfactory criteria. We live in a society of *political scarcity,* although the level of economic development favourably compares Yugoslavia to the lower bracket of the middle developed countries.

Contrary to the usual opinion, the economic and political system as it is today, is not in opposition to the *existing* institutions of workers' self-management and social self-government. The monopolization of the basic decision-power by professional politicians is in full accord with the atomization of self-management and self-government. The Yugoslav political system is only in conflict with the vision of the integral system of the workers' self-management and social self-government.

It is impossible to deny that the post-revolutionary dictatorship in Yugoslavia has been significantly *liberalised* since 1950, but this should not be allowed to blind us to the absence of real democratisation. The impetus created by the initial de-Stalinisation has been quickly exhausted. Creativity and planned experimentation have been replaced by political inertia and improvisation. Economic and social reform failed first politically and then economically, and was finally reduced to stabilization; socialist changes during the past few years have been more quantitative than essential.

The basic centres of social power are still dominated by forces which are unwilling to allow radical socialist changes in the existing system. Therein the 'mystery' of the occasional revolutionary proclamations unaccompanied by its practical realization is explained. It is not surprising that lay people are often confused and unable to understand why such declarations are never put into practice.

Under pressure from the more progressive elements in the Party, the centre, as well as the conservative wing of the Party, occasionally will consent to radical political declarations. However, no one should confuse mere verbal acceptances of a principle with a genuine disposition to use it as a guide for action, and therefore fall into the misconception that the right wing and the centre could actually favour the realization of their declared aims. This balance of forces in Yugoslav professional politics explains why the most successful politicians are those who are radical in their programme and rhetoric, somewhat left of centre in their criticism of the current situation and centrist in their practical attitudes. What other explanation could there be for the shifting from reform to stabilization; from one reorganisation to another?

There can be no hope of breaking away from this circle until the Party is transformed from the guardian of the existing order into the initiator of the communist movement. It is well known that for Marx, communism was foremost a movement, but in the last thirty or forty years the majority of communists have become so rigid that the Party has become synonymous with the Movement. In all revolutions, until now, however, the active movement has been considerably broader than the Party. It was only after it had seized power that the Party eliminated all other participants in the movement from the political scene. Is the democratisation of the post-revolutionary dictatorship conceivable without returning to the original idea of the Movement?

In addition to the Party, the Yugoslav communist Movement should include, above all, industrial workers, and leftist students and intellectuals. It goes without saying that the Movement would grant no special privileges to the Party. In order to gain influence in the Movement, the Party would have to rely on persuasion, argument, and example. But the uncertainty evolving out of such a situation seems harmless when compared to the certainty that there can be no developed socialism until the Party is *forced* to act in this way. A benefit which is freely granted does not have the same significance as that which has been fought for and won. Real and secure democracy can never be a gift of the benevolent political leadership – the masses must conquer it.

Many Party members wish for a communist movement, but are unwilling to face any kind of spontaneous initiation from below. The trouble is how to get out of this circle: in times of crisis the officials are too afraid to risk democratisation, and yet, a socialist solution for the crisis is impossible without democratisation.

The fundamental reform of the Party will also continue to retreat like a mirage if there is no effective pressure from below. 'The materialist interpretation of history is no cab to be taken at will; it does not stop short of the promoters of revolutions.' (Max Weber, 'Politics as a Vocations' from *Max Weber, Essays in Sociology,* H. H. Gerth and C. Wright Mills, eds., p. 125). The Party apparatus is under the illusion that its motives are the historical interests of the working class rather than its own immediate interests. This altruistic self-satisfaction can only be dispelled by the pressure of the proletariat expressing its real interests. The real question is not why the Party doesn't enable the working class to enter the political scene, but rather in whose *interest* it is, in the Party, to allow and support the political activity of the working class.

The point is that the Yugoslav Party created the conditions for the development of the working class and not conversely: classical Marxism was mistaken in supposing that the industrial revolution could not follow but must precede the socialist revolution. The Party tried, of course, to create a working class which by its atomization and even 'serialisation' would correspond to the political monopoly it had in society. Atomized self-management is certainly not favourable to the development of the workers' *class* consciousness. The trade union hierarchy is bent on doing everything in its power to prevent the development of a class consciousness from the fragmentary consciousness of workers isolated from each other by the opposed interests of their self-managing firms.

The view that the class consciousness of the working class could be formed by Party preaching and lecturing has long been discredited, at least in theory, in Yugoslavia. It is well known that the workers cannot develop from a 'class in itself' to become a 'class for itself' until they are politically active and organised. The myth that the working class is the ruling class in Yugoslavia is nevertheless very influential, although the working class *as a class* is not present on the political scene. To justify this state of affairs, the politocracy usually points to the backwardness of the working class. However, Yugoslavia already has large industrial centres, and the political position and function of the workers there is also quite insignificant. It is not enough to have a working-class ideology; what is necessary is a politics really inspired by working-class interests. Gramsci rightly maintained that the proletariat will achieve its historical emancipation from the fetters of immediate existence through simultaneous constituting and suppressing itself as a class. Yet, in socialism so far, there have been few signs of the self-suppression of the proletariat; we find instead its repression by the Party which has effectively prevented it from constituting itself into a class.

History shows that a social crisis which cannot find a solution on the left, will very probably be resolved by a shift to the right. The historical responsibility for the strong emergence of the nationalist right on the Yugoslav political scene lies, therefore, with those circles within the Party which in 1968 and later decided to quash the leftist student movement that might have instigated the political engagement of the working class and a general shift to the left. In 1968 the Party hierarchy felt for the first time threatened from the left, and so the majority of the leadership opted for the suppression of the student movement as a 'group-in-fusion'. This is one of the points in the history of the LCY that might be as far reaching as the suppression of the workers' opposition was for the Bolsheviks.

Our crisis cannot be genuinely overcome by a centrist politics which successively resorts to attacks against the left and against the right or against both at the same time, in an effort to keep the balance that safeguards its interests. The guardians of the past are still too strong in the party to allow the democratic-communist wing to rely *openly* on support from below. Radical socialist democracy will remain unattainable until both these conditions are realized: differentiation within the political hierarchy and the spontaneous rise of a leftist workers' and intellectuals' movement from below. Both the Stalinists and the anarchists – though of course for opposite reasons – never had any faith in the possibility of this fruitful union between political organisation and political spontaneity. It would be insincere to say that such a union in Yugoslavia, at present, could be realized, but conscious commitment to a future course of action and preparation for it is sometimes more important in history than the length of time necessary to attain it.

Workers' councils in Yugoslavia: successes and failures*

Goran Marković

The Socialist Federal Republic of Yugoslavia was the only country in world history which experienced self-management throughout almost its whole existence. Self-management purported to be the essence of the Yugoslav social system, and workers' councils lay at its core. The achievements and failures of this experience take on great practical importance today because of the revival of ideas of participatory democracy and self-management in some parts of the world and in some currents of the workers' movement. If the Yugoslav experience had proved that self-management as such is impossible, then it would be useless to revive the idea because every version of it would eventually fail. But if the failure of Yugoslav self-management was not caused by man's inherent imperfections, then other explanations must be sought. At the same time, the fact that workers' councils lasted for forty years is in itself evidence that the project had some positive sides that should not be underestimated.

Historical background of the creation of workers' councils

Workers' self-management was not part of the original program of the Communist Party of Yugoslavia (which took power in 1945). According to the Party, the economy had to be under state control while nationalization had to lead to overall state ownership. The Communist Party Politburo was the decisive political body; trade unions were under party control and were treated as mere transmission belts. Workers' councils were created for the first time in 1949. They were to serve only as consultative bodies while decision-making remained in the hands of CEOs imposed by the state. Workers'

---
* This article was first published by *Socialism and Democracy Online*, 29 December 2012, <http://sdonline.org/57/workers-councils-in-yugoslavia-successes-and-failures/>. Copyright © The Research Group on Socialism and Democracy. It is reprinted here by permission of Taylor & Francis Ltd, <http://www.tandfonline.com> on behalf of The Research Group on Socialism and Democracy.

councils became organs of workers' management only after June 1950 when the Federal People's Assembly adopted a law putting state enterprises and higher economic units under management by work collectives.

Workers' councils were introduced not as the result of conscious struggle of the workers' movement, but rather as a by-product of the conflict between the Yugoslav CP leadership and Stalin. It is unlikely that workers' councils would have been introduced if this conflict had never occurred. The conflict confronted the Yugoslav party leadership with two problems. First, it had to prove its own legitimacy and fidelity to Marxism in order to justify its challenge to the Soviet leadership. Second, the conflict itself prompted reconsideration of the then existing social order, which was a mere copy of the Soviet one. It would have been strange and impossible to explain why the two leaderships came into conflict if there was no difference in their social systems.

Of course, the Yugoslav leadership could have chosen another way to distance itself from Soviet Union. However, it is not perchance that it decided to introduce self-management as an alternative to the Soviet system. First, most of the top Yugoslav leaders were well educated Marxists. Therefore it is not surprising that they decided to 'go back to Marx' and to accept ideas which, in one way or another, were present during the Paris Commune and the October Revolution. Second, the concept of workers' self-management, already known in the workers' movement and in Marxist theory, represented a natural and definitive contrast to the Stalinist practice of bureaucratic domination over society as a whole, particularly over the economy. Third, it was obvious that workers in a centrally controlled economy lacked sufficient economic motivation. This suggested the need for decentralized management. Although decentralization did not necessarily entail worker control, in the Yugoslav context it was the most appropriate solution. Fourth, during the National Liberation War of 1941-45, self-organized people's liberation committees emerged all over Yugoslavia as new institutions of power. Principally, they were under the political leadership of the National Liberation Army and National Liberation Front, although they included many non-Communists and members of pre-war bourgeois parties. Although this phenomenon lasted only a few years, Yugoslav leaders saw it as a good starting point for the development of workers' self-organization and self-management.

The Yugoslav Revolution was an authentic one, emerging from the fight against Nazi occupation. The Yugoslav leadership had at its disposal at the end of World War II an 800,000-strong army and a very well organized and experienced Communist party with 141,000 members[186.] It received some support from the Soviet Red Army only at the end of war. Out of its independent struggle, the Yugoslav leadership wanted to pursue an independent policy. This led to an inevitable conflict with the Soviet leadership.

Because of the Stalinization of the Yugoslav CP in the 1930s, the concept of so-called state socialism was accepted and implemented during the first post-war years. It was also called revolutionary etatism by leading ideologists of the time and was proclaimed as a necessity in an underdeveloped society. However, the existence of so-called revolutionary etatism, even temporary, led to creation of a bureaucracy as a de facto new ruling class. It was a bureaucracy which in its own interest introduced self-management, with workers' councils as its first organizational form. This was the basic contradiction of the Yugoslav system of self-management which eventually led to its failure.

There was no strong and autonomous workers' movement in Yugoslavia at the moment of introduction of workers' councils. Trade unions were under the control of the CP, which was strongly centralized. Pre-World War II trade unions had long been controlled by a tiny and regime-oriented social-democratic cadre, and when the Communists won decisive positions in many of the larger (100,000+-member) trade unions, they were banned by the government (1940). The political wing of the workers' movement also was not strong. While the legal Socialist Party was firmly connected to the regime and ruling class yet without any real influence among the working class, the CP was strictly illegal although stronger among workers in the 1930s. So, at the end of 1940s, the workers' movement lacked autonomy and there was no developed political culture among workers which would make them independent of state, party, and employers.

The economic and cultural backwardness of Yugoslav society had a great impact on the development of self-management. The small size of the working class at the end of World War II – with 75% of the population living on agriculture[187] – also influenced the prospects of workers' councils.[188] Yugoslav workers were mostly of peasant origin. They lacked educational or professional skills, not to mention the culture of organization and struggle against authorities. Many of these newly mobilized workers were in fact half-workers, half-peasants, with some private property, and were not attuned to work discipline or to the functioning of workers' councils. Their outlook remained petty bourgeois.

Moreover, Yugoslav society never developed the type of democratic political culture which is necessary for self-management. It has always had an authoritarian political culture, where strong leaders played the most important role in social life while the state was often seen as an organ for taking care of people. This is one of the reasons why Yugoslav workers did not resist the bureaucratic degeneration of self-management. At the same time, the party leadership was caught in a dilemma. On the one hand, it had to deepen the process of socialist transformation in order to mark Yugoslav society off from the Soviet system and legitimize itself in the eyes of Yugoslav workers. On the other hand, it could not overcome its own lack of democratic political culture which originated from its subordination to Stalinist ideology and its highly centralized internal relations. In practice this discrepancy could be resolved in one way only: by introducing a form of workers' self-management in which bureaucracy and working class operated jointly – but with clear prevalence of the former.

This social situation caused doubts in the party leadership about workers' readiness for self-management. According to Yugoslav leader Josip Broz Tito, workers' self-management was introduced with some delay for this reason.[189] It was one of the inevitable contradictions which marked the first stage of workers' self-management: self-management requires certain levels of cultural development and professional and managerial skills; time and practice are needed to achieve them. According to one analysis of workers' councils in the city of Užice, Serbia, most members of workers' councils rarely took part in discussion, while CEOs played a decisive role. Decisions were made mostly by administrative and technical officials while workers tended to uncritically accept their proposals.[190]

Legal solutions

Workers' councils were introduced in state enterprises by a December 1949 Directive. Councils were formed in 215 selected enterprises; half a year later, their number had grown to around 800. But they did not have managerial authority. They could only give advice and proposals to CEOs, while the latter were not obliged to accept them. For example, according to Article 3 of the Directive, workers' councils could discuss economic plans of enterprises, draft rules of order at the workplace, propose measures for improvement of production or for better organization of work, discuss work norms, etc. The CEO had to consider the workers' council's conclusions. If he opposed them, he had to submit them to an administrative-operative chief for a final decision. Until this official resolved the case, the CEO could disregard the workers' council's input. However, if the workers' council opposed the rulings of the administrative-operative chief or other state organs, the CEO nevertheless had to apply them. Thus, the powers of workers' councils at the enterprise level were very modest while at the branch or national level they were non-existent. The first workers' councils, established between December 1949 and June 1950, were organs of workers' participation and not of workers' self-management.

The first appearance of workers' councils was welcomed by the working class and by Yugoslav society as a whole, but it was clear from the outset that the limitations under which they operated were unacceptable. A new Basic Law, ratified by the federal parliament on June 27, 1950, provided the legal basis for workers' self-management. It had to abolish excessive bureaucratization of the economic system, to introduce more democracy into it, and to 'gradually establish management of state enterprises and higher economic associations by work collectives according to the socialist principle that producers themselves have to manage social production' (Preamble of the Basic Law).[191] In Article 1 of the law it was stated that work collectives manage state enterprises, which are under people's ownership, in the name of the community and in the framework of the state economic plan. Work collectives fulfil this duty through workers' councils and Managerial boards. Workers' councils were elected by all workers in the collectives for a one-year term (Articles 2 and 3). The workers' council as a whole, as well as its individual members, could be recalled at any time (Article 3/2). This made council members – in contrast to parliamentary representatives, who could not be recalled – accountable to those who elected them.

The first weakness of this model of workers' self-management was that management boards as executive organs had great influence on management. It is true that they were defined as organs elected by and responsible to workers' councils, but they were also responsible for the management of enterprises and, together with the CEO, for their day-to-day running. For their decisions, management boards were accountable not only to workers' councils but also to state organs. This severely limited self-management, despite certain restrictions (in Article 6) on the powers of the management boards. A further limitation in the Basic Law was the stipulation that the CEO of an enterprise would not be elected by workers but rather nominated by the state or by a management board of a higher state enterprise. A CEO was thus responsible not to the workers' council but to a management board and higher CEOs.

Workers' councils had between 15 and 120 members. The larger councils were more like workers' assemblies or workers' parliaments,[192] and they did not have day-to-day contact with workers. Exacerbating this lack of contact was the fact that council members were not formally obligated to follow workers' opinions on particular issues. It was a contradiction: workers could recall members of workers' councils if they disagreed with their policy, but they could not oblige them to follow a particular policy during their mandate.

All workers in the enterprise, regardless of skill-level, could elect and be elected to the councils. Elections, held annually, were direct and by secret ballot. By law, workers' councils had the following prerogatives: acceptance of basic economic plans of an enterprise, adoption of policy measures for the enterprise, election and dismissal of a management board, deliberation on particular decisions of a management board, allocating a portion of the enterprise's surplus.

The relationship of workers' councils to management boards was analogous to the relationship of parliaments to governments. This was particularly the case when workers' councils were large. Their size often compromised their efficiency while small-size management boards, composed of more educated cadres, prevailed. And although workers' councils could shape the general economic policy of enterprises, management boards had control over their day-to-day affairs.

Workers' councils strengthened their legal position from 1950 on. They achieved their legal peak with the 1974 Constitution and the 1976 Associated Labor Act (in Serbo-Croatian *Zakon o udruženom radu* or ZUR), which strengthened their authority and introduced new organizational forms based on the principle of delegation. Large enterprises were subdivided into smaller units known as basic organizations of associated labour (BOAL), numbering 300-400 workers, which were in turn divided into still smaller units within which workers performed their jobs and elected delegates to workers' councils.[193] At the level of the BOAL, workers could decide all important matters. But, insofar as the BOALs were subordinated to larger regional and national organizations, their possibilities for independent decision-making remained limited.

The basic institutions of self-management were workers' assemblies and workers' councils. The assemblies, composed of all workers, met from time to time to set basic priorities, while the councils met more frequently and decided on the most important issues. Here it is important to distinguish two rights given to workers in their relationship to workers' councils. First, workers had a right to recall council members. They had this right from the very beginning but they used it only occasionally. Another right which they obtained only in 1970s was to give council members obligatory instructions how to vote. If workers were not satisfied with council members' behaviour, they could recall them.

According to the 1974 Constitution (Article 100), workers' councils had the right to elect executive organs and CEOs, draft statutes of their enterprises, enact economic policy, and define measures for its execution, etc. But they had to follow directions imposed on them by their electors, which meant that they could not follow their own policy.[194] Workers' councils had more discretion in deciding on surplus and accumulation. Council-members had to be in constant touch with their electoral base – workers themselves – and they could not, as in the first phase of workers' self-management, act independently. This surely broadened self-management and further democratized it. Workers' councils, by a two-thirds vote, elected CEOs or collective executive managing organs that were responsible to them. Nominations, however, were made by special commissions composed of workers' delegates, members of trade unions, and representatives of socio-political communities (municipalities).

Workers' councils and reforms of the system

Workers' councils had to deal with many reforms of the Yugoslav system from 1950 to 1990. At the beginning, the system was characterized by bureaucratic control over the economy from a single centre. Subsequently, there was a gradual broadening of workers' councils' autonomy. Between 1952 and 1956, workers' councils could not direct allocation of resources and distribution of income.[195] The state determined the system of salaries as well as use of funds. The decentralizing reforms of the 1950s did not at first significantly change the role of workers' councils, for they depended on decisions of republican[196] and local instead of federal institutions. After 1957, wages were no longer fixed by public authorities, and workers' councils had the right to decide on allocation of resources remaining after taxation.

The fifteen years after introduction of workers' councils could be described as a period of gradual decentralization of the economy, devolving power onto federal units and municipalities as well as broadening the autonomy of workers' councils. The first elements of market economy were introduced in the early 1960s. This contributed to recruitment of managerial strata which tried to replace state officials at the head of enterprises. Formally, managers were under the control of workers' councils, but in practice they imposed their power on workers' councils who in most cases simply rubber-stamped their directives.

In the first half of 1960s the state maintained considerable control over prices and workers' incomes. Workers' councils could make decisions on production only in the framework of prices established by the state. In 1965 the political elite decided to start radical reform of the economic system, introducing more elements of a market economy and widening the autonomy of enterprises. The dominant faction of the political elite proclaimed that market and self-management were inseparable. Its argument was that the market was a precondition for limiting bureaucratic state intervention in the economy, which in turn was necessary for the greater autonomy of enterprises led by workers' councils.[197]

The 1965 reform caused a radical reduction of economic planning especially at the macro level. Workers' councils were not able to make adequate decisions, particularly in the area of investment. The overall impact of the reform was mainly negative. By weakening economic planning, it strengthened the market and hence managers as the real decision-makers in enterprises. On the other hand, it caused strong social differentiation and a rise in unemployment. The federal government was no longer able to secure harmonious economic development of country. In terms of self-management, introduction of the market did not have the effect of strengthening workers' councils and other self-managing institutions. The most important beneficiaries of the reforms were managers, who replaced state bureaucrats as the most important decision-makers in enterprises. Managers were seen, because of their competence and knowledge, as a guarantee of economic efficiency. They joined forces with republican political elites that wanted to weaken the federal centre through market reform and also to repress self-managing workers and their institutions.

The early 1970s saw an attempt to reverse this course. The new goals were: to reaffirm economic planning, to reduce the scope of the market, and to facilitate workers' self-management by subdividing enterprises and introducing the delegate system. The reaffirmation of planning did not mean centralized planning – not only because this was equated with Stalinism, but also because strengthened republican political elites could not accept such a reform. Therefore planning had to be reintroduced from below, from enterprises. Yugoslav planning had to be the sum of microeconomic plans. At the same time, the political elite decided to reinforce the leading party through particular parliamentary chambers composed entirely of party functionaries and through the party's influence on election of CEOs, of whom 76% belonged to the League of Communists.

The results were disastrous. Although the number of workers in workers' councils and other organs of self-management increased, this did not lead to any real strengthening of self-management because workers had little influence over decision-making in the framework of their BOALs. BOALs belonged to wider organizations of associated labour – working organizations (ROs) – and were not economically independent. Sometimes BOALs and ROs united into composite organizations of associated labour (SOURs) which operated in the framework of an entire republic and sometimes of two or more republics. The most important micro-level decisions were enacted in ROs or SOURs while BOALs could not significantly influence them.

In order to create BOALs after 1974 and 1976, existing enterprises had to be divided into smaller, relatively independent economic units. Each BOAL behaved as a separate entity with particular interests. The reforms of 1974 and 1976 did not establish either institutions or mechanisms which could promote integration of the Yugoslav working class. Economic planning was seen, as mentioned above, as a process of negotiation and accommodation of republics and autonomous provinces, while federal or republican institutions lacked efficient mechanisms to implement economic plans.

The new system led to bureaucratization and an overproduction of legal acts. Between 1.25 and 1.5 million different legal acts were adopted in the first years after the reform, while the number of administrative workers increased by 44.3% between 1972 and 1978.[198] Decision-making was also very complicated[199] and workers, who often took their right to self-management very seriously, were eventually disappointed, feeling that the system was less legitimate and efficient than before the reform.[200]

The Yugoslav political elite promoted the idea of republican or ethnic working classes (as opposed to the united Yugoslav working class advocated by President Tito). This idea went hand in hand with the process of confederalisation of Yugoslavia. Republics and autonomous provinces built eight economic systems loosely connected to each other. They had their own economic plans, and republican political elites often tried to create a kind of social pact with the working class in their republics, by giving them inordinate wage-increases. This severely reduced the impact of workers' councils. Thus, while decentralization was carried out at the federal level, republics and autonomous provinces were not decentralized in favour of working collectives. The Yugoslav political elite never accepted the concept of self-management mixed with democratically organized central planning.

Successes

The essence of workers' self-management is to enable workers to become the dominant subject in the economy and society as whole. This was not achieved in Yugoslavia. But if we accept a more limited definition of self-management – as participation in decision-making at the micro level – then the Yugoslav experiment can be called a success.

In the first place, hundreds of thousands of workers were elected to workers' councils,[201] which was a very important experience for them. Being a member of a workers' council was not just a formal function. Workers' councils had some real power in enterprises although they were not the ultimate policy-makers. Workers themselves did not perceive the councils in such a way. However, workers' councils succeeded in what was possible at that moment: they achieved a partial redistribution of power between the bureaucracy/technocracy and the working class. This was no small success considering the monopoly over social power in the hands of bureaucracy before 1950 and also the fact that, apart from workers' councils, the working class had no autonomous organizations under its own control.

Second, workers' councils broadened their prerogatives over time and thus became, at least legally, more powerful than they were during the first phase of their existence in 1950s. For example, while during that first phase CEOs were not responsible to them, later they were. Also, with the introduction of the delegate system in the 1970s, the authority of the councils was increased as their members became workers' delegates who could not act independently of their electorate. There is evidence, however, that this did not greatly impress the workers, as the CEOs of self-managed enterprises still retained the authority to administer work, conclude contracts, hire and fire workers, secure work discipline, and suspend acts of the management board that they judged to be illegal.

Third, the material basis for workers' council activity broadened. In the first phase of workers' self-management, enterprises had at their disposal only 25-30% of overall accumulation.[202] Self-management advanced steadily from 1953 to 1963, starting with the 1953 Constitutional Law and ending with the 1963 Constitution, often called 'The Charter of Self-Management'.[203] According to 1971 constitutional amendments, overall income belonged to BOALs. Workers had the right to determine distribution of income because it was from the products of their labour.

Fourth, the introduction of workers' councils fundamentally changed the role of the working class in society even if it didn't become the dominant social subject. The official ideology of socialist self-management in Yugoslavia gave the worker greater legal rights and a much better social and working position than a worker in the East or the West. Yugoslav workers, as self-managers, had job security; they could not fire themselves. Bureaucracy and technocracy, although dominant in society, had to take into consideration workers' opinions and moods. Otherwise, workers could try to impeach their management, organize a strike,[204] or appeal to the party. Although a CEO could count on support from the local bureaucracy, it was not certain that he would survive a workers' revolt. The bureaucracy had to adhere to the ideology that viewed workers as key players in decision-making, so it had to accept workers' complaints and decisions whenever workers were strong enough and conscious enough to insist on them.

Fifth, workers' councils were a kind of replacement for autonomous workers' organizations, which were lacking in Yugoslavia. The only existing party was bureaucratically controlled, and workers formed only a relative majority of its membership. Trade unions were a transmission belt for the party, without real power in decision-making processes. Autonomous trade unions did not exist, nor did other political parties. The only chance for the working class to play an autonomous role in society was through the workers' councils. They took advantage of this opportunity to some extent, displaying a generally positive attitude toward self-management despite their awareness of its subordinate position in the overall system.[205]

Workers' self-management, with workers' councils as its basic form, had wide legitimacy among Yugoslav workers for many reasons: it stood at the centre of a social system which secured significant economic, social and cultural development;[206] it provided some relief against bureaucratic domination; and it provided levels of job-security and workplace-participation unknown anywhere else in the world. Formally, workers could decide about all aspects of their enterprises' functioning. Moreover, self-management was not limited to the micro level: through various layers of assemblies and through the delegate system, workers could participate in decision-making about economic, social, cultural and political issues at all levels of socio-political organization (municipalities, provinces, republics, and federation).

It is not easy to say to what extent workers' self-management contributed to Yugoslavia's dynamic economic development between 1950 and 1980. Workers' councils, despite their powers, remained in the shadow of managerial structures and informal groups in enterprises (organizations of associated labour) and bureaucratic structures. Nonetheless, it can be said that self-management contributed to economic development in that it tapped workers' initiative and motivation, thereby reducing the need for non-market bureaucratic intervention.

Yugoslav economic development rested on a combination of workers' self-management, limited market, and limited state intervention. These three mechanisms of the economy corresponded to three basic social subjects – working class, technocracy and bureaucracy. In comparison to workers' participation in Western Europe, workers' self-management guaranteed to workers more power and rights.[207] Therefore Yugoslav workers could be more motivated to contribute to the economic success of their enterprise, which belonged to society as a whole and not to state or to any individual or group. It could not be argued that workers saw enterprises as belonging to their own collectivity more than to society as a whole. This was because they clearly saw that the political elite and managerial strata had in many formal or informal ways influenced the economic policy of enterprises as well as the process of selection of executive organs and CEOs. Also, workers formally and to some extent in practice were the only decision-makers who could motivate them to work harder and better. The International Labor Organization confirmed that workers' participation strengthened labour discipline and also strengthened work collectives relative to management.[208]

To be sure, workers sometimes followed their particularistic interest in allocating themselves wage-increases. But it would be one-sided to attribute this to any inherent deficiency in self-management. There were other causes for such behaviour. First, the political elite retained for itself final say in case of an enterprise's bankruptcy. For that reason the workers' interest in self-management was often limited. Second, although the Yugoslav system had strong elements of market economy and self-management, the state continued to play a key role through price control and macroeconomic measures. Workers' councils functioned on the micro level. Their competences and autonomy were limited by macroeconomic decisions made elsewhere. It is thus not surprising that they showed less initiative and responsibility.

The political elite understood this well and tried to institutionalize workers' self-management at all levels of economic and political organization. In 1953 the Council of Producers was established as a chamber of the Yugoslav parliament (Federal People's Assembly). It was elected by workers and had competence in making decisions on economic issues at the macro level. Similar councils, with different names and structure, were established in the 1963 and 1974 constitutions at the level of municipalities, republics, and the federal state. However, most members of these councils belonged to the League of Communists. This fact did not necessarily prevent council members from acting in accordance with workers' wishes, but party discipline had always been an obstacle to their autonomy. On the other hand, the federal government drafted an economic policy which limited the autonomy of these specific councils of self-managers.

Although some authors thought that workers were not interested in the economic development of their enterprises, many examples proved the opposite.[209] In certain cases when management ruined enterprises and caused much economic damage, workers acted quite unselfishly to try to make things better. There was some irony in the system's functioning. Where self-management was not developed enough, workers played only a secondary role in decision-making. But if management was incompetent, workers could revolt and impose personnel changes. On occasion, workers voted reductions in their own wages in order to find enough resources for economic recovery.[210]

Failures

If one compares the level of democracy in Yugoslavia before and after 1950, or if one compares it with the level attained in the Soviet Union, then one has to rate workers' self-management as relatively successful. Despite this measure of achievement, however, the project fell short in a decisive way, in that workers' councils did not become basic institutions of Yugoslav society.

Although workers participated relatively actively at meetings, less than half of them thought they influenced decisions.[211] Their levels of education and information remained deficient.[212] Some authors view such differences in informational levels as insurmountable.[213] Lack of information and the role of experts and executive organs in preparing council meetings led in many cases to formal adoption of proposals prepared in advance by management. Very often workers were informed after the decision was made. Workers were not acquainted with alternative solutions, and workers' councils often decided without presentation of the consequences of one or another decision. Workers were often unaware of the legal options offered by self-management, not to mention basic economic concepts relevant to enterprise policy.[214] Seeing management as the real decision-maker in an enterprise led workers in conflict situations to bypass organs of self-management and to attempt negotiations directly with the CEO, his assistants, and even organs of socio-political communities, primarily municipalities, which had legal authority to intervene under certain conditions (for example, enterprises in financial troubles could count on budgetary injection). All that was left to the workers' council would then be to monitor the implementation of any agreement.

Workers' councils were obstructed in their work by informal groups that existed in enterprises, composed of those who had real power in the decision-making process. Many CEOs came from the political elite or had good connections with it. Therefore they could impose their authority over that of workers' councils and other organs of self-management.[215] Overall democratization would be needed in order to prevent this, but economic democracy at the micro level did not lead to political democracy. Although the political elite developed democratic structures in political institutions after 1953, the League of Communists leadership retained its monopoly. Informal groups could be allowed to function because self-management had an insufficiently strong material basis while one and the same group maintained control over society as a whole.[216] The state continued to intervene in the economy, many CEOs had political ties, and the party had supreme power.

This did not mean that the party always controlled the process of decision-making. It depended very much on the concrete situation in each enterprise. For example, an informal group composed of a CEO, party activists, and experts could try to impose its proposals and to ensure their acceptance.[217] What chances did unorganized workers – or even members of a workers' council – have against such groups? Their ability to resist depended on their developing a self-managing consciousness. If a workers' council was composed of independent individuals who were not under the control of informal groups, it could trace an independent policy.

But self-management failed to become the dominant social relationship. Workers' councils had some impact on decisions at the micro level, but they were not able to essentially question the dominance of technocracy and bureaucracy.[218] Yugoslav society between 1950 and 1990 was marked by constant class struggle between the bureaucracy and the working class and by tensions between etatism and self-management. Although the bureaucracy voluntarily gave up some of its prerogatives, it retained its overall dominance. Self-management was introduced from 'above,' by decision of the political leadership and not by the action of an autonomous working class. This is the real reason why self-management developed only gradually and with constraints.

Conclusions

Despite its limitations, self-management was not a merely formal arrangement. It worked to some extent, and its positive results as well as the legal openings it offered encouraged workers to implement it. Two arguments should be taken into consideration. First, self-management was a constitutional principle; its realization was therefore a legal obligation of governance in Yugoslavia. Not only enterprises but also political institutions were meant to be run in accordance with its principles. The degree of power exercised by workers' councils in practice, however, depended not only on legal precepts but more on the relationship of forces in each enterprise between managerial strata and party bureaucracy on one side and workers on the other. Second, workers' self-management was solidly grounded in communist ideology. Its realization was thus essential for preserving the legitimacy of the party leadership. Thus, somewhat paradoxically, although the party might be threatened by self-management, it had an interest in assuring its basic viability.

Workers' consciousness was a key factor. It was tested by issues such as surplus-allocation and regional inequalities. Conscious workers who acted as good managers would not spend most of an enterprise's revenues on their own wages. They would probably think about improvement of their economic activities. Also, if workers did not think of enterprises as belonging just to their own group, they would be able to offer solidarity and material support to less developed regions or enterprises. Of course, the scope of their discretion remained limited. Workers' councils acted on a micro level, where policy had to be executed and not created. More precisely, they had to make decisions within the general framework of economic policy decided on at the federal or republican level. Although councils of producers and later councils of associated labour existed as specific chambers in the framework of different parliamentary bodies, Yugoslavia could not be clearly defined as the 'Republic of Workers' Councils' because these 'macro workers' councils' had to share power with parliamentary chambers composed entirely or predominantly of members of the political elite. Economic policy, the politics of price control, and alleviation of regional inequalities were decided by the federal government and federal parliament. Workers had no influence on the federal government [ministries] but they could influence parliament's decisions through their delegates in 'macro workers' councils,' i.e. councils or chambers of workers' delegates in federal and other parliaments.

Studies from 1985 showed that consumption was a very important motive for workers to participate in decision-making.[219] The Yugoslav political elite wanted to improve living standards. They saw this as a major means for preserving the system's legitimacy. They also used it to offset workers' disappointment at not being able to realize the full potential of self-management. Had the workers been entrusted with greater responsibility, it is more likely that they would have been able to look beyond their personal well being and the success of their own enterprise. At the beginning of 1960s, workers' councils applied their expanded autonomy to grant themselves intemperate wage-increases. A few years later the authority of the councils was reduced as a result of recession and inappropriate allocation of revenues. It is impossible to say whether workers' councils would have continued to behave in this manner if they had continuously had authority over the whole budget, especially if the state had abandoned its policy of saving bankrupt enterprises.

The Yugoslav system of self-management with workers' councils as its basic cells functioned as a mixture of market socialism, state socialism and self-managing socialism. This specific combination allowed two diverse results. On the one hand, the more developed republics developed faster taking advantage of the market economy, while on the other hand the federal government intervened through a special fund in order to promote development of the less developed republics. The results were contradictory. While underdeveloped republics grew rapidly, the gap between them and the developed republics in some cases widened.[220] This result of market socialism caused dissatisfaction in the less developed republics, which thought that they were being exploited by the more developed republics. This problem arose especially after 1966 when the market economy became more important while the new system of self-management was introduced. The inability of the system to clear up the feeling of less developed republics that they were being exploited led to a weakening of the legitimacy of self-management and eventually to its replacement by nationalism as the dominant ideology. This occurred because self-management was presented by the political elite as a basis for socialism and socialism as a system was perceived as the main cause of regional inequalities.

Of course, regional inequalities are a consequence of many factors acting on the macro level. The negative impact of market mechanisms could be prevented only by state intervention. The role of self-management here becomes clear if one understands that it entails a self-managing state, i.e. a state which is going to wither away in the Marxist sense. In other words, elected delegates of workers' councils in federal and other parliaments had to decide on the scope and content of state intervention in order to prevent regional inequalities and therefore dissatisfaction with self-management. This is precisely what failed to happen, however, because political elites of different republics tried, often unsuccessfully, to find a middle way between market and state intervention. The resulting society was perceived as unjust. As self-management was defined as its basis, people more and more accepted the idea of replacing self-management with some other system. Workers' impotence in decision-making just reinforced this reaction, especially when economic crisis led to a deterioration of living standards.

Introducing elements of the market economy in 1965 helped the development of self-management because it enabled workers' councils to act more independently from the state. Self-management could not succeed in practice if the state controlled economic activities, because workers' councils would lack a material basis for their autonomous decisions.[221] On the other hand, the functioning of the market economy contributed considerably to sharpening social inequalities and raising the level of unemployment. At the same time, the introduction of 'market socialism' benefited managerial strata more than it did self-managing workers, because CEOs, executive organs and informal centres of power rather than workers' councils regained some of the authority previously reserved for the state. In the more democratic legal framework, however, where workers' councils had more formal authority, workers could try to improve their position in the decision-making process and in some cases they were able to do it. Workers' councils were democratic institutions where workers could exercise more power than in any other institution at micro or macro level, and they often tried to take advantage of this opening.

We thus find a contradiction originating in the tension between market, state intervention, and self-management. Workers' councils could not really act as organs of self-management – especially on matters of income – if state institutions had wide legal prerogative to intervene in the economy. Decentralization did not help because it meant only that republican rather than federal institutions influenced the economy. For workers' councils it did not make a big difference whether federal, republican or local institutions intervened in the economy. The problem sharpened when republican political elites could not agree any more on allocation of investment. Therefore the market was introduced as a mechanism to relieve inter-republican tensions as well as to allow greater enterprise-autonomy. If state or local authorities decided on economic issues, workers' councils could not be real organs of self-management.

The impact of the market economy on workers' behaviour depended on the extent of their real participation in decision-making. They had an economic interest in 'their' enterprises being as successful in the market as possible in order to earn a bigger income. On the other hand, self-management is an inherently socialist concept, which led to another natural consequence: workers as self-managers in the socialist sense had also to concern themselves with the well being of society as whole. This could be achieved only by limiting the economic selfishness of particular enterprises through 'global' or 'macro' workers' councils in the form of local, republican and federal councils of producers or councils of associated labour. Unfortunately, this aim was not achieved because these councils did not really act as organs of self-management at the macro level although they were conceived as such.

It was often said in Yugoslavia that the gradual introduction of self-management was an expression of economic and cultural underdevelopment. Ostensibly, self-management would become more effective as the society advanced in other respects. But this did not occur. It is true that self-management developed in many ways – institutionally, legally and practically. Institutionally, it developed in the sense that many new self-managing institutions were created, both at micro and macro levels. Self-management existed not only in the economy but also in the political system, social services, culture, education, sport, and other spheres of social life. Legislative bodies also were organized along self-managing lines, including a delegate system after 1974. Practically, self-management decreased the power of bureaucracy in comparison with the pre-1950s period of 'revolutionary etatism' or 'state socialism.' But these improvements did not change the nature of society. The ruling bureaucracy knew very well that legal and institutional changes could not challenge basic features of the system – one-party rule, state dominance over the economy, etc. These features contributed to the final failure of workers' self-management.

The other contributing factor that has to be considered is the workers' own performance as self-managers. For example, it has often been said that workers didn't show enough economic rationality and conscience because they 'ate the accumulation,' i.e. they tended to spend the surplus rather than use it for economic or technological improvements in their enterprises. Furthermore, workers' councils were not able to raise workers' motivation and secure work discipline, especially during 1980s. These arguments, however, are at best half true. Although in some cases workers made irresponsible decisions about distribution of surplus, it is hard to assess the generality of such behaviour. On the other hand, however, workers had ample cause to be not much interested in the functioning of workers' councils. First of all, they were well aware that the councils often functioned without regard to their wishes and attitudes. They could see in practice the existence and dominance of informal groups – bureaucracy and technocracy. Second, the very concept of social ownership in Yugoslav theory and in the legal system gave some authority to the state to intervene in economic affairs. One of the mechanisms of this intervention was so-called socialization of risk or socialization of losses. If an enterprise worked badly, its losses would be covered from a budget. This negative solidarity, where the community and successful enterprises had to pay for bad decisions of unsuccessful enterprises, led to lack of work discipline and economic efficiency of workers, and discouraged initiatives on the part of workers' councils. For workers understood that their councils could not work independently and that the bureaucracy was interested in covering losses from bad economic performance. Therefore they had little incentive to struggle for more workers' council powers, nor did they think it was possible to achieve them.

Although the official attitude was that Yugoslavia had a system of socialist self-management, in practice it was a mixed system which combined elements of self-management and etatism, with prevalence of the latter.[222] This basic feature of the system determined all the others. Officially, Yugoslavia had a system of integral social self-management which was exercised in all spheres of society. The political system therefore was also organized along self-management lines with socio-political organizations (the League of Communists being the most important) as only one of its components. Thus social self-management, and workers' self-management as its component, was a macro phenomenon. However, workers' councils still were the organs of self-management where workers could exercise most of the power belonging to them.

As a general conclusion, it could be said that workers' councils, to the extent that they really were allowed to manage the economy, were efficient, democratic and humane institutions, whose economic, political and ethical scope could not be denied. But their actual social powers were severely limited. Yet if political democracy had been introduced in Yugoslavia, with pluralism in the political and trade union spheres, then workers' councils might have been able to evolve from organs of participation into organs of self-management.[223]

OTHER POST-CAPITALIST EXPERIENCES

Plan, market and democracy: the experience of the so-called socialist countries*

Catherine Samary

Introduction: theoretical, political and methodological questions

Up until the collapse of the Eastern European countries and the USSR in 1989-91, debates between supporters of the plan and supporters of the market were often argued out on 'purely economic' grounds.

Planning versus market? Or what kind of society do we want?

Planning advocates stress the well-known evils of market relations: unemployment, cyclical crises, the narrow scope of needs registered and satisfied by the market. They rightly counterpose the virtues of a system which assumes collective responsibility for satisfying needs in the long term, and ensures the full use of material and human resources by rising above local and short-term criteria of profitability.

Market advocates point to the repeated experience of bureaucratisation that has afflicted, to various degrees, the countries which tried hyper-centralised planning, from the USSR through China, Vietnam and Eastern Europe to Cuba. They emphasize, also quite rightly, the economic waste caused by management subordinated to commands from the seat of political power.

* This chapter is an edited version of *Plan, Market and Democracy* published in 1988 by the IIRE (International Institute for Research and Education, Amsterdam). *Plan, Market and Democracy* was translated from French to English by John Barzman and Patrick Baker. It can be downloaded at <https://www.iire.org/node/663>. Reproduced here are large extracts dealing with general theoretical, political and methodological questions relating to bureaucratically centralized planning, market oriented reforms, 'market socialism' and self-management, and the Soviet debate on the 'law of value'. The conclusion deals with comments made by the Czechoslovak reformer Ota Sik and Charles Bettelheim, on how to determine the 'socially necessary labour' and democracy in a post-capitalist society in transition to socialism.

Naturally, the former may include officials who derive privileges from the plan. The latter, on the other hand, may draw strength from their radical critique of existing institutions – from their rejection of minor readjustments which solve little or nothing.

Our argument is not located on the plane of this counterposition of the market and plan.

A false alternative

To summarise our view, we would say that reformers of bureaucratic planning who reject Stalinism without a radical critique of its political system, are very quickly led to theorise a false alternative: either bureaucratic planning (and state totalitarianism) or the rationality of the market (and freedom). Many also assume that the market enhances self-management and makes regulatory norms unnecessary.

But theirs is not the only type of reaction to attempted reforms of bureaucratic planning. There also exists, in the very same societies, a massive rejection of the 'rules' of marketplace competition. This pragmatic rejection emanates not only from conservative forces attempting to protect their incompetence against any form of penalty. It comes also from workers who cannot accept being treated as a 'factor of production' that can be fired at will, for the sake of some pseudo-economic rationality totally alien to them. The current reservations and even hostility of Soviet workers towards the reforms now underway confirm this observation.

In other words, it is not only the welfare state that should be subjected to critical scrutiny, but also the generalised market. For hidden under the latter's cost and efficiency criteria, with their false claims to universality, and under world market prices, lies definite social relations which must be rejected.

This is clear in the case of Yugoslavia's present problems: its crisis cannot be explained in the first place by failure to respect the requirements of the world market. It is due above all to a failure to respect an internal imperative, essential from the socialist standpoint the need for a prior and explicit decision about relations between human beings and between communities. In other words, what was disregarded was the need to subordinate production and exchange (both domestic and international) to a political choice about what sort of society one wishes to build together. This, of course, poses the question of a radical democratisation of society.

The 'external constraint' exists and sharpens the internal crisis! It is a key problem in all countries whose comparative productivity is lower than that of the dominant economies, in a world in which the latter can impose their own criteria. The real choice is not between autarky and participation in world trade. It concerns rather the choice of the criteria that will determine how a national economy inserts itself in world trade. The real question is: should these criteria be primarily 'internal' to a given community, and therefore democratically controlled by it?

Unforeseen turn of events

Between capitalist society and communist society, there stands the period of the transformation of the one into the other.
Karl Marx, *Critique of the Gotha Programme.*

Karl Marx, Critique of the Gotha Program

Marx and Engels left some well-known indications on how they conceived socialism. They were grounded in a critique of the contradictions of the capitalist system, of 'generalised commodity production'. The superiority of socialism/communism could emerge only by organising human labour on a new basis, on a scale at least as developed as that of the most advanced phase of capitalism. The internationalisation of production and the worldwide division of labour promoted by capitalism offered humanity a chance to develop its productive forces in an unprecedented way – but at a growing social cost.

The subordination of the economies of the capitalist periphery to the needs of the imperialist metropolises enabled capitalism to pass its most explosive contradictions onto the less developed societies. In this respect, the October revolution, as well as the Yugoslav revolution, were the national products of an organic whole, a world system structured hierarchically.[224] As a result, they combined features of the bourgeois democratic revolution (land reform and national sovereignty) and of the proletarian revolution (in their anti-capitalist dynamic), features of the most modern capitalist development and the legacy of pre-capitalist societies. In these revolutions, the question of a socialist transformation was posed in a context in which it was out of the question to avoid going through 'the detour of the market'.

The discrepancy between the actual circumstances of these revolutions and the writings of Marx and Engels raised some new terminological problems, that is whether one could call the immediately post-capitalist society a socialist society. More importantly, substantial new problems grew up under the terminological dispute: the risk of growing social differentiations fostered by the bureaucratic apparatus, and/or the market, appeared. Cultural, social and economic underdevelopment was conducive to the delegation of power and to the crystallisation of privileged layers defending their own interests.

On the plane of terminology, Marx and Engels often used socialism and communism interchangeably in their writings, even after their well-known statement that the socialist mode of distribution corresponded to a lower stage of communism. In any case, the 'associated producers' were supposed to manage directly the product of their labour from the moment that capitalism was overthrown – in this respect, socialism was already communism.

Did this mean that the USSR under the New Economic Policy (NEP) should be labelled socialist? Or that it could be socialist? For the Bolsheviks, it was a transitional society to socialism, major parts of whose economy were still capitalist or based on petty commodity production. In adopting the name Union of Soviet Socialist Republics, they intended to stress their goal of transformation, not the immediate reality. Lenin stressed this point:

> No one, I think, in studying the question of the economic system of Russia, has denied its transitional character. Nor, I think, has any Communist denied that the term Socialist Soviet Republic implies the determination of Soviet power to achieve the transition to socialism, and not that the new economic system is recognised as a socialist order.
>
> But what does the word 'transition' mean? Does it not mean, as applied to an economy, that the present system contains elements, particles, fragments of *both* capitalism and socialism? Everyone will admit that it does.[225]

The Bolsheviks' conception of what this transitional economy could be, or should be, was particularly unclear because they had not imagined that the revolutionary victory could remain isolated in backward Russia.[226] They did not even consider the idea that socialism could be achieved in a national framework, that is a framework less developed than capitalism which was already a worldwide system. On this point, the Bolsheviks' theoretical position stood in the fullest continuity with Marx's thought: they conceived socialist transformation as a world process that only began in the national arena, after the seizure of political power.

In other words, socialist revolution would not stop with the seizure of power, or even with nationalisations. The historical function of the transition was to carry through this 'revolutionary transformation of capitalism into communism' during which regressions would be possible, even to the point of jeopardising the socialist future.

Trotsky's theory of 'permanent revolution' was an extension of

Marx's conception into which it integrated the actual conditions in which revolutions were developing, in the social formations of the capitalist periphery. The Left Opposition to Stalin believed that it was possible to begin to build socialism in a country like the USSR, provided one did not harbour the illusion that one could succeed on one's own. It was vital for the USSR to raise itself out of its backwardness and isolation. It should therefore not ask that everything, particularly the possibility of revolutions in other countries, be subordinated or sacrificed to the (impossible) task of building 'socialism in one country'.[227]

You said impossible? But by the late 1930s, Stalin officially proclaimed that socialism had been built in the USSR. He imposed this 'fact' both domestically and internationally. The Yugoslav Revolution was the first breach in this edifice built by Stalin, because it refused to bend to the diplomatic interests of the new 'great power'.

Designating the new formation

Faced with anathema from Stalin, the Yugoslav Communists were forced to explain what had really happened in the beloved 'homeland of socialism' they had idolised until then. Milovan Djilas wrote:

> Given in particular that the USSR was for a long time the only socialist country, a rather backward country at that, surrounded by the capitalists, and that the conscious participation of the masses to the building of socialism played a relatively minor role there, and that revolutionary forces inside as well as outside the country turned out to be rather weak, what emerged in the end was the creation of a privileged layer of bureaucrats and bureaucratic centralism; the state was transformed provisionally into 'a power above society'.[228]

The only problem was that this 'provisional' situation has proved to be quite lasting and has been repeated, in other forms, elsewhere, notably in Yugoslavia. It is well known that there is no consensus, not even among Marxists, around a unanimously accepted characterisation of this new historical phenomenon.

This new type of society has been variously called 'socialist' (sometimes with the addition of an adjective such as 'bureaucratic', 'state' or even 'market' in the case of Yugoslavia), 'capitalist' (with a range of contradictory variants) or 'new class' society. The economic and political criteria used in these analyses are heterogeneous and need not be discussed here.

We subscribe to a fourth option which also has several possible variants.

We analyse these societies, unforeseen by Marx, as hybrids, neither capitalist nor socialist, and devoid of a new ruling class, playing an independent and coherent role in the relations of production. This approach stands in the continuity of Lenin's and Trotsky's when they characterised the USSR as a transitional society. It can be placed in a broader view of history in which transitional periods arise between stabilised 'modes of production,' a conception developed by Ernest Mandel[229] and, somewhat differently, by Bettelheim.[230]

The notion of a transition to socialism is also upheld by several Yugoslav authors.[231] Official Yugoslav terminology has fluctuated. But the term 'socialist' is generally understood to designate the goal of development, not an actually classless society free of any social conflicts (contrary to the touching picture-book images spread by Stalin).[232]

The debate on the so-called socialist societies of the world today seems to us to gain in depth and richness when it is linked to an overall reflexion on the transition between capitalism and communism.

Nevertheless, the notion of a 'transitional society between capitalism and socialism' raises certain problems. 'In a transitional society', Ernest Mandel writes, 'there is a hybrid combination between elements of the past and future. But this combination gives rise ... to something specific, to relations of production specific to this transitional stage.'[233] In other words, the concept of a 'hybrid' formation does not imply that there is a 'socialist sector' on the one hand, and other sectors which are not yet socialist (as Lenin's and Preobrazhensky's terminology seemed to imply). 'One of the essential distinctions between transitional periods and the great 'progressive stages' of history, as indicated by Marx in his *Preface to a Contribution to the Critique of Political Economy*, is that transitional periods do not have a mode of production that is specific to them[234] whereas the great progressive stages of humanity are, by definition, characterised by specific modes of production.'[235]

One should note, however, that there is an objection to this approach when applied to contemporary so-called socialist countries. On the theoretical plane, the idea of a transition to communism, even when one inserts a pre-socialist period, implies that there is no real stabilisation at any given intermediate stage, that elements really belonging to the future are already present, just as socialism was already a form of communism. The problem is that the bureaucratic deformation of these elements obviously poses a difficulty in this respect. The direction of their evolution is no longer guaranteed. The society can undergo a regression towards capitalism or a blockage of the transformation of social relations as a result of bureaucratisation. This is why we prefer to describe these societies as post-capitalist societies, insofar, of course, as capitalism has not been restored. We shall return to this point: in our view, this term is more neutral, but at the same time, does not preclude the possibility of analysing these societies in the context of the general contradictions of the emergence of socialism.

We agree with the many authors who argue that the elimination of private ownership of the means of production does not immediately confer the quality of 'social property' onto these means. In fact, the Yugoslav experience shows many more possible relations between the real – not only juridical – content of property and the various conditions of surplus appropriation.[236] On the socio-economic level, one can uncover, depending on the context, forms of 'socialisation' of juridicaly private property and, conversely, forms of 'privatisation' of 'juridicaly social property'.

Once the overall nature of a society has been grasped as 'post-capitalist,' one must still identify and analyse the direction of evolution of its components and, when the case arises, the qualitative leaps – towards socialism or towards capitalism. Such an analysis is not easy. The theoretical problems encountered in the first case are not the same as in the second.

How should advances toward socialism be identified?

Simply rejecting the equation that 'Stalinism = socialism' (even if one adds the adjective 'underdeveloped') does not resolve the problem, far from it. But any attempt to go beyond that and define socialism runs the risk of elevating certain normative criteria, selected on the basis of subjective preferences, above others: Have the means of production been nationalised? What percentage? Is there a plan? What kind of plan? Is there democracy? Beyond what threshold can one say that democracy is present?

We prefer to adopt the same approach to socialism as we adopt towards social property – they are in fact simply different facets of the same problem – namely that it involves the transformation of social relations in the direction of the withering away of relations of oppression and exploitation, and the re-appropriation by each individual – and therefore by all – of labour as a creative activity.

We adopt W. Brus's approach and extend it.[237] Brus posits and analyses the process of transformation of state property into 'social property' in the strict sense – which means property actually controlled by society, and not just by the state as an institution separate from the citizens, nor even simply by one particular group of workers. The difference is that Brus does not question the 'socialist' content of the societies described in this way. For us, on the other hand, there can be no socialism without social property, nor advance towards socialism without an advance towards the transformation of property relations. We will deal with socialist self-management in line with this approach.

Socialist self-management

The problem is that the idea of self-management can be promoted by certain ruling classes or castes to preserve their power under new forms. It is then designed, in the best of cases, only to get the workers to participate more actively in their own exploitation. This sort of atomised self-management is sometimes proposed when it is realised that the compartmentalisation of work slows down the rate of growth of productivity. At other times, self-management can be the watchword of particular layers who hope to gain more responsibility and influence. The point is to obtain a new delegation of power along with a shift in the balance of forces within the privileged layers. This, incidentally, can cause the emergence of breaches 'at the top,' of which those 'at the bottom' can take advantage. Overall, though, the result will be not that alienated wage labour withers away – to the benefit of all – but that new stratifications emerge.

If one means by socialist transformation a process whereby, as Marx put it, 'a mass of instruments of production are subordinated to each individual and property is subordinated to the whole', [238] then the socialist transformation can be blocked. It can happen as a result of the emergence of new social stratifications. The juridical question is not the main argument. But this does not mean that it plays no role whatever. 'Property rights' are relations between human beings, not relations between human beings and things.[239] We will see that rights guaranteed by official ideology can be circumvented or made more effective. In either case, their existence changes people's behaviour and consciousness. We will also see that these rights can be challenged directly when a process of capitalist restoration sets in.

The question of capitalist restoration

Capitalism can exist in many forms. Moreover social formations considered capitalist are the product of the uneven and combined development of different social forms. This raises the question of when the qualitative leap can be considered to have taken place. We would answer that capitalism has been restored when capitalist domination is guaranteed, legitimated and protected by the state power and its institutions. Capitalist exploitation implies that the logic of accumulation has a particular social content – that it is subordinated to the search for profit in the framework of specific class relations.

We are not faced with two options only. The fact that the workers do not exercise social control over the surplus does not automatically mean that the appropriation of this surplus is 'capitalist' – unless one wishes to give this term a dull and a-historical content applicable to all forms of class society and exploitation.

There exists a decisive test of capitalist restoration: whether the system can raise the productivity of labour by treating labour (in reality, labour power) as a mere 'factor of production, a thing,' a cost on the same plane as other costs and factors; or, if you prefer, whether there exists a social mechanism which incites units of production to introduce machines against workers, relying on the weapon of unemployment, on 'the industrial reserve army.' This process is finally consummated when it is legalised and protected by the state.

But long before capitalist restoration is completed, the role of money can be transformed – and with it, the social relations underlying credit and the forms of appropriation of the surplus, with the result that money tends to operate as 'capital'.

But one should not confuse a tendency and the final product. Capitalism was born in the midst of societies which it did not yet dominate. Some people – notably Bukharin and many Yugoslav economists – have argued that the elimination of private property at once eliminates all dangers of capitalist exploitation and precludes the development of new antagonistic social stratifications. We do not agree with this view.

But stating that such dangers do exist, does not provide a ready-made answer to the question of whether market relations and private property – and capitalist investments for that matter – are indeed necessary in a given post-capitalist society, and, if so, in what proportions. In other words, believing that the extension of the market and private property work against the achievement of the socialist goal, does not automatically mean that one should not resort to them. What it does mean is that the process must be consciously controlled.

We are convinced that mere readjustments of bureaucratic planning will prove ineffective and that what is needed is a radical critique of Stalinist practice and pseudo-theory. But it is also necessary to analyse the causes of the dead-ends – and current crisis – to which market-oriented reforms have led Yugoslavia. We will try to demonstrate that any system which tries to make the market the essential, fundamental link between firms self-managed by the workers, must inevitably run into these dead-ends.

In fact, if reformers really want transparency and democracy, the first thing they should do as they propose new reforms, is to make a public balance sheet of similar reforms already attempted elsewhere with all those concerned.

Apparently, this is not what *glasnost* is about. What we are saying is that it is not the extension of market relations which should be radical, but democratisation. In all other domains, mistakes are possible and can be corrected.

One of the problems with the debate on the place of the market is that the word encompasses different interpretations and situations. One of our goals is to make more explicit the different definitions.

Beyond Definitions

The word 'market,' used in everyday language (including by economists), can describe very different realities and social dynamics. The same is true, in fact, of the word 'planning.' During the post-capitalist transition, there is necessarily a certain dose of market relations (how much? that is the question!). The debate can be clarified if participants explicitly state which areas and which choices are assigned to the market, and with how much leeway in each case.

But even words like 'sale' or 'purchase' may cover different operations. On the whole, Mandel stresses precisely the tendency for forms of planning increasingly to penetrate and moderate the spontaneity of the market. This was, in fact, one of the characteristic features of the long post-war boom of capitalism. But it is precisely the overall dynamic which must be evaluated. The economic crisis, or more accurately the two types of economic crises in the two systems, have acted as a revelator. If you look at the overall dynamic of the capitalist system in crisis, you can see to what extent it is still dominated by *ex post* regulation, through the market, through bankruptcies and through unemployment.

Three models

For the sake of this necessary process of terminological clarification, we will distinguish, along with Brus, three major 'models', each one of which displays significant differences in the role of market mechanisms. They correspond to three types of economic systems which have really existed or were proposed at one point or another in the so-called socialist countries.

1. Bureaucratically centralised planning

These are the systems in which money plays a passive role. Prices are formed by the planners. One could argue that, in theory, the methods and criteria used by the planners in price formation are not arbitrary. In fact, specialists have debated this point quite extensively. But in practice, the lack of real transparency about the labour actually expended in the Soviet economy means that prices have often acquired a high degree of arbitrariness. At any rate, the notion of passive prices does not necessarily imply arbitrary prices, except in the mind of economists who believe the only possible prices are the 'true' market prices.

This first model corresponds to the planning system in effect in the USSR under Brezhnev. It has existed, with variations and historical specificities, in all post-capitalist societies, from Vietnam, through Eastern Europe, to Cuba. It was the basic reference in all so-called socialist countries until reforms were attempted (in general in the 1960s). In some cases, as in Czechoslovakia after the Soviet intervention, it was restored after the reforms were reversed. It is the model which the Polish regime has been trying to reform since the 1970s. (Price changes had caused riots in Poland before the advent of Solidarność.) Even Romania, despite its overtures to the outside world, remains totally centralised.

This model is compatible with the existence of specific economic circuits where money plays a more 'active' role (that is, where prices influence the economic decisions of the 'agencies' involved). For instance, there exists a partial recourse to market mechanisms in the distribution of the labour force, since workers are free to choose their job on the basis of the more or less attractive level of wages, among other factors. Likewise, in the sector of consumer goods, one can purchase items freely with one's wages, the only limit being the short supply of these items. But this does not mean that supply and demand operate freely to determine the choices of production. Nor does it determine which sector, the private or the state sector, should produce what is missing. Once again, this – the insufficiently 'active' role of money and of the market – is precisely where certain reformers find fault with the system.

This model is also compatible with non-market-oriented reforms designed to improve its efficiency. In East Germany, for instance, reforms have been introduced to change the indexes used to measure performance, to create new channels between the centre and the firms, and to allow for the signing of contracts between firms after validation by the plan. Of course, the particular type of political system which implements this model can also make a big difference in how it operates.

2. The use of market mechanisms by the plan

This second model enables money and prices to play a more active role – yet without the 'law of value' becoming the regulator of the economy. What this model actually involves is the use of market mechanisms by the plan – not the pre-eminence of the market. That pressures in favour of elevating the status of the market exist in this model, is another matter. The model can be implemented without workers self-management, as it was in Hungary in the 1960s, or with workers self-management, as it was in Yugoslavia from 1952 to 1964, before 'market socialism' was introduced. This model also inspired the reforms put forward by Soviet economists Liberman and Trapeznikov in the 1960s, implemented in the USSR under Kosygin from 1965 to 1968, and taken up by Ota Sik in Czechoslovakia and Wlodzimierz Brus in Poland around the same period.

For the time being, the reforms now being proposed in the USSR belong to this category of reforms too. To summarise what they are about, we could say that this model combines the supremacy of centralised planning (which has, until now, been bureaucratic, but need not be) over strategic development decisions with more room for decentralised initiative on the basis of market relations (in the sense of 'purchases and sales') in other spheres. In this set-up, the decisions of firms are influenced by the pricing system because they must operate on the basis of an economic calculation of costs and profits. Precisely who in the firm decides is another matter; we will examine examples both with and without workers self-management. But this does not mean that the prices on the basis of which the calculations are made are free market prices reflecting the law of value. Nor does it mean that the major investment decisions obey this law.

3. 'Market socialism'

In theory, this third model aspires to restore the full coherence of the operation of the law of value – its automatic responses and criteria. The only case where such reforms were actually put into practice was in Yugoslavia, during one of the different reform periods, between 1965 and 1971. But this model was advocated by various 'experts' and 'advisers' in Eastern Europe, most notably in Yugoslavia, Hungary and Poland by the IKK (executive committee) of Solidarność. It was also the logic behind the proposals of certain Soviet economists, such as Shmiliov. In any case, one should distinguish the decision to have a reform from its actual implementation.

A typology of post-capitalist societies based on the various functions performed by the plan or market mechanisms is a useful approach to grasp the common socio-economic contradictions of all post-capitalist societies. But it is not sufficient to interpret the relations between the rulers and the ruled, and to understand the different obstacles against which the reforms have run up in each of these countries.

To conclude: economics and politics

The full importance of the political factor must be understood if we wish to avoid a reductionist approach.

On the one hand, the reforms discussed here have never been tried in combination with the fullest political democratisation at all levels. As a result, the ability to master the socio-economic effects of the reforms was considerably reduced.

On the other hand, even though all so-called socialist countries are ruled by a one-party system, the relations between the party leadership and the population are not the same everywhere. This has an obvious effect on the degree of obstruction encountered by the reforms and the audacity of the reformers themselves. In general, one should distinguish the regimes brought to power by a popular revolution (Cuba, Yugoslavia, Vietnam, Mao's China) from those where the rulers have been designated by a crystallised *nomenklatura*. Moreover, both the process of bureaucratisation and the process of de-Stalinisation have had a different profile in each country, and each national bureaucracy, even the most loyal to Moscow, has sooner or later sought to develop its own roots and legitimacy. Kadar in Hungary is not the same as Ceaucescu in Romania. The problems of bureaucratisation and bureaucratic government (one-party rule) cannot be reduced to the question of Stalinism. The experience now underway in the USSR emphasises the fact that a bureaucracy can develop different policies and methods of rule, even in the same country (Stalin $\neq$ Khruschev $\neq$ Brezhnev $\neq$ Gorbachev $\neq$ Ligachev, etc.).

In line with this remark, the goal of the present lectures is limited. Their point is to clarify the major stakes and contradictions of the planning and market systems experienced in the so-called socialist countries, not to provide a substitute for the necessary study of each experience in all its historical and political specificity.

Until now, all attempts at reform of bureaucratic planning have ended in failure. There is much to be learnt from this. Unfortunately, it seems that each new turn in the so-called socialist countries is immediately accompanied by new justifications, new state truths which sometimes praise the very things which, only a few weeks earlier, were denounced as 'anti-socialist deviations.'

This is particularly harmful because nations who wish to escape the logic of capitalist development, without closing themselves off to the world capitalist environment, desperately need a critical review of these experiences. What is the best way to advance against the stream of world trade, towards a socialist goal, without living in autarky? Can one borrow some mechanisms of the capitalist system (such as the logic of profit as an incentive and a criterion for the orientation of economic development) without being saddled with all its evils? Can the market and its laws be introduced and given a socialist content?

These questions were already at issue in the debates about the NEP in the USSR of the 1920s. Stalinism closed these discussions and brutally interrupted the NEP. It is therefore necessary to unearth the real content of these discussions and evaluate them in light of the experience since then.

From what angle should one approach these problems? Alec Nove[240] has declared a war on the use of Marxist concepts in the study of 'really existing socialism.' He also blusters against those who identify as Marxists and naively view socialism as a society without conflict or complex choices. While Nove is thus able to avoid dogmatism, his investigation rapidly becomes a description which, although often fascinating, provides no real criteria for forming a critical judgement – except a short-term one, namely that this or that reform has 'worked' to a greater or lesser degree. Since he has pledged to remain within the confines of the 'feasible' (which we also think is important) but without being guided by any vision of 'utopia,' his critical edge is dulled. He does not raise the question of whether the market is socially neutral, that is whether it is a 'mechanism' compatible with any social relations.

In trying to deal with these questions, we have been guided by one postulate only: the belief that the communist perspective makes sense only if it means the emancipation of 'each individual and therefore of all.'

To avoid getting lost in the maze of different situations and preserve one's critical spirit, to develop criteria which are objective but not dogmatic, it is necessary to keep in mind the goal towards which one is striving – provided one thinks it is worth the effort – namely the withering away of all classes, privileges and relations of oppression and exploitation. We should note here that this does not mean a uniform, conflict-free or even easy to manage, society. The theoretical hypothesis that this emancipating goal remains relevant today can be grounded only in a common analysis of the contradictions of both the capitalist and post-capitalist systems.

In other word, we will not adopt a dogmatic approach that argues: 'Marx said' that there could not be socialism with a market, 'therefore' we oppose market reforms because they take us away from socialism 'by definition.' On the other hand, we will not bend to the reverse intellectual terrorism which commends market reforms *a priori,* in apologetic, a-critical fashion, as 'un-dogmatic.' We will follow Marx only – but that is quite a lot – in adopting the method which grounds the emancipating perspective in a critical analysis of the contradictory social relations of a given society – whether this society was foreseen by Marx or not, whether it be capitalist or socialist, a 'state' or a 'market' society.

Social relations and the plan

Relations between bureaucrats and workers

What sort of relations exist between these two categories then? We have already mentioned the existence of alienation – work performed outside the control of the worker. Should one also speak of the existence of exploitation? If the term is not used to designate only capitalist-style exploitation, then it might be relevant to describe a system of bureaucratic dictatorship which fosters privileges. For these privileges represent a share of the social surplus to which a layer or caste with specific interests lays claim in private fashion.

It is a parasitic form of exploitation: the rule of the bureaucracy rests upon an act of political expropriation. The privileges are camouflaged, not legitimated. They are limited by the fact that they are conferred as perquisites for ruling in the name of a 'really existing' class. In other words, the bureaucracy does not play an independent role in a coherent new mode of production. It does perform certain economic functions, of course, but it undermines their efficacy because it manages things with its own consumption privileges in mind. This is why the applicability of the notion of 'class' to it is debatable and does not provide an accurate picture of the specific relationship between the bureaucracy and the working class. The simple fact that the former rules in the name of the latter does not lessen the magnitude of their conflicts but makes them more complex. The bureaucracy's lack of any independent and coherent economic base renders it more fragile: the more centralist its system, the closer to political death (that is, in this case, death pure and simple) will even the slightest independent workers movement, bring it. Hence this paradox: although the workers have fewer democratic rights than in capitalist countries (developed ones, of course! People in Eastern Europe too often forget the dictatorships of the West), they have a far greater capacity to resist market mechanisms, the reason being that the bureaucracy can concede quite a lot, as long as it retains political power.

The bureaucracy does not rule only, or even mainly, through police mechanisms in the long 'normal' periods. It avails itself of a complex array of socio-economic and institutional means that must be analysed in their proper context: from social benefits, such as the prospect of a promotion, that can be suspended should a challenge be made; to recruitment and propagandising in various mass organisations; granting decentralised management rights to a firm; and the ability to fire or demote workers for political reasons. Whatever the method used, one thing must remain constant: the monopoly of the party, which guarantees that the workers will remain politically atomised.

But this monopoly is compatible with different forms of government and management of the economy.

Overall social content of the bureaucratically centralised plan

It is not enough to merely state that the plan is bureaucratic. But it is, of course, first and foremost bureaucratic, and this from two angles: the bureaucracy is both a political and social category.

We stated earlier that the goals of the central planners could not be reduced simply to the task of harmonising the sum of the requests emanating from local bureaucrats. The plan is bureaucratic both because its strategic orientations are defined by the regime, 'from the top down,' albeit in the framework of its relationship with the citizens/workers; and because the very mechanisms of planning integrate at every stage and level the bureaucrats' own particular social interests (in this respect, the reforms can lead to more complex differentiations among the bureaucrats, depending in particular on how the market will affect them, or on the type of skills or function they hold).

The central government and local bureaucrats share many common interests (privileges) but conflicts do appear: the political bureaucracy can, for reasons of its own, decide to purge its intermediate relays. Their relations have sometimes been compared to those of the bourgeois state with multiple competing capitals. The difference is that private capitals are guided by an economic rationale (to maximise profit) which endows the overall system with a coherence of its own, whereas bureaucratic interests undermine the efficiency of the plan. Various currents of the bureaucracy may compete for the allegiance of the workers, as in the Soviet Union today, or in Czechoslovakia in 1968, for political or social reasons. But they cannot gain the workers' support without granting them some concessions, not to mention by making their situation worse!

Distinguishing various market-oriented reforms

There are two main models of market reform, the term 'model' being used here to refer to a simplified representation which retains only the main features of a given system of production and exchange. Observers have highlighted different features to distinguish the various reforms. Some have singled out the recourse to a 'socialist market' or 'economic' instruments (by contrast with 'administrative' instruments used in planning by direct command) as typical of the first type, whereas they describe the second as a system of 'market socialism'.[241]

We prefer the following distinction, used by the Polish economist Brus:

- the first type corresponds to the use of market mechanisms by the plan in a system in which the plan is dominant whereas
- the second type corresponds to an economy in which the market regulator is supposed to be dominant (self-management in 'market socialism' without plan: Yugoslavia 1965-1972).[242]

Yugoslav 'market socialism' with self-management

Impact of 'market socialism' on self-management

At the Second Congress of self-managed workers held in Sarajevo in 1971, V. Bakaric emphasised that between 1961 and 1968, firms had paid out more than half of their business fund as interests on credit. In most firms, assets were no longer sufficient to cover debts that had fallen due and interest on loans contracted earlier. The reproductive potential of the firms, composed of the business fund and the fund for depreciation, expanded in absolute value – but shrank in substance and relative value. From 1964 to 1968 (with the exception of 1966), investments made by firms out of their own resources represented a smaller and smaller share of the total sum for depreciation: about 37% in 1967, 32% in 1968 and 17% in 1969, according to Bakaric's report in Sarajevo.[243] There were many instances when wages had to paid out of the business and depreciation funds. In this regard, self-management had already lost some of its substance.

In the period under review here, 'compulsory inter-firm credit' became a general trend, a characteristic feature reflecting the 'cash shortages,' that is, the discrepancy between material production and financing, troubling the entire economy.

'Self-managed' workers as wage earners

The recourse to strikes, despite the existence of self-management rights, testifies at the very least that self-management had gotten bogged down. From 1968 to 1971, social tensions were expressed particularly openly as strikes were now tolerated.

In practice, the search for professional management skills overtook political appointments – the technocracy replaced the 'politocracy'. The Workers General Meeting lost its powers to the various management bodies; in the Workers Councils themselves, the percentage of workers decreased, from about 76% in 1960 to about 67% in 1970, according to official Yugoslav statistics.

The management teams decided in substance how to orient accumulation and finance the firm, and then more or less formally submitted their decisions to the General Meetings, to which experts also presented a mountain of technical documents. Self-management was also smothered by real difficulties of institutional and socioeconomic origin: Josip Zupanov and several other Yugoslav sociologists have mentioned in particular 'the sea of rules which imposes an enormous amount of red tape and raises the operating costs of the economic structures'. Frequent jurisdictional changes, sometimes designed to protect self-management, but whose meaning was not understood by those most affected, did little to help. Cultural differences were widely exploited to bypass actual control by the workers. The size of firms and the fusion and take-over processes underway in this period enhanced the autonomy of the management teams.

But this rise of technocrats took place in a society which had enshrined workers rights. Although a large gap had developed between the law and reality, self-management did exist, 'as a negative.' It limited the powers of management teams, particularly in matters of redundancy. Here is what Vladimir Bakaric said about it: 'No workers council would agree to dismiss large numbers of workers. In other words, no modem technique could be introduced and put into practice other than at the cost of new, important investments, far exceeding the funds available to the firm in question.'[244]

The Second Congress of Self-Managed Workers in 1971 made similar remarks:

> In the mining and steel combine at Zenica, the principle that no worker would be made redundant due to modernisation or the reconstruction of production workshops or work units was recognised. A system of life-time training of all those directly involved in production and of experts was also instituted to ensure the necessary mobility and a rational division of labour. In the Bor mining and steel basin, the principle that no worker would be made redundant due to excess labour and that an equivalent job would be found for him in his own workplace or in another, was also given legal sanction.[245]

These remarks touch on the most sensitive question of the reforms in Yugoslavia as well as in Eastern European countries: the right to work.

As soon as one places the worker at the heart of a society's value system, the conditions under which he or she may be recycled or transferred, become a central political problem. The defence by each individual worker – or each collective – of the job situation that they have achieved, is not always rational for society as a whole. But only two solutions exist: either the conflict is resolved expeditiously by 'the laws of the market,' or else, mechanisms are found, that can involve those affected in the overall problem and arrive at solutions which do not harm their interests: that is by shortening and redistributing the necessary work time among all, and by ensuring that transfers or reconversions improve status and recognised skills and take family obligations into account – the 'additional burden' created by such procedures would be not only compensated, but outweighed by people's enthusiasm for a government that made the right to work its guiding principle and the deepening of democracy in production its preferred problem-solving method. We are led once again to the very core of the argument.

Under the conditions of the Yugoslav reform, there was no solution to the problems posed, only two conflicting, contradictory logics: hence the 'wage system-like' relations in the management of investments, that is, the fact that workers' rights to self-management could only be defended by massive resistance to lay-offs and attacks on their living standards.

As for the firm managers, it is clear that lacking 'real' ownership of capital and the means of production, they could hardly implement the capitalist rationality of maximising profits and minimising production costs. Wasting means of production and financial irresponsibility were not a particular problem for managers whose position remained insecure. In this respect, there was no qualitative difference with the position of the bureaucrats towards the plan, only far more powerful centrifugal forces.

'De-statisation' without real socialisation of the means of production

Formally, in the period studied here, the 'social sector' continued to expand in the Yugoslav economy at the expense of the private sector.

But if one wishes to look at the substance of things, the real trend was towards less control over the economy ('social property') both at the macroeconomic level and in the workplace.[246]

An examination of the private sector will provide further evidence for this negative balance sheet.

The present and future place of the private sector and its relations with the socialised sector have been the subject of much debate in Yugoslavia. Certain authors, such as R. Bicanic, consider the controversy which divided the Bolsheviks at the time of the NEP of little relevance to the present. Given that the Yugoslav economy and its socialised sector have attained their present level of development, the 'feeling of insecurity' and the fear of a revival of relations of exploitation are 'difficult to understand,' they aver. Theoreticians like Branko Horvat[247] developed a radically new approach to the problem: in the framework of the decentralised 'associative socialism' model which he advocated, personal labour on private means of production could be a form of direct self-management. Thus, he believed that the market and private property (albeit without wage-exploitative relations) had a future under socialism. In the same vein, Alexander Bajt, another Yugoslav economist, developed the notion of 'social property – whether collective or individual,' a form which existed provided that the private producer 'did not appropriate a larger part of the social product than that issuing from his labour'.

But the prevailing opinion remained suspicious and pragmatic. The private sector would be allowed to develop in those areas where the socialised sector was found deficient (by lightening taxes on private means of production). Nevertheless, restrictions remained in place: no more than five wage earners in one's employ or 10 hectares of land in one's possession. At the same time, the inauguration of competition between firms in the two sectors took place after the dismantling of the plan and its redistributive functions. Under the circumstances, the reform caused a radical reversal of the way in which the two sectors of production had begun to interact, that is a reversal of the trend towards increased voluntary cooperation.

In 1964, there were nearly 1,300,000 members of cooperatives. In 1971, there were hardly more than 860,000. The drastic reduction of the subsidies granted to the socialised sector (in its entirety) was certainly the chief cause of this turn-around. But this is not all there is to it.

There was also undoubtedly a negative feeling about the administration's suspicion of, and general relations with individual peasants in the cooperatives. This explains the fragility of earlier advances towards cooperation. The peasants had directly experienced too many broken contractual obligations and suffered too often from an unequal balance of power, conflicts over the distribution of revenues earned jointly, and defeats in their attempts at self-management. In effect, they could only cast an indicative vote in decisions concerning their cooperatives and had no representatives as such.

These problems having been noted, it was not indifferent for the future direction of agriculture whether the focus of criticism and the key to the recovery effort would revolve around greater democracy and respect for the peasants within the cooperatives, or whether it was necessary to encourage the private sector to seek greater autonomy and spur it to compete more vigorously with a dismantled social sector. Whether or not this was the intended result, the policy of the reform actually pushed the peasants towards a retreat into individual solutions.

The incentive to cooperate was considerably reduced when private peasants perceived possibilities of improving their social position by making use of the margins of individual development still opened to them. The trend was all the greater in that the peasants felt their status was not stabilised, defined and recognised.

Joining the socialised sector became less attractive because the latter's position was deteriorating rapidly.

For a while at first, rising agricultural prices favoured agriculture as a whole in relation to industry: the reform had planned increases of 35%. In the first two years of its application, the rise was of the order of 66% (as against 28% in manufacturing industry and 59% in retail trade). But at the same time, the system reduced subsidies to agriculture to the lowest level in Europe. Federal funds for the financing of investments were also drastically reduced, in the general spirit of the reform. Very rapidly, the rise in industrial prices tended to catch up with that of agricultural prices and made inputs more expensive at a time when credits were also more expensive. Losses increased.

The fact is that, under the constraint of market prices and new methods of financing investments, state combines and farms reduced their consumption of fertiliser by a third, the number of employees by half (particularly skilled personnel who were more expensive to hire), and the number of tractors and heads of livestock by about the same proportion: a fair proportion of these were resold to the private sector (whence the absolute fall in the number of tractors in the socialised sector). In the context of this general movement, cooperatives became less attractive and individually owned tractors more competitive. The number of cooperatives was cut by half.

The rise of conflicts 1968-1971

By 1971, the rise of workers strikes combined with the movement of the students and left intelligentsia of 1968, directed at once against the market-oriented reform and the bureaucracy (see the two articles written at the time below), and the growth of nationalistic tensions caused a new institutional turn. The extension of market mechanisms was called to a sudden halt. But the dismantling of the system and of the various forms of solidarity which had existed, had reached the point of no return. Two articles of that period give a good picture of the situation.

The students drafted a *Political Action Program*,[248] which was published in *Student*, their official journal. Here are their demands:

> To bring about a most rapid and efficient solution to the fundamental problems of our socialist society and self-managed community of one people and several equal and free nations, we feel it necessary:
>
> I.
>
> - To adopt measures that will rapidly reduce the great social inequality in our community. To this end, we ask that the socialist principle of

distribution according to one's work be applied systematically; that the criteria used to determine personal incomes be defined clearly and precisely; that a minimum income and a maximum income be instituted; that differences in personal income based on non-socialist, privileged positions connected to the monopoly exercise of power, be abolished. Actions must be undertaken against the accumulation, in non-socialist fashion, of private property. We call for the immediate nationalisation of unjustly acquired property. The privileges of our society must be liquidated. Excessively high incomes must be taxed progressively.

- To resolve the problem of employment rapidly and genuinely, a long-term perspective for the development of our economy must be adopted, based on the right to work throughout the country. An investment policy allowing for full employment and the improvement of the material and cultural conditions of our people must be adopted. The hiring of young skilled workers must be made possible and therefore overtime and volunteer work must be reduced to a minimum or banned. Vacant positions must be filled by those who have the necessary skills.

- Measures must be implemented to rapidly institute self-management throughout our society and destroy the bureaucratic forces which have fettered the development of our community. We must systematically develop self-management, not only in the workplace, but at all levels, from communal to federal, so that the producers can exercise real control over the organs of production. The key to the development of genuine self-management is the ability of workers to make the decisions about working conditions and the distribution of surplus value completely independently. All self-management bodies must be responsible for the fulfilment of these tasks and socially responsible if they fail to achieve them. Personal responsibility must be given its rightful importance.

- In parallel with the self-management bodies, all social and political organisations, particularly the League of Communists, must be democratised. In particular, a fundamental democratisation of the means of public expression must be accomplished. Finally, democratisation must make it possible for all rights and freedoms recognised by the Constitution to take effect.

- An immediate halt must be called to all attempts to break social property down into private property. Attempts to transform individual labour into individual or group capital must be stopped. Legal measures to decisively eliminate such tendencies must be taken. Real estate law must be amended immediately to prevent speculation on social or private property.

- The commercialisation of culture must be rendered impossible and the opportunity for creative cultural activity opened to all.

II.

- The educational system must be reformed immediately to answer the needs for economic and cultural development and the development of self-management.
- The right of all young people to equal educational conditions must be guaranteed by the Constitution.
- University autonomy must be inscribed in law.

Apart from the information which has been published on the students' revolt in Belgrade, there has been an almost complete silence on the subject of the trade-union congress which met from June 26 to 29, 1968. However, this Sixth Congress of the Confederation of Trade Unions of Yugoslavia (CTUY) was the arena for an explosion of workers' discontent which surpassed the anger of the students in size and social importance.

For four days, speakers from different industrial sectors and regions of Yugoslavia spoke from the podium one after another, and criticised, in often-brutal terms, the consequences of the 'economic reform.' The worker Milos Kicovic, speaking in the name of the metalworkers of Skopje, Ljubjana and Zagreb, protested: 'We have had enough of socialism on paper!' and called on the trade unions to defend the just material demands of the workers. On the eve of the congress, *Borba* published a letter from a metalworker containing very sharp criticisms of the government's policy. 'We should recognise,' he wrote, 'that now, when workers self-management is fairly developed in our country, it has produced a pauperisation of the working class; this refers to the producers. And while the latter have to fight for their elementary rights, others get richer. Those who possess houses, villas and cars can take holidays overseas or go on excursions. This is why it is no surprise that the trade union is slowly dying off ... I condemn the trade union because it has allowed the income of a metalworker to become hardly enough to live on. Our workers either move abroad or become unemployed here. It is the higher organs of the state who are to blame. We have given them their high incomes and their villas. We squabble with each other in the factory, but our money is going elsewhere. The trade union should defend the interests of the workers and not those of the government.' *(Borba,* June 1, 1968)

So powerful was the discontent expressed at the congress of the CTUY that Tito repeated the same manoeuvre that he had already tried at the time of the student revolt. He took the stand at the Congress and gave a strong indictment of the negative consequences of the 'economic reform'.[249]

Updating the Soviet debate on the 'law of value'

To avoid confusion, it is now essential to unravel two separate issues: on the one hand, the question of the timing and method by which the NEP was ended; on the other, the nature and extent of the real conflicts and contradictions which the NEP created.

For it is possible to believe, along with Trotsky and the Left Opposition that both industrialisation 'at a snail's pace', as advocated by Bukharin, and the policy of forced collectivisation and frenzied industrialisation decreed by Stalin were mistakes. One can feel that Bukharin had a certain feel for the peasant question, and more generally for the need to marshal all existing know-how, while Preobrazhensky displayed a certain 'objectivism'. This inclination towards 'objectivism' is perhaps part of the explanation of why Preobrazhensky ultimately endorsed the industrialisation imposed by Stalin. In other words, simply stating that one agrees with 'Bukharin's ideas' or with those of his opponent, mixes up two different questions, two aspects and two periods of Stalinist policy. It is more profitable to explain exactly to which issue one is referring.

In our opinion, there is no doubt that the way in which the NEP was interrupted, has had lasting negative consequences on Soviet society. Neither forced collectivisation, nor the 'physical liquidation of the kulaks as a class,' nor the pace and unbalanced options associated with industrialisation were fatal and acceptable policies. Our criticism on this score is thoroughgoing. But it does not lead us to dodge another necessary debate which is the one that concerns us here: what was the NEP supposed to achieve? What could it achieve? And more generally what is the role of market relations in the building of socialism?

Our purpose here is not to make a systematic analysis of these debates.[250] Moreover, once Stalin had imposed forced collectivisation and industrialisation, the contending positions shifted fundamentally in relation to each other: the criticisms levelled by Bukharin at that point were quite close, in many respects, to those put forward by the Left Opposition (which, by that time, Preobrazhensky had left).

Whatever our disagreements with Preobrazhensky and Bukharin, we cannot but note with admiration the high quality of the debates which they initiated, without the benefit of hindsight, in the early 1920s. The practical and theoretical questions which they raised then are still at the core of the problems facing all post-capitalist societies. These debates must be retrieved and brought up to date, beginning with a direct return to the true thought of the theoreticians involved – dismissing, therefore, the caricatures of their positions bequeathed by Stalin.

We shall focus here on the two questions outlined above: first, what social differentiations occur when the market is extended, and second, the theoretical debate about the economic laws governing the transition to socialism – and then, the necessary updating of the debate.

Is the market 'socially neutral'?

The phrase 'socially neutral' refers to the notion that the market is a mechanism usable interchangeably in societies of different class nature. If true, this would imply that the market, in of itself, does not foster any specific social relations.

How did Bukharin and Preobrazhensky differ on this issue? Bukharin, like Preobrazhensky, was both a revolutionary and a Marxist theoretician. But unlike the latter, he held that the overthrow of the bourgeois state sufficed to insure the superiority of 'socialist' industry in its competition with the private sector. This being the case, the market should be treated as an instrument that allowed 'equal' exchanges to take place between the state sector and private producers; the operation of the market in this framework would enhance cooperation and therefore move society forward towards a socialist transformation. In this framework, the slogan put forward by the Bukharinists (the call on the kulaks to 'enrich themselves') was intended to stabilise the 'worker-peasant bloc,' and even to bring about a decline of social conflicts: 'We will not reach socialism directly through the process of production; we will reach it through exchange, through cooperation.'[251]

In this article, Bukharin waxes ironic about Preobrazhensky's 'uncertainties': for although the latter believed that cooperation could lead to the socialisation of agriculture, he held that this was only one – the most positive – of several possible directions of the evolution of cooperation. Bukharin, on the other hand, believed this direction of evolution was guaranteed:

> Indeed, we are not evolving towards the consolidation of class relations, but towards their elimination. And the more rapidly accumulation takes place in the socialist economic environment and in its periphery undergoing socialisation, the more the opposition between the proletariat and peasantry will diminish.[252]

This particular dynamic stood in contrast to what happened under capitalism, he argued, since in the latter situation, the integration of petty commodity production into the capitalist system sharpened the antagonisms between the interests of the bourgeoisie (the ruling class) and the small peasants.

Bukharin interpreted Preobrazhensky's doubts as a misplaced distrust of the peasantry, indicative of his 'anti-peasant deviations.' (We should note that Bukharin did not fear to use the sort of polemical style which later became notorious).

'What strikes one here, is Preobrazhensky's unpretentiousness; he does not polemicise with Lenin …; he merely asserts that one cannot make a theoretical analysis of something which does not yet exist, of what is called upon to rise.' 'According to Preobrazhensky,' Bukharin continues, 'the evolution of the peasant economy can go in three directions: 1) petty production remains petty production; 2) petty production, through capitalist cooperation, becomes capitalist; 3) petty production becomes cooperative through a still unknown socialist path, of which agricultural cartels and communes are the first stages.'

And Bukharin comments:

> … Preobrazhensky does not understand the specific character of the paths available to the proletarian dictatorship. He imagines that the laws of evolution of the rural economy have remained the same under the rule of the proletariat as they were under capitalism. While under bourgeois rule the cooperative organisations of the peasant masses were integrated inevitably into capitalism, this will no longer be the case under the proletariat, with its proletarian ideology, banks, credit and organisers.[253]

So, Preobrazhensky had doubts about the direction of evolution, as stated by Bukharin. One of the reasons was that he did not believe the superiority of so-called socialist industry (the state sector) was assured from the outset of the transition (we shall return to this point). He believed that social differentiation would inevitably grow in the countryside itself along with the extension of market relations. He had foreseen the rise of social conflicts so clearly that he wrote a small work of anticipation about it, entitled *From NEP to Socialism*. Its script involved the market breeding a new layer of 'Nepmen' who then turned on the workers' state and attempted to strangle it. More fundamentally, the author of *The New Economics* identified the contours of potential conflict areas with the rich peasants: on the one hand, in relations with the world market; and on the other, as a result of the inadequacy of industrialisation and its inability to satisfy the needs of agriculture.

The first point was connected with the overall need to supply goods for export (mainly agricultural goods) to pay for the equipment necessary to industrialise the country. The state monopoly imposed low prices on the peasants, so that they were less favoured than if they could have freely sold their goods on the world market.

Generally, Preobrazhensky stressed that any boundaries set on capitalist accumulation would be a source of tension.

The second point concerned the general state of the country. Preobrazhensky believed that it was naive to hope to build a stable alliance with the rich peasantry: increasing agricultural prices conflicted with the social goals of the regime (improving the workers' standard of living) and the state itself was not yet ready to supply the farmers with what they wanted: equipment, infrastructures, fertilisers, skilled personnel capable of bringing about improvement in the productivity of agriculture and the standard of living of the countryside.

> But the dictatorship of the proletariat could be placed in jeopardy not only insofar as we do not succeed to live 'on good terms' with the peasantry because of mistakes in our policy on relations with the countryside, but because our economic base will develop slower than the capitalist offsprings of our economy bred by the market economy.[254]

Preobrazhensky therefore felt that it was indispensable to assign top priority to the industrialisation of the country by skimming some of the income off the rich private agricultural sector – and providing it, in exchange, with the equipment, electrification, transport networks, etc. which it needed. He believed that the tax policy should make a clear-cut distinction in favour of the poor peasant who produced no surplus and whom the state should assist. This does not mean, as suggested by the caricature of this debate, that Preobrazhensky advocated imposing a rise of industrial prices on agriculture that would have smothered its élan – let alone that he favoured accumulation at the expense of the standard of living of the population.

> My real opinion on this question can be summarised as follows. A just price-setting policy for products of state industry should try and meet the following three goals: it should provide accumulation for the enlarged reproduction and renewed technical outfitting of industry, it should raise wages, and it should reduce prices. Can these three goals be achieved simultaneously? They can. A contradiction would arise only if the economy remained in a stable condition, if the volume of incomes, both those of the state and peasant sectors, remained in a stable situation. Only

then, would accumulation be possible only at the expense of a cut in wages or a reduction of prices ... But with an increase in the productivity of labour, the three-fold problem can be resolved simultaneously. ... Apportioning the benefits of productivity gains among these goals does not just depend on an increase in production and the productivity of labour, but also appears to be itself the indispensable condition of such an increase.[255]

It is clear from this quote that the real debate revolved in the first place around the search for productivity gains through a better organisation of work; and in the second place, around the search for the optimum level of accumulation – not the maximum, as the Stalinist industrialisation policy later chose to present things – for the possibility of achieving productivity gains depends on raising the standard of living of the people, as Preobrazhensky stressed in this article.

One of the obstacles to achieving this optimum rate, the author wrote, is the fact that private trade is still in the hands of the private sector. As a result, in a situation of relative shortage, the latter could use the lowering of industrial prices for accumulation in its own sector – rather than to lower the prices paid by the consumers.

Moshe Lewin's book, *The Making of the Soviet System*,[256] gives a very precise account of this period of Soviet history. He demonstrates quite effectively that Stalinist policy was not a pre-determined project, but a bureaucratic response to the build up of problems and tensions. His study re-establishes the historical truth in exposing the inaccuracy of Stalinist claims that the repression meted out at that time was directed exclusively against 'kulaks'. Stalin's distortions aside, the NEP did generate genuine problems. Moshe Lewin shows that real social differentiation had taken place in the countryside – but, in his opinion, rather between the poor and middle peasants, than between the latter and the kulaks who had basically disappeared. He emphasises the chain of political mistakes which led to a more and more dramatic situation, culminating in the cessation of wheat deliveries and food shortages in the cities which threatened to strangle the regime. In this context, Stalin's policy appears as a blind forward plunge, over a wall erected by his own methods. Lewin's book does not deal specifically with the criticisms of Stalin made by either the Left Opposition or the so-called 'Right' wing – which remained a loose current. But he carefully mentions the policy advocated by the Bukharinists – as well as their illusions that their price policy could solve the problems of relation with the peasants.

Other experiences since the NEP make a more precise balance sheet possible. The market-oriented reforms of planning in Yugoslavia, Hungary and China had definite positive – albeit short-run and contradictory – effects. We have examined the sort of conflicts and issues they generated in the lectures.

Stalinist charges of 'capitalist roaders' directed at reformers, make it particularly important to distinguish the rise of social tensions as a result of the extension of market mechanisms from the actual restoration of capitalism. The Stalinists' Manichean view has left deep marks; in reality, though, everything cannot be reduced to the bourgeois versus proletarian opposition. Between social tensions and even antagonisms within the previously existing system, and the restoration of capitalism, there is a major gap, but also – let us not be naive in the name of rejecting caricatures – some rather sturdy bridges. A clear grasp of the distinction requires a very concrete analysis of the context and unfolding process. Previous experience with reforms shows that a section of the bureaucratic apparatus reacts to the social tensions created by the reforms long before the threshold of a qualitative change to capitalist restoration has been reached. But this apparatus itself is crisscrossed by restorationist tendencies – particularly if the political system does not allow such tendencies to express themselves elsewhere. The Yugoslav example shows that social disintegration can reach a critical point.

Moreover, the tensions and differentiations do not take place only between the private sector and state sector. They affect the entire social organism in each one of its parts. We already mentioned the need to look beyond the formal juridical status and uncover the relations of private appropriation existing within 'social property,' the horizontal inequalities and vertical differentiations created by the market within self-managed firms, processes which developed quite extensively in the Yugoslav reforms for instance.

Finally, it has become clear that a complex analysis is needed to determine the exact role and direction of evolution of petty commodity production. Bukharin was right to emphasise that the sector of private petty production could be socialised through the extension of cooperatives. We can also note now that the weight of petty production will probably last longer than foreseen in Marx's writings. This is true both in capitalist and post-capitalist society: certain sub-contracted services and the production of certain goods are probably better handled by artisanal or small-scale units than by the prototype of large-scale socialised industry, and will probably remain so for some time. (Alec Nove emphasises quite properly the fact that bigness does not always yield economies of scale.) But this does not prejudge of the property forms.

On the other hand, there is not one and only one possible dynamic for the private sector. In particular, the elimination of bourgeois rule alone – possibly even with the elimination of the ability to hire wage earners – cannot guarantee a positive dynamic. In this respect, Preobrazhensky was right to voice his doubts. One tendency that can arise is for the private units to retreat into self-sufficiency; another is for them to seek to accumulate at the expense of the state sector; finally, they can advance towards socialisation through cooperation and new forms of the division of labour. The Yugoslav experience has shown that the very same juridical property relations on the land (with 15% in the hands of the state and 85% in private hands) can produce opposite overall dynamics: Yugoslav agriculture evolved towards cooperation between 1955 and 1964, and towards increased real privatisation later. The fundamental difference was the qualitatively greater scope of market relations thanks to the dismantling of the plan in the latter period, combined, of course, with increasing bureaucratisation.

Now, if the market is not socially 'neutral,' should one accept to be ruled by its laws? And if not, is the only alternative to accept the arbitrary dictates of a bureaucracy?

The question of the 'economic laws' of the post-capitalist transition period

We already discussed the law of value in the introduction to these lectures. On this question too, which has its own specificities and pitfalls, Bukharin and Preobrazhensky put forward different positions.

Bukharin believed that the law of value is the only regulator and this view is widely held in all the current debates, either in its Marxist guise or reformulated in 'neo-classical' (free-enterprise) terms.

Let us first review the formulas most often expressed among Eastern European reformers of bureaucratic planning.

According to this approach, there exists a universal, inescapable 'objective economic law,' the law of regulation through the market (or law of value). The 'true' prices determined by this market law should be allowed to form freely – that is, unfettered by any state intervention (unless the function of the state is defined precisely as enforcing the rule of market prices, as in Oscar Lange's model). In this view, market prices serve as indicators helping to funnel investments towards particular sectors: a rise in prices as a result of insufficient supply leads to higher profits and attracts investors; on the other hand, a fall in prices as a result of overproduction or difficulties in selling a shoddy product leads to closing down that production line. This makes clear what are the appropriate specialisations for competing on the world market – provided the capital of firms showing a deficit (at those price levels) is allowed to flow towards the more profitable branches. This implies that cheap credit and other forms of subsidies should cease to be lavished on lame duck firms. Many Hungarian and Yugoslav economists believe that, under these conditions, the overall equilibrium between branches of the economy would be re-established and the foreign debt would be reduced.

This neoliberal free-market world is, paradoxically, sometimes advocated by reformers who identify with socialism and Marxism.

'Neo-classical' free-market theoretical models have a real attractive power among economists of Eastern Europe. These models seem to operate 'above' class relations since they deal only with the 'producer' and the 'consumer' 'in general'. They claim to be universal. Many reformers of planning in Eastern Europe believe that these theoretical models can be adapted to a socialist framework and even that they are compatible with a Marxist approach. This was the standpoint of Branko Horvat in Yugoslavia.

Without entering into the finer details of all these debates, the basic idea of these pro-market reformers identified with socialism is that the Marxist critique of capitalism concerns mainly capitalist private property.

In other words, in their view it is the hiring of wage earners by private firms which is the decisive criterion, which is why they propose stringent legislation on this point. Once capitalist private property is eliminated, or severely restricted, they believe criticism of the market as such is considerably less warranted. They argue that the state should oppose the accumulation of income from work performed by others – but that individual work performed on private means of production is another matter, as indeed it is. In that perspective, the role of planning is mainly indicative: providing firms with all the necessary information on the market for them to make the right choices, in other words, consciously implementing the laws which wild capitalist competition enforces blindly, at great cost, through trial and error and cyclical crises.

As we have seen, this outlook can be fleshed out as a self-management scheme in which firms managed by their workers must respect the strictures of competition for their own benefit and that of all society: this competition is supposed to make it possible to produce at cheaper costs and to adapt to consumers' demands more flexibly while enabling the self-managed firm to maximise its profit. (See for instance the self-managed models elaborated by Jaroslav Vanek in the United States.) More 'Keynesian' versions of this approach assign the state a greater role: they argue that while the system should allow market prices and competition to serve as its key regulators, the centre should guarantee that investments are allocated in the right proportions to bring about full employment.

These reform projects cannot be simply (or simplistically) labelled 'pro-capitalist' – any more than it would be acceptable to label Bukharin a pro-capitalist. For Bukharin too, after asserting that the only possible regulator was the law of value, proposed at the end of the 1920s that the plan should consciously enforce the orientations that a perfectly pure competitive market would have enforced. 'The plan constitutes "an anticipation of what, in the context of spontaneous regulation," would have been established after the fact'.[257]

But once you accept that the plan should restrict itself to consciously applying the rules of the market, it is easy to see why reformers in the former 'socialist countries', given their experience with ponderous planning bureaucracies, preferred to eliminate the plan altogether. In other words, the hypothesis of a 'socialist' use of the law of value (or of the market as a regulator, on the basis of neo-classical models) leads quite logically to the proposition that the plan should be dismantled – rather than to the simulation of a market mechanism, as advocated by Oscar Lange.

One of Bukharin's arguments against Preobrazhensky in this debate was that it was necessary to conceive economics as labour-saving economics under socialism as well as under capitalism. We already pointed out that this interpretation identifies all labour-saving economics with one particular historical form: the law of value.

In summary, according to Bukharin the law of value was universal in its substance. Only its form would change: just as it had undergone a change in the transition from petty commodity production to capitalism, so would it change again in the transition out of capitalism: this time, the chief difference would be that society could move towards its conscious implementation. The elimination of capitalist private property, and its corollary, the anarchy of decisions taken independently of each other, would make it possible to overcome the cyclical form of the capitalist crises.

Contrary to Bukharin, Preobrazhensky believed that two antagonistic laws would coexist and clash in the immediate post-capitalist transition: on the one hand, the law of value (bolstered by the influence of the capitalist world market, among others), and on the other hand, a new law which he named 'the socialist law of primitive accumulation.' What were his arguments? How do they stand up now, in the light of experience?

For Preobrazhensky, the law of value was rooted in history. It corresponded to specific social relations – the existence of both a capital market (with mobile competing capitals) and a labour market (in which labour-power was treated as a commodity), which, together, allowed the market to function as a regulator. These capitalist relations of production corresponded to a generalised market as distinct from the partial commodity forms which survived in the 'socialist transition:

> The socialist-market system and pure commodity production belong to two different types of economic structures.... It is impossible to separate the regulatory mechanism from the economic structure in which it arises.... The law of value precisely reproduces the relations of a market economy, and can only function as a regulator thanks to the development of these relations.[258]

Preobrazhensky's interpretation was based on the Marxist theoretical tradition in quasi-philosophical fashion. Marx's writings beautifully explained how each society sets its priorities and evaluates its needs and costs differently. Proceeding in the exact opposite way than the 'neo-classical' method mentioned earlier, Marx sought to uncover, behind the 'producer' and the 'consumer,' the real property relations, the real forms of appropriation of the surplus, the specific overall class logic which each production system promoted.

In other words, for Preobrazhensky, the various ways in which social labour was 'measured' in different systems, were not simply a formal matter (more attention to planned calculations) that did not alter the ultimate acceptance of the same proportions, as argued by Bukharin:

> Finally, to reduce the whole problem of the two different regulators corresponding to two different systems of social reproduction, and the whole question of the different material consequences caused by the regulator, to a difference in regulation mechanisms, in the narrow sense of the term (...), was to substitute one aspect of the problem to the problem as a whole.[259]

The post-capitalist society whose 'laws' Preobrazhensky proposed to analyse existed, and would exist, he pointed out, in a new historical situation:
- It had to eliminate the existence of a labour market forthwith and confer a new and central status in the logic of production, upon the worker, as such; that is to liquidate unemployment forever.
- It had to try and eliminate capitalist private property while continuing to use the latter's resources domestically and in foreign trade.
- The market would no longer be dominant but would remain necessary on both the domestic and international plane.
- Moreover, experience had shown that the proletarian revolution would

occur first in the weakest links of the world capitalist system. The problem of furthering the transition to communism on the basis of a lower productivity than that of the most highly developed capitalism, was therefore not only that of the USSR at that moment, but of Europe later, as it faced the United States.

Preobrazhensky attempted to think through the theoretical problem of the transitional period economy in the really existing historical circumstances, unforeseen by Marx, in which it arose: not in a society breaking with the most highly developed capitalism, nor in an immediately socialist society, as foreseen by classic texts in which the 'associated producers' could dispense with the 'detour of the market'; but in a framework in which the market was alive and kicking, although no longer dominant; a framework in which time would be needed to draw out the proletariat's own sources of productivity.

> At the present time, our state economy is both technically and economically weaker than Europe's and America's capitalist economy. The Soviet economy will be weaker ... than capitalist America's economy. In its initial period of development, lacking both the material preconditions for the rebuilding of its technical base and the means to raise the culture and education of the proletariat, the socialist form cannot develop all the distinctive advantages organic to socialism ....' At the same time, 'it forfeits some [of the advantages] characteristic of a capitalist economy. [Preobrazhensky refers here to the coercion of the market, particularly the threat of unemployment as a capitalist mechanism to increase productivity – C. S.] The capitalist economy, 'on the other hand, remains in full battle gear (...), which means that, even in the period of decline of capitalism, the socialist form generally has to compete and struggle with capitalism from a position of equality.'[260]

As a consequence, relations with the world market – and the law of value – would be conflict-ridden. Preobrazhensky believed that autarky would be a regression and should be avoided. On the contrary, relations with the capitalist world would be a vital necessity. The question was, on what basis, with or without protection?

> ... presenting the struggle waged in different forms against the private economy, including in the form of forced collaboration with capitalism, as a peaceful, 'golden legend,' amounts to idle superficial chatter above the real phenomena ....[261]

And further:

If economic relations were formed on the basis of the free play of the law of value of the world economy, in our country, at this time, this is what would happen: given the current prices on the world market and the over-industrialisation of Europe, two thirds of our large-scale industry would be eliminated because it would show a deficit and prove unnecessary *from a capitalist standpoint, from the standpoint of the world division of labour on a capitalist basis*. [Emphasis in original.] Conversely, while our agriculture would eventually be deeply and durably transformed by the transformation of the country into an agricultural semi-colony of the world capitalist system, it would initially, during the first years, benefit from this [opening on the world market] because industrial prices would be lower and exchanges more favourable on the world market ....[262]

Preobrazhensky added, for the Mensheviks' benefit, that allowing the law of value free play on the territory of the USSR would not have served the cause of the development of a national capitalism, but would have subordinated the national economy to the requirements of world capitalism, of its division of labour.

This question of the confrontation with world capitalism was central for Preobrazhensky – whereas Bukharin proposed to leave it to the side:

'Abstracting the foreign market from the discussion means abstracting our reciprocal relations with the world economy; it means abstracting our completely exceptional relations of value with it, our monopoly of foreign trade ..., the fundamental conditions of our existence ....'[263]

This aspect of the debate is often omitted in overviews of the period, but it is the one which best illustrates Preobrazhensky's viewpoint: to make use of the market while resisting its implicit criteria.

The new historical problem to be resolved was how to ensure the transformation of the starting relations – not their reproduction, expanded or otherwise. To be socialist, such a transformation required both the development of material resources and the lessening of inequality and relations of oppression, which the market tended to reproduce:

Only by always taking into account both poles of the entire process (the initial pole and the final pole) can we understand the historical location of any transitional form, and avoid to lose our way in details or fall into vulgar economics which tries to pawn a superficial description of the present off as a scientific analysis of a concrete system.[264]

Note how far this is from the apologies of bureaucratic planning as 'developed socialism.'

But, if the law of value cannot be the regulator of the new society, is the latter under the sway of some other law of accumulation? This is the hypothesis which Preobrazhensky advanced, while emphasising that he was not yet able to define fully its content: only experience and scientific investigation would make it possible to make its contours more precise, retrospectively. He nevertheless gave a name to this new law to be discovered: 'the socialist law of primitive accumulation' (primitive being used by analogy with the expression 'primitive, i.e. initial, accumulation of capital').

He argued that this law should 'dictate to the state' its decisions on relations – and transfers of value – between the state sector and private sector, since industrialisation, in particular, required accumulation at the expense of the rich section of the peasantry.

We know how Stalin was able to refer back to this point, in caricatural form, to argue in favour of forced industrialisation at the sacrifice of agriculture – and of the *nepmen* and private producers of all types.

Preobrazhensky's historical approach remains fundamentally fruitful on the theoretical and experimental levels. All attempts to use the market as a regulator, far from solving the problems of bureaucratic planning, far from being a socially neutral measure, and far from fostering socialist self-management relations, led in practice to a dead-end on these three levels.

More broadly, all countries which posed the problem of breaking with under-development and dependency were confronted with a central question. The same question will face all countries who attempt to follow that path: they must have relations with the capitalist environment, but cannot submit to its criteria if they are to remain true to a logic of satisfaction of the needs of the people.

This is not a plea for autarky. It is an argument for protection against the law of value, for a multiform defence which, though it may not insulate a country from the currents of the dominant economies, will enable it to steer a course against the stream. The more accurately it knows the forces with which it is dealing, the easier and better it can chart such a course. Yugoslavia's crisis is all the sharper that it opened itself wide to 'healthy competition,' that it assumed precisely that the latter was strictly 'healthy'.

We have found Preobrazhensky's historical approach to the law of value essential and illuminating in interpreting the Yugoslav self-management experiment: the law of value 'needs' a generalised market to function as a 'regulator.' It 'needs' both a labour and a capital market. In other words, it needs social relations that reduce 'labour' (the worker) to a thing, to a cost to a commodity that one (who? the workers self-management body?) can 'substitute' or combine with other 'factors of production.'

Our balance sheet will therefore be paradoxical: the logic of 'pro-self-management' market reforms leads to the elimination of self-management.

But the acknowledgement that the old criteria applied to the new society lead to a dead-end, does not in and of itself provide an obvious answer as to what a socialist 'measurement' of useful labour might look like. The task then becomes the discovery of a new space-time (which can no longer be local and short-term once it is not defined by the market) and new mechanisms (actors) which will make it possible to judge what is useful labour.

This is the vantage point from which Preobrazhensky's view deserves some criticism.

We do not believe that Preobrazhensky's formula of the two antagonistic 'laws' should be retained. We prefer the broader formula of 'two regulators.' Competitive capitalism is the only instance in history when the economy seems to be imposing its 'law' independently of the will of any human. (One can, of course, analyse the social relations hidden by the market and discuss the theoretical and practical role of the state in the mechanisms of competitive capitalism.) It is the fact that these apparently automatic responses are so widespread in the market that gives the notion of economic 'law' its value.

In the case of the 'socialist' mode of accumulation or better yet, of the socialist transition, the term 'law,' although used out of respect for a scientific approach, seems less adequate, or even confusing.

For the author of *New Economics* presents the law of value as 'the natural law of commodity production' – which makes sense – but, proceeding by analogy, states that one must equally seek 'the natural laws of socialist accumulation which are known only in outline'[265] and which 'dictate to the state ... on the basis of necessity, first, determinate proportions in the distribution of the productive forces ..., and secondly, determinate proportions for accumulation ....'[266]

'... Which dictate to the state': this seems to imply that a single set of specific proportions – differing from those indicated by the law of value – is waiting to be discovered and that scientific investigation suffices to discover them.

But the range of possible choices is widening, a fact which the term 'law' cannot emphasise. There are of course certain necessary constraints and requirements for consistency. These must indeed be discovered and made explicit – which amounts to saying that regulatory mechanisms suited to the new goals of social transformation must be found. The conflicts and imbalances which arise at each stage, as a reaction to each set of institutions and social relations, are a revelator of a search for consistency. But this is a long shot from a 'natural law of socialist accumulation' above the actions of men and women.

Satisfying the needs and fostering the fullest development of each and every individual is a goal which imparts a qualitatively greater weight to certain subjective, cultural and social imperatives in the optimal 'proportions' of accumulation and in the very definition of the criteria by which these proportions should be determined.

The bureaucracy was absent from *New Economics*. Who could 'dictate to the state' the necessary choices? The 'law' of socialist accumulation rapidly was transformed into a 'decree.'

The centre of gravity of our approach therefore shifts the discussion from the issue of 'plan versus market' to the issue of 'who should decide?' according to what criteria, in line with what class interests and by what institutional devices? These questions hold whether applied to the market or to the plan (and to their combination). Preobrazhensky's historical and social approach to the law of value remained essential. But the bureaucratisation of the plan proved to be a new source of social stratification which also threatened the socialist future.

As Preobrazhensky predicted it, market reforms yielded increased inequality – but the main threats of capitalist restoration were to emerge within the so-called social sector itself.

Putting an end to the rule of the market did make it possible to put on the agenda an economic logic which subordinated investment choices to the satisfaction of needs, in the broadest sense – focusing on the need to transform the nature of labour and social relations themselves.

But the question posed at that point – and still not resolved to this day – was that of a mode of regulation which took into account, as an explicit imperative, 'subjectivity,' the choices made about society after a transparent presentation of their consequences.

In other words, the question of democracy as a factor of production must be placed at the core of the mechanisms of socialist accumulation. This is why we prefer the term 'regulator' to that of 'law' used by Preobrazhensky. We can then speak of the existence of a conflict between two regulators in post-capitalist society:

- one, based on the market, derives its consistency from the competition between different capitals, from free enterprise and its right to hire and fire labour power, treated as a commodity;
- the other, 'socialist,' places solidarity, the reduction of inequality and the conscious determination of the most important social needs (including

full employment) at the core of its priorities.[267]

Any attempt to reject Preobrazhensky's hypothesis about the two regulators must necessarily take one of two paths: it must either demonstrate what cannot be demonstrated, namely that the market can be a regulator that meets the criteria of socialism; or renounce the goals traditionally upheld by socialism.

We propose not to reject, but to make a critical update of Preobrazhensky's approach. To do so, one must accept the hypothesis of two conflicting regulators while rejecting explicitly the idea that the socialist goals can be achieved by bureaucratic means – or by a state that substituted for its citizens/workers.

The very great similarity between people's resistance to the decrees of the bureaucratic plan and their resistance to the laws of the dictatorship of the market reflects an underlying social consistency struggling to emerge.

Conclusion

How to determine 'the socially necessary labour'? Economic democracy as a relation of production and distribution

Individuals cannot master their own relations before having themselves created them.
Karl Marx, *Foundations of a Critique of Political Economy*

In 1981, commenting on the Yugoslav experience and crisis, Ota Sik recalled the solutions he had advocated in 1968, during the Prague Spring.[268] In this interesting critical re-examination of his position, he averred that it was 'necessary to subordinate the process of distribution to democratically determined social objectives'.[269] This led him to challenge the freedom which Yugoslav firms had had to distribute their net income:

> 'In the first place,' he said, 'such a mode of distribution does not permit one to insure a macro-economic balance. This ill-proportioned development produces high inflation. In the second place, this mode of distribution does not allow … coherent differentiations of income, according to the performance of firms, due to a monopolistic income-formation structure…. Third, this mode of distribution prevents the achievement of democratic objectives based on developing the entire economy on the basis of alternative choices.'[270]

At the same time, though, Ota Sik maintained the proposition that investments should be allocated on the basis of the market and firms oriented on the basis of a search for the highest profit.

The precondition for a real debate on these questions is that each choice be subject to a real democratic discussion and decision-making process, whatever the level at which the decision is now made. Only then can one begin a theoretical and practical discussion, based on experience, to determine which problems can be solved more effectively at which levels (overall, regional or local), what advantages and disadvantages market mechanisms might bring in a given context and which problems they might be able to solve.[271]

Ota Sik's answer suggests three remarks.

The first remark is that if the freedom of self-management remains confined to a local level and oriented to maximise income, it will necessarily conflict with the desire for a macro-economic equilibrium and the control of inflation. There are three possible responses to this:

- One can return to a system in which self-management is constrained by rules set down by the central state (as in Yugoslavia in the 1950s), but this means returning also to the conflicts and contradictions characteristic of that system described earlier.
- One can eliminate all forms of workers self-management and renounce the goals of socialism.
- Or, one can expand self-management to a national level. This implies revamping the system in such a way that the choices made on distribution at the central level emanate no longer from an institution alien to the self- managed workers who have to put them into practice, but from the workers' own decision taken at another level. The workers' interest in making these choices and abiding by them would stem from the possibility of resolving the problems which they encounter as consumers of consumer and production goods in the face of inflation; from the possibility of a better solution to the problems of employment; and, finally, from the possibility of broadening their horizons as producers/managers. This is the key problem which remains to be solved.

This was the rationale of the proposals made by the Student movement in 1968, influenced by the Marxist professors of the *Praxis* review: for 'self-management from bottom to top', 'against the 'red bourgeoisie'. Those criticisms were 'appropriated' by Tito, Kardelj and Bakaric after having repressed any independent movement: the Titoist leadership organised the second congress of self-management in Sarajevo (1971), where concrete criticisms were expressed against the banking system and technocratic forces, introducing amendments to the 1974 Constitution: a broad part of them was an attempt to break to destructive dynamic of the market reforms by the introduction of a self-managed planning, chambers of self-management at different territorial levels, 'self-managed community of interests'; they were combined with the dismantling of the banking sectors and of big factories in favour of the new 'Basic Unit of associated labour' supposed to consolidate workers self-management against technocrats. But this was combined with concessions to the national demands – in particular the republican control on foreign exchange (expressed in the 'Croatian Spring' in 1971), and the absence of a federal chamber of self-management. The whole Constitution was therefore contradictory and unable to produce a consistent system able to resist market and nationalist threats.

The second remark is whether there is a convergence between individual interests and social needs.

Which questions would be better solved by democratic central choices than by market procedures must be deduced – as Ota Sik does – from the macro-economic imbalances. But the distinction also depends on which hypothesis is upheld with regard to the possible sources of a convergence of individual interests and social needs.

The role which Ota Sik and other theoreticians of market reforms attribute to the market flows from an idealisation of the virtues of the market and a static and 'pessimistic' view of individuals' behaviour at work. Sik says it explicitly in his study: he sees no other way than the market to stimulate more productive labour of a better quality. Otherwise, he writes, each person 'tries to maximise his or her income with the least expenditure of labour.'[272] This negative observation leads him to argue in favour of a model in which the organisation of production and choices about investments must remain subordinate to market profits.

We have attempted to show that this sort of mechanism for accumulation cannot have the virtues of capitalist management without having its disadvantages as well – and others besides. The 'imperfect' reality of the really existing market in Yugoslavia will solve neither the problems of over-investment, growing costs and waste, nor those of the low productivity of labour. It will produce inflation and inequalities while postponing the socialist objectives of full employment and the dis-alienation of labour, producing more and more conflicts along the way. The social cost of a 'perfect' model of maximisation of micro-economic competitive profit would be even greater.

Put another way, there will be growing divergence, not convergence, between individual interests and social needs if resources are allocated according to their potential for profit on the market.

Why not try to transform the motivations of individuals instead?

On the one hand, the inability of Taylorism, work broken into pieces, to raise productivity gains beyond a certain limit is well known. On the other, the positive results achieved by Hungarian agriculture when margins of responsibility were increased; the way in which workers criticised waste in Hungary when social control developed in 1956, and in Poland under Solidarność; the suffering observed in workers prevented from 'doing a good job'; the 'professional scruple' analysed by Komai' even when the system as a whole makes the effort ineffective, all testify to the existence of deep-rooted aspirations thwarted by bureaucratism as well as market relations.

These aspirations have far more to do with the content of labour than with its remuneration – provided the latter is adequate and each individual enjoys some regular improvement of her or his living standard. Once this sort of security is achieved, individuals can turn their attention towards other latent concerns. The idea that only the risk of redundancy and the individualisation of remuneration can stimulate an improvement in the quality of labour is by no means demonstrated – quite apart from the fact that such incentives have perverse side effects. As soon as labour becomes interesting in itself (and provides a standard of living judged socially equitable in a given context by consensus), routine and conservatism can easily be combatted through comparing results, through the pressure of teams working together, through the pressure of consumers of the goods or services, and through the pleasure of job well done.

But such progress and creativity of labour cannot be fully realised in a single workshop or on the basis of financial management turned to the lure of profit. If work is still piecemeal, then the worker might as well do the least possible for the greatest possible income. Likewise, if workers exert their energy, and imagination in vain because the system does not generalise such efforts, or worse yet, because they benefit the private interests of a privileged layer, then the workers might as well stay put and fix up their own home.

Workers self-management of the accumulation fund – 'deferred consumption' – imposes a coherent system in which the objectives, the means, the relations of production and distribution, the criteria for measuring labour and the incentives used reunite the producer, the consumer and the manager.[273]

This leads us to a third remark about Ota Sik's position which concerns differential pay according to the performance of the firm and that the means must be consistent with the ends.

The Czechoslovak theoretician is right to emphasise 'the monopolistic structure of incomes' in Yugoslavia. But it should be clear that, underlying this feature, there is a strong tendency (also noticeable in capitalist countries when the workers movement is strong) to generalise the advantages won by those with the best 'performance,' or to disconnect personal income (or wages) from competitive mechanisms[274] – trends which make monetary incentives counter-productive and a source of inflation. No one will challenge the necessity for material incentives. It is their place and nature which is a matter for debate.

Shortening the work week, eliminating the most tedious and strenuous jobs, allowing time for training, education, management tasks and leisure, providing men and women with the means to control the conditions that affect their lives, can be forms of non-monetary material incentives – along with the development of a taste for decision-making for its own sake.

These wellsprings of energy and creativity have not been tapped, even when self-management made them a real possibility. Would it not be better to take the goal itself–transforming social relations and raising productivity to reduce the work week – as an incentive and phase out those (monetary) incentives which have a disintegrative effect – and have neither been applied fairly nor demonstrated fully their alleged virtues? Reuniting the worker with his or her labour, encouraging the free public expression of needs and promoting a debate on the incentives themselves, would help to discard inadequate solutions to the problems. Democratic management of distribution networks could link raises in monetary income to increases in the general productivity of the system; this would incite workers to disseminate all advances achieved in their particular location, stimulating those with the 'highest performance' to associate with others and pass on their know-how. At the same time, it could allow all kinds of incentives linked to improvements in the organisation and quality of labour, to operate on a local level. This raises once again the question of what is the best time/space set in which the consumers can judge these advances and improvements. Should they measure it in the opaque, compartmentalised dimension of value? Or in the dimension of the entire chain of social labour and use value?

It is clear that the very tight connection between relations of production and relations of distribution, emphasised throughout Marx's work, appears in a very complex context when people's habits remain shaped by market incentives. As Che Guevara put it: 'The pipe dream that socialism can be achieved with the dull instruments left to us by capitalism …'

The basic contradictions are probably insurmountable. Ernest Mandel writes:

> The survival of bourgeois norms of distribution reacts against planned relations of production, in the sense that it creates – in the context of a

system prone to shortages – a strong incentive in favour of linking income not only to labour inputs, but also to the relative productivity of the latter, since it is calculated and therefore known. This link can be individual or collective; it can break up or accentuate the solidarity of workers in a firm or locality or a branch of industry. It will always [emphasis in original] accentuate inequality among the totality of the associated producers and will thus be a force tending to dissociate the latter subjectively.'[275]

'Bourgeois norms of distribution,' based on equality before the law in a situation where pre-existing inequalities survive and embodied in the formula 'To each according to his labour,' have been interpreted and applied in practice in a variety of ways. It is not obvious to us, beyond the need to overcome deformations which serve as a cover for privilege, which criteria should be retained to achieve the optimum distribution in the context of 'socialist' accumulation. In a seldom quoted letter, Engels shed an interesting light on Marx's views on this question.[276] Referring to the debate about the mode of distribution under socialism, he wrote:

> We have dealt with this in a very materialist way in contrast to certain idealist juridical expressions … But none of the participants (in the discussion) appear to grasp socialist society as something in continual change and progress … However, in a rational approach, one can only 1) try to discover the mode of distribution with which it began, and 2) try to find the general tendency in which the new development proceeds.[277]

This is a far cry from a normative vision of socialism 'defined' as a society in which the mode of distribution must be 'to each according to his labour.' Already today, distribution according to needs has taken on growing importance everywhere. Yet have material incentives which can at once improve and transform labour, really been discovered?

> Pursuing the pipe dream that socialism can be achieved with the dull instruments left to us by capitalism (the commodity as the basic economic cell, profitability, individual material interest as a lever, etc.) risks leading as to an impasse … To build communism, it is necessary, simultaneously with the new material foundations, to build the new man,
>
> That is why it is important to choose the right instrument for mobilising the masses. Basically, this instrument must be moral, without neglecting, however a correct use of the material incentive, particularly of a social character.[278]

Under capitalism, the commodity analysed by Marx is a contradictory unit use value (produced by 'concrete labour' with specific physical qualities) and value (produced by 'abstract' labour, a product of human energy in general,' the substance of exchange value). Value cannot be realised without use value. But capital subordinates use value to exchange value because profit is the objective and it does not exist without market value. Needs are of little concern. Only solvent demand (a need with cash in its pocket) matters, provided it can ensure a 'sufficient profit.' As soon as the profit from sales is no longer judged 'sufficient,' capital sacrifices the use values produced and the unsatisfied needs. In the final analysis, the 'socially necessary labour' analysed by Marx therefore incorporates a three-fold judgement whose mechanisms are at once connected and hidden by the market: a judgement about costs, a judgement about demand, and in close association with the first two, a judgement about the 'suitable' social relations for a given society. The commodity as an economic unit embodies these three aspects.

In post-capitalist society, market mechanisms and money subsist. But their functions can change and eventually wither away to the extent that other mechanisms – other social relations – are able to assume these functions better. Conversely, when the former fail to materialise, the latter will re-emerge. Even when they are no longer commodities, goods remain the product of concrete labour (specific, not measurable) and abstract labour (comparable to other labours). The latter must be saved while the first is transformed (by reducing unpleasant labour and developing skills and mechanisation). Nevertheless, the commodity no longer rules as the economic unit – the crisis of bureaucratic planning is not a crisis of overproduction of commodities: it is the crisis of bad (over/under) production of use values and the wastage of human labour.

In a 'collective ownership' system, it is completely absurd to destroy any use values produced on the sole grounds that their cost of production – the labour expended on them – was (too) high, or that the entirety of the links in the chain of use values necessary for the production of a good is interrupted by a bottleneck (bad planning). The results can be analysed and rectified without this adjustment requiring a change in prices to ensure 'economic recovery.' This is the reason why even incorrect prices do not prevent the system from functioning – albeit poorly, since expenditures should be measured in proportion to needs.

In *Calculs économiques et formes de propriété,* Bettelheim rightly stressed that transitional society had not yet developed 'concepts adequate for the measurement of social labour, which is never given in the dimension of physical labour.'[279]

He noted in particular how difficult it was to 'measure' labour 'useful' for the satisfaction of alternative social needs which the system was capable of meeting at a given moment. In this regard, he wrote, the 'socialist' equivalent of 'socially necessary labour,' related to 'useful social effects' has not yet been found. Does not this theoretical problem lead us, we might ask, to an analysis of bureaucratic relations?[280]

The particular combination of private labour and social labour can be transformed. In competitive capitalism, a commodity is primarily the product of private labour: it is manufactured in the context of free enterprise, by private decisions taken independently of each other. Responsibility for this production is private – this is the price a capitalist has to pay for keeping his profit. The risk, if the private labour expended is not recognised by the capitalist market as 'socially necessary' – in other words as corresponding to a demand which incorporates a 'sufficient profit' – is bankruptcy for the firm, meaning unemployment for the worker. Planning, even bureaucratic planning, confers on labour expended a certain direct social content – at the same time as it shares risks collectively.[281]

This is not the only difference. The market in combining the various aspects of a commodity, renders verdicts which punishes waste. On the other hand, socialism, more than any other society, requires a value judgement on the quality and quantity of labour – from the standpoint of the worker as a producer as well as a consumer. The risk can be assumed collectively. But it remains necessary to correct faults and errors; the system must find its own equivalent to 'socially necessary labour'. Quality control and the verification that needs are actually satisfied are indispensable. The judgement of the user (whether an individual consumer or a firm receiving equipment goods) must be expressed.

The act of purchasing can be one of the means for this verification. But it does not necessarily follow that money is the sole or best means of judgement. The fact that a good or service is not purchased gives no clue as to the reason why it was not purchased. Likewise, defective goods might be purchased and the defect not reported. Prices can be allowed to reflect insufficient output. But if the rare goods are also essential goods, a debate over how they should be distributed is necessary. Otherwise, the price increase will benefit the rich. Moreover, it is not desirable for increases in free prices to provoke a disorderly rush of investments towards the newly 'profitable' industry. On the other hand, such price increases could be taken into account to make a specific market study and avoid the anarchy of overproduction of commodities. Public discussion can assign various needs a grade of priority and reserve sufficient centralised resources to ensure that everyone's 'absolute needs' are met. Other needs could be left to the purview of decentralised collective initiative and individual initiative. Computers are an essential means for recording needs, making choices clearer for the producers, and taking macro-economic constraints into account in decentralised choices.

Communities affected by particular undertakings could pass direct, periodic judgements on the latter, thereby contributing to bring them more in line with the overall goal of satisfying needs more thoroughly.

If it came after all these mechanisms, money could cease to be a means of private accumulation and therefore a source of speculation. It could cease to be the means by which private labour is recognised as social – at least through the dramatic procedure of declining sales and bankruptcy as an individual risk. On the other hand, it could remain a means of circulation, a means of verification of the actual use of a social expenditure (thanks to a relationship between the private and the social).[282] And if the direct judgement of those affected (the producers and consumers) confirms the uselessness of an unpopular product, the means for a reconversion and better use of the means of production and labour involved could be determined by society. It is the communities of workers and consumers affected by the same production of goods or services who should be able to determine whether a job performed less effectively than another remains nonetheless useful – and how it can be improved.

In the same way as the commodity as the basic economic cell incorporates a three-fold judgement on costs, needs and social relations, social control must extend its sway over these three fields: but the techniques for recording costs and inventorying needs must be subordinated to overall social choices.

What needs to be challenged is not – in Bettelheim's words – 'the theoretical space of the plan' ruled by use value, but who controls the plan and who determines which space is under its sway – or under the market's.

As long as really expended, 'physically controllable,' labour is hidden by the bureaucratic plan – which covers all waste, feeds parasites and perpetuates alienated labour – or, alternately, as long as it is 'reified' by the market, the bureaucracy will have the upper hand and labour will reject all attempts to measure it 'socially.'

The commodity has begun to wither away as the basic economic unit, but without allowing economic democracy, its dialectical antinomy, to replace the market, without passing its powers to judge the social expenditure of labour on to the 'associated producers' themselves. Granted eliciting the producers' judgement is not easy, but without the will to do so, it is impossible.

We admit, then, to a continuing 'prejudice' against the market as a regulator (as distinct from the partial use of market mechanisms). The problem is that one cannot let all the functions performed by the market simply wither away along with the market itself: other methods of determining costs, waste and needs must be invented. The debate then shifts to another terrain in which the standpoint of society as a whole is the starting point of a new economic logic – and not a footnote, a sentimental wish or a band-aid repressive centralism put in place by Lenin and Trotsky applied after the damage is done. Once this terrain is accepted, the focus shifts to a case-by-case discussion of which social needs should be met first and how – drawing the balance sheet of experience for all to see. This approach therefore requires that a distinction be introduced among various needs, as suggested by Ernest Mandel in his debate with Alec Nove, between those which are considered (by those affected themselves) essential, strategic and to be met before all others; and those which are diversified and can be met by decentralised means, on the basis of other forms of financing and distribution criteria. The whole process could be subject to periodic balance sheets and adjustments. For clarity of choice, the advantages, disadvantages of each particular option must be fully discussed and the coherent set of decisions and mechanisms which its implementation would require, made explicit. The quality of life and work, relations with nature, ethical preferences, fundamental desires for national and international solidarity are all 'needs' which cannot be expressed by the market and should be the subject of debate and explicit judgements, and present in all decision-making procedures.

The process of dis-alienation of labour should be the goal consciously pursued at each stage: whether the choice concerns priority needs or the institutional, cultural and socio-economic methods to meet them. This is the function of democracy.

The democratic process described here is neither simple nor always direct. It must free itself from the fetishism of commodity relations at one end and the bureaucratism of administrative orders at the other. Experience shows that this requires a complex set of institutions, mechanisms and means.

The problem is not mainly technical, although computers and audio-visual methods are essential to solve the questions posed in this process: the choices available to an industrialised society are many and varied, as are the social interests present. Class differences will disappear slowly. They can revive, even in post-capitalist society. To these are added other forms of stratification and conflict. In addition, the same individuals do not necessarily have immediately convergent interests as consumers and as producers. National and community aspirations, sexual and cultural differences will also remain durable sources of tension.

In this context, it is best to take the perspectives bequeathed by Marx and Engels for what they are: general guidelines for another mode of social organisation in which the development of productive forces stems from the dis-alienation of labour, in which the conscious extension of each new gain for the benefit of all replaces equal competition among the unequal and in which the criteria of profit and solvent demand ceases to limit the satisfaction of needs. Their perspectives are not indications on how to get to such a society and how to organise it. But what they are is not insignificant for the critical analysis of 'really existing socialism.'

On this point, Alec Nove dissolves the Marxist argument into an overly general and therefore irrelevant point.[283] He is right to emphasise the naïveté of a vision of socialism without differences, without conflict, without specialised professional skills, where each individual would be interchangeable with the other in every task. Granted also that direct democracy does not resolve all problems in and of itself, contrary to the impression one might gain by taking Marxist texts too literally. But it is the substance of the matter which is important to us: can one and should one strive towards a society in which a monopoly of power based on privileges no longer exists? In which differences would no longer foster relations of oppression and exploitation? These questions pose the need for an experimental evaluation of the conscious, political means to combat the spontaneous mechanisms which have used differences to reproduce or produce and crystallise relations of oppression and exploitation.

Each and every individual cannot decide everything all the time.

Bringing the decision closer to those who are most directly affected by its effects can help to define the necessary institutions.

From this viewpoint, the 'associated producers' should have the decisive say over the organisation of their work. Another clear imperative to counter exclusive and therefore oppressive decisions, is that various communities (nationalities, women, youth) be given freedom of speech and the right to organise.[284]

The fact that society must pay a high social, economic and cultural cost when an important dimension is denied expression and smothered, is probably the only rational force that can motivate the search for a consensus. Conversely, when substantial social and cultural differences persist, counterposing appeals on the people as a whole to work out their problems 'all together' rather than engaging in allegedly old-fashioned struggles, is at best naive, and more often than not, a deliberate mystification. Consensus has no chance of becoming an effective method of decision, capable of reducing antagonisms, unless the antagonisms have already been reduced as a result of a more egalitarian distribution of labour and a more egalitarian appropriation of its results. This is why institutions of power cannot be discussed separately from property relations and the socio-economic decision-making mechanisms.

Just as direct democracy 'needs' institutions to avoid being purely formal, so it 'needs' a process of reduction of social and cultural inequalities.

When efforts to resolve these different aspects of the same overall problem are applied separately, at different times, power arrangements and antagonisms can crystallise and become more difficult and costly to challenge.

The idea that the main economic choices should be the purview of the Party (or of several parties) is as much a mystification as that which reserves these questions exclusively for 'experts.' But it would be equally false to oppose to these two impasses the naive vision of a direct democracy which could do without either political debate or experts. The mistrust of economists who raise certain partial theories and methods to the rank of universal – and therefore undisputable – rationality is mirrored by the mistrust of politics perceived as pure manipulation and hunger for power.

Economics is like a weapon, Serge C. Kolm notes quite accurately; all depends on who is using it. The same is true of politics.

The pluralism of expert opinions, the right of every institution of direct democracy to resort to a 'counterstudy' by another expert, is just as essential as the pluralistic expression of political options, whose function should be to fight the languages of experts. But scientific institutions, like parties and other political groupings (whether in party form or not), should not wield the actual power of decision. Groupings in political communities can give an overall view of the problems and stimulate self-activity. The possibility of resorting to the judgement of experts can give confidence. The guarantee of being able to defend oneself against abuses of power also contributes to making recognised rights credible. In other words, both self-management as an integral system, and direct democracy require scientific institutions and political groupings.

If, on the other hand, parties or experts substitute themselves for direct democracy, the people will remain confined in the narrow horizons of everyday life and growing conflicts of interest will emerge.

But as long as any form of 'central' choice, that is of choice affecting society as a whole, is identified with 'statism' and dictatorship – because repeated experiences have anchored this in people's minds – the debate will remain on a false basis. Localist, regionalist or corporatist interests will be inevitable, whatever the formal decisions taken on the harmonisation of interests.

The future: socialist utopia

'Utopia means nowhere, in other words a society which does not exist. Not one which is impossible.'[285]

Socialism will not mean uniform individuals, raised in the same mould – fortunately! On the contrary, it will mean new differences and new conflicts. The wager expressed in socialist utopia is not that a society without contradictions can exist, but that with a certain level of socio-economic and cultural development, human society will be generally freer.

Bibliography

Bakaric V., 'Intervention au Congrés du PCY- Ljubliana 1958', *Les Nouvelles Yougoslaves,* no. 221, 9 mai 1958.
– *Les fondements théoriques de la reproduction sociale dans le socialisme*, Belgrade: Questions actuelles du socialisme, 1975.
– 'Reproduction élargie et intégration sur des bases autogestionnaires', *Rapport au 2ème congrés de l'autogestion,* Sarajevo, 1971 (typewritten document).
Benassy J. P., Boyer R. and Gelpi R. M., 'La régulation monopoliste,' *Revue économique,* May 1979.
Bensaid D., *La revolution et le pouvoir,* Paris: Stock, 1976.
Bettelheim C., *Problemes théoriques et pratiques de la planification*, Paris: PUF, 1946.
– *Class Struggles in the USSR*, (2 vols. First Period, 1917-1923. Second Period, 1923-1930), Hassocks, Sussex: Harvester, 1976 and 1978.
– *La transition vers l'économie socialiste*, Paris: Maspero, 1968.
– *Economic Calculation and Forms of Property*, New York: Monthly Review, 1975.
Boncoeur J., 'Le traitement du travail dans quelques modules théoriques de la planification' in Lavigne M., (ed.), *Travail et monnaie en système socialiste,* Paris: Economica, 1981.
Brus W., *Socialist Ownership and Political Systems,* London: Routledge and Kegan Paul, 1975.
– *Problemes généraux du fonctionnement de l'économie socialiste*, Paris: Maspero.
Bukharin N. I., *The Path to Socialism in Russia*, New York: Omicron, 1967, <https://www.marxists.org/archive/bukharin/library.htm>
Després L., 'Politique économique et fonction objectif du plan, la notion d'optimalité praticable dans un module de planification de l'économie nationale' in Lavigne M., (ed.), *Economie politique de la planification en systeme socialiste,* Paris: Economica, 1978.
Djilas M., *Sur les voix nouvelles du socialisme,* Le Livre Yugoslave, 1950.
Djurdjevac V., 'Essai sur la propriété étatique et la propriété sociale', in Lavigne M., (ed.), *politique de la planification en systeme socialiste,* Paris: Economica, 1978.
Duchêne, G., 'Les limites de la recherche de l'efficience dans la politique économique soviétique', in Lavigne, M., (ed.), *Economie politique de la planification en systeme socialiste,* Paris: Economica, 1978.
Ellman, M., *Soviet Planning Today,* Cambridge: Cambridge University Press 1971.
Godelier, M., *Rationalité et irrationalité en économie,* Paris: Maspero, 1974.

Guevara, Ernesto Che, 'Socialism and Man in Cuba,' *Che Guevara and the Cuban Revolution,* Sydney: Pathfinder, 1987.
Horva B., An *Essay on Yugoslav Society,* New York: IASP, 1969.
– *The Yugoslav Economic System,* London: Routledge, 1976.
– *Towards a Theory of Planned Economy,* Belgrade: Iser, 1964.
Kardel E., *Les contradictions de la propriété sociale dans le système socialiste,* Paris: Anthropos, 1976.
Kolm S., *La bonne économie, La réciprocité génerale,* Paris: PUF, 1984.
Kowalewski Z., *Rendez-nous nos usines,* Paris: La Brèche, 1985.
Lavigne M., 'Optimum et croissance en système socialiste' in Lavigne M., (ed.), *Economie politique de la planification en systeme socialiste,* Paris: Economica, 1978.
Lenin V. I., 'Left-Wing Childishness and the Petty-Bourgeois Mentality' (May 1918). *Collected Works, Vol. 25,* Moscow, Progress.
Lepage H., *Capitalisme et autogestion,* Paris: Masson, 1978.
Maksimovic I., 'Social Property', in *Le socialisme dans la théorie et la pratique yougoslave,* Belgrade, 1976.
Mandel D., *The Petrograd Workers and the Soviet Seizure of Power,* London: Macmillan, 1983.
Mandel E., *Marxist Economic Theory,* London: Merlin, 1962.
– 'Du nouveau sur la question de la nature de l'URSS. Lutte entre la 'loi de la valeur' et 'la logique du plan', *Quatrième Internationale,* no. 45, Sept. 1970.
– 'Ten theses on the social and economic laws governing the society transitional between capitalism and socialism', *Critique* 3, Autumn 1974.
– *The Formation of the Economic Thought of Karl Marx,* London: New Left Books, 1977.
Marković M., 'Socialisme et autogestion', in *Etatisme et autogestion,* Paris: Anthropos, 1973.
– 'New Forms of Democracy and Socialism,' *Praxis International,* 1981.
Marx K., *L'idéologie allemande,* Paris: Pleïade,
Mihailovic K., *Ekonomska stvarnost Jugoslavia,* Belgrade, 1982.
Nove A., *The Economics of Feasible Socialism,* Oxford: Routledge, 1987.
– *The Economics of Feasible Socialism,* London: Allen and Unwin, 1983.
Preobrajensky N., *From NEP to Socialism,* 1921, London: New Park, 1973, <https,//www.marxists.org/archive/preobrazhensky/1921/fromnep/index.html>
–– *The New Economics,* Oxford: OUP, 1965, <https://libcom.org/files/[Preobrazhensky,_Evgeny_Alekseevich]_The_New_Econo(BookZZ.org).pdf>.
Rosdolsky R., 'La limite historique de la loi de la valeur. L'ordre social socialiste dans l'oeuvre de Marx,' *Critiques de l'économie politique,* no.6, 1972.
Sik O., 'Pillars of a Democratic and Socialist Economic System', Typewritten papers of the international symposium, 'Les Lessons du Printemps de Prague' held in Paris, October 1981.
Tartarin R., 'Schémas de reproduction et politiques d'industrialisation' in Lavigne M., (ed.), *Economie politique de la planification en systeme socialiste* Paris: Economica, 1978.
Trotsky L., *The Third International After Lenin,* New York: Merit, 1970.
– *The History of the Russian Revolution,* New York: Monad, 1980.

Preobrazhensky E., *The New Economics,* Oxford: OUP, 1965, <https://libcom.org/files/[Preobrazhensky,_Evgeny_Alekseevich]_The_New_Econo(BookZZ.org).pdf>.
– *De la NEP au socialisme*, Paris: CNRS, 1966.

The law of value in relation to self-management and investment in the economy of the workers' states*

Ernest Mandel

The Cuban magazine *Nueva Industria – Revista Economica*, organ of the Ministry of Industry, published two polemical articles in the issue of October 1963 of great interest, one written by Ernesto Che Guevara and the other by Commandante Alberto Mora, Minister of Foreign Trade. This polemic also testifies to the vitality of the Cuban Revolution in the field of Marxist theory. It deals with a number of questions of the utmost importance in the construction of a socialist economy: role of the law of value in the economy during the epoch of transition; autonomy of enterprises and self-management; investments through the budget or by means of self-investment, etc. Involved in these issues is the problem of the ideal model for the economy in the epoch of transition from an underdeveloped country, a problem of absorbing interest to the Bolsheviks during the 1923–1928 period and which arose again, even if on a rather low theoretical level, in Yugoslavia, Poland and even in the Soviet Union in recent years.

The Law of Value in the Economy During the Epoch of Transition

The question of the 'application' of the theory of value in the planned and socialized economy of the epoch of transition has been subjected to the worst confusion, mainly because Stalin, in his last work, posed it in a both gross and simplistic way: 'Does the law of value exist (*sic*) and does it apply in our country? ... Yes, it exists there and it applies there.' This is an evident truism. To the extent that exchange occurs, commodity production

---

* Originally published in *World Outlook* No.14, 1963, Paris. Republished in *Fourth International* No. 18, 1964, Paris. Ernest Germain was the name under which Ernest Mandel wrote this article. Transcribed by Joseph Auciello and marked up by Einde O'Callaghan for the Marxists Internet Archive. It is available online at <https://www.marxists.org/archive/mandel/1963/xx/value-self-man.html>.

survives, and exchange is thereby objectively governed by the law of value. The latter cannot disappear until commodity production withers away; that is, with the production of an abundance of goods and services.

But this does not answer the *concrete question* around which turns the fundamental discussion begun in 1924-25 between Preobrazhensky and Bukharin which has continued to develop, with ups and downs, among Marxist economists and theoreticians up to now: *to what exact degree* and *in what sphere* does the law of value apply in the economy during the epoch of transition?

Stalin himself, while muddying the issue, had to admit a fact which the Khrushchevist economists are nevertheless beginning to draw into question; namely, that in the 'socialist' economy, the law of labour-value cannot be the *regulator of production*, that is, cannot determine *investments*.

In developed capitalist economy, the law of value determines production through the play of the rate of profit. Capital flows toward the sectors where the rate of profit is above the average and production increases there. Capital recedes from the sectors where the rate of profit is below the average, and production decreases there (at least relatively). When the means of production are nationalized, so that there is neither a market for capital nor its free entry and withdrawal, nor even the formation of an average rate of profit with which the rate of each particular branch can be compared, clearly there is no longer a possibility for the 'law of value' to be directly the 'regulator of production.'

If, in an underdeveloped country which has carried out its socialist revolution, the 'law of value' were to regulate investments, there would be a flow preferentially toward the sectors where profitability is the highest *in relation to prices on the world market*. But it is precisely because these prices determine a *concentration of investments in the production of raw materials* that these countries are underdeveloped. To escape from underdevelopment, to industrialize the country, means to deliberately orient investments toward the sectors that are least 'profitable' for the time being according to the criterion of the long-term economic and social development of the country as a whole. When it is said that the monopoly of foreign trade is indispensable for industrializing the under-developed countries, this means precisely that it cannot be accomplished until these countries are able to 'pull the teeth' of the law of value.

But perhaps this qualification applies only to the 'law of value on the world market'? Cannot the law of value at least alter investments on the national scale, once world prices are left aside? This is wrong again. The industrialization of an underdeveloped country cannot be carried out rapidly and harmoniously except by deliberately violating the law of value.[286]

In an underdeveloped country, and precisely because of its underdevelopment, agriculture tends from the beginning to be more 'profitable' than industry, handicrafts and small industry more 'profitable' than big industry, light industry more 'profitable' than heavy industry, the private sector more 'profitable' than the nationalized sector. To channel investments according to the 'law of value,' that is, according to the law of supply and demand of commodities produced by different branches of the economy, would imply developing monoculture for the export trade by priority; it would imply preferential construction of small shops for the local market rather than steel plants for the national market. The construction of comfortable lodgings for the petty bourgeois or bureaucratic layers (an investment corresponding to 'effective demand') would have priority over the construction of low-cost homes for the people which clearly must be subsidized. In short, all the economic and social evils of underdevelopment would be reproduced despite the victory of the revolution.

In reality, the decisive meaning of this victory, of the nationalization of the means of industrial production, of credit, of the transportation system and foreign trade (together with the monopoly of the latter), is precisely to create *the conditions for a process of industrialization that escapes from the logic of the law of value*. Economic, social and political priorities, *consciously and democratically chosen*, take the lead over the law of value in order to lay out the successive stages of industrialization. Priority is placed not on immediate maximum returns, but on the suppression of rural unemployment, the reduction of technological backwardness, the suppression of the foreign grip on the national economy, the guarantee of the rapid social and cultural rise of the masses of workers and poor peasants, the rapid suppression of epidemics and endemic diseases, etc., etc.

That is why the industrialization of the workers states follows a different road from that of the capitalist countries where industries are built beginning with the sectors that will most easily satisfy 'effective demand.'

To violate the law of value is one thing; to *disregard* it is something else again. The economy of a workers' state can disregard the law of value only at the price of *losses* to the economy which could be avoided, of *useless sacrifices* imposed on the masses, as we shall later demonstrate.

What does this mean? In the first place, that the whole economy must be carried on within the framework of a strict calculation of the real costs of production. These costs will not determine investments; these will not automatically go toward 'the least costly' projects. But to know the costs means to know the exact amount of subsidies which the collectivity grants the sectors which it has decided to develop by priority. In the second place, that it is necessary to have a stable yardstick for these calculations; without stable money, no rigorous planning. In the third place, that all sectors where economic or social priorities do not dictate any preference are to be actually guided by the 'law of value,' (for example, different crops aiming at the domestic market). In the fourth place, so longs as the means of consumption remain commodities, and aside from the commodities and services deliberately subsidized or distributed free by the state (pharmaceutical products, school and training materials, books, etc.), the preferences of the consumers will freely operate on the market the law of supply and demand will affect prices, and the plan will adapt its projected investments to these oscillations (within the limits of what is available in finances, equipment, raw materials, etc.).

In the light of these initial remarks, we can consider the importance of the two problems raised in the Guevara-Mora polemic: What is value? Are means of production commodities in the transitional epoch? Mora affirms that value is not essentially abstract human labour; that it is 'a relation existing between the limited disposable resources and the growing needs of man' (p. 15). Still better: he holds that value is a 'category created by man under certain conditions and for certain (!) ends' (p. 15).

It is clear that we are faced here with a *subjective deformation* of the Marxist concept of labour-value, of which Marx specified the essence to be *abstract human labour*. It is not by chance that Mora refers to the 'neo-Marxist' Soviet economists[287] who have been attacked, in the USSR itself, and rightly so, as wanting to introduce surreptitiously the marginal theory of value. His conception, according to which the 'law of value is the economic criterion for regulating production' in the epoch of transition (p.17) – while he affirms that it is not the *only* regulator – necessarily involves the notion according to which 'exchange of the means of production' occurs even when these are completely nationalized, that 'sale of commodities' occurs even when these means of production pass from one nationalized enterprise to another, and that the 'contradictions' between the state enterprises justify the assertion that a 'change in ownership' occurs at the time of these exchanges (p.19). All these affirmations are contrary to the reality and to Marxist theory. On all these questions, Che Guevara is entirely right against Mora.

Mora states that if in investments, one leaves aside the law of value, one must 'pay the price'; in doing this, you automatically limit the social resources available to satisfy other needs. This is true, and we, likewise, underline the necessity for strict calculation of production costs in all fields. But in limiting oneself to this economic truth, the social content of the epoch of transition is done away with; that is, in *abstracting from the class struggle*, Mora leaves out a whole important side of the problem.

In fact, it is impossible to operate in the economy of the epoch of transition – any more than in any other economy containing different social classes – with aggregates like 'social revenue,' 'social costs,' 'social price of investments,' without at the same time posing the question: 'Who is to pay this price to whom?

The society of the epoch of the transition to capitalism to socialism is not homogeneous. In conducting an appropriate policy of investments, of prices, wages, foreign trade, etc., the workers state can act in such a way that the *social benefits of priority investments* (numerical reinforcement of the working class; elevation of its standard of living, skill, culture and consciousness; reinforcement of its leading role in the state and economy; accentuation of its participation in political life, etc., etc.) *are paid economically by other social classes*; the residue of the former owning classes; imperialism; the small commercial entrepreneurs and independent peasants. In an expanding economy, this economic price, paid particularly by the merchants, artisans and independent peasants can moreover be accompanied by a rise in their standard of living, on condition that this rise is less than it would have been in the framework of the 'free play of the law of value' (thanks, for example, to a progressive income tax).[288]

The Law of Value and Foreign Trade

All the preceding evidently constitutes only a general framework for replying to the specific problems which the question of economic calculation and the orientation of investments raises in each particular workers state. Here, Mora is right when he stresses (p. 18) that in a small country like Cuba, which depends strictly on foreign trade for the current functioning of its industry (spare parts and raw materials) and for the equipment of its new enterprises, the necessity for rigorous economic calculation is imposed with all the more reason than in a big, largely autarchic country like the Soviet Union.

Exports are made according to prices on the world market. So that these exports will not constitute a constant drain on the national economy (they must be met in any case in order to keep industry and industrialization going through imports), it is necessary that the production costs of exported goods should as a whole be below the prices obtained on the world market. It is necessary to fix the objective on progressively suppressing all exports at a loss, so that exports are not only a means supplying the national economy but, in addition, an important source of accumulation, a means of defraying part of the expense of industrialization – a part of the costs of not observing the law of value on the national market! – from abroad. The tendency for current prices of sugar to rise on the world market creates, moreover, a favourable framework for the success of such a policy. The *progressive diversification of exports*, to render the Cuban economy independent of future fluctuations of current sugar prices on the world market, must point to the selection of other export, products where production costs remain below the prices obtained abroad (that is, average prices on the world market).

But Mora mixes up the need to carry out all these calculations in the most strict way with the extension of the field of application of the law of value in the Cuban economy. The two phenomena are not identical; they can even be directly contradictory.

The law of value determines the exchange value of commodities according to the quantity of labour socially necessary to produce them. The concept of 'socially necessary' labour is determined in turn by the average level of the productivity of labour in a country, and by the concept of the effective demand of society – which must never be confounded with human needs or social needs from an objective point of view. In an underdeveloped country like Cuba, *all* production of many industrial branches can correspond to an 'effective demand,' that is, all labour in these branches can appear as 'socially necessary,' despite a very low level of productivity. The reference to the law of value, far from thereby resolving the problem of rapid improvement in the productivity of labour, of the technological transformations which these industries must undergo, can only obscure it. Because the law of value will have a tendency to *keep alive* archaic enterprises, as long as the state of scarcity exists, from the moment there ceases to be free movement of capital and free imports of commodities which could stimulate competition with these enterprises.

Far from being a field of application of the law of value, the dependence of Cuba on foreign trade thus implies the necessity of *economic calculation of comparative international costs*, which could provide a choice of economic criteria, independently of any rigid 'law.' The necessity to assure the country's supply of spare parts and raw materials *imposes* a certain volume of exports, even if these are carried out at a loss. The necessity to maintain and develop the existing level of industries dependent on foreign supplies imposes searching, as quickly as possible, for profitable exports *in relation to prices on the world market* – even if this means switching investments toward branches that are already profitable *in relation to the national market* (branches that already sell their commodities at their exchange value). The possibility of exporting at a profit, of gaining supplementary resources from exports, of transforming trade into a constant source of socialist accumulation, will moreover permit just the *liberation of the economy* from the tyranny of the 'law of value,' that is, will permit the development of new industries despite the fact that their production costs at the beginning will be higher than the prices of imported products, without lowering the standard of living or the rate of accumulation in the country. This is an aspect of the real dialectics of the dependence on foreign trade and the play of the law of value that is decidedly more complex than Comrade Mora thought!

The Law of Value and Autonomy of Decision at the Enterprise Level

In the debate which has raged in some of the workers states, the problem of the area of application of the law of value is intimately linked with the problem of autonomy of decision at the enterprise level in the field of investment. The Yugoslav authors have even formulated with regard to this a veritable new dogma which requires critical analysis: 'Without the right of the self-management collectives to dispose of a considerable part of the social surplus product, no genuine self-management.'[289] [4] This analysis must examine the problem from two aspects: economic efficiency (criteria for choosing one investment project rather than another), social and political efficiency (success in the struggle against the bureaucracy and bureaucratization).

The more backward a country is, the more conditions of almost universal scarcity rule not only in the means of production sector but also for much of the industrial means of consumption (at least for the great majority of the population), and *the more detrimental the practice of self-investment is*, the more detrimental is it to permit the self-management collectives to determine for themselves the projects for priority of productive investments.

It is evident in fact that under conditions of almost general scarcity of industrial commodities, *almost all* the investment projects can be economically profitable, no matter how gross the economic errors that are committed. Almost every profitable industrial or agricultural enterprise (providing funds for investment) is like an island in a sea of unsatisfied needs. The natural tendency of self-investment is therefore to attend to what is most pressing, both locally and in each sector.

In other words: if the self-management enterprises hold large funds for self-investment, they will have a tendency to orient their investments either toward the commodities which they lack the most (certain equipment goods; raw materials; auxiliary products; emergency sources of energy), or toward the commodities which their workers or the inhabitants of the area lack the most. Thus, criteria of local or sector interest are placed above national interests, not because the law of value is 'denied,' but precisely *because it is applied*! This means, once more, to orient industrialization toward the 'traditional road' which it followed in the historic framework of capitalism, in place of reorienting it according to the requirements of a nationally planned economy.

An attempt can be made to reconcile national planning requirements and allocating self-managed enterprises considerable funds for self-investment. The means chosen for this aim can be a levy-tax in behalf of national development funds and equalization funds for regional development. This is evidently a step in the right direction, but it does not at all resolve the problem.

Since an underdeveloped economy is characterized precisely by the fact that the enterprises of high productivity are still the exception and not the rule, it is sufficient to leave them a part of their net surplus product and the inequality of development between the industrialized localities and the non-industrialized localities, the inequality of development and of revenue between the archaic enterprises which enjoy only an average level of productivity and the enterprises technologically 'up to date' will increase instead *of diminishing*. It is necessary, moreover, to insist on this fundamental idea of Marxism: any economic freedom, any 'autonomy of decision' and any 'spontaneity' *increases the inequality* so long as there exist side by side strong and feeble enterprises or individuals, rich and poor, favoured and unflavoured from the point of view of location, etc. This is the reason why, it should be noted in passing, that according to Marx the mechanism of the law of value leads to its own negation; competition inevitably ends in monopoly.

The economic logic of a planned economy therefore speaks completely in favour of *productive investment by budgetary means* at least for all the big enterprises. What must be left to the enterprises is an amortization fund sufficiently large to permit *modernization of equipment with each renewal of fixed equipment* (gross investment). But all *net* investments should be made in accordance with the plan, in the branches and places chosen according to preferential criteria selected for the society and its economy as a whole. In this respect, too, the thesis of Comrade Guevara is correct.

The problem has been obscured, above all in the USSR, through associating it with the problem of *heightening the material incentives in enterprises*. Numerous Soviet economists have criticized the stimulants still employed today in the economy of the USSR to incite the enterprises (?) to carry out the plans. This criticism is in general pertinent. It has but to repeat what anti-Stalinist Marxists have said critically for many years. Yet, it is only necessary to examine closely the arguments of these economists to see that what is involved in reality is *heightening of material incentives for the bureaucracy* for whom the growth of revenues must in some way be the essential stimulus for the expansion of production in the enterprises.

This is where certain partisans of self-management, particularly in Yugoslavia, maintain that *decentralization of the decisions on investment would be a powerful guarantee against bureaucratization*. This thesis is based on a fallacy. The Yugoslavs are right in stressing that the power of the bureaucracy grows in relation to its freedom in disposing of the social surplus product. But the technicians and economists of the planning commission 'dispose' of the surplus product only in the form of figures on paper; the real power of disposal is situated *at the level of the enterprise*.[290] The more that means other than consumption funds (distributed revenues and social investments) are left at the free disposal of the enterprises, *the more is precisely bureaucratization stimulated*, at least in a climate of generalized scarcity and poverty; also the greater the temptation becomes for corruption, theft, abuse of confidence, false entries – temptations that do not exist at the level of the planning commission, if only because of multiple checks. The concrete experience of Yugoslav 'decentralization' has shown, moreover, that it is an enormous source of inequality and bureaucratization at the level of the enterprises.

But doesn't the possibility of complete centralization of the means of investment at the state level create the danger of the *economic policy as a whole* favouring the bureaucracy, as was the case in Stalinist Russia? Obviously. But then the cause does not reside in the centralization itself; it lies in the *absence of workers democracy on the national political level*.[291] This means that a genuine guarantee against bureaucratization depends on workers management at the enterprise level and workers democracy at the state level. Without this combination, even the autonomy of the enterprises will eliminate none of the authoritarian, bureaucratic and (often) erroneous character of economic decisions made at the government level of the plan. With this combination, the centralization of investments – priorities being democratically established, for example through a national congress of workers councils – would not encourage bureaucratization, but, on the contrary, suppress one of its principle sources.

The Law of Value and Self-Management

'Heightening material incentives' in the enterprises cannot be a 'stimulant' in the question of investments. But 'heightening material incentives' in the self-management collectives can actually stimulate continual growth of production and productivity among the enterprises.

Certainly, under a regime of genuine socialist democracy, creative enthusiasm, the free development of all the capacities of invention and organization of the proletariat, constitute a powerful motor for the growth of production. But it would be a grave idealist and voluntarist error to suppose that in a *in a climate of poverty* – inevitable in an underdeveloped country immediately following the victory of the socialist revolution – this enthusiasm could last long *without a sufficient material substructure*.

The example of the Soviet Union, where the proletariat gave proof of an enthusiasm and spirit of self-sacrifice without parallel in the first years after the October Revolution, is instructive in this respect: a long period of deprivation ended inevitably in mounting passivity of the workers, daily material concerns taking precedence over attentiveness to meetings.

It is therefore imperative to link self-management to the poss-ibility for the workers to immediately judge the success of each effort at increasing production *by the elevation of their standard of living*. The simplest and most transparent technique is that of distributing a part of the net revenue of the enterprise among the workers in the form of one or more months of bonus wages, the amount increasing or diminishing automatically with the level of revenue. *The increasing collective material interest* of the workers in the management of the enterprises moreover is superior to piece wages, inasmuch as it does not introduce division and conflicts in the workers' collectivity, inasmuch as it corresponds better to contemporary technique, which place less and less importance on individual output and more and more importance on the rational organization of labour.

Self-management (and not mere workers' control) seems to be the ideal model for organizing socialist enterprises. But it by no means hinders more or less unlimited competition among the enterprises, which flows from their autonomy in the domain of prices and investments. This autonomy cannot but reproduce a series of evils inherent to the capitalist regime: monopoly positions exploited in the formation of prices and revenues; efforts to defend these monopolies by 'hiding' discoveries and technical improvements; waste and duplication in the field of investments; high cost or errors in decision, revealed *a posteriori* on the market (including the shutting down of enterprises); reappearance of unemployment, etc., etc. Useless and detrimental from the economic point of view, it by no means constitutes a sufficient guarantee against bureaucratization, as we have indicated above.

In this connection, the polemic of Lenin and Trotsky against the theses of the 'Workers Opposition' is still completely valid. Marxism is not to be confused with the doctrine of anarcho-syndicalism. The genuine guarantee of workers power lies on the political level; it is on the state level that it must be established; any other solution is utopian; that is, unworkable in the long run and a source for the reappearance of a powerful bureaucracy.

For all these reasons, self-management does not at all imply wider recourse to the 'law of value' in relation to centralized planning.[292] The fundamental data of the problem remain the same. It is necessary to carry out strict calculations of production costs to show in the case of each commodity whether its production has been subsidized or not. But nothing calls for the conclusion that prices must be 'determined by the law of value,' that is, by the law of supply and demand. If such a conclusion still has some meaning with regard to the means of consumption, it is senseless for the means of production which, we repeat, are not commodities, at least in the great majority of cases. And even means of production which are still commodities – those produced by the private or co-operative sector for the delivery to the state, and which the state furnishes to private enterprises or co-operatives – cannot be 'sold at their value' without encouraging under certain conditions private primitive accumulation at the expense of socialist accumulation. But, if the means of production are not sold 'at their value,' the 'value' of the means of consumption is itself profoundly modified.

Prices are, then, instruments of socialist planning and cannot be anything else in the epoch of transition from capitalism to socialism. If you say instrument of planning you likewise say instrument for *determining the distribution of the national revenue between consumption and investment, an instrument for determining the distribution of revenues among the different classes and layers of the nation*. To leave the determination of this distribution to the 'law of value,' is to leave it in the final analysis to the 'laws of the market,' to the 'law of supply and demand,' that is, to economic automatism. And economic automatism would rapidly take us back to an economy of the semi-colonial type.

But to say that prices cannot be *determined* by the law of value does not at all signify that they can be *independent* of the latter. Society can never distribute more values than it has created without progressively destroying its accumulated wealth and impoverishing itself increasingly in the absolute sense of the term. The total sum of prices must therefore be equal to the total sum of value of the commodities produced (granting that there has been no monetary depreciation). The distribution of certain products – in goods or vouchers – below their value (subsidies!) automatically signifies a distribution of other products above their value. Without strict calculation of production costs; without book-keeping aided by an objective criterion; without a kind of double entry system that faithfully registers, for each product, alongside the price fixed by the state, the real cost and the subsidy (or the tax) there is not only no possibility for genuine scientific planning, there is above all no stimulus for the fundamental economic dynamic of the epoch of transition

– the dynamic that progressively elevates one new branch of industry after another to the point of rendering it 'competitive' in relation to prices on the world market, up to the time socialism announces its next triumph when socialist industry as a whole operates with a productivity superior to that of the most advanced capitalist industry.

At the moment, the 'law of value' could theoretically govern the dynamic of the workers state (or more exactly: the workers states as an international whole; because it appears excluded that this situation could be first obtained 'in a single country'). But at the precise moment when it is on the point of triumphing, its reason for being disappears. The highest level of productivity attained under capitalism in all its branches cannot be surpassed without approaching such a level of abundance that commodity production withers away. In the workers state 'law of value' cannot channel investments except to the precise degree that it withers away and to the degree that along with it all the economic categories, products of a relative scarcity of material resources, likewise wither away.

Building socialism in Cuba*
As pressure for economic liberalization grows, what would it take to turn Cuba into a socialist democracy?

Samuel Farber

In July 2016, thanks to a 20 per cent reduction in oil shipments from Venezuela, Cuba's economy minister Marino Murillo announced a 6 per cent cut in electricity and a 28 per cent cut in fuel. Meanwhile, he ordered an immediate drop in public sector energy use, with consequent working-hour reductions for state employees, and warned of possible blackouts, raising the spectre of the dark and hungry days of the Special Period of the nineties.

This turn of events delivered another blow to Raúl Castro's attempts to establish a Cuban version of the Sino-Vietnamese model, which maintains a one-party state while opening the economy to private enterprise and the market.

In the political realm, this has meant a relaxation of state control over the citizenry. But this hasn't been matched with democratization. For example, the 2012 emigration reform facilitated Cuban citizens' movement in and out of the country, but did not recognize travel abroad as their right.

In the economic realm, the government has implemented a modest and contradictory strategy. For example, the agricultural sector's structural reforms provide land leases for a maximum of twenty years; the Chinese and Vietnamese governments, in contrast, established much longer and, in some cases, permanent contracts.

The government now allows self-employment in few occupations (a little over two hundred). Had it opened it up for the whole economy – reserving only those sectors regarded as high social priorities, like medicine – the reform would increase available products and services.

Complementary changes introduced to bolster these structural reforms

* This article first appeared in *The Jacobin*, 10 December 2016, <https://www.jacobinmag.com/2016/10/alternative-cuba-socialism-left-opposition-worker-control>

– like the establishment of wholesale markets and commercial bank credits – have been inadequate and ended up negatively impacting the reform program. In addition, the bureaucratic and inefficient Acopio – the state agency with the monopoly power to buy most agricultural products at prices established by the government – has slowed agricultural production. As a result, harvested produce has spoiled while waiting to be processed at government plants.

The Castro regime's half measures will, more likely than not, push Cuba closer to a form of state capitalism without democracy. But there is a feasible alternative for the country.

No Recovery

Until this new crisis, the Cuban economy had partially bounced back after the worst years of the Special Period, which devastated the country in the wake of the collapse of the Soviet bloc in the late eighties and early nineties.

The country hit bottom between 1992 and 1994, when extreme food shortages led to an outbreak of an optical neuropathy epidemic that affected some fifty thousand people. Since then, the Cuban economy has surpassed the GDP it achieved in 1989.

But other indicators – such as real wages and pensions, which in 2014 were still at 27 per cent and 50 per cent of their 1989 level, respectively – never came back.

Meanwhile, social spending is still falling, and family consumption is expected to decline 2.8 per cent in 2016 and 7.5 per cent in 2017.

Although the hunger of the early nineties is gone, Cubans still struggle to find enough food. The much-praised development of organic and urban agriculture on the island represents a relatively small part of agricultural production. As Cuban economist C. Juan Triana Cordoví pointed out, declining domestic production has forced hotels to import vegetables, including yucca, the root-vegetable mainstay of the Cuban diet. The small progress in sustainable agriculture doesn't make up for the fact that food production has never regained its 1989 level and that more than half of Cuba's food supply comes from imports, at an annual cost of $2 billion.

Many of the revolution's gains in education and health have also been lost. The teachers who fled the educational sector's low pay haven't been fully replaced, and private tutoring – often provided by public school teachers in their spare time – has grown exponentially. In addition, numerous school buildings, libraries, and laboratories are crumbling. Before the start of the current school year, 350 schools were closed after they were found to be in dangerous physical condition.

The same applies to many hospitals and other medical facilities, which now operate with skeleton crews: the government sends large numbers of general practitioners and specialists to Venezuela and other foreign countries in exchange for oil or hard currency.

The regime's contradictory reforms will likely pass with the historic generation of leaders. Second-generation bureaucratic officials are likely to fully commit to the Sino-Vietnamese model, perhaps tilting somewhat toward Russia's capitalism, which combines massive oligarchic theft of state property with a nominal 'democracy' that would give US Congress the political cover it needs to repeal the 1996 Helms-Burton law and remove the island's economic blockade.

Besides winning the United States' enthusiasm, this new generation of leaders will enlist foreign capital and at least a sector of Cuban American capital by reassuring them that the government will maintain total control over the state, the mass media, and the mass organizations – including state-controlled unions – to guarantee their new capitalist investors, foreign and Cuban, peace, law, and order.

Yet there are other economic models that are being talked about inside and outside the government, although in a rather discreet fashion due, in great part, to the political system that does not allow a full and candid exploration of ideas.

Free and Rational

Mainstream critics have for some time been arguing for the establishment of a free-market economy, which they present as the only 'rational' alternative to the bureaucratic economic management of Communist Party rule.

This group covers a wide spectrum, ranging from a hard free-market stance to a more social-democratic welfare state perspective. In this latter grouping, moderate critics overlap with sections of the island's academic economists, including members of the Center for the Study of the Cuban Economy at the University of Havana.

Yet hardly any of these critics have openly addressed the question of what to do with the most important part of the Cuban economy, the larger state-owned enterprises. Instead, they focus on establishing private PYMEs – the Spanish language acronym for small and medium size enterprises – although they haven't clarified what 'medium' actually means.

They have also supported the government's move toward replacing the universal rationing system with one that subsidizes categories of people instead of products. Today, all Cubans, regardless of income, can receive a number of products at low, subsidized prices. The new system would only provide these products to the poorest and most disadvantaged, thereby rationalizing agricultural markets and reducing the government's budget. The government's recent reduction of the number of products distributed by this system marks the first step in this means-tested direction.

Finally, they imply that the state monopoly of foreign trade should end, and Cubans should be free to import all they can afford from abroad.

Tito in Cuba

Like all of the regime's opponents, the nascent critical left – mostly composed of anarchist and social-democratic currents – has had to operate under close state monitoring and repression.

These left-wing formations resist reductions to state benefits and – unprecedented in the Cuban left's history – call for a worker-managed economy.

Interestingly, they never mention democratic planning or coordination among economic sectors. As a result, their version of worker self-management would create an economy of self-sufficient firms in competition with each other. This resembles the system implemented in Tito's Yugoslavia from the 1950s until the 1970s.

This market socialism was locally self-managed, but regionally and nationally controlled by the League of Communists. It did increase worker input, decision-making, and productivity at the local level but, because of its competitive and unplanned nature, also created unemployment, sharp trade cycles, pay inequality, and notable regional disparities that favoured the northern republics.

The workers' powerlessness to decide on anything beyond what happened in their workplaces encouraged parochialism, isolating them from broader, national economic decisions. Workers felt no reason to support investment in other enterprises, particularly those located far away.

In the last analysis, as Catherine Samary points out in Yugoslavia Dismembered, Yugoslavian self-management could not confront either the bureaucratic plan or the market. The 1970s was the last decade of growth. Eventually a $20 billion debt led to the International Monetary Fund's intervention.

The Yugoslav model is a fraught one to emulate in Cuban, then. Further making any kind of worker control unlikely, none of the government's left-wing opponents have explained how it might be implemented in the absence of a workers' movement or how it might operate if workers aren't motivated to fight for those goals.

There are other voices on the critical left that reject any concession to private enterprise and capital on the grounds that capitalist enterprise by definition contradicts socialism. But they have been unable to answer the critical question of how a socialist and democratic Cuba could emerge from poverty and economic stagnation without concessions of any kind.

What is possible

A growing number of Cubans on and off the island, see socialism – whether democratic or authoritarian – as an impossibility. A diminishing number of Cubans still regard it as either desirable or likely. Certainly, the island's current economic conditions – combined with extraordinarily powerful international capital – make it hard to imagine a fully fledged form of socialism.

This view derives from a specific application of the general Marxist theory that rejects the possibility of socialism in one country, particularly when that country is economically underdeveloped and exists in a capitalist world currently unthreatened by socialist revolutions.

Besides having to face the hostility of its imperial northern neighbour, autarkic 'socialist' economic development won't fit for Cuba because the country still depends on oil imports. Further, its reliance on tourism and medical service, nickel and, to a lesser degree, pharmaceutical product exports and the dramatically shrunken sugar industry underline the foreign-trade character of Cuba's economy. The island's considerable integration into the capitalist world market prevents the establishment of a full socialist democracy.

This does not mean, however, that Cuba should abandon socialism. Instead, critics must think in terms of a transitional economy, a holding operation that can realistically be implemented until an international situation more favourable to socialism develops.

Classical Marxist political economy provides a model for what that possible holding pattern could be. This theory recognizes the greater role that individual, family, and small-scale production and distribution play in less-developed economies like Cuba.

In *Socialism: Utopian and Scientific*, Friedrich Engels distinguishes between modern capitalism – where production is a social act, but the social product is appropriated and controlled by individual capitalists – and socialism – where both production and its appropriation are socialized. Following this distinction, the productive property requiring collective work becomes the proper object of socialization, leaving aside individual and family production as well as personal property.

A transitional economy in Cuba would therefore allow for small, productive private property. This accommodation derives from a fundamental Marxist analysis of capitalism, not an opportunistic adaptation to liberal, free-market politics.

In Cuba, as in many other less developed countries, a transitional economy would subordinate a private sector of small enterprises ruled by market mechanisms under a commanding state sector that administers the island's big industry – pharmaceuticals, tourism, minerals, and banks – through workers' control and democratically coordinated and planned in a democratic polity. The government would strive, through its knowledge of market conditions and adequate economic forecasts, towards harmonizing the state and self-employed economy according to a definite plan.

Economic obstacles

But we must first honestly assess the Cuban economy, which, even before a reduction in Venezuelan oil shipments provoked the current crisis, had been in a marked state of deterioration.

For one thing, its all-encompassing public sector is floundering. As the Cuban economist Pedro Monreal reminded us, the government has openly admitted that 58 per cent of state enterprises function 'deficiently or badly.'

Also, the island's economic growth has been generally low, a situation that will only be aggravated by the current crisis. Cuban economist Pavel Vidal Alejandro estimates that Cuba's GDP will not grow in 2016 and will likely shrink by almost 3 per cent in 2017. This would mark the first year of negative growth in the last quarter century.

Important voices in the left opposition have argued against economic growth for ecological and other reasons. But improving most Cubans' material conditions is a condition of a successful democratization. The alternative – continual stagnation and declining living standards – will encourage massive emigration. This represents a tragedy in itself, but would also undermine potential democratic and progressive – let alone socialist – opposition movements.

Alarmingly, the rate of new investment, necessary to replenish the existent capital stock, has become among the lowest in Latin America, dropping below 12 per cent of GDP. Government forecasts indicate that investments will fall 17 per cent in 2016 and 20 per cent in 2017. This will result in a rate of gross capital formation slightly over 10 per cent, barely half the rate of investment considered necessary for economic development

The deterioration of Cuba's capital stock makes it impossible to maintain the current economic output and living standards, much less to expand them. As a result, the substantial increase in tourism – from 3 million visitors in 2014 to 3.5 million in 2015, and a projected 3.7 million by the end of 2016, sparked by the resumption of US-Cuba relations in December 2014 – has strained Cuba's tourist capacity to its limit.

Further, President Obama's elimination of restrictions on the remittances sent to the island by Cuban Americans has significantly worsened food and beverage shortages. Supply cannot meet the increase in demand.

The Cuban economy's productivity also lags. Agricultural yields – with the exception of potatoes – are well below the rest of Latin America. In industry, biotechnology is the only sector that enjoys high productivity relative to the region.

Rising productivity isn't just a profit-driven capitalist scheme. An economy that prioritizes reducing backbreaking labour, improving living standards, and maximizing leisure time can only do so if it also prioritizes making more with the existing workforce.

Che Guevara advocated what in effect was the 'sweating of labour.' But better organization, technology, and – most importantly – worker control would have the same effect.

Control, in itself, represents a powerful motivator. The current low productivity comes from a bureaucratic system that systematically creates disorganization and chaos and does not provide workers either with political incentives – allowing them to have a say and control over what they do – or with material incentives – typical of the developed capitalist world – to motivate them. Guevara's moral incentives failed: they were a method to get workers to take responsibility without power and to work harder without control or pay.

Ecological obstacles

Much of the island's left opposition to economic growth is grounded in environmental considerations. Cuba now confronts many serious ecological problems, including the increasing number of breakages and leaks in the old and poorly serviced water pipes all over the island. This has led to a massive loss of water, which often spills into streets and empty lots, and to the frequently inappropriate storage that many residents have been forced to resort to in response to the lack of water. Consequently, the Aedes Aegypti mosquito, which transmits the dreaded Dengue illness, has proliferated.

Moreover, the growing number of pigs, poultry, and house-grown crops – part of the much-vaunted, but very problematic, urban agriculture movement – has combined with deteriorating garbage collection services to considerably increase the risk of urban health crises.

The recent government claims to have held off the Zika epidemic and almost eliminated the Dengue fever must be met with scepticism as long as these and other conditions that propitiate the spread of diseases remain.

Anti-growth sentiment among Cuban left-wing oppositionists was reinforced when, on a recent visit to Havana, the economist Jeffrey Sachs recommended that 'the Cuban people don't progress into the twentieth century.' As the left-wing journalist Fernando Ravsberg explained, Sachs argued that Cubans should not forget sustainability and concentrate on the development of organic agriculture, sowed without tractors and grown without using chemical fertilizers or pesticides.

If Ravsberg's account is correct, Sachs's argument fails to weigh the relative costs and benefits of environmentally conscious measures. Small and economical tractors, like those the Cuban government is planning to produce in association with US capital, do still consume oil. But oil's negative environmental effects do not compare to the cost of human- and animal-powered agriculture. The latter model produces less food while requiring massive energy inputs from workers and animals.

Cuba's history already proves this: the forced abandonment of motorized agricultural vehicles at the beginning of the Special Period constituted, in net terms, a huge setback for the Cuban people.

Also in the nineties, urban transport was demotorised, and many city residents turned to bicycles. They were later abandoned – not because Cubans abstractly preferred the infrequent and overcrowded buses or the expensive urban collective taxis (only a small proportion of Cubans own automobiles), but because bicycles don't let workers arrive on time from distant working-class suburbs nor do they protect riders from tropical rains and winds from June until November.

The Chinese government has encouraged individual car ownership, which has contributed to the country's overwhelming urban pollution. This should serve as a warning sign for Cuba to aim for the adoption of an effective mass transit system as an alternative environmental policy.

Finally, at a minimum, Cuba needs to improve on the 5 per cent of its electricity derived from renewable sources, which is a quarter of the Latin American average.

The politics of a socialist alternative

The move toward a socialist society does not only require a program, but also a politics. This requires using principled strategic and tactical considerations to engage with the government's and various oppositionist currents' proposals.

In doing so, Cuban socialists might find areas of overlap with the liberal Catholic and social-democratic critics. Those include proposals that would promote agricultural production and productivity, such as codifying individual farmers' usufruct rights, eliminating the compulsory sale of agricultural produce to the government at prices dictated by the Acopio, and creating wholesale markets for small firms and individual producers.

In the field of urban employment, these proposals include forming cooperatives based on the initiative of interested workers, rather than on government diktats trying to dispose of so-called lemons – unprofitable enterprises or businesses that are difficult to administer on a centralized basis, like small restaurants.

At the same time, this new left will need to counter other proposals from those same groups. For example, they call for legalization of all forms of self-employment, including occupations that should be run on behalf of the public interest, like education and medicine.

The Left can respond to the call for free importation by arguing that a democratically run state should allocate foreign exchange on a strict priority basis, with social criteria that favour the most economically deprived sectors of the population and the purchase of capital goods that would most support the country's economic development. Otherwise, affluent Cubans might waste the country's relatively scarce foreign exchange on frivolous imports, such as expensive vehicles or luxurious furniture and household effects.

Socialists should also resist the dominant view – held by both critics and an increasing number of government economists – that the government should subsidize people, not products, that it should replace its universal subsidies with a system that provides for only the neediest citizens.

To be sure, those universal subsidies unnecessarily benefit wealthier Cubans. However, the critics of this program never mention their proposal's downside, which is that it undermines social solidarity. International experience has shown that income-tested programs for the poor produce stigmatization and, as a result, lose political legitimacy over time, thus threatening their long-term funding and viability.

One answer to this problem would be the introduction of a sliding scale where everybody benefits in inverse proportion to their income. This would recognize differential need while maintaining maximum political support.

Socialists in the Marxist tradition understand that subsidies must be selective: if, under current conditions, everything was provided free of charge or sold below production costs, an economy would collapse in short order. Moreover, a relatively underdeveloped economy like Cuba's has a much smaller surplus to leverage for free and subsidized goods.

But keeping the idea of universal subsidies alive leaves the road open for their future expansion as the Cuban economy becomes more productive and wealthier.

Liberal critics and the government itself support foreign investment as a means to deal with the Cuban economy's undercapitalization. Many on the Left have opposed it, seeing it as the Trojan horse of capitalism and foreign domination. However, a policy of controlled and selective foreign capitalist investment is indispensable in the absence of a domestic developed-goods industry. These imports could bring in new machinery and renew transportation and utility infrastructure.

New investments from abroad can also have significant employment and multiplier effects that trigger the development of entirely new industries that complement and further develop the established ones.

Further, the impact of foreign investment on wages and working conditions could be negotiated by independent unions, which, among other things, should prioritize the immediate abolition of the Cuban government's practice of collecting salaries owed to Cuban workers from foreign investors and then turning over to their citizens only a small fraction of the money collected. The government claims that they do this to finance social spending and other government operations. But the same goal could be achieved through a transparent and equitable tax system rather than through the government monopoly of the sale and control of labour.

It is true that worker-controlled production and powerful unions may deter foreign investment. However, an honest public administration and tax system as well as the existence of natural and human resources not reproducible elsewhere can also serve as a draw that supersedes those disadvantages.

Right-wing critics and oppositionists play down – if not ignore entirely – the crucially important issue of Cuba's growing inequality.

For the Left this presents a unique opportunity to push for independent unions, which, along with a progressive tax system, could be a more effective policy than the current one, in which the proliferation of bureaucratic rules harasses small firms and the self-employed.

This is not to do away with regulation entirely; it is necessary in occupational safety, health, pensions, and union rights. If these rules were administered – under worker control and supervision – by professional organizations rather than by a central bureaucracy, they would surely benefit workers, not owners. But to do so will require distinguishing between rules designed to protect the interests of the workers and those that protect the interests of bureaucrats.

Engaging with the specific proposals put forward by both the undemocratic government and by the pro-capitalist opposition sector, the Left will have the opportunity to formulate specific demands and to mobilize people to fight for them. This would build a movement – or at least a clear organizational pole – in spite of government repression and popular scepticism.

Cuba's present regime will not permit the existence of other legal political parties, independent unions, or a free mass media. Of course, these elements constitute precisely the political setting that would facilitate the kind of transitional social and political system outlined here.

Nevertheless, the left opposition must talk about an alternative model that openly acknowledges both the possibilities and the difficulties involved in building a socialist democracy. This empowers people, rather than making them feel that nothing can be done to push the country in an anti-capitalist, radically democratic, and socialist direction. But there is an alternative.

SUMMING UP AND FURTHER DEBATES

Chile and Portugal in the 1970s: the left, nationalisations and 'workers' control' in the revolutionary processes*

Franck Gaudichaud and Raquel Varela

We will stop the 'denationalisation' process, each time more important, of our industries and jobs that submit us to the foreign exploitation. (...) It is the task of the people's government, that is, of each of us here, I repeat, to create a just state, capable of giving the maximum of opportunity to all who live within our territory.
Speech given in 5 September 1970 at the National Stadium in Santiago by Salvador Allende[293]

Through the control of the democratic state on the basic sectors of the economy, until now in the hands of large monopolies, it will be finally possible to prevent capital flight and to put savings at the service of the people.
Portuguese Communist party press release, 14 March 1975[294]

Introduction

The history of the nationalisations of enterprises, the debates about workers' control and 'people's power' reached their climax in Chile during Popular Unity government (1970-1973) and in Portugal during the Carnation Revolution (1974-1975).

Salvador Allende, a charismatic freemason, physician and long-standing Socialist MP, won the 1970 presidential elections in Chile, a country then living with mass mobilisations. Chile, a dependent country of the Southern Cone of South America, situated in the backyard of the American imperialism, had at that time a combative and very organised working class movement, especially with the powerful Central Única de Trabajadores (CUT – the

* The authors would like to thank Waldo Mermelstein for the translation, comments and suggestions, and also the historians António Simões do Paço and Valério Arcary for their comments.

central trade union federation).²⁹⁵ The working class, who elected Allende president, mainly wanted a profound transformation of economic structures but also a rupture with the past policies of the local elites. Popular Unity (PU – Unidad Popular) was a left coalition that tried to coordinate a broad alliance stretching from the Communist Party (CP – Partido Comunista de Chile, the heavyweight in the alliance) to the small Radical Party, including the Socialist Party (SP – Partido Socialista de Chile, a heterogeneous Marxist party which was rapidly growing), and eventually the Christian parties (such as the MAPU – Movimiento de Acción Popular Unitaria, and the Christian left – Izquierda Cristiana). The strategy of PU, with its project of an alliance with the 'progressive national bourgeoisie', was seen as a continuation of the popular fronts of the 1930s, but under the hegemony of the two big parties with large working class constituencies: the CP and the SP. The programme of PU was characterised by audacious social and anti-imperialist reforms, within a country that suffered from an unequal 'ill-development', particularly centred around a mining enclave, the world's largest reserve of copper. Allende wanted to prove that the 'Chilean road to socialism' was possible, without having to follow the soviet bureaucratic road or the Cuban armed struggle while respecting the institutions that were established by the liberal Constitution of 1925. This project, largely influenced by the theory of a 'peaceful road to socialism' of the communists, had at its core a programme of nationalisations with working class participation but which was subordinated to a strategy of 'stages' and gradualism. This experience will be rapidly marked, on the one hand, by the appearance of tensions between Allende and a part of the working class which aspired to a real workers' control and 'people's power', and on the other hand by the violence of the coup d'état of September 1973 which ended all revolutionary aspirations and in particular the experiences of occupations of factories and the 'cordones industriales'.

The events of Portugal have been less studied than those of Chile. Portugal underwent the most radical revolutionary process in Europe in the post-war period, and in 1975 was a central target of US President Ford's administration in the diplomatic field.²⁹⁶ The Portuguese Carnation Revolution may be widely compared to the Chilean case in the way that the working class, left political parties, and the popular front government were involved in the process of nationalisations and workers' control.

The social subjects had different origins in the Portuguese and the Chilean revolutions, and this mostly explains the fact that the severity of the crisis of the state was more pronounced in in Portugal than in Chile, and that the nationalisations came as greater surprise in Lisbon than in Santiago do Chile. The Portuguese Revolution began on 25 April 1974 following a military coup against the Salazar-Caetano regime and its colonial war, and was defeated only 19 months later, again by a military coup on 25 November 1975. In April 1974, three social factors converged to create a historical situation that made the Portuguese events the most radical social revolutionary process in Europe after the war, and was the last of the twentieth century in Europe to question the private ownership of the means of production. The anti-colonial revolutions in Guinea-Bissau, Angola and Mozambique had weakened the Portuguese military hierarchy, and opened a crisis within the army, the main support of the state[297] and deeply weakened the Portuguese ruling class. In addition, a young urban working class[298] had arisen, concentrated on both banks of the Tagus River in Lisbon, and which had organised itself more or less spontaneously. It had also set in motion forms of self-organisation that escaped the control of the traditional social democratic and communist parties as they were not yet consolidated following the fall of the Salazar-Caetano dictatorship.

It was during the Portuguese Revolution that the main sectors of the economy – banks, insurance and energy – were nationalised. The first nationalisation was imposed by workers as early as May 1974, but the bulk of nationalisations only occurred after March 1975, when the GDP had already fallen more than 4 per cent.[299]

The nationalisation of banks, insurance companies and factories in Portugal, which took place roughly between March 1975 and May 1975, was propelled by the workers who were in control of banks and companies through a situation of dual power. Neither the MPA, nor the Portuguese Communist Party (PCP) or the Socialist Party (SP) – the three main political and military organisations that were dominant in the government and in the state – had a strategy of nationalisation in the 1974-75 period.

The outcome of the nationalisation process was the state control over firms, with the combined result of rescuing businesses in the midst of an economic recession, and private ownership of property and the means of production being disputed by the workers. In the medium term – a decade later – the banks and nationalised industries were returned, with compensation, to their former owners. When the nationalisations occurred they represented a victory for the workers, a defeat for the capitalist system, and a sharpening of the class struggle as they challenged private property and power. The history of the revolution from then on was also the history of the extraordinary self-confidence that workers and the intermediate sectors of society had acquired. From moment of the unsuccessful coup d'état of the 11 March 1975 onwards, they were confident they could win by challenging the private ownership of the means of production. That confidence spread like wildfire throughout the country, as was at the root of the revolutionary crisis which began in July 1975, the so-called 'hot summer'.

As in the case of Chile, the analysis of the governmental coalition is essential to understand how the state managed the situation of dual power which originated in the workers' control of factories and enterprises which appeared mostly spontaneously, especially from February up to May 1975. A particular focus should be placed on the role that the Portuguese Communist Party exerted in the governmental coalition through its alliance with sectors of the Portuguese bourgeoisie which the party leadership considered 'progressive'.

The debate about 'workers' control', nationalisations and 'people's power'

In the 1970s, workers' control was a common demand, for example among young left-wing members of the British Labour Party and reformist trade unionists.[300] These different sectors were not speaking about the same thing when they used the term 'workers' control'. This subject has been comprehensively studied by several major works. Maurice Brinton, for example, considers that workers' control is a way of 'distracting' workers from self-management, the only way to challenge profits.[301] Ernest Mandel has also defended that, beyond the democratic control of capitalist enterprises, the definition of workers' control could include self-management, but that it only would make sense as a transitional measure.[302] John Hammond uses a minimal definition: collective control by workers in enterprises, leaving open the degree of control, which could be over management issues, such as dismissals, but also over distribution and production.[303]

In Portugal, in 1974-75, workers' control over the enterprise meant either 'participation in the management', 'publicising salaries' or 'control over the production'.[304] Political organisations and trade unions did not distinguish clearly if workers' control meant control over the management, production and/or distribution, and if it was carried out by democratic assemblies of workers or by the trade unions.

In the Chilean case, 'workers' control' was scarcely used by the parliamentary left (mainly the Communist party and Socialist party), although it is often found in documents of sections of the left wing of the SP, which was very influenced by Trotskyism. Within trade unions and the CUT (the central trade union federation dominated by the Communists and Christian-Democrats), the term 'workers' participation' was used more frequently, and referred particularly to wage demands. The extra-parliamentary left, of which the MIR (Revolutionary Left Movement – influenced by the Cuban

Revolution) was the main far-left organisation, called for the building of 'people's power', a loose notion which comprised 'the poor of the cities and rural areas', with the aim of generalising workers' control of production with a perspective of 'dual power'.[305] Allende's political programme advanced ideas of 'people's power', 'workers' participation' and 'people's control', but scarcely provided a precise vision of what the PU government understood by these terms. Most of the time, this fluidity left a space for a diversity of interpretations, which were the reflection of the divergences within the left. The term of 'people's power' was regularly used in the texts of PU and the speeches of its leaders, but it was a minimalist version rather than a more radical one. It meant simply support by the organised popular base for the government's policy of new relations of production with a perspective of a rapid transition to socialism. The programme of PU stated nonetheless, that the 'structural transformations proposed are revolutionary transformations', and it underlined the need of 'controlling the political and economic power by the organised people, expressed in the state area of the economy and its overall planning. The people's power will be the one to ensure the accomplishment of the tasks highlighted'.[306] In general, the mention of 'people's power' by the Chilean left referred to a broad alliance of the popular layers, as noted the historian Hugo Cancino:

> The word 'popular', which was present within the tradition of the Latin-American and Chilean movements, designs and refers to the call of social subjects situated beyond the worker-proletarian universe: it comprises the peasants, the middle classes, the petite-bourgeoisie and, in general, the subaltern sectors.[307]

In this study we use a narrow definition of workers' control: the democratic control by workers over the production and distribution in enterprises managed by capitalists, which implied the abolition of commercial secrecy. Such a definition does not consider both co-management and self-management, and defines workers' control literally, but in its historical meaning, that is as a transitional measure towards collectivisation. In this meaning, workers' control puts the enterprises, managed by capitalists and not by workers, under the control at the level of production and distribution (for which the abolition of commercial secrecy and of the opening of books is essential) by workers' commissions or other rank-and-file organisations and not by the trade unions.

This definition is based on several presuppositions: there is no real workers' control except in revolutionary situations; workers' control is, because of this, less than self-management in terms of management, but politically its application is incompatible with capitalist accumulation (while self-management is not), as it is a transitional measure that either evolves towards the conquest of power by workers or degenerates into co-management. The essence of workers' control resides in the fact that the state or the capitalists still manage the enterprise/factory, but cannot do so against the workers. This is the reason why a correct historical understanding of this form of expression of dual power has to analyse the concrete cases of struggles within factories and companies. This definition is based on two essential premises: the dynamics of the national class struggle and the process of accumulation of capital.

Workers' control is a process of dual power that consists of the organisation of workers at the level of production – whether formalised or not – with a view to taking political power. It is a moment in the process of a struggle in the midst of a revolutionary process and not a structure or an institution. The existence of workers' control is actually part of what defines the very concept of a period as being revolutionary. This specific phenomenon is quite distinct from self-management (a form whereby the workers become their own bosses) and from co-administration (whereby, normally, the workers through their trade unions, manage the factories or companies in a partnership arrangement with the bosses/owners and/or with the state).

It is also quite common to find in some works, an association of workers' control with situations of organised dual power where authors do not acknowledge the existence of workers' control because structured forms of council-type organisation (e.g. soviets) do not exist. This is mistaken because in certain situations, workers' control can be much stronger than dual power in the political sphere. In other words, the disruption in the economic sector may be far more extensive than the crisis of the state. This was apparent in the Portuguese revolution, but also in other processes of workers' control such as in the industrial belts in Chile or the councils in the Bienno Rosso of 1919-20 in Italy.

In the 1970s, workers' control was widely discussed on the basis of the experiences of 1917.[308] However it was actually the theory developed by the revolutionary leaders in the period from 1848 up until the 1930s, namely, Karl Marx,[309] Lenin,[310] António Gramsci,[311] Karl Korsch,[312] Leon Trotsky,[313] Pannekoek,[314] and Adler,[315] which addressed the question more profoundly.

Thus there is no substantial theoretical body of work dedicated to this question. What follows is therefore succinct descriptions of the main schools of thought and aspects of the theoretical debate.

Based on the historical experience of the Paris Commune (1871),

Karl Marx analysed this question stressing the importance of workers' management experiences but not defending the idea of self-management which he believed, could only effectively exist after the 'proletariat had taken power'. He described this as 'workers self-government of production', because the role that self-management could play in the political learning process through the experience that workers acquired from it.[316]

During the two years of revolutionary upsurge in Italy (1920-1921), Prime Minister Giolitti, faced with the occupations of the factories presented a draft bill to parliament for the establishment of workers' control. In his analysis of workers' control, Antonio Gramsci considered that:

> For the communists, addressing the problem of control (...) means addressing the problem of workers' power over the means of production, the problem of conquering the state (...) Every law on this emanating from the bourgeois power has a single meaning and a single value: it means that in reality, and not just verbally, the terrain of the class struggle has changed, insofar as in this new terrain the bourgeoisie is obliged to make concessions and create new legal institutes; and it has the real value of demonstrating the organic debility of the ruling class.[317]

Leon Trotsky developed the analysis on the basis of a debate with German anarchists at the beginning of the 1930s about the legislation of the factory workers' councils in Germany. Trotsky, who had been the president of a soviet in Russia in 1905, stressed the issue of dual power and belittled the institutionalisation of forms of workers' control under a bourgeois government. Trotsky raises a question that we consider to be central to any explanation of the Portuguese revolution, namely that in certain situations workers' control may become more powerful than dual power in the political sphere. In the Portuguese case, the conditions (see below) were favourable for the development of workers' control, especially as there was not the existence of a 'vigorous fascism' because the dictatorship had collapsed in the first week after the coup of 25 April 1974.

An advanced regime of dual power, as one of the highly probable stages of the proletarian revolution can develop in different countries in different ways because of different conditions. Thus, for example, in certain circumstances (a deep and persevering economic crisis, a strong organisation of workers in the enterprises, a relatively weak revolutionary party, a relatively strong state keeping a vigorous fascism in reserve, etc.) workers' control of production can be considerably ahead of the development of political dual power.[318]

It is far more difficult to recognise the existence of workers' control because it represents a *de facto* situation which, according to Trotsky, has no institutional recognition and often it does not even have a political recognition. In Portugal, however, there were government decrees about workers' control but designed to put an end to it. It is a form of power that challenges institutional power and therefore its recognition is weak or even non-existent. In the case of Portugal, however, there is an exceptional abundance of sources referring to workers' control, perhaps because of the period in which it occurred, and also because of the militant intellectuals who studied the factories which led the Carnation Revolution.

In a discussion on workers' control in the nationalised companies, Lenin, who was responsible for the first ever decree on workers' control in 1917, stressed the need to nationalise the entire banking system (not just part of it) and that also meant the nationalisation of the great industrial and commercial corporations. He pointed out that 'unless the commercial secret, the control over production and distribution, is abolished, it [workers' control] will not go beyond an empty promise'. He declared that it would merely be a bureaucratic measure and not one of true workers' control. The issue was a central one for the Russian revolutionaries and not just a theoretical issue. After taking power on the 7 November 1917, they adopted on the 27 November this decree on workers' control:

1. Workers' control over the production, storage, purchase and sale of all products and raw materials shall be introduced in all industrial, commercial, banking, agricultural and other enterprises employing not less than five workers and office employees (together) (...)

2. Workers' control shall be exercised by all the workers and office employees of an enterprise, either directly, if the enterprise is small enough to permit it, or through their elected representatives, who shall be elected immediately at general meetings (...)

3. The elected representatives shall be given access to all books and documents and to all warehouses and stocks of materials, instruments and products, without exception.[319]

Obviously the discussion of workers' control also embraced the organisational form that sustained it, whether spontaneous or formally organised, namely the workers' councils. One of the authors who discussed this issue extensively was Anton Pannekoek. He refers to 'labour democracy', declaring that 'organisation in the form of councils is the only way that working humanity organises its vital activities without the need for a government to run them'.[320] Karl Korsch developed the concept of 'industrial democracy' whereby he opposes the idea of a struggle to wrest power from the state, arguing that 'the final decisive combat is waged for domination of the economy (or of the organisation of labour) and not in the dispute to gain control of the state's governing bodies'.[321]

Chile 1970-1973: Allende's government and the nationalisations

For the Chilean communist party (CP), the major party and supporter of Allende's government, the socio-economic strategy of Popular Unity (PU) consisted of the formation of new productive structures serving the great majority of the country's population. If the government spoke about the 'deepening of democracy and workers' rights', it was first of all in relation to respecting freedom for the trade unions and their right to participate in the different levels of the state apparatus.[322] Nonetheless, what is almost absent are the issues of incorporation of the popular masses in the administration of the economy, of self-management and workers' control. In effect, the participation of workers was very coyly dealt with: in the programme of PU there was only one allusion to the participation of working people in the functioning of the nationalised enterprises.[323] This did not seem to mean a qualitative change in the relations of production. With regards the private companies, which, according to the programme, would remain the big majority, there was nothing in it about the right of workers to oversee their operation or about the opening of their bank and commercial accounts. The only right recognised was that regarding 'just wages and working conditions', while at the same time, PU repeated that it was ready to help the employers in the private sector mainly by means of planning. Nevertheless, a close study of the programme enables us to distinguish two types of social mobilisation from which PU wanted to draw support.[324] The first one was centred around the traditional organisations of the workers' movement, above all, the trade union movement (the CUT, and industrial, professional and peasant unions). The next level was the organisations of the poblaciones (poor neighbourhoods), essentially the committees of neighbours (juntas de vecinos) that had been promoted by the Frei administration, with the aim of channelling the demands of the most marginalised sectors of the population.

Popular Unity also wanted to escape from the rut of the previous governments, by giving back to the state the ability for powerful economic intervention and regulation, while speeding up the agrarian reform. The country's 'new economy' would be divided into three sectors: 1) The sector of 'social property', Area de Propriedad Social (APS), formed by the already state-owned companies, to which were added the companies being nationalised and which would be administered by representatives of the state and of the workers; 2) The privately-owned sector; 3) The sector with mixed ownership, which combined public and private capital.

In his last speeches during the presidential campaign, Allende stated that his intention would be that the state would control, in a co-administration with the workers, the production of raw materials, the banking system as well as the 'strategic industrial monopolies', and the companies 'that condition the country's economic and social development'. It was envisaged that compensation would be paid to the owners of companies being nationalised, the majority of which was the property of foreign capital. The government constituted a list of 147 companies that would prioritised to pass over into the APS, an ambition which was eventually reduced when Allende took office in La Moneda (the presidential palace) to 91 enterprises (of which 74 were industries), and in 1973, to 49 companies under the pressure of the owners and the right-wing.[325]

When he started his presidency, Allende's concern was to control copper, 'Chile's salary', which was overwhelmingly in the hands of American companies. The administrative order of nationalisation of 1971 announced that:

> By means of an act of national sovereignty, Chile has decided to recover the property of the most decisive and productive sources of wealth for the present and the future. It is from these resources that depends the result of Chile's combat to take its people away from material misery, and the exploitation of men by men within the country, and by the foreign subordination from abroad. Two-thirds of our incomes in foreign currencies and the financing of nearly one-fourth of the country's budget come from the exploration of copper.[326]

When calculating the compensation that it would pay the big copper mining companies, the government decided to deduct the 'excessive profits' extracted between 1955 and December 1970 by these multinational companies. The 'excessive profit' amounted to 774 million dollars, which was in the end greater than the compensation foreseen. The American companies were therefore expropriated without compensation and they even owed money to Chile. This expropriation incurred the anger of the Nixon government, which intended to bring down Allende by any means necessary and started to prepare the military coup of 1973.[327]

The nationalisation-expropriation of the copper mining companies was unanimously approved by the Chilean Congress, including by representatives of the right. But it was in the application of the rest of its programme that PU met numerous difficulties. Being in a minority in the Congress[328] and aiming at an 'institutional road to socialism', Allende was committed to respect legality, whatever the costs. For any progress to be made in the building of the APS, he depended on a judicial arsenal, mainly created by the oligarchy which he was fighting, and on a Parliament in which the left was in a minority. From the start of its administration, PU had to negotiate with the Christian-Democrats which controlled, with the help of the right-wing Partido Nacional, two-thirds of legislative branch of the state. The 'constitutional guarantees', which linked PU to the Christian-Democrats, were aimed in particular at protecting the private property of the means of production and to limit the possibilities of the expropriation of capital. The government started then a real 'judicial guerrilla war' to find the means of creating the APS without going beyond legality. This whole process has been studied in details by Zimbalist and Espinoza in a work about the 'economic democracy' under Allende.[329] The companies could be integrated into the APS in five ways: 1) The government could create new public companies; 2) A constitutional reform could allow the president to indicate the companies to be nationalised, but this decision had to be submitted to Congress for approval; 3) The government could buy shares in the private companies; 4) The labour code and the law on internal security authorised the Ministry of Labour to 'intervene' into strategic companies in which there was labour problems which interfered with normal production; and 5) An administrative order under a law of 1931 enabled the Ministry of Economy to control temporarily strategic enterprises where economic problems could cause an important fall in production. It was essentially using the last two judicial mechanisms, which did not need Congress approval, that certain ministers extended the APS. This occurred essentially under the pressure of the workers' movement which demanded the development of the 'social area'.[330]

The nationalisation project initially targeted only a limited part of the economy, essentially the modern sector (steel industry, production of intermediate goods, etc.). Only 10 % of the industrial workforce, or 55,800 people, and less than 1 % of Chilean enterprises were initially affected (in Portugal, only 8% of workforce will be part of state sector). In Chile the nationalisation process not only left out the big majority of wage-earners in the small and medium industries, considered as 'non strategic', but also entire sectors of the textile, construction and food industries. According to Fernando Mires, it was also a political strategy that 'marginalised' numerous workers from any possibility of participation.[331] The programme of nationalisations involved no more than 141,046 wage earners of the big industry, thus leaving aside 281,289 wage earners, an important fraction of the working class, and the same thing occurred in the construction sector. According to the economist Hector Vega:

When the economicist project of PU was proposed, 65% of workers remained outside of it. The limits of the programme of action have a double consequence: on the one hand the strength of workers incorporated into it was severely limited, and, on the other hand, it was in favour of an alliance with the middle sector that in practice would show its limits.[332]

Nonetheless, as the APS was being progressively implemented, an interesting experience developed of participation of workers in co-administration alongside the state functionaries. As a result of the implementation of the APS, the CUT underwent a progressive integration in the management of the nationalised companies, and then participation in government, which did not occur without generating tensions with its rank-and-file. It was under pressure that Salvador Allende declared in the 1 May of 1971: 'Strengthening and consolidating people's power means making more the unions powerful, making them aware that they constitute one of the fundamental pillars of the government'. At the beginning of November 1972, a civic-military cabinet was established to prevent a civil war which was smouldering. It included the three chiefs of the armed forces as well as Minister of Agriculture Rolando Calderón (SP member and general secretary of the CUT) and Labour Minister Luis Figueroa (CP member and president of the CUT). The government was in a more and more difficult position, stuck in a hostile constitutional game, confronted by an increasingly deeper social polarisation, and also having to enter into negotiations with the Congress which were blocked by the opposition. Therefore, the history of nationalisations during Popular Unity government was also the history of the struggles and tensions between, on the one hand, some sectors of the mobilised working class which wanted to speed up the reforms and was suffering from the pressure of the employers, and, on the other hand, a government that sought to respect its commitments with the popular classes, while still committed to its legalist conception of transition to socialism, and hence eventually on its agreements with the bourgeoisie in Congress. The extension of the nationalised sector was thus the fruit of a rank-and-file social movement that pressurised Allende, who remained for numerous workers 'their' president. This dialectic was masterfully documented in the documentary *The Battle of Chile* by the film director Patricio Guzmán.[333] As noted by a young researcher, Mariana Ferreira Gomes Stelko:

> Under these circumstances each enterprise had its own history in the middle of social effervescence. Each organised collective had its way to proceed in the change of management and/or owner. As the factories were occupied, the workers demanded that they be integrated into the

APS. The government decided case by case how to proceed, due to the relation of forces within PU, and, also to the conjuncture of the moment.[334]

Finally, at the moment of the coup d'état, it was estimated that there were more than 200 enterprises that were under the trusteeship of the state, a consequence of multiple 'interventions' by the Ministry of Labour under the pretext of paralysis of the production. The 'interventions' were not nationalisations in the narrow sense because they were not recognised by Congress and were almost always systematically rejected by the Contraloria de la Républica.[335] One of the best studies, carried about this complex dynamic of nationalisations and class struggle in Chile is without doubt the book *La lucha de clases en Chile* by the sociologist Manuel Castells.[336]

Portugal 1974-1975: nationalisations against workers' control

The first nationalisation following the 1974 Carnation Revolution took place just one month after the fall of the regime. On 21 May 1974, the workers at the Companhia das Águas (Water Company) occupied the company's offices and demanded that it should be nationalised. The name was changed to Empresa Pública das Águas de Lisboa (Lisbon Public Water Company – EPAL).[337] Nationalisations only started again after the adoption of the Law of Colonial Independence in the summer of 1974. In September 1974, Decrees 450, 451 and 452/7 ordered the nationalisation of the Banco de Portugal (Bank of Portugal), Banco de Angola (Bank of Angola) and the Banco Nacional Ultramarino (National Overseas Bank). This wave of nationalisation, according to Medeiros Ferreira, was 'the first step for the state to occupy the only place in the management of the financial consequences of decolonisation that had come about with the enactment of Law 7/74, dated 26 July'.[338]

Indeed, decolonisation had forced Portuguese capitalism to take refuge in nationalisation and state intervention to save as much as possible of its capital tied up in the colonies. However, one should not underestimate the role played by the revolutionary struggle in the metropolis in bringing about those measures. In the first instance, the very decolonisation process itself was determined by the revolutionary dynamics in the metropolis in the period after 25 April. The bank workers union had been involved in vigorous struggles since 25 April 1974. In the aftermath of the defeat of the right-wing coup headed by general António de Spínola on 28 September 1974, the state increased its powers of inspection of credit institutions with the issuing of Decree540-A/74 dated 12 October.

Most of the nationalisations were carried out between March and May 1975. On 11 March 1975, bank workers occupying bank installations demanded the nationalisation of the banks. On the next day, the Revolutionary Council, which had been set up that very day, announced the nationalisation of banks with the exception of foreign banks, and on 24 March it was the turn of the insurance companies. On 14 April, there were massive demonstrations in Porto and Lisbon in support of the nationalisation of the banks.[339] On 15 April, the Fourth Provisional Government nationalised dozens of companies belonging to the expropriated financial groups, including companies in basic sectors of the national economy such as petroleum, electricity, gas, tobacco, breweries, steelworks, cement, marine transport, cellulose, shipbuilding and repair, trucking, and urban and suburban collective transport. As previously mentioned, many of these companies were linked to the big economic groups that had grown extremely rich during the 1933-1974 period of the 'New State' of Salazar and Caetano such as CUF, the Champalimaud group, the Espirito Santo Group.

Many companies, including some reasonably large ones, managed to escape the wave of nationalisations, among them the cork processing, sugar refining, textiles and wine exporting industries which were mainly located in the north of the country. It was precisely through these companies that the first nucleuses of the new private groups such as Américo Amorim, were constituted. The New State doctrine had revered private enterprise but the Sector Empresarial do Estado (State Corporation Sector – SEE) also experienced a vigorous development in that period, as Silva Lopes[340] had noted, with the state holding the positions of command or influence in the fields of transport, refineries, electricity, banking, etc. It is estimated that, prior to the nationalisations, companies integrated to the public sector employed 2/3 of the workforce that the SEE came to employ after the nationalisations. In the first year after the 1975 nationalisations, the SEE employed around 300,000 workers, equivalent to 8% of the active population, and generated gross added value of somewhere between 20% and 25% of the GNP. As Silva Lopes remarks, Portugal ended up with one of the biggest public sectors in Western Europe, achieving a situation that was not unlike those of France, Italy, the United Kingdom and Germany. In those countries the public sector employed, on average, 8% of the workforce.[341]

The nationalisations were carried out in the context of a generalised, worldwide capital accumulation crisis and to some extent the way they were carried out, without workers' control, suggests that the Portuguese bourgeoisie used the nationalisations as an expedient to 'lose a ring but save its fingers'. It was a way of putting an end to social conflicts inside the companies and rescue them from the capital accumulation crisis. This is confirmed by the rhetoric of the parties forming the governmental coalition who, without exception, appealed for an end to the struggles inside the nationalised companies. They used the argument that the companies then belonged to the Portuguese people but omitted the fact that the state was still capitalist and so were the companies that it administered. Medeiros Ferreira, for example, argues that the nationalisations made it possible for the military to take control of the financial system[342] and Silva Lopes points out the effects that had on the economic situation.[343]

The importance of the nationalisations carried out during the revolution does not essentially lie in their economic impact or the eventual design of an economy with a socialist aspect – because the economy and the state both continued to be capitalist and the foreign companies and banks continued to be exempt from interventions.

As mentioned above, in 1975 the nationalised companies employed 8% of the active population. The importance of this, and it is actually a specific feature of the Portuguese revolution, lies in the fact that the nationalisations were made under pressure from the workers who often came together in large meetings, occupying the company installations and demanding their nationalisation. Other extraordinary workers' victories accompanied the nationalisations such as considerable wage increases in a period of high inflation (20-30%) and other social benefits. Furthermore, the nationalisations were made without any paying any compensation. Mirroring the acute critical stage of the class struggle, many capitalists, among them some of Portugal's wealthiest individuals, were either arrested after the coup of 11 March and/or fled the country, mostly going to Brazil. They would only return to Portugal at the end of the 1970s when the governments began to outline a process of compensation or of handing back the companies. The compensation values were determined by the terms of Act 80/77 dated 26 October.[344]

Co-administration and 'battle for production' versus cordones industriales and people's power?

At the beginning of the 1970s, the Chilean left was not the only one to advocate a stronger participation of wage earners in the enterprises. It suffered from the strong competition of the Christian Democrats (CD) on this issue. The Christian Democrats were also historically more interested in the subject of self-management than the left, which remained extremely 'statist' and centralist.[345] How was thus implemented the participation of workers within the nationalised sector (APS – Area de Propriedad Social) during Popular Unity government? The agreement signed between the

CUT and the government on 7 December 1970 referred explicitly to the need of participation in the process of national transformation, especially at the level of the economic management. However, neither the government nor the CUT were those who directly suggested the idea of establishing 'workers' committees'. It was eventually due the rank-and-file pressure that the idea of workers' control was introduced by some union representatives, in such a way that it was finally debated during the ninth conference of the CUT in Valparaíso. One study accomplished by a CUT-government commission, produced the 'Basic norms for the participation of workers in the direction of Enterprises of the Social and Mixed Areas', a legal framework for this participation.[346] There was no relationship with the issue of 'workers' control', in the Leninist sense of the word, or even to self-management, but to the 'participation' and co-administration. This document invoked two levels of participation. The first one was at the level of economic planning. For this, a national development council was established, which was comprised of six 'representatives of wage earners', who would debate the economic policy at the national level. These representatives were the leaders of the CUT. The second level was the direction of the enterprises of the APS. In this case, the workers' assemblies, presided by the leadership of the union, elected five representatives to the administration council. The later was thus composed of five representatives of the state, five representatives of the workers' elected in their assemblies and one representative of the presidency of the Republic who presided over the council (the Interventor). This council was the organ that directed the enterprise, in collaboration with the 'production committees' where the elected workers also had seats. State representatives, in fine, had the majority within the direction of the nationalised enterprises.

Undoubtedly, the numerous testimonies that have been collected prove that the establishment of this system within the enterprises was a rich collective and democratic experience that left its mark in the memory of left-wing militants. It was a moment of important disruptions within the factory: of the hierarchies, of the representations of the workers, a moment of liberation of the workers' self-expression. For example, this is the case with José Moya, a worker and member of the MIR, who was nominated president of the factory's production committee within the big radio-television monopoly IRT (ex-RCA). For José Moya, co-administration was a moment of recognition of the essential role of workers by president Allende and Popular Unity. Nonetheless, he highlighted also the limits of that system and pointed out that it corresponded to a period of intensification of labour in response to the strong increase in demand.[347] Each experience of co-administration could give room to a specific study and monograph, as it depended on the relation of political and social forces within the enterprise. This is what has been brilliantly shown by the historian Peter Winn in his study of the textile enterprise Yarur, where the struggle for participation was also a source of tensions and of numerous debates among the left-wing militants.[348]

However, more globally, the participation within the Social Area consisted essentially of ensuring at the level of the enterprise, the implementation of general economic norms fixed 'from above'. Given the lack of a real organic system of democratic and participative planning, the objectives of the companies of the Social Area had their role reduced most of the time to increasing production by means of the 'production committees'.[349] The participation of union representatives at the regional level was never put in place and the CUT limited itself to a consultative role within the different governmental economic organs. In this sense, we can, as Víctor Farias did, state that the importance of a real transformation in the relations of production was not taken into account by Popular Unity. If for certain left-wing militants, the APS should have initially embodied the seeds of workers' control of the future socialist society, it represented most of the time a tool in the 'battle for production' undertaken by the government. This call was put out in particular by the Communist Party who made it one of its priorities. Highlighted by the new administration, it was based on a real mobilisation of the rank-and-file of one part of the workers integrated into the APS. Allende, in his speech to the workers on the 1 May 1971, declared: 'It is essential to obtain the biggest sacrifices and the biggest patriotic effort from all workers...and produce more, because in this way you are about to ensure the future of the homeland and the defeat of those who conspire against Chile and the workers' government'.[350] In its annual report of 1971, the government announced that 'the participation of workers means that they conduct with enthusiasm the battle to increase the production, as they know that from now on the beneficiaries are themselves'.[351]

Several government reports described an unprecedented productive success in the enterprises that had passed into the control of the state. For example, it was underlined that there has been an increase of production in 1971 which surpassed 100 % in certain textile factories; and more than 50 % within the electronics sector. It was possible to see in the distance a kind of Chilean Stakhanovism, but in a way much less refined and systematic than in the Soviet Union. Seen from this angle, the CUT and the Communist Party insisted on workers' 'responsibility'. Examining the left-wing press we can have an idea of the magnitude of this propaganda. Thus, on his return from the Soviet Union, Luís Figueroa[352] remarked that in 'the homeland of socialism', one of the ways chosen was also the intensification of production and the increase in productivity.[353] According to the CUT, the priority for workers was from that time onwards to 'Produce and Study'.[354] At the beginning of 1972, the theoretical magazine of the CP explained clearly that the main goal of the participation was to increase production and that the workers in the APS would be rewarded, including financially, according to their productivity.[355] The union militants and leaders were responsible for diffusing this initiative to the rank and file. For numerous union militants, the main political battle of that period was, therefore, the 'battle for production'. This battle was perceived by the Popular Unity militants (especially the communists) as that for socialism. The consequence was this meant a categorical rejection of all those who could make any criticism of that position. It was the case of the MIR, for whom prioritising production was a typical error of state capitalism, while the fundamental issues of power and the bourgeois state were not yet resolved in favour of the workers.[356] The French Marxist Henri Lefebvre, in his study on the Chilean 'state mode of production' also confirmed the potential dangers of that slogan of the governmental left: 'Produce for the homeland', this slogan, which could so easily be used by the right and the generals, could be read on all walls of Santiago'.[357] Even today, some enquiries restore the memory of this state of mind of that 'battle', despite the rupture that could have meant the dictatorship (1973-1989).[358]

But this orientation, if it had any immediate beneficial economic effects, tended to restrict the workers of the APS to a race for production, without any assurance that the surplus would not be re-accumulated by the private sector by means of the middlemen of distribution (whose majority were private capitalists). This issue, that started to be raised by critical sectors within the left, was amplified when the economic policy of PU, which was showing severe signs of running out of steam.

However, thanks to the crisis of the policy of the year 1972, the issue of workers' control and people's power brutally reappeared 'from below'. As the heir to a long tradition of struggles and pushed by the popular radicalisation, a part of the Chilean workers' movement gave birth to a movement of self-organisation, unique for its extension in Latin America. During the confrontations of October 1972 and the great mobilisations of 1973, the economic demands were articulated with the political demands of the more radical workers: that connection was translated noticeably by the formation of the cordones industriales. During the 'red October' of 1972, when the big bosses, middlemen, liberal professionals profited from the strike of truck drivers (financed by the CIA) trying to paralyse the country's economy, a fraction of the industrial working class occupied the factories and some workers succeeded to partially restart them under their control. The same thing happened in the field of distribution in which a part of the militant youth supported the workers by supplying goods to the popular neighbourhoods and markets. The cordones industriales were formed on the basis of a horizontal territorial coordination of several dozen factories, independently of their economic sector or whether or not they were private owned.[359] The cordones were essentially directed 'from above' in the urgency of October by the union leaders and the militants of the SP or the Revolutionary Left Movement (MIR – Movimiento de Izquerdia Revolucionaria). Later, there were workers' assemblies in the most combative factories (e.g. Sandra Castillo Soto) whose declared goal was to elect two or three representatives, revocable at any moment, who would make the decisions within the assembly of the cordón representatives. However, rapidly, the workers of the cordón confronted the limits of the governmental left. These forms of alternative organisations further advanced towards the unification of their struggle by creating in July 1973 the coordination of cordones industriales of the province of Santiago. During the crisis of October 1972, after the military uprising of the colonel Souper in June 1973, and then after the new lockout by bosses in July of that same year, these forms of what we may call 'constituent people's power' experienced a significant extension across the whole the country. The word 'people's power' claimed by an entire part of the left was embodied then as a transitional reality:

> The democracy of 'all the people' threatens the form of representation and delegation of doing politics. The dynamics of socialisation of struggles is spread along all the territory and returns in a multiplied way within the enterprises. 'People's participation' starts to transform into 'people's power.[360]

In Santiago, the cordones Cerrillos and Vicuña Mackenna played the most important role, beside the cordones O'Higgins, San Joaquin, Santa Rosa, Recoleta, Mapocho-Cordillera, Santiago Centro and Panamericana-Norte. In the capital, the cordones concentrated several thousand workers, but they were also found from the North down to the South: in Arica, Concepción and also in Talcahuano and Punta Arenas. This original form of development of workers' control was also facilitated by the parallel dynamics of the movement of pobladores, which since the end of the 1960s has been organising in the urban outskirts (the poblaciones). However, the 'comandos comunales' that should, according to the revolutionary left, regroup workers, students and pobladores did not succeed to develop in the absence of a stable conjunction between the different social actors. A bitter debate even existed among militants to know if the priority should be given to the workers' cordones, according to the SP, or directly to the comandos, according to the MIR. It seems that this debate was moreover the reflection of where each party was present. In practice, the cordones industriales were dominated by socialists such as Hernan Ortega (cordón Cerrillos) or the trade unionist Armando Cruces (cordón Vicuna Mackenna), whereas the MIR was primarily present in the sectors of the urban semi-proletariat. These militants succeeded, nonetheless, to administer very effectively entire neighbourhoods, such as the Nueva La Habana, a real self-administrated village within Santiago.

Beyond its diversity and contradictions, this urban people's power may be defined as a 'power in movement', in the sense understood by the political analyst Sidney Tarrow.[361] It is undeniable that these initiatives were not 'spontaneous', being actually the fruit of an accumulation of militant experiences, of struggles, and of the building of a popular identity within the mobilised urban space: this is what the historian EP Thompson called a 'class experience'.[362] This big self-organisation wave fed by the left-wing militants PU (radical sectors of the SP, Christian Left) and by the MIR, meant essentially the crisis of the organs of historical mediation and leadership of the workers' movement. It has also accentuated the fratricide divisions within the left and weakened Allende's government. They were accused of parallelism by the CUT and the CP, which actively tried to slow down the constitution of the cordones industriales, rejecting any 'creation of an alternative power to the government'[363]. The MIR, under the leadership of Miguel Enriquez, replied to this by calling for the birth of a real dual power, refusing to 'maintain the subordination of the masses to bourgeois democracy' and to Allende's strategy. As to the SP, which was seeking an impossible synthesis, it acknowledged 'the development of a people's power as an alternative to the bourgeois institutions, but not to the government'.

The distance between Allende and 'people's power' grew as the economic policy of the left ran out of steam, and eventually sunk into paralysis with the appearance of the black market and hyperinflation. From January 1973, the cordones industriales openly opposed the project of the Communist Minister Orlando Millas who, in collaboration with the military that had then integrated the government, planned the restitution of 123 enterprises occupied or requisitioned during October, and the reduction to 49 of those integrated in the APS. Such a project accelerated the tensions between the government and the cordones, who strongly mobilised in opposition. According to the cordones, the CP and the 'reformist' sectors of PU acted against the revolutionary process.[364] In March, the government could reassert its legitimacy as a 'people's government' by obtaining more than 43 % of the votes in the legislative elections. But during the whole of 1973, the armed forces, far from being a neutral force, started their repression. Taking advantage of a law of 1972 about the 'control of arms', the military intervened in the workers' strongholds, confiscated the few arms they found and evaluated the resistance. After the crisis of June, when the medias (almost all in the hands of the opposition, starting with the newspaper El Mercurio) warned hysterically against the dictatorship of the proletariat, the CUT reiterated its appeals to return some of the occupied factories to their bosses. On 9 August 1973, a civic-military of 'national security'cabinet was established, which included three generals and the commander in chief of the police. Armando Cruces, the socialist leader of the cordón Vicuña Mackenna, declared: 'the military in the government, as in October, represent a reassurance for the bosses and not for the working class'. This was in vain, because one month later, general Pinochet, recently nominated as chief of staff after the resignation of the legalist General Carlos Prats, launched the coup d'état. Several days later, only a few dozen of battle-hardened militants confronted tanks and fighter-jets in la Moneda, the presidential palace which was in flames, while soldiers invaded the cordones industriales and popular neighbourhoods with the support of Washington.[365]

The struggle for political power: workers' control in the Portuguese Revolution

As in Chile, the issue of the control over the production was crucial and divided the left in Portugal. During 1974 and 1975, the term workers' control was used indiscriminately for 'management participation', 'publication of accounts', and 'control over production'. Political organisations and trade unions argued with each other to imbue the term with a meaning that was in consonance with their particular political strategy. During that period, the concepts became intertwined and toppled over one another reflecting the diversity of the evolution of the struggles in the factories and enterprises. Almost daily, companies were passing from the stage of democratic conflict (persecution of PIDE informers) to one of occupation. The state would intervene in a company and shortly afterwards it would enter into a regime of self-management or sometimes the self-management began even before state intervention. Sooner or later, the question of workers' control would arise in an establishment and following that, or sometimes before, it would evolve into a proposal for an embryonic form of coordination of that particular establishment with others in the same area or sector.

It was also possible or even probable that within the same factory or company there would have been a daily political struggle between those who argued for maintaining the ownership and/or control of the state over it and for forms of co-management; those who declared the need for a 'battle for production' without questioning ownership and arguing in favour of co-management or self-management as the way to concretise their proposal; those who believed in self-management and the development of technical mechanisms of control over production but outside the framework of a 'battle for production'; and those who, within a process of workers' control, sought to insert control over companies in a national political framework that would impose the total disruption of the state.

There are undisputable records of that power struggle in various companies. In the Lisnave shipyards, a document was produced declaring that workers' control should be implemented in the sense of 'showing the class that increased productivity and the solution of the unemployment crisis cannot be achieved by merely changing bosses', and that:

> If workers' control at the factory floor level is the working class' first step towards controlling the bosses' administration, workers' control at the level of all shipyards, then at the level of the metalworking and mechanical branches and lastly at the level of all the workers' commissions throughout the country, are the second, third and fourth steps that the class will take and that it needs to take to ensure that the bosses do not play cat and mouse with us.[366]

In her study of workers' control, Fatima Patriarca gives dozens of examples of declarations issued by factory and company assemblies that rejected the 'battle for production proposal and argued in favour of workers' control as a measure in the fight against capitalist exploitation and as a form of workers' movement to create leaders and class awareness, and eventually abolish the system of capitalist relations altogether. Lisnave's Conselho de Defesa dos Trabalhadores (Workers' Defence Council) rejected measures that it said were 'inserted in an economic battle that did not merely mean producing more'.[367] At that time too, workers at the Margueira shipyards defended the idea that 'there is no workers' control if we merely intend to manage the bosses' businesses'. In May 1975, workers at the Sacor Company, in the north, proposed that gas and fuel should be supplied to companies with economic problems where the bosses had fled. They also defended the idea that workers' control could only be meaningful if it 'leads to increased awareness (on the part of the workers), that is to say, if it enables them to increasingly see where their real interests lie and leads them on to the fundamental issue: the conquest of power'.

With few exceptions, it is possible to synthesise an analysis in which the history of workers' control during the revolution is divided essentially into three major periods: 1) atomised forms; 2) workers' control coordinated by sectors; 3) workers' control disseminated at the national level and coordinated in an embryonic form at district and national levels.[368]

In the social fray, starting from 25 April 1974, workers' control existed in the form of radical protests (strikes, kidnappings, occupations). That control, which was not the same thing as trade union demands (e.g. for better wages), existed above all in the sphere of the struggle that forced the administrations to alter their composition (e.g. purges). During that stage, workers' control was dispersed: the focus was still on the company and not the political power of the state. The struggle was for recomposing the administration and not to gain total control over production. Furthermore, there was no national coordination, not even the most embryonic one, of those forms of collective action.

In the period from April 1974 to February 1975, there were various processes of radical struggle that were taking place in the companies and at their heart they were of a claiming and demanding nature. There were also several processes of self-management quite distinct from workers' control insofar as they defended the idea of the ownership of the companies being in the hands of the workers themselves.[369] Workers' control expanded but it was sometimes limited to certain sectors of a company, as was the case with airline TAP, and sometimes to their entirety (Lisnave, Jornal do Comércio) but even then it was quite restricted in terms of the national panorama.

Driven by motives of a democratic nature (to guarantee freedoms), workers pressurised the companies in order to be able to determine the composition of the administration. To achieve this, workers spontaneously organised themselves in workers' commissions. That form of organisation made it possible to place an agenda of claims and demands right at the heart of the workers' commissions' activities insofar as it brought together in assemblies social subjects whose common interests were the improvement of labour conditions and relations. These assemblies, by then unified in the form of a commission, were destined to determine the evolution of political awareness, partly due to the influence of the youth groups of the radical left and of the inability of the regime to avoid growing unemployment in a context of deep recession.[370] The struggle, in a democratic manner, for jobs and improved conditions opened the political horizon towards the fight for socialism.

From February 1975 onwards, workers' control emerged as a condition of political struggle and of challenging the power of the state. It was organised on the basis of the factory and was designed to achieve the realisation of economic demands. That factory-level control was not alienated in any way from the development of control at the neighbourhood level conducted by the residents' commissions.

The development of workers' control, starting in February 1975, is one of the factors that explains the nationalisation of the banks. In the Portuguese case, it was not restricted to a mere nationalisation was more an expropriation because it was carried out without any compensation. The nationalisations and the political crisis of 11 March 1975 gave workers' control a new boost due to the state taking control of several companies belonging to the biggest corporate groups, which were in turn nationalised and following that, the question of workers' control came up for discussion. On the other hand a fierce social struggle by workers in companies (among them Central de Cervejas and Lisnave) broke out in an effort to achieve their nationalisation. The recession continued: inflation, galloping increases in food prices and transport fares and, above all, the presence of unemployment which reached its height in that period were all at the heart of that process.

Thus a political struggle broke out inside the companies, especially after March 1975. This struggle was between on the one hand, those who organised themselves in an endeavour to exercise workers' control based on the commissions to control production (and profits and wages as well) with the intention of 'the workers taking power' (a position which was strongly represented or dominant in many factories), and for that reason they attributed the organisational aspect to national bodies coordinating the sector-based control commissions with the satellite company or inter-commission entities. The struggle pitted on the other hand, another group of workers led by the PCP and government party supporters which took the defensive stance of favouring co-management involving administrators, workers and the state. They tended to emphasise the defence of the 'national economy' and the 'battle for production', to reject wage control, and for the nationalisation of foreign companies.

The predicted inability of the government to avoid what would be the downfall of the Portuguese bourgeoisie, namely the setting up of a national body coordinating the workers' commissions, which would constitute an alternative national power, a counter-power to that of the state (as it was described in several documents recording the plenary sessions of assemblies in various companies) headed by the industrial workers and strongly concentrated in three cities. In our opinion, this is what led to a rupture with the government and the mobilisation by the church, and the right wing forces, and unleashed the violence of the 'hot summer' against sections of the working class and left wing political parties. It would also lead to the decision in August 1975 to set up a new broad front bringing together the SP, the church, sectors of the MFA and the right-wing. This new broad front was in preparation for a coup that would block the revolution, but it was not to block the Communist Party, as was wrongly assumed for a long time, as the party actually opposed workers' control.

The breakup of the governmental coalition, however led to a split in the MFA and after September 1975, the question of establishing workers' control at the level of companies and neighbourhoods began to involve the army which up until then had been to some extent been restrained by the *sui generis* alternative power of the MFA. The MFA had made a great but unsuccessful effort to establish equilibrium and avoid a clash. When the MFA was dismantled, some of its members joined the right-wing but part of the left-wing military, occupying key posts in the armed forces, tended to support very embryonic forms of dual power (SUV – Soldados Unidos Vencerão – soldiers' committees) and that led to clashes within the PCP itself. Most members of the party leadership were reluctant to allow things to evolve into an open confrontation and put their hopes on recovering the equilibrium by forming a political front with the PS.

In spite of the construction of a history largely originating from the PCP that reintroduced the idea that the fall of the Fifth Government, which curiously enough the PCP never really supported, would have been the end of the revolution (associating revolution with government, regime and state), but the history of workers' control demonstrates just the opposite. The crises of state and government actually loosened all the admittedly tenuous bonds that still restrained the revolution – power in the hands of the people and the workers – from being imposed on the state. The revolutionary crisis, the moment when there is a change in those holding the levers of power and there is a forced breakup of the political equilibrium that allows for the reestablishment of capitalist relations production, actually began in September 1975 and it is euphemistically referred to as the 'political-military crisis'. The MFA was the one that dragged down with it the last refuge for the stability of the state.

To help our systematisation we can use a saying from the Russian revolution, which is that a revolutionary crisis is when 'those at the top can no longer govern and those below no longer want to be governed as they were before'. We can see that in the Portuguese revolution, unlike the Russian revolution, there was no single hegemonic revolutionary party, but instead, there were various fragile, molecular ones. Nevertheless their members had performed a fundamental role in the process of workers' control that had its roots in the strength of ideas and organisation in the schools and the universities during the period of Marcelism (Marcelo Caetano was the dictator from 1968 to 1974 after Salazar). They were influenced by the Cuban revolution, Latin American guerrillaism, the Sino-Soviet conflict and even more directly by the European events of May 1968.

The last period of workers' control in November 1975 was marked by the gradual construction of embryonic coordinating bodies of workers' control at the national level, that is, by the exponential development of the strength of the workers' commissions, and by the preponderance of political claims and demands towards the state and companies. Among the demands were the construction of socialism, the abolition of mercantile relations, the abolition of class-structured society, control over profits and refusal to accept the appeal for national reconstruction. That situation and the Fourth Government's inability to govern, gave an added boost to the creation of the embryonic forms of coordination of the workers' commissions. This coordination materialised with great force but also with serious internal dissent in Lisbon, which was where everything was decided due to its position as the capital city and with a high concentration of industries. On 7-8 November 1975, at a meeting of the workers' commissions of the Lisbon industrial belt, workers' control and the national coordination of the workers' commissions were two of the items that divided opinions among the local commissions represented.

After the Fourth Government and the MFA Revolutionary Council had seized control of the banks in a bid to protect a sector that was then under the threat of workers' control, it adopted the 'battle for production' strategy, which had historical antecedents such as in 1945 France. The strategy, which in effect was to curb workers' control, was developed by the PCP, then at the heart of the government, and was supported by all members of the coalition government.

The PCP definition of what it understood workers' control to be was a form of co-management, and it spread the concept by means of the Intersindical (the trade union federation).[371] Workers' control for the PCP was the organisation of workers in all kinds of associative bodies – unions, associations, cooperatives, peasants leagues, residents' commissions and others, with a view to defending the revolution and ensuring success for the 'battle for production', which was 'the main battle front of the working class'.³⁷² It meant that such organisations participated in, but did not control, production alongside the unions in establishing the companies' plans, processes, salaries, etc.³⁷³ and this was all strictly bound up with the overriding objective of the success of the 'battle for production'. The State Secretary of Labour, Carlos Carvalhas, a PCP member, explained in *Avante* how the party saw the scope of 'workers' control': 'This battle for the restructuring of the entire production apparatus has two main guidelines: produce better and with lower costs'. ³⁷⁴

Thus 'workers' control' was subservient to the 'battle for production'. There was another policy associated attached to the 'battle for production', which was to curb what the PCP described as 'unrealistic demands' made by workers. That was against a background in which, even after all the nationalisations, 90% of the workforce was still working for a private employer and the state continued to be a capitalist one.³⁷⁵ At a PCP rally held on 18 May 1975 in Vila Franca de Xira, Álvaro Cunhal declared that 'the great task of the moment was the 'battle for production' and it had to be fought to put an end to 'unrealistic demands' and the strikes'. At another rally held on 28 June at Campo Pequeno, Veiga de Oliveira, communist Minister of Transport and Telecommunications in the Fourth Government, reminded people of the victories achieved with the nationalisation of the railways, of TAP, marine transport, and dozens of road transport companies, and he criticised the wave of demands and strikes being called in those companies which he said was 'sabotage' and 'reactionary'.³⁷⁶

That policy achieved a broad consensus in both the coalition government and the Revolutionary Council of the MFA. The SP and the conservative PPD declared that the difficult situation called for the moderation of demands and claims.³⁷⁷ Costa Gomes, the President at the time, stated that working was 'a way of being with the revolution',³⁷⁸ and Prime Minister Vasco Gonçalves's speech on Labour Day was perfectly in tune with the policy that the PCP defended:

> I hereby call on all workers, on all patriots, to engage in the Battle for Production because the future of the Revolution depends on our victory in that battle. The Battle for Production is a necessary stage in overcoming the economic crisis and creating conditions for the future development of the economy along the road to socialism.³⁷⁹

The nationalised companies were to be the high points of that policy. The nationalisation of the banks, insurance companies and, following that, various strategic companies belonging to dominant Portuguese economic groups, took place roughly between March and May 1975. It was a policy forcefully imposed on the political parties and the MFA by the workers who, in the dynamics of the revolution, obliged the MFA Revolutionary Council and the Fourth Provisional Government to implement it by decree. It was the evolution that placed the nationalisations at the heart of Portuguese history in 1975. Neither the PCP, the Partido Socialista (Socialist Party) nor the MFA adopted nationalisations as one of their strategies in the two-year period of 1974-75.

The history of the nationalisations is fairly complex because they seem to have actually strengthened state power while apparently taking it away from the companies. It has Bonapartist aspects but it is contradictory as the outcome of the nationalisations was the state taking control of the companies with the twin result of rescuing, in economic terms, companies that were suffering from an economic recession, but at the same time safeguarding the property that objectively was about to be targeted by the workers with of workers' control.

Just one decade later, the nationalised banks and companies were handed back to the private sector. That process, however, has a history: it has a beginning and an end. When the nationalisations took place, they represented the victory of the workers, a defeat for the capitalist system and a heightening of the class struggle that directly targeted private property. The history of the revolution was the history of the extraordinary self-confidence that the workers and some parts of the intermediate sectors of society acquired from 11 March 1975 onwards, the day the right wing coup was defeated and which led to the generalisations of embryonic organs of dual power. It was the confidence that they could win and that they could question the private ownership of the means of production – sentiments that spread like wildfire throughout the country – which was at the root of the crisis that began in July, the so-called 'hot summer'.

Conclusions

The Chilean and the Portuguese revolutions are an immense laboratory for the study of the relation between the state and the workers in moments of intense social conflict. We focused in this article on a specific aspect of this relation, the one that was built during nationalisations. It was a contradictory and complex process that synthesises within the same economic relation the contradiction between workers and capitalists and helps us to understand the role performed by the state and the government.

Chile and Portugal and different, moreover due to the distinct role the military had, by their place in the international system of states (Chile was a peripheral country, whereas Portugal was the last and decadent colonial empire), and by the different conclusions of both revolutions. In Chile there was a horrible bloodbath while in Portugal there was a legal and democratic counter-revolution, a predecessor of the Carter doctrine.

But both countries have much in common, starting with the role of the workers, who had unique experiences of democratic control and management of their lives; the appearance of embryonic organs of dual power (*cordones industriales*, workers' commissions), the degree of urbanisation of their societies, the close link between these revolutions and the crisis of accumulation of the 1970s, the international impact of both political processes that, apart from Vietnam, were the centre of international social tension in that period. This article aimed to contribute towards a better understanding of the relationship between these political processes, not only within a comparative dimension, but also by means of the role of the communist parties.

In conclusion, we underline what seems to be most urgently reflected upon.

A history of workers' control in Chile and Portugal in the 1970s cannot be developed in isolation from a global history of communism. It is necessary to go beyond a comparative history, that is, it is necessary to reflect on the role of the communist parties and their close relationship with the foreign policy of the URSS. We have seen that not only the policies in the two countries were similar – the theory of the peaceful transition to socialism; the co-management between unions and the state; the policy of peoples' front; the battle for production – but that the vocabulary used by the parties and the trade union federations which they led (CGTP and CUT) was identical, despite being separated by a huge ocean.

In the heat of the events, the state regulation that limited workers' control, and which had less effect in Portugal than in Chile, was developed, as we have seen, by ministers and Labour Secretaries of State who were members of the communist parties of both countries. As a matter of fact, the extent and the complexity of the internal processes of each country cannot disguise the role of Stalinism. This was an international apparatus that contributed decisively in both cases to limit the independence of the working class and popular and middle layers and to subsume the organs dual power to the need for participation in governments based on multi-class alliances. This policy, which served the interests of the foreign policy of 'peaceful coexistence' of the URSS, created a permanent tension with important sectors of the working classes of both countries.

Consequently, the history of nationalisations in Portugal and Chile was also the history of the struggles and tensions between, on the one hand, some sectors of the mobilised working class which fought to speed up the reforms and which was suffering from the pressure of the bosses, and on the other hand, governments that sought to respect their commitments with the popular classes while still basing themselves on a gradualist conception of transition to socialism, and hence *in fine* on its agreements with the sectors of the bourgeoisie. This led to the policy of the governmental left abdicating responsibility for nationalisation, and therefore also for management and control of the state, and also calling for restraint in social struggles in the nationalised companies. However state intervention and workers' control of production appear in Portugal and Chile incompatible and the direct role of the state in nationalised firms limited *de facto* the scope of workers' control.

Three elements, in our opinion, combined but contradictory, determined the character of the participation of workers in the nationalised sector in both countries: the hegemony of the union structure and of the state representatives; the insertion of the organs of participation around the objective of the 'battle for production', and the virtual inexistence of a national democratic planning system based on the participation of representatives elected by workers.

In Chile, the production increased during the first period in a spectacular way, whereas the surpluses generated were scarcely transferred from the APS to the other social sectors. The combination of these three elements had the consequence of raising the standard of living of workers in the APS and the amplification of the existing differentiations within the working class, of which a majority remained excluded from the nationalised sector. In Portugal, when the battle for production started, it was defeated in the factories and enterprises in a explosive combination of, on the one hand, contestation by the workers to the policy of intensification of productivity, and, on the other hand, a profound political crisis. This combination led to the fall of two governments within 4 months, exactly when this policy of the 'battle for production' was being implemented. Within a very short period, no more than three months, it led to a revolutionary crisis which unfolded from September to November 1975. This revolutionary crisis ended with a coup d'état by social-democratic sectors, that is the SP and the 'Group of Nine' (reformist army officers) allied to a right-wing block and the Catholic Church, and with the open abandonment of any resistance by the PCP and its central trade union federation. This coup d'état met with little resistance by workers, who had never achieved a level of national cohesion and organisation of the workers' commissions and were thus unable to resist the coup.

Since its origin, both popular front governments were struck by a major tension: they were the product of a huge popular mobilisation and wished to create a new 'people's power', but at the same time they did not want 'people's power' to challenge directly the state institutions and the army, or its project of transition to socialism by stages.

However the notion of workers' control and people's power overwhelmed the entire political framework of the big left parties. In Chile in particular, militants, through of the '*cordones industriales*' in Santiago and other cities, demanded first of all the extension of the nationalisations to their factories, but also workers' control, the organisation of defence committees, the dissolution of the Congress, the setting up of a Constituent Assembly, the cleansing of reactionary officers from the army, and the nationalisation under popular control of the distribution in order to prevent the black market.

In Portugal, nationalisations were a milestone in the Portuguese Revolution because they had repeatedly been made under pressure from the working class in massive meetings of workers or where establishments had been occupied and workers were demanding their nationalisation. Nationalisation was also accompanied by extraordinary victories of workers in significant improvement in real wages during a period of high inflation (20 to 30%) along with other social benefits, which were all made without compensation. As a reflection of an acute class struggle, many capitalists, including some of the richest men in the country, were arrested after the coup of the 11 March 1975 and/or ended up fleeing to Brazil. They only returned to Portugal at the end of the 1970s or later, when governments began to outline a method of compensation which was first to be established by Law 80/77 of 26 October 1977.

As a first balance sheet, it is unavoidable to underline that despite the scale of the phenomenon of dual power, these forms of constituent people's power did not have more than an rudimentary and temporary character. Their actions were carried out in a defensive and ill-planned manner. Their coordination remained often a weak superstructure led by some trade union and political activists, and it was not a mass organisation which originated from the assemblies of organised workers. Neither the cordones industriales in Chile nor the workers commissions in Portugal succeeded in uniting beyond a local level, or even to be base themselves on a political alternative project to that proposed by the governments. Lastly, with regards to the historiography, although advances have been made recently by a new generation of scholars, these experiences of 'people's power' have yet to more profoundly studied as they still constitute today one of the big gaps in the study of Popular Unity in Chile and the Carnation Revolution in Portugal.

Latin America: state, popular power and class struggle*

Franck Gaudichaud

Bryan Seguel (BS): The concept of 'popular power' became lodged in the Latin American imagination, from the 1970s onwards, in various contexts and, in this framework, different uses were made of it by the social movements and the revolutionary political organisations: how do you understand this idea or theory of popular power and what elements are – in your view – fundamental for analysing it.

Franck Gaudichaud (FG): Certainly, as you say, the notion of popular power is very heterogeneous, it has no single definition, far from it. Its flexibility is its strength and also its weakness, given that we have to adapt it to each real process to understand it fully. In a collective book on popular power, the Argentine theorist Miguel Mazzeo has stressed, humorously, the danger of having a 'bat notion' (a concept derived from the Italian theorist Vilfredo Pareto, who said 'Marx's words are like bats. One can see in them both birds and mice') that is an understanding of popular power so heterogeneous that its very nature remains barely determined, so that if it was an animal, it could be a bird or a rodent, or a mixture of the two. Personally, I like both birds, capable – like utopias – of flying very high in the sky, and rodents which, like Marx's 'old mole' are capable of undermining the dominant order 'from below'! Joking apart, the concept of popular power can effectively be the subject of various antagonistic readings and is located within different perceptions: from anarchist or libertarian currents to orthodox Marxism, via heterodox Marxism or council communism

---

*   This interview of Franck Gaudichaud by Bryan Seguel was carried out in November 2014. It is the second part of an interview published in Spanish in March 2015 by the Political and Social Studies Group (GESP) of the University of Santiago (USACH) and Tiempo Robado editoras. The interview was published in French by *Contretemps* in 2015 <www.contretemps.eu>. This version has been translated from the French by Bernard Gibbons.

and so on. For example, in Latin America, some anarchist groups argue: 'Popular power remains a notion centred and articulated around the state, so it doesn't suit us' whereas numerous libertarian currents on the contrary identify with it as a central force of their engagement. In my view, the demand for popular power is related to what Daniel Bensaïd called 'the smile of the spectre' of communism and it refers essentially to the organised eruption of the workers' movement and subaltern classes on the political scene and to the self-managing mobilisations of the dominated and exploited faced with capitalist, productivist and patriarchal hegemony. In certain historic conjectures, these social sectors, through their subaltern position and by the strength of their mobilisation and self-organisation, begin to create spaces of autonomous and (partially) counter-hegemonic power, thus in part subverting the dominant social order. This power which shoots up is never 'pure' and exempt from multiple contradictions, for sure; it can be local, communal, indeed regional, leading – in exceptional historic moments of pre-revolutionary crisis – to a dualisation of power, territorial and/or at the state level, which throws into question the legitimacy of the existing order and, notably the state's monopoly of violence and the organisation of social relations of production. But to concretise itself, this 'popular power' needs to develop starting from *real* social subjects with a material basis, the reason for which the experiences of popular power take on a specific revolutionary force when they emerge among employees and the workers' movement, because their resistance directly threatens the ownership of the means of production and the reproduction and accumulation of capital. Thus, historically, in Chile, the praxis of popular power was particularly incarnated through the cordones industriales, which succeeded in controlling – and in a transitional manner – sectors of the apparatus of production during the turbulent 'Chilean road to socialism' (1970-1973): this is what I have tried to show by several years of research, interviews with workers of the period, archive work and publications on this theme. Currently, in Argentina and Brazil, there are dozens of enterprises that have been taken over, several of them functioning under workers' control or more often in the form of cooperatives of production. These are embryos of what I call the logics of class-conscious constituent popular power.

In this respect, the importance of new trade union and workers' struggles in several countries of the continent show that the theories of the 'end of the proletariat' or 'of work' are profoundly wrong. Trades unionism and workers' class struggles remain very much alive and are even on the upturn in certain countries: the significant mobilisations of employees during the recent period in Argentina, accompanied by a strong recomposition of the anti-capitalist (Trotskyist) left; in Chile, the action of the copper miners and the dockers in the portside union or the recent conflicts in the services sector (Walmart and Jumbo supermarkets, pharmacy, call-centres); in Mexico, the struggles of the electricity trade unions; in Peru, the national resistance to the Humala government's reform of the labour code and so on. Nonetheless, since the 1990s, the traditional trade union form is globally in retreat and in crisis across the whole continent (as shown by the example of the COB, the Bolivian trade union federation) along with flexibilisation/precarisation-outsourcing of work. To wish to rediscover today the glorious industrial working class of the 1970s of the semi-industrialised countries like Argentina, Chile or Brazil is a romantic (or dogmatic) illusion. There has been a profound transformation of the workforce under the blows of neoliberalism, and it is starting from these new social formations which are partially rebuilding, and often painfully, the trade union spaces. For this reason, we must also understand and value the new dynamics of struggle and forms of Latin American community and horizontal-territorial organisation, thanks – to a great extent – to the impulsion of the indigenous movements or those of 'unemployed workers' (like the piqueteros). Constituent popular power thus also starts from the territorial space of the neighbourhood or rural area, around the 'poor of the countryside and the town', and inside the communities of indigenous peoples in resistance. For 20 years, we have seen this force of the peripheral urban or indigenous-peasant territories where a (re)appropriation of living spaces is taking place, generating a collective counter-power faced with the constituted power of the extractivist multinationals, of the neo-colonial state, of the big landowners, local authorities and governments. This counter-hegemonic power is being transformed, in certain cases, into an alternative social appropriation, demanding horizontal democracy from below, the struggle against patriarchy, the right to the town, to new forms of agricultural production and so on. That is what we have tried to show in a little collective book published by Syllepse in its French version on the 'emancipations in construction'. We think for example of the Commune of Oaxaca (Mexico) in 2006. In my view, this was a key experience if we are talking about popular power in the 21st century, because what was affirmed there was a level of radical, popular, indigenous and trade union democracy which was exceptional: perhaps the first great 'Commune' of this beginning of the century as the Paris Commune was at the end of the 19th century? Also interesting is the contradictory experience of the Communal Councils in Venezuela, as expression of local political power, in link with the Bolivarian governmental power. These Communal Councils have a better potentiality when they feed off the trade union and workers' movement, and come to demand a greater autonomy in relation to the bureaucratic or central clientelist power, while avoiding 'neighbourhood caudillismo'. Another example, among many others, is the region of Cauca (Colombia), where an original indigenous and agro-ecological experience is developing, with rotation of leadership functions, control of production and alimentation: an alternative bio-power, a constitutive power made from self-management, self-organisation, with capacity to control its mode of life, of feeding itself, without depending on institutions or agribusiness... We can also, of course talk about Chiapas and neo-Zapatism, a concrete utopia essential to the neoliberal era, or again the resistance of the ronderos of Conga (Peru) against the mining multinational Yanacocha, where we find moreover the active support of historic figures of the Latin American revolutionary movement, like Hugo Blanco (and his monthly *Lucha indígena*). These many experiences allow us a certain optimism of the will for the future, despite a global panorama where a reasoned analysis generates a certain pessimism. Nonetheless, none among them can avoid the strategic discussion on the manner in which these constituent local powers could construct a capacity to change society on a larger scale and thus offer an alternative anti-capitalist and eco-socialist 'project-country'.

BS: Is it your view that a praxis of popular power solely anchored in a local experience cannot survive in the long term, if it does not contest hegemony on the national or global level?

FG: Sometimes, they can persist for decades, like Chiapas and become a planetary example for numerous movements worldwide. Some very rich practices of community-based popular power should be recognised for this, and I think one of the most emblematic in Latin America remains that of the Zapatistas, who have just commemorated twenty years of resistance at a significant territorial scale. Recently, Jérôme Baschet has sought to make it an anti-capitalist example to follow, without making it a model to copy. The Zapatistas have shown that one can do away with authoritarian forms of organisation and build other forms of life, defending common goods on the basis of a plural community and indigenous subjectivities, according to a vision and practice of power which is more respective, more democratic in the real sense and subversive of democracy – as well put by Jacques Rancière: that is, more horizontal, with rotation of leadership functions, control of the social base over its leaders, 'good government councils', and so on. But the social and political situation in the rest of Mexico has not improved, very much to the contrary! It continues to worsen: poverty, the exploitation of labour and violence increase. The Mexican narco-state involves such levels of social decomposition that it has been possible to kidnap 43 students in Iguala, with complete impunity and with the collaboration of the mayor of this area, a member of the supposedly 'centre left' PRD party. This is only the visible part of the problem, whereas for the last five years we have seen tens of thousands of killings and disappearances, a veritable internal war. Hence the importance and urgency of the strategic discussion on the theme 'how to change the world' by everybody collectively taking power. But where to begin?

Some activists think that what is at issue here is a dispute on the question of 'revolutionary subjects' and the search for the 'principal contradiction'. For example, in Chile, I have heard debates concerning 'popular power versus workers' power', insisting on the unavoidable centrality of the working class. I think that it is necessary to restore a dialectical thought and understand that the concept of 'popular power' encompasses the notion of workers' control, it includes it but offers a broader and more dynamic vision. Personally, I assume fully that in case can we claim to dissolve the contradictions of classes and the central role of the labour-subject and replace it with the constitution of abstract or ethereal forms of popular power: if popular power aspires to anti-capitalism, it must needs be articulated around the struggles of those who experience the domination of capital, in their workplace but also beyond it. In Chile, the industrial workers' movement was the cradle of some of the most advanced forms of popular power with – as I have noted – the fleeting but essential appearance of the cordones industriales in 1972-1973. The cordones sought an alliance with the inhabitants of the poorer and self-constructed neighbourhoods (the pobladores), with the students and other sectors of employees. Forty years later, we must again discuss the strategic alliances to be articulated to form a counter-hegemonic class-conscious bloc, but in the light of the current social formations, diverse and with fragmented identities (sometimes it's better that way). That is, by abandoning a heroic, somewhat phantasmal vision of the working class as if thirty years of neoliberalism had not transformed the salariat, representations and also common sense (the work of Ricardo Antunes is essential here). For example, today in Argentina, the experiences of self-management born from the movement of laid off workers, outside of the workplace, and also those of a new generation of the working class which is more educated, as seen in the 'manufacturing without bosses' at Neuquén (FASINPAT), formerly Zanón. It is necessary also to assume the existence of the 'diagonal' of the social conflict (Bensaïd),[380] a conflict which is not reduced to work alone: conflicts of gender and with the patriarchy, conflicts for the defence of well-being faced with the destruction of nature and living environment, ethnic conflicts, of 'race' and in favour of the self-determination of peoples and so on. As the Chilean writer Luis Vitale said more than 30 years ago, Latin American Marxism should take on three insufficiently integrated challenges: feminism, the colonialism of power (Quijano) and the ecological and climate crisis (Vitale, 1983). The reason for which critical though should seek to put in relation, think about the intersectionalities and link the different oppressions in an articulated manner: 'race'-class-gender-colonialism constitute in Latin America parts to be linked to a dependent and combined totality, that cannot be cut into little pieces without the risk of fragmenting our knowledge of reality and social praxis. As if, for example, women's struggles for their emancipation were totally delinked from the ecologist, indigenous, working class and anti-imperialist struggles and reciprocally.

BS: In understanding that the reference to popular power in Latin America depends very much on the context of each country, it appears that there are diverse experiences where this notion has been used as a central element in the construction of projects of socio-political transformation. For example, there is its current use in Venezuela with the Bolivarian Republic and in Cuba since the 1960s and in another context, by the Argentine organisation Frente Popular Darío Santillán, in Colombia by the Congress of the Peoples or, finally, the reference made in Chile in the field of 'Mirista culture' (the reference is to the MIR – Movimiento de Izquierda Revolucionaria) or inside the activist culture of the ex-PRT-ERP (Partido Revolucionario de los Trabajadores – Ejército Revolucionario del Pueblo) in Argentina. How can the same concept produce such distinct political practices? How can the same word articulate politics which are so different indeed antagonistic, from a Leninist conception centred on a classic idea of duality of power to a more horizontal conception of participatory democracy?

FG: Your question confirms that the demand for popular power can be broad, contradictory and flexible, just like the notions of democracy, revolution, liberty and finally many other central elements of political discussion. This concept is powerful, but it requires debate, demystification and above all, strategic definition. In Cuba, the notion of popular power is a heritage of the 1959 revolution, but today, it has above all been transformed into a rhetoric used by a party-state which leaves little margin to plurality and to political differences in the context of the revolution (if the latter are not expressed internally to the party and/or in subterranean fashion). This is totally different to the notion of popular power demanded by the Frente Popular Darío Santillán (Argentina), a territorial autonomist movement which globally rejects the figure of the state, which demands self-management based on the movement of workers and unemployed to construct a, shall we say, more libertarian political reference, but which, unlike Castroism, has not faced a 50 year criminal blockade by the United States and the everyday management of a small impoverished Caribbean state a few kilometres from the main global power of the 20th century!

In the case of the historic experiences you cite, it is certain that in Chile, the MIR was the organisation which most clearly demanded – and theoretically developed – the notion of popular power. Its slogan, chanted on the demonstrations in Santiago up to today, is globally known: 'Create, create popular power!'. Especially under Popular Unity (1970-1973), the movement led by Miguel Enríquez tried to advance this demand from the areas where it operated, notably in the movement of the pobladores and in an area like 'Nueva Habana', a very interesting experience of local popular power. But it is always necessary to compare discourse and praxis, theoretical demand and political-social action. Inside the MIR, there has always been a tension between a 'revolutionary vanguard organisation' which continued to be very vertical, structured around political-military groups (GPM), and appeals to 'create popular power', to develop the Communal Commandos. The MIR was Marxist-Leninist (with a Guevarist, focoist influence) and adopted the theory of dual power, in particular from 1972 onwards, but it lacked a massive insertion in the workers' and trade union movement. It also hesitated on how to critically support Allende's democratic government while fighting the reformism of the Communist Party (CP). Combining a theory of 'popular power' with certain levels of immediate pragmatism, the MIR concentrated on the construction of broader Communal Commandos, seeking to group workers, pobladores and students. Unlike the activists of the left wing of the Socialist Party (PS), very much present in the factories, it lost view of the fact that at this moment of the 'Chilean road to socialism', faced with the attacks of the bourgeoisie and the Nixon government, it was above all urgent to give priority to the real germs of constituent dual power: the cordones industriales. Some traits of the PRT-ERP (Argentina) are also linked to the notion of 'prolonged peoples' war', that is to a central political-military aspect, and to a sometimes abstract mixture of theoretical Marxism with strong traits of pragmatism and vanguardism (as the historian Pablo Pozzi has suggested); which, in the periods of vigorous ascent of popular struggles (the 1970s in Argentina) entered into tension with horizontality, the massive size of the mobilisations and with what the historian Peter Winn calls the 'revolution from below'. One of the lessons to be drawn is certainly the need to consider the political-military and self-defence elements as an integral part of the transition, but put at the service of processes of popular self-management and self-organisation, and not of a professional militant apparatus, an enlightened vanguard, often external to the class and the social movement. Obviously, this is easy to say seen from today. The difficulty is how to organise in this manner when the state tends to brutally and immediately repress all forms of self-defence. Today undoubtedly in both Latin America and Southern Europe, the centre of the discussion is how to articulate the force of popular power, favour it and the conquest via the ballot of institutional spaces, including a popular government which is committed to a programme of democratic and social rupture.

In Venezuela – a 'peaceful, but armed' process as Hugo Chávez put it – there is a demand which is very much present of popular power formulated by the Bolivarian government. In fact, all the ministers are supposedly 'of popular power' which is a contradiction and an oxymoron! In fifteen years of 'Bolivarian revolution', original spaces of participation have been created like those I have already mentioned, especially the Communal Councils. In a country where the social movements were previously weak, albeit very explosive – as was the case during the Caracas uprising (the 'Caracazo') in February 1989 – original forms of participation were attempted, like the Bolivarian Circles, the Urban Land Councils or the Communal Councils. I have visited Venezuela several times in recent years, and I think that the 'battle of Caracas' – as Atilio Borón has suggested – has a key importance on the continental geopolitical terrain. I have been able to participate in the meetings of Communal Councils in the popular neighbourhoods of the capital and to read several serious academic studies on this theme. Conclusion, these are complex and ambivalent realities: some Communal Councils function in a phenomenal, genuinely democratic manner, while others are co-opted by small and not very representative groups. Generally, they effectively allow the improvement of the concrete situation of the population, empowering the poorer inhabitants, allowing discussion of neighbourhood problems and the management of a participatory public budget. The limit of these bodies is that these are very limited spaces, of a participatory power dependent on the state, and particularly the presidency which grants the budget and sets the powers of the Council, its territory and its norms. It is an embryo of local popular power, fragile and very little institutionalised, impelled mainly 'from above', thanks to a close relationship between the Bolivarian people and the charismatic leadership of Hugo Chávez.

Again, we find the tension between the 'constituent power' and the constituted powers, but not precisely in the sense developed by the Chilean historian Gabriel Salazar, who centres this discussion on aspects like 'the construction of the state by the people, alongside the market and civil society'. Salazar's view seems to me to, firstly, overvalue the social in relation to the political (he says that the citizens' social movement could be *by itself* an alternative to the dominant institutional system, without evaluating the problematic of the political organisation); secondly, this view is misleading, because he writes on the need to cease to think in terms of the class struggle (reduced to an economic struggle). Seen in this way, constituent power seems to crystallize as a praxis of a set of various corporatized social sectors: inhabitants of poor neighbourhoods, intellectuals, workers, entrepreneurs, citizens, all together constituting – 'from below' – the state and the market. Among Salazar's ideas which I consider interesting on Chile, we cite those on the social memory of the people, his reminder of experiences like the Constituent Assembly of employees and intellectuals of 1925 or his criticisms of partisan vanguardism and the parliamentary lefts. But, constituent popular power cannot be reduced to attempts to write new constitutions or even to (self) construct the state; and it has above all as fuel and motor the social classes, and not an imaginary and ahistorical elaboration of an overall construction of employees, civil society and employers, diluting the basic conflicts of society.

BS: While you were developing this analysis of popular power, I began to formulate some questions. On the one hand, a tension between form and basis, that you indicate in the case of the MIR, which demanded a revolutionary democratic background, but whose specific political practice was contradictory, that is to say the links between the parties and the 'mass' movement. Another tension is that between the local and the national, in the sense that the concrete experiences tend sometimes to be isolated from national contexts, which generates problems in the area of representation and in the scope of the latter. The final tension, indicated by the Bolivian vice-president and sociologist Álvaro García Linera as 'creative tensions of the revolution', that is the relationship between constituent powers and constituted powers. Do you think these three elements could explain the different orientations taken today by popular power(s) in Latin America?

FG: These three elements are fundamental, effectively, but in thinking precisely of García Linera (Bolivia) and Gabriel Salazar (Chile), I would like to again stress the fact that the debate on popular power should take place within the strategic discussion on the relations of classes and the mode of production, the models of ecological and economic accumulation and the anti-capitalist scenarios. If not, we could empty of its content this capacity of transformation that the demand for constituent popular power represents. Can we conserve the perspective of transforming the social relations of production? Do we want to insert the dynamic of popular power in the capacity of the employee, the student, the indigenous woman or the Afro-descendant peasant and all the subaltern sectors to take power in hand and exercise it democratically? Today, García Linera – a brilliant intellectual – is situated, from the fact of his position as vice-president, more in the context of the state constituted power than in that of the construction of the communal and trade union form, which he himself defended for years as a heterodox Marxist sociologist in the Comuna group (a very fecund group of Bolivian intellectuals). A little while ago, I attended one of his lectures at the former national congress in Santiago, Chile. García Linera gave the speech of a statesman, a figure of government, identifying the state 'as art and supreme form of politics'. In fact, he said it several times. Unlike his writings on indigenous and trade union struggles, he defended the Bolivian popular (pluri-national) state and Andean-Amazonian developmentalism, rather to the detriment of the notion and the conquest of post-capitalism and post-extractivism.

BS: If we examine how the Argentinian Miguel Mazzeo refers to popular power in his books, we could indicate that he sees it rather as 'performative' political praxis, anticipating in basis and form the construction of the society of tomorrow, anti-capitalist and socialist. What do you think of this line of argument?

FG: I think that this idea of experimentation here and now is very important and that inside the revolutionary Marxist left, we have forgotten it, or we have not known how to practice it. Today, it is urgent to recover the 'hope principle' to which Ernst Bloch referred and to proclaim our desire for 'concrete utopias': we need to demonstrate by praxis and not only announce it learnedly, to theorise it or demonstrate it, that another world is not only indispensable but also possible. The challenge is to take on today what we could begin to construct tomorrow, on other scales. Hence the importance of occupation-recuperation of sites of work and production, to show that the worker can democratically carry out production, as has taken place in several hundred enterprises in South America today. To show also – with the Zapatistas of Chiapas – that we can reject the authoritarian state and at the same times construct the 'snails', stress that in other countries we can create alternative and community-based means of communication or again demonstrate that we can re-appropriate educational spaces and practice popular education and so on. These concrete demonstrations, which sometimes we have depreciated a little because they have not been concretized by an immediate or conscious perceptive of dualisation of power or of 'taking of power' are nonetheless fundamental. They are both 'prefigurative' and performative. They allow us to practice, to get it wrong, to know ourselves, to see all the difficulties which are before us, our weaknesses, our strengths and our collective potentialities. These spaces can help us go further, to accumulate forces without cutting ourselves off from the popular classes and steer us towards global struggles against the state, capital, militarism, patriarchy. Hence the interest of Miguel Mazzeo's reflections on popular power as means and as end, as road and objective of the emancipation in construction, that as not according to a simple 'utilitarian' logic at the service of a party of professional revolutionary cadres, nor by following the tyranny of enclosure in the impotence of localised micro-powers.

The invitation is then to the constitution of a popular power built from below, from the workplace, the neighbourhood and the rural community, from production and territory, but which aspires also to combat the hegemony of the dominant, their state, their culture and their laws on a general level. A dialectical thought between the below and the above of social transformation is the key, this appears very basic to say this, above all if we reread the classics of critical thought, but – to a certain extent– this political compass has become lost in the ideological fog of the 1990s and faced with the modes of essentialised autonomism and, its opposite, the social liberal or 'progressive' official governmental vision. The two trends coexist and respond to each other in the global and Latin American lefts. We should seek to avoid the dichotomy between a movement of the 'indignant' without political organisation or programme and the uncritical defence of reasons of state by the functionaries of the ministries and the organic intellectuals of social liberalism or 'light' progressivism. A vast programme? Certainly, but the stakes are considerable.

BS: But what then could be the relationship between the experiences of popular power and left institutional expressions? Are the former necessarily located outside the dispute on institutional transformation or are they related to it? Is popular power a form of institutional transformation? How do you relink the notion of popular power to elements like left governments, parties, trade unions?

FG: This debate has traversed the whole of Latin America and the European horizons, just like the movement of the indignant or *Occupy Wall Street* in the USA. The debate on tools is an old debate, still before us, above all henceforth with Syriza in Greece and Podemos in Spain, after 15 years of a 'left turn in Latin America': party and/or movement? Elections and/or social struggles? And what type of movements to construct and what type of parties? How to conquer government by the ballot box without losing one's soul and keeping one's promises? The discussion on the state is also a great theme, just like that on violence: what do you make of armed force? How is the violence of those from above and those from below exercised? That goes together with the exchange of ideas around power and its definitions. A rich reflection on the relationship between 'might' (potentia) and 'power' (potestas) inaugurated by John Holloway and Raúl Zibechi in Latin America and which has taken place also in France with Daniel Bensaïd, Michael Löwy, Philippe Corcuff and others in the review *Contretemps*[381], as well as with the intellectuals collaborating with the review *Herramienta* (Argentina) under the direction of Aldo Casas. These are essential problems. With a sometimes fetishistic vision of the social and a somewhat abusive over-generalisation of Zapatismo, Holloway argues that it is necessary to create the potentia and reject the potestas, that we need to create rebellions outside the state to better fissure it. In another register, Raul Zibechi – basing himself on the observation of struggles like El Alto (Bolivia) after 2000 or the Commune of Oaxaca – sees more the need to resist in the 'interstices' of the state and the 'crevasses' of the system, to 'dissolve' and even 'disperse' it. This author, an activist in many popular collectives, has an original and creative approach to the emancipations and mobilisations in Latin America, forcefully raisin the territory-self-government-autonomy trilogy. In his observation-action of several collectives on the continent, he succeeds in highlighting common elements and key ideas, including the territorial rooting of the movements and the space where the community is created; autonomy as form of organisation faced with the clientelist practices of the state and parties; the cultural component and the decolonising identities of the struggles; the essential role of women; the relationship with nature and the environment. But, like Michael Löwy and others, I continue to believe that it is not enough to think only from the crevasses of the system or a hypothetical 'dissolution' of the state: any politics of emancipation must finally combine potentia and potestas, social movements and forms of political organisations, centralisation and assemblies. To check and defeat the reactionary forces or the domination of the bourgeoisie, hostile to change, it remains indispensable to organising, attaining minimum levels of institutionalisation and including plebeian violence against the dominant. Any life in society has standardised or institutionalised spaces, conventions and rules of functioning – a trade union is an institutionalised space, a collective always has an organic or 'bureaucratic' level. How could a massive movement of emancipation which claims to 'change the world', society, the state, not have them? As argued in Antoine Artous's book, *Marx, l'État et la politique*,[382] the thousand Marxisms today must transcend the 'mythology' of a possible rapid disappearance of the state and the installation of a direct democracy in an ideal society free of conflicts, distributing goods 'to each according to their needs'. A critical reading of the young Marx and a certain under-estimation of the legal moment of emancipation, at the same time as the authoritarian disasters of the 20th century, oblige us to (re)think democracy and the affirmation of politics (and its institutional mediations) as specific and key moment. We cannot dissolve or 'drown' the political in the social, just as we cannot cease to reflect on the future institutionalised forms of a possible self-managing democracy, accompanied by its fundamental rights and indispensable forms of popular representation (single chamber, constituent assemblies and assemblies of social movements, mechanisms of control from below and of recall of mandates, end of the professionalisation of politics and rotation of elected representatives, forms of participation and popular deliberation, universal and proportional voting rights, and so on).

At the end of the day, Chiapas and Zapatismo have not 'dissolved' the state. They have created new institutional forms, based on common goods, community autonomy and self-government, as explained by the studies of the anthropologist Jérôme Baschet. Holloway is completely right to stress this advance and its creativity faced with any dogmatisms. So, agreed: emancipation also consists in emancipating oneself from the state, but as Atilio Borón recognises in his harsh critiques of Holloway's theories, the ideal would be to create from today a democratic society without the state – as Marx said in his studies on the Paris Commune and the civil war in France. Nonetheless, faced with the global emergency of the capitalist disaster in which we find ourselves and at a few steps from a planetary ecological collapse, we have to think of 'emergency' forms of transition, have a concrete tactical programme and a strategic agenda which does not *proclaim* the 'dissolution' of the bourgeois state, but allows in the long term: a construction with successive ruptures, in 'permanent revolution' as Trotsky would say, towards a libertarian self-managed democracy, a world which houses all the worlds (a Zapatista slogan). How to elaborate together this long term of post-capitalist, post-developmentalist and post-patriarchal emancipation? There are no set rules.

It is however urgent to propose non-bureaucratic and non-authoritarian paths to radically democratise the institutional field and, at the same time, 'revolutionise' society, so that all can take and transform power, without being taken by power as Besancenot puts it. This could be the road of a democracy of self-managed communes, based effectively on individual liberty and collective autonomy, self-determination and the full political participation of free men and women, the redistribution of emancipated labour from the yoke of capital and with the right to leisure, culture, sexual diversity, respecting nature and so on. But – and here I cite Bensaïd – in this discussion on 'from nothing becomes all' (*Communist Manifesto*), it is necessary to avoid the short cuts of anti-politics, anti-power, 'the illusion of the social' which are still very strong in certain collectives. What are our tools to confront imperialism, the multinationals, the oligarchies, the patriarchy, the coups d'état like in Chile in 1973 or in April 2002 in Caracas, the 'soft' destabilisation and the manipulations orchestrated by the global media enterprises? We can resist this only by local self-management and diverse experiences of 'might'? No, certainly not. That is what is under discussion in certain spaces of critical Chavismo in Venezuela or in collectives like Pueblo en Marcha in Argentina. As Daniel Bensaïd says, parties and political movements can serve as 'strategic accelerator' so as to favour collective reflection, avoid the collection of egos or specific interest, also rein in the phenomenon of caudillismo or Bonapartism. This, without fetishism of the party or cult of the leader, by assuming and criticising the bureaucratic or electoralist risk, by imposing strict measures of control of leaderships: recall referendums, parity of gender and rotation of mandates, to do away with vanguardism, 'machism-leninism' and authoritarianism inside our own organisations. And there we must also humbly recognise that the Europeans have nothing to teach, nor offer Latin Americans, very much to the contrary! It is rather the on-going experiences of the continent that should critically inspire the European lefts.

As the Venezuelan sociologist Edgardo Lander puts it, the coming challenges of transformation consist in seeking alternatives beyond capitalism, developmentalism and the (post-)colonial/liberal state. And in this, we need to draw essential lessons from the past century and the traumatic Stalinist experience. I quote:

> The struggle to build a post-capitalist society in the 21st century – what could be called the society of well-being or 21st century socialism – particularly in the South American context, must needs respond to the challenges and demands which go far beyond the imaginaries of social transformation of the last two centuries, and more especially those of the socialism of past centuries. An alternative to capitalism and liberal democracy, in this context, must necessarily be a radical alternative to the socialism of the 20th century. I refer to three basic questions characterising these societies: their blind confidence in progress and the productive forces of capitalism, their mono-cultural character and their severe limitations

in the area of democracy... A post-capitalist society of the 21st century must necessarily be more democratic than capitalist society. It is about, as Boaventura de Sousa Santos put it, the democratic construction of a democratic society. If we present the idea of 21st century socialism as a new, radically democratic experience, which incorporates and celebrates the diversity of the human cultural experience and the ability to build a harmony with all the existing forms of life on the planet, we need to make a profound critique of this historical experience of the 20th century. (Lander, 2013)

In summary, Lander offers a radical perspective from Latin America calling us (according to a Mariateguist optic of the 21st century) to the construction of an Info-Afro-Latin-American eco-socialism. It is about demanding to live well, understanding that a:

reorganisation of all modes of production and consumption is necessary, based on criteria external to the capitalist market: the real needs of the population and the defence of the ecological balance. That means an economy of transition to ecological socialism, where the population itself – and not the 'laws of the market' or an authoritarian political bureau – decides, by a process of democratic planning, priorities and investments. This transition would lead not only to a new mode of production and a more egalitarian society, more solidarity-based and more democratic, but also to an alternative mode of life, a new eco-socialist civilisation, beyond the kingdom of money and the infinite production of useless commodities.[383]

Undoubtedly, more than ever, to attain this 'new civilisation', we must invent, experiment, fight, think and again dream to 'create, create popular power'. But at a time of global crisis of capitalism and the threat of ecocide for all human beings, Latin America could be the laboratory continent for the construction of alternatives for the 21st century.

Bibliography

A. Acosta, 'El correísmo: un Nuevo modelo de dominación burgesa', *SinPermiso*, 2013.
A. Artous, *Marx, l'État et la politique*, Paris, Syllepse, 1999.
J. Baschet, *Adieux au capitalisme. Autonomie, société du bien vivre et multiplicité des mondes*, La Paris, Découverte, 2014.
D. Bensaïd, 'La Révolution sans prendre le pouvoir ? À propos d'un récent livre de

John Holloway', *ContreTemps*, Paris, February 2003.

D. Bensaïd, *Le Sourire du spectre. Nouvel esprit du communisme*, Paris, Éditions Michalon, 2000.

D. Bensaïd, *Clases, plebes, multitudes*, Caracas, El Perro y la Rana, 2005.

F. Betto, 'América Latina: Impasses de los gobiernos progresistas', *Revista América Latina en Movimiento,* No. 500, December 2014.

E. Bloch, *Le principe espérance*, 3 vol., Paris, Gallimard, 1976, 1982, 1991.

A. Borón, *Aristóteles en Macondo: notas sobre democracia, poder y revolución en América Latina*, Valparaíso, Construyendo América, 2013.

B. Dangl, *Dancing with Dynamite: Social Movements and States in Latin America*, Oakland, AK Press, 2010.

P. Dávalos, *La Democracia disciplinaria. El proyecto postneoliberal para América Latina*, Santiago, Editorial Quimantú, 2013.

F. Fuentes, 'Cuando el árbol del 'antiextractivismo' no deja ver el bosque', *Rebelión*, 2014.

Á. García Linera, *Las Tensiones creativas de la Revolución*, La Paz, Vicepresidencia del Estado Plurinacional de Bolivia, 2011.

F. Gaudichaud, 'Venezuela : 'La question aujourd'hui est de savoir comment freiner la violente offensive de la droite néolibérale', Interview with Valeria Ianni, Revista *La Llamarada*, 2014.

F. Gaudichaud, *Chili (1970-1973). Mille jours qui firent trembler le monde*, Rennes, PUR, 2013.

F. Gaudichaud (ed.), *Amériques Latines. Emancipations en contruction*, Paris, Syllepse, 2013.

F. Gaudichaud (ed.), *Le Volcan latino-américain. Gauches, mouvements sociaux et néolibéralisme au sud du rio Bravo*, Paris, Textuel, 2008.

E. Gudynas, 'Estado compensador y nuevos extractivismos', *Nueva Sociedad*, 2012.

M. Harnecker, *Amérique latine. Laboratoire pour un socialisme du XXIe siècle,* Paris, Editions Utopia, 2010.

J. Holloway, *Changer le monde sans prendre le pouvoir*, Paris, Syllepse/Lux2008, (*Change the World without taking power*, London, Pluto, 2002)

J. Holloway, *Contra y más allá del Capital. Reflexiones a partir del debate sobre el libro 'Cambiar el mundo sin tomar el poder'*, Buenos Aires, Universidad Autónoma de Puebla, México/Ediciones Herramienta, 2006 (*In, Against, and Beyond Capitalism*, Los Angeles, PM Press, 2016)

J. Holloway, *Agrietar el capitalismo. El hacer contra el trabajo*, Buenos Aires, Ediciones Herramienta, 2011.

C. Katz, *El porvenir del socialismo*, Buenos Aires, Herramienta – Imago Mundi, 2004.

E. Laclau, *La razón populista*, Buenos Aires, Fondo de Cultura Económica, 2005 (*On Populist Reason*, London, Verso, 2005)

E. Lander (y otros), *Promesas en su laberinto. Cambios y continuidades en los gobiernos progresistas de América latina*, La Paz, IEE, CEDLA, CIM, 2013.

V. Lenin, *State and Revolution, 1917*.

M. Löwy, *Écosocialisme: L'alternative radicale à la catastrophe écologique capitaliste*, Paris, Fayard/Mille et une nuits, 2011.

D. Machado et al. (ed.), *El correísmo al desnudo*, Quito, Editorial Montecristi, 2013.

K. Marx, *The civil war in France,* 1871.

M. Mazzeo, *Introducción al poder popular. 'El sueño de una cosa'*, Santiago, Tiempo Robado editoras, 2014.

M. Massimo, 'Revoluciones pasivas en América Latina. Una aproximación gramsciana a la caracterización de los gobiernos progresistas de inicio de siglo' in M. Modonesi (coord.), *Horizontes gramscianos. Estudios en torno al pensamiento de Antonio Gramsci*, México, FCPyS-UNAM, 2013.

F. Nahuel Martín and M. Mosquera, '¿Qué organización para qué estrategia? Poder popular, herramienta política y estrategia socialista', *Democracia Socialista*, March 2014.

O. Acha (and others), *Reflexiones sobre el poder popular*, Santiago, Tiempo robado editoras, 2014.

P. Pozzi, *Partido revolucionario de los trabajadores – ERP*, Concepción, Escaparate, 2013.

J. Rancière, *La haine de la démocratie*, Paris, La Fabrique, 2005.

I. Rauber, *Revoluciones desde abajo: gobiernos populares y cambio social en Latinoamérica*, Buenos Aires, Ediciones Contin Rauber ente-Peña Lillo, 2012.

F. Ramírez, 'Mucho más que dos izquierdas', *Nueva Sociedad*, '*América latina en tiempos de Chávez*', 2006.

R. Regalado, *La Izquierda latinoamericana en el gobierno: ¿Alternativa o reciclaje?*, Cuba, OceanSur, 2012.

P. Salama, *Economies émergentes latino-américaines. Entre cigales et fourmis*, Paris, Armand Colin, 2012.

G. Salazar, *En el nombre del poder popular constituyente (Chile, siglo XXI)*, Santiago, LOM, 2011.

P. Stefanoni, 'La lulización de la izquierda latinoamericana', *Le Monde Diplomatique*, Buenos Aires, May 2014.

M. Svampa, 'Consenso de los commodities, giro ecoterritorial y pensamiento crítico en América Latina', *Observatorio Social de América Latina*, Buenos Aires, CLACSO, N. 32, 2012.

M. Le Quang and T. Vercoutère, *Ecosocialismo y Buen Vivir. Diálogo entre dos alternativas al capitalismo*, Quito, IAEN, 2013.

L. Vitale, 'El marxismo latinoamericano ante dos desafíos : feminismo y crisis ecológica', *Nueva Sociedad*, 1983.

R. Zibechi, *Progre-sismo. La domesticación de los conflictos sociales,* Santiago, Quimantú, 2010.

R. Zibechi, *Dispersar el poder: los movimientos como poderes antiestatales*, Santiago, Quimantú, 2008.

Eastern Europe: revisiting the ambiguous revolutions of 1989*

Catherine Samary

Twenty years after the fall of the Berlin Wall, Timothy Garton Ash wrote that 'in 1989, Europeans proposed a new model of non-violent, velvet revolution.'[384] Some years earlier, instead, he has used an interesting neologism – 'refolution'[385] – to describe the kind of systemic changes that had occurred, combining features of revolutions and of reforms from above. I want here to support and develop the neologism against the 'pure' epithet, as being more accurate to analyse the very ambiguities of the historical transformations that put an end to the 'bipolar world'. I will argue, that the mobilised democratic movements, which occurred before 1989, were both against the ruling *nomenklatura* and not in favour of the main socio-economic transformations introduced since 1989. It is necessary to look behind labels and ideological discourses to take into full account the role of 'bipolar' international 'deals' still at work in 1989, but also the role taken by leading figures of the former single party in opaque forms of privatisations: that means the lack of any real democratic procedure of decision making about the main reforms which have had plenty of counter-revolutionary substance. Popular aspirations were expressed massively in revolutionary upsurges against the single party and Soviet domination like the Polish Solidarność movement in 1980-1. And this movement was closer to the Prague autumn of workers councils in 1968 against the Soviet occupation, than to the 1989 neoliberal shock therapies. Those embryonic revolutions towards a third way were repressed and dismantled by the bipolar world's dominant forces through different episodes, because the mobilised democratic forces were an alternative to the existing political order which tried to impose its own end, a reality hidden by Cold War concepts and the transformation that followed 1989.

* This contribution was first published as a chapter in *From Perestroika to Rainbow Revolution*, Vicken Cheterian ed., London, C. Hurst & Co, 2013. This version has been slightly edited with some additional notes.

The 20th anniversary of the fall of the Berlin Wall in 1989 has been a particular opportunity for many countries to commemorate that historical event, leading to systemic changes up to the end of the Soviet Union in 1991. In spite of different scenarios in Eastern Europe, 1989 has been described as 'year of revolutions'. Timothy Garton Ash stresses how different those 'revolutions' were from the usual violent 'model' of such radical changes elsewhere: 'in 1989, Europeans proposed a new model of non-violent, velvet revolution'.[386] But the specificities are probably elsewhere.

Ideological bias of Cold War concepts

Without engaging here in semantic debates or accepting rigid 'models' or norms, one can certainly reject the reductionist identification of revolutions with organic violence. And we can reasonably take for granted that this notion covers two interlinked features and meanings: a broad popular (social) mobilisation against fundamental aspects of an existing system on the one hand, and on the other hand the result of those movements, that is getting rid of the ruling structures and dominant social forces of the system and introducing new ones with symbolic and ideological dimensions. Even if gaps (disillusionment) always exist between the popular hopes and demands and the accomplished changes, the 'revolutions' express an organic link between both aspects: that is mass movements being needed for radical changes. It is rather obvious that the use of the term 'revolutions' in liberal-oriented milieus and media to characterise the 1989 historical turn associates popular (democratic) rejection of the repressive dictatorships with what is described as 'the end of communism'. In so doing, a democratic legitimacy is given to the changes and four implicit equations are established: the former rule of Communist parties (CPs) are equated with 'communism'; popular rejection of those past bureaucratic and repressive regimes is identified with demands for the political and socio-economic changes introduced after 1989, as part of the neoliberal capitalist globalisation; the latter is identified with democracy; and all opponents of the past (communist) regimes are identified with anti-communists. Those dominant equations are all but convincing.

As a matter of facts, labels were and are still confusing, especially 'socialism' and 'communism' which cover, first, ideals of a non oppressive society without classes and aiming at the satisfaction of human needs through their individual and collective direct full responsibilities. This does not give a 'model' but only principles and aims that are shared by those who still believe in that 'concrete utopia'. It includes in their thoughts the means to go towards these ends, and a critical approach to all experiences, including those which claimed to be socialists. The second meaning of those worlds covers systems or parties as concrete historical formations, having adopted

EASTERN EUROPE: REVISITING THE AMBIGUOUS REVOLUTIONS OF 1989   281

those labels at a certain moment of their history, and developed concrete institutional 'models'. Inside or outside those systems or parties, individuals or movements can criticise the concrete model or experience because of its distance from the ideals. The main historical reasons for the gap between ideals and reality, and the resulting ideological ambiguities and confusion behind labels lies on the one hand with the international evolution of 'socialist parties' towards integration in the capitalist world order and more recently towards its neoliberal variants, and on the other hand the Stalinisation and more generally the bureaucratisation of the 'socialist revolutions' of the 20th century, and since the 1980s the role played by many ex-communists (or even, in China, still 'communists') in the process of privatisation and insertion in the capitalist world order. The classical 'right' and 'left' divisions are themselves often opaque.

I will not deal here with the conceptual debates which have divided – and still divide – even Marxists themselves about how to characterise the Soviet Union and its sister countries.[387] The main crises and social upsurges within the former 'communist' societies and the concrete process of their transformation since 1989 convinced me that 'pure' concepts to characterise them (either 'socialist' or 'capitalist', or 'new class') cannot permit to grasp their main contradictions – namely, the historical context of the 1980s leading at the end of that decade to a specific turn of large parts of the bureaucratic apparatus of the Communist parties' (CPs) bureaucratic apparatus towards insertion in the world capitalist system, and the popular ambivalent feelings and specific conflicting relations to those states/parties – which played a key role in the opacities of the capitalist restoration. Those parties were ruling on behalf of the workers (which meant a non-capitalist and paternalist form of social protection) – but at their expense (repressing all autonomous movements of the workers). Considering those parties as classical political bodies is obviously wrong. But reducing them to the (real) feature of state apparatus denies any historical and political influence on their way of functioning, and the role the socialist ideology which they used to legitimate themselves. This is also reductionist, one-sided and misleading.

The same dual aspects lies behind the analysis of the kind of bureaucratic 'social ownership' which characterised – under different variants, including decentralised self management – the former regimes claiming to be socialist. They suppressed private property as a dominant feature not in limited circumstances but as a 'constitutive' and ideological factor that limited the domination of market in such a way that the money could not play the role of 'capital' (money invested to 'make money', that is profit). The party/state *nomenklatura* managed the economy, but did not own shares and could not transform its privileges of power, consumption and management into real ownership rights that could be transmitted to heirs: the official (legal) 'real owners' were the workers (every one and no one in particular) or even the 'entire people'. But all that also meant there were neither the right to carry out economic lay-off nor to enter into bankruptcy procedures. The right to strike was forbidden (the workers would not strike against themselves, said the regime). And the trade unions were the transmission belt of the decisions of the party, not organs of defence for workers. But the way the labour force was stabilised in big factories was through the distribution of increasing 'social income' under the form of flats, products, health care or childcare services associated with jobs – and a 'good attitude'. The dominant, paternalist and repressive role of the party prevented any independent and consistent power of decision making for the workers, but the single party was ruling on behalf of socialist ideals and claiming to implement them. The 'socialist' legitimation of the regimes was established through a high level of social protection, ideological praise of the labour force's creation of the wealth, and relatively high 'egalitarianism'.

The party's strength would have been reduced if it was only an apparatus. The integration from rank and file members of the party, and in its broad 'mass organisations', of the 'best' socialist workers and intellectuals was both a mean to channel, control and if 'necessary' repress their initiative and to give a legitimacy or a 'social basis' to the regime. The popularity of the official ideology was reflected by ambiguous relationships: dominant trends of resistance and alternative movements have been, consciously or *de facto*, aimed at reducing the gap between the official socialist ideals and the reality. Many rank and file members of these CPs simply tried to implement those ideals which were popular. That is also why so many party members were involved in the huge upsurges that occurred in 1956 in Poland or Hungary, in 1968 in Czechoslovakia and Yugoslavia, or even in the Polish Solidarność, in 1980-1. But all of them suffered repression by the ruling apparatus as it feared the loss of its privileged position of power and control.[388]

All this cannot be analysed without going behind the dominant labels. As already stated the former 'communist' party/state was of course not a real political party (e.g. there was no right for alternative tendencies, no real and free votes in congresses). But it combined different features: an apparatus with bureaucrats having privileges of power; but also a set of mass organisations attached to the party, among which the cultural ones played a kind of political role with a fair amount of critical approaches. In spite of Stalinisation (even analysed not only as deformation but as a kind of counter-revolution within the revolution[389]) the regime continued to use a socialist ideology to legitimise itself both nationally and internationally (within the anti-capitalist and anti-colonialist social, trade-union, political scene). In the period of real 'catching up' (up to the 1970s) with a high extensive growth of production and improvement of standards of living, these regimes could be perceived as an alternative to capitalism, and an improvement in the global balance of forces for those who resisted imperialist colonial policies. But the Stalinisation of the Soviet Union had also transformed it into yet another 'great power' wanting to control its 'sister countries' as much as its own workers.

Membership in these parties in power could be sought for a broad range of (changing) motivations, ranging from cynical use of the party card to get privileges to sincere communist and anti-imperialist convictions. The practical choice to try and reduce the gap between the official ideology and the reality included both explicit involvement in intellectual and popular anti-bureaucratic criticisms and upsurges, and simple daily promotion of horizontal fraternal relationships and activities. In between, there were all those without sophisticated ideologies who were born into the system and were looking for positive aims and concrete gains for themselves and the people around them by using the rules and with a little help of the party card – so long as such gains did exist. Ideological bias and Cold War concepts provide limited complex objective sociological and political analysis about these specific conflicting societies.[390] The relationships between these regimes and their populations have generally been presented in black and white – from both sides of the bi-polar world.

The Stalinised Soviet Union behaved as a 'great power' dealing with (in Yalta) or conflicting with (during the Cold War) other 'great powers' over the back of 'fraternal regimes' and people. The Yugoslav Communist regime (called 'Titoist' from the name of his leader, Josip Broz known as 'Tito') was 'excommunicated' in 1948 by the Kremlin. This meant absolute isolation, political and physical repression of all links with the Yugoslav regime within the international Communist movements (especially in Hungary, Poland, Czekoslovakia). After Stalin's death, Khrushchev came to Belgrade in 1955, and made apologies and promises to respect different socialist 'models'. But in spite of that (and of the hope of a 'de-Stalinisation' of the Soviet Union at the 20th Congress of the CPSU where 'K' denounced Stalin's crimes and the Gulag), Moscow continued – in 1956 in Hungary and in 1968 in Czechoslovakia – to slander and repress alternative socialist movements and figures by fear of uncontrolled democratic dynamics. Past official communist movements supporting the Soviet Union as the motherland of socialism censored and repressed as 'anti-communists' all of its opponents. And, in general, that included all movements or individuals who criticised the gaps between socialist ideals and the reality who were looking for a 'socialism with human face'. Social gains introduced by these regimes were supposed to 'prove' their socialist reality; but they were in fact far from real social rights because autonomous activities and initiatives which they could have de facto stimulated, were under the control and repressed by an apparatus which wanted to keep its monopoly of power.

Anti-communist ideologies at the time were too pleased to identify these regimes with any kind of communist ideals as such, and to reduce communism to the repressive aspect of the Soviet reality. Like new official 'democratic' (pro-market) regimes – especially when dominated by former members of the communist *nomenklatura* – they tended to deny or (now) suppress recognition of any progressive gains from those past regimes, which are reduced to Gulag. The whole short 'Soviet century' is now presented as an artificial parenthesis in a European history and civilisation which is only 'western' and supposed (wrongly) to have been unified in the past: the slogan 'return to Europe' is heard as very arrogant and ignorant for the majority of these populations.

There was a paradoxical convergence of Cold War approaches (defending the communist regimes or cursing them) in claiming that the former societies were 'communists' and therefore all opponents, or simply critical citizens could only be anti-communists dissidents. The reality was certainly otherwise: different kind of political currents and aspirations existed, including in period of crisis of the former systems. But it remains to analyse what aspirations and dynamics were dominant, which we will try to do in the last part of this text. Hence '1989', or more broadly the different national scenarios and phases of crisis and changes in the Eastern European countries is an issue at stake in alternative interpretations and memories.[391]

Popular demand for individual and collective freedoms in past (or present – in Cuba or China) 'communist regimes' do not 'belong' to a particular current. They were expressed in broad fronts in 1989 and before then, as in Czechoslovakia in the dissident movement called Charter 77 or the Civic Forum it established in 1989 where Communists and anti-communists individuals coexisted and fought together for their freedoms. Similar demands were put forward in democratic upsurges against single party dictatorship and the Kremlin's domination, in 1956 in Poland and Hungary, 1968 in Czechoslovakia and Yugoslavia, 1980-1 in Poland. So the very question of continuities and discontinuities between those democratic upsurges and 1989 are at the core of conflicting views. That is the very question I will discuss at the end of this text.

International factors and Cold War deals before 1989

The opening of archives and commemorations of 1989 in 2009 leave no doubt about the key importance of international hesitations and 'deals' in a specific context around the issue of Germany. But although 1989 was a 'turning point', it was neither a sudden 'event' nor a pre-conceived and controlled scenario. We have briefly to go back to the 1970s, to remind ourselves of a crucial period of crises and changes in the international capitalist world order, while the neo-Stalinised world became itself more and more fragile.

From the stagnation of the 1970s and the arm race to the fall of the Berlin Wall

The 1970s had been dominated in Eastern Europe by the freezing of internal reforms. Whatever had been their limits, these reforms were aimed at increasing a certain degree of decentralisation (in general at the benefit of managers, but in Yugoslavia with increasing workers rights of self management) and some market pressure to reduce bureaucratic waste. Their main contradictions were socio-economic and political: on the one hand they increased inequalities and instability according to market pressure – which was rejected by workers as contradictory to egalitarian values and by conservative sectors of the bureaucracy who feared to lose their domination. On the other hand, precisely in order to overcome social resistances, the reformist wings of the apparatus opened the doors to more freedoms – but then, social and intellectual movements from below would develop without respecting the limits of the reforms of the single party regime: this was illustrated by the development of spontaneous workers councils in 1956 in Poland and Hungary, demands for 'self-management from top to bottom' and self-managed planning opposing the market reforms and the 'red bourgeoisie' in Yugoslavia in June 1968, and all features of a 'socialism with human face' like in the Prague Spring and Autumn of workers councils (to which we will come back at the end of this text).

So the reforms were blocked after repressive episodes, and the intervention of the Warsaw Pact tanks in Prague. But a new decade of relative growth (by comparison with western countries) occurred based on increasing credits and imports in some key Eastern European countries. This opened the floodgates to western products in order to modernise their economies and so respond to consumer aspirations of the population. The rather high rate of growth in the South and in the East by comparison with the 'stagflation' in the core capitalist countries was attractive for western banks: they increased their international loans, looking to use in a profitable way the deposits they had received in dollars from Arab countries after the oil price hikes.

The 1970s had also been a decade of relative 'stagnation' in the Soviet Union when the Kosygin's reforms had been pushed back and the old guard around Leonid Brezhnev clamped down. It was therefore a period of high social protection both for workers and for the bureaucrats in power but of slowing down of productivity and growth.

At the end of that decade, the Soviet intervention in Afghanistan opened up the last phase of the Cold War and of the arms race with a radically different effect in the two parts of the bipolar world. The huge military expenses and foreign borrowing legitimised by the 'Star Wars' programme against the 'communist danger' helped the new US President Ronald Reagan to relaunch the US economy (with a considerable budget deficit) and begin to re-establish the deteriorating hegemony of the US. The 'neoliberal' turn in Britain in 1979 under Margaret Thatcher and in the US in 1980 with Ronald Reagan turned out to be a counter-offensive against all systems, programmes and labour rights which, after the Second World War under the pressure of the bipolar competition, had reduced inequalities, promoted the welfare state and protected the labour force from market competition. The technological revolution was mobilised in order to reorganise the productive space and dismantle trade union bastions or other forms of collective capacities of negotiation. Meanwhile, the free flow of capital and suppression of social and national protections required the imposition of generalised market competition under the new rules of US-led international financial institutions. The debt crisis (in the post-colonial countries of the 'South' and in some Eastern European countries) became the central vector of 'conditional credits' and policies of 'structural adjustment' aimed at opening these societies to generalised privatisation and competition – what has been called the 'Washington consensus'.

The arm race weighted heavily on the USSR – unlike the US: military expenditure caused a drain in other areas of the budget, in particular spending on infrastructure and Soviet industrial equipment, which were fast becoming obsolete. And during the very same period, relations at the heart of the Comecon (Council for Mutual Economic Assistance) became strained by years of foreign borrowing in hard currencies that were without precedent in many of the key Eastern European countries: Poland, Yugoslavia, Romania, Hungary and East Germany.

The increase in interest rates in the United States (with a radical monetarist policy) at the beginning of the 1980s provoked a chain reaction on the variable interest rates of those international credits contracted from private banks. This increased suddenly the level of the debts in Eastern European countries (as well as in the South) while reimbursement through exports was difficult in the context of the slowdown in world growth and the weak competitiveness of their products.

The response of the Communist parties in power in Eastern Europe to this debt crisis differed. In Poland, the Gierek government decided on a price increase for consumer goods that produced the explosion of strikes leading to the establishment of the first independent trade union (with some ten millions workers) in Eastern Europe, Solidarność (Solidarity). After its first and last democratic congress, martial law was imposed by the (communist) General Jaruzelski followed by nearly a decade of repression and absolute fall in production up to 1989.

In Romania, President Ceausescu imposed the repayment of the entire debt over the course of the 1980s, through a violent dictatorship enforced against his own people. His peers were in favour of trying to keep their own power, while making the dictator pay for his unpopularity, by way of his assassination during a pseudo 'revolution' at the turn of the 1990s.

In Yugoslavia, the 1980s were marked by the paralysis of central institutions, which were incapable of making people accept the federal policies of repayment of a debt that was opposed by both workers and the republics. Soaring inflation reached triple figures and multiple resistances was expressed through thousands of scattered strikes combined with an increase in nationalist tensions. The widening of the gap between the republics, which had become the real centres of decision making since the decentralising reforms of the 1960s, and the disintegration of solidarity foreshadowed the break-up of the federation. The last Yugoslav government of Ante Marković, tried to impulse a radical liberal shock therapy and transformation of social ownership in 1989, but he was confronted by different republican nationalist strategies and the decision of the richest republics to leave the sinking boat while nation-wide bureaucracies were trying to consolidate a 'nation state' able to control the appropriation of wealth and as large a stretch of territory as possible...

In Hungary, the Communist leadership was the only one that tried to repay the debt by selling the best businesses to foreign capital as early as the 1980s. In the context of the Gorbachev's signs of 'disengagement', they bargained the opening of their borders to Austria in September 1989 (in return for financial compensations), making the fall of the Berlin Wall unavoidable.

But the key indebted country was the GDR, the German Democratic Republic, whose increasing imports from the West had been encouraged by Moscow during the 1970s, as a way to oppose US-led prohibition of technological export to the Soviet Union. Honecker's GDR was in fact 'released' from November 1987 by Gorbachev, who hoped that agreeing to get rid of such an unpopular regime and the Wall – and perhaps accepting a unification of Germany – could be the best solution for his own policy. It was hoped that German subsidies would help the repatriation of the Soviet army, reduce the cost of the arms race and allow concentration on internal reforms, while the Soviet withdrawal would stop the western embargo on credit and facilitate the import of new technologies. Gorbachev's tone was that of 'peaceful coexistence' and no longer that of the Khrushchev's regime in 1956, aiming to catch up with capitalism by 1980.

From this point on, the USSR wished to disengage from its essential international politics of political-economic aid notably in Cuba and Nicaragua, in order to go ahead with the new international 'deals'. But the USSR also wanted its sister countries in the framework of the Comecon to pay back their debts in products – and was more and more interested in turning its exports of oil and gas towards those countries which paid in hard currencies. Yelstin pushed forward the logic behind the dissolution of the USSR, which enabled the Russian Federation to ask the new independent states to pay in hard currency for their energy imports.

Behind the scene, financial deals with the Hungarian regime (to open the first holes in the 'Wall') and Moscow (to accept the unification) were associated with Gorbatchev's popular visits in Germany – and his orders to the East German security services not to repress popular demonstrations. But his idea was to propose the dismantling of both NATO and Warsaw Pact coalitions. He shared with Mitterrand a project of 'a common European house' based on a peaceful coexistence and reforms in both parts of Europe – along some kind of Council of Europe and Helsinki agreements like those which were in the 'Paris Charter'.[392]

The dynamic of German unification was determined by Chancellor Kohl's decision, supported by the US, to establish a monetary union. The exchange rate (one to one) was a disaster for the East German economy but attractive in the short term for its population. Such an absorption/destruction of the GDR was far from the initial discussions Gorbachev had held with Kohl about a new constitution for both parts of Germany. Mitterrand's French government made all possible efforts to integrate the unified Germany within the European construction (with the Maastricht Treaty and its rigid monetarist approach a condition for convincing the Bundesbank to leave the DM). But for the US administration, NATO was the stake – Germany had to be in, and NATO had to be maintained and expanded in spite of the Warsaw Pact's dissolution in 1991.

During the 1990s, the US used the Bosnian and then Kosovo issues (in the context of the failure of European and United Nations 'peace plans') to push the former Cold War Alliance eastwards and establish new protectorates.[393] The internal dynamics of Soviet policies changed the balance of external relations and put Gorbachev in the corner; he has no choice but to accept western political decisions. The dissolution of the Soviet Union, Yeltsin's coup against the Duma which was opposing radical market reforms, and international reciprocal agreements about measures against terrorism opened the door for a new period.

Democratic revolutions or opaque 'refolutions'?

Let us deal here with factors that prevented social 'revolutions' from occurring and, moreover, contradict the 'democratic' nature of the changes.

Bipolar external factors

International behind-the-scene negotiations between Gorbachev and western governments are not sufficient grounds to deny the character of 'revolutions'. The past had demonstrated the possibility of revolutions breaking the bipolar world's agreements: the Yugoslav Revolution leading to the Titoist regime resisted both Stalin and the western major powers, the Non-Aligned movement. It was able to impose itself despite (and against) Yalta's agreements according to which Yugoslavia was supposed to be a monarchy again with western and USSR's influence 'shared' fifty-fifty. The capacity to resist to such international 'deals' was rooted in several factors: the deep popularity and legitimacy of the partisan-led antifascist struggle, the distribution of land to hundreds of thousands of armed peasants, and a new self-administration on the liberated territories crystallising the new federal project against inter-ethnic hatred, all of this associated with a radical rejection of the Serbian Kingdom which dominated the first Yugoslavia in a dictatorial way.[394] Our hypothesis is that the decisive role played in 1989 by international 'deals' in the dynamics of changes illustrates, on the contrary, the weakness of popular mobilisations, unable to really determine the contain of the transformations, which occurred 'from above' (and from outside). They were sufficient to get rid of the most corrupt and inefficient regimes and open a process of pluralist elections. But this was introduced in the Soviet Constitution without any 'revolution', under Gorbachev's rule and appeared as a possible 'norm' as soon as Moscow had accepted the fall of the GDR's regime.

The former Czech dissident of Charter 77 and later President, Vaclav Havel, expressed that clearly in an interview to a French newspaper,[395] given in the context of the 20th anniversary of the 'Velvet revolution': 'in

1989, we were first looking carefully at the East German exodus, which was a huge flow passing partially through Prague (...). I understood that the course of history had changed'. And as the journalist asks 'Did the 'Velvet revolution' began naturally in Berlin?', Vaclav Havel stresses, of course, the deep aspirations and struggles for freedoms in all societies and adds that, in spite of there being no guarantee for peaceful events, one could guess that 'the Soviet Union could no more intervene unless it would have opened an international crisis and a break in the new policy of Perestroika'. But he stresses: 'the dissidents were not ready (...); we have had only a marginal influence on events themselves. But when the power began to look for a dialogue, he made us its interlocutors. There was no organised political movement with which it could speak. That was when we established the Civic Forum'.

In other words, 'the Velvet Revolution would not have been possible were it not for the monumental events unfolding in the other Communist Bloc countries', first of all, the Soviet Union.[396]

But it remains to be explained how very unpopular radical socio-economic transformations could be introduced if not through revolutionary mobilisations at least (apparently) without resistance. Other sources of ambiguities appear in those issues.

Unclear labels

The first source of ambiguity for the dynamics of the changes is the fact that all the new fronts or new parties coming out of the former single party were very heterogeneous, and rapidly split, without agreements on what to do. In the same interview Vaclav Havel reminds us what was the programme of the Civic Forum: 'Our ideals were still the same. The first reforms were reduced to the dissidence principles: free elections, pluralism, market economy, citizen rights, and protection of individual freedoms. And then our priority was to dismantle and get rid of all those who were responsible of communist exactions'. In reality, behind those vague formulations, high disagreements existed about all those issues (including 'lustration' – kind of witch hunting anti-communist campaign) among former members of the same Charter 77. Everywhere, new parties emerged with increasing difficulty in establishing stable majorities in parliaments. And the experience of neoliberal first 'market reforms' led quite rapidly people voting the former communists back in, hoping they would maintain or reintroduce social protections. This happened first of all in Poland, only three years after the neoliberal shock therapy.

And there was then another factor making the picture unclear. Dominant figures of the newly elected parties or of former communist parties now renamed social democrats, had carried a membership card of the Communist party only some months earlier. And from Russia to Poland, most of the new leaders came from the former apparatus – even from its secret police.[397] That was one of the reasons why the population did not clearly understand what was at stake.

Getting rid of the single-party regime and introducing pluralism enjoyed popular support and therefore were not difficult to accomplish. But the party/state was at the same time both infrastructure and superstructure and dismantling allowed a radical transformation of the system from the top, through changes in fundamental laws without pluralist debates on new constitutions. The lack of democratic life in the past but also the opacity of the economic transition facilitated that process. It was enough that the newly elected leaders attacked the foundation of the socio-economic order through a set of new laws established without transparency. The populations, in particular those involved in Solidarność (the Polish independent trade union) at its congress in 1980, never expressed or demonstrated in favour of a project of generalised privatisations. Their aim was to live better and freer. The hope was often to benefit from the best in each system – looking much more towards a very social-democratic Swedish or German model of the 1960s, rather than towards the Anglo-Saxon capitalism of the 1980s.

The transformation of a large cross-section of former Communists into new liberals and property owners occurred in general in Eastern Europe because they wanted pragmatically to protect their privileges of power and consumption and could no longer do so through the former mechanisms. Because of the debt crisis, increasing waste and low productivity, they could not 'pay for' stability through the guaranteed social protection. So they looked to privatisation for themselves and used their knowledge of the system and former social relations to invent convenient reforms. In general, the former party was the main source of qualified elites, and there was no private capital to buy the factories. That is why they became the dominant actors and beneficiaries of the privatisations and new political system.

Two slightly different cases must be stressed where former communists could not play that role. The first case is the unified Germany, because a real German bourgeoisie with real capital able to buy the factories did exist. That is why a radical anti-Communist purge and in particular a denigration of the past regime was imposed (we will come back on that point later). The second case is the Czech Republic, because there, the neoliberal social democratic party which was established, had its roots in the pre-war past (and could be reconstituted) and not in the former transformed Communist party. So unlike for instance Poland where the population brought back to power the ex-communist transformed into 'new' social democrats, the Czech population could vote for another social-democratic party, after the first years of domination of the right – which refused any alliance with the CP (the only one to keep its name in Eastern Europe). Staying in the opposition (like the PDS – Party of Democratic Socialism – in Germany), that CP was not directly involved in the neoliberal policies implemented by all the social democratic parties (be they from 'communist' origin or not). And this 'marginality' became initially an advantage with electoral support rising among the losers of the privatisations (especially pensioners and unemployed), both in the Czech Republic and in Germany. There, the PDS fused with some other left currents to build *Die Linke* – the Left[398] – with some electoral successes.

But a deeper issue has to be raised to understand the opacity of the whole transformation: that of the form taken by privatisations, without historical precedent.

The 'refolutions' in ownership: politics and/or economy?

We use here Timothy Garton Ash's neologism[399] to describe the core of the 'great transformation' which, from the end of the 1980s affected the USSR and Eastern Europe in extremely unexpected ways: the reforms 'from above' would revolutionise the system and change it radically, but the self dissolution of the single party was not a 'revolution'. Generalised market and privatisations were the 'bench-marks' of the break with the past regimes, indicators of the 'transition's success' for external 'experts', creditors or negotiators. But what did they mean for the population?

A certain kind of market for goods did exist. The popular image of the market was obtained by travelling to the West or from pictures showing beautiful and attractive shop windows. That was surely the reason of the attraction of the Deutsche Mark and the immense joy of East German people crossing the former frontier and discovering the real abundance in western German shops. Later on they will have to discover new market rules.

So what about 'privatisation'? The notion was even more abstract and blurred. Small private sectors did exist and could be useful. Surveys in Poland[400] asking the people if they were for or against privatisation gave a dominant 'for' as a general possibility, and 'against' as a concrete question for the factory where the person was employed (even if in certain cases or periods, the hope that a foreign owner could bring higher income could lead to a positive assessment on privatisation). In general, far from a clear capitalist form of ownership (linked with the market 'laws', constraint and risks of bankruptcy and unemployment), the word 'privatisation' itself was used in a very opaque way to express the change in ownership. And in electoral slogans, the 'experts' pushed forward a kind of equation: 'market + privatisation = efficiency + freedom'. That was certainly optimistic and, at the least, not precise. What were the criteria of efficiency? What individual and collective freedoms and rights were related to property rights?

The on-going reforms were called 'transition to market economy' by international 'experts' during the first years after 1989. It was a confusing and imprecise formulation: what is a 'market economy'? Is it an economy with a market? What kind of market? Is that Yugoslavia? Sweden? Mexico? Great Britain? France or Germany? And when, in what periods? The 1960s? Now? But in spite of being imprecise, the notion of 'transition to' seemed to indicate a clear and unique possible choice for the future, with a non-explicit normative neoliberal 'model'. Who had determined such a future choice?

By presenting themselves as scientific, neoliberal precepts had a voluntary, dogmatic and normative character – falsely claiming that successes elsewhere in the world were attributable to them. In practice they were imposing their criteria and excluding their choices from democratic debate.[401] In Eastern Europe not only did they benefit from the strength of the institutions of globalisation (with the IMF and the World Bank having a direct role in the re-organisation of budgets and accountancy and later the European Union's commission playing a leading role); but they also benefited from the zealous support of former members of the Communist parties.[402]

Practically, the process of privatisation had to fit into the ideological context inherited from the former system of formal rights and find some 'democratic' legitimacy. Therefore the dominant feature was at the beginning of the 'transition' was to recognise that the ownership had first to be taken from incompetent and corrupted bureaucrats and given back to the workers and people who had produced the wealth for decades (and additional owners were put forward as 'legitimate': those who had been expropriated in the past). To be popular, the discourse had to focus against the privileges fitting with the dominant egalitarian ideology. Yeltsin first 'profile' and the '500 days' Chataline's programme of privatisation in Russia at the beginning of the 1990s, were based on that ideology. And this very same orientation was also expressed in the East German initial proposals before the monetary unification of 1990.

That does not mean that the scenarios and contexts were all the same. There were choices and the Slovenian cases shows a slightly different 'model' because of different factors: a relatively favourable context (that republic had the highest level of life and of export of the whole Yugoslavia, and the most efficient self-management system); a radical reorganisation of the former official trade-union into a real independent force helping to express a massive mobilisation and therefore public debate on privatisations resistance to neoliberal recipes at the beginning of the 1990s and later on. As a result, in spite of recurrent pressures from the European commission to 'open' the economy to liberal criteria, the state kept the control of public financing of strategic big factories instead of systematic privatisation and lack of credit; the forms of privatisation kept an important part under the control of municipalities and factory employees; the taxes on income and factories and the wages were not submitted to neoliberal criteria (to be 'attractive' for private foreign capital as a general rule); growth was based on internal mechanisms and regulations without accepting the logics of 'competitive advantage' to reduce workers' income and taxes; the main assets of the past system in culture and health care were not destroyed[403].

But if the case of Slovenia was in the initial phase slightly different, it was not because elsewhere the populations were more in favour of liberal recipes but just the opposite: it was because it was more difficult elsewhere for the populations to defend their social gains. They could only express more and more disagreements in elections. The party which had been most involved in privatisations (like the first liberal coalition around the Balcerowicz's shock therapy in Poland in 1989) even lost the capacity to come back later on in Parliament, or to establish stable parliamentary majorities. They could claim to be dismantling the arbitrary rules and waste of the former state-party system; but their aim was mainly a dismantling of social protections – something that was generally kept quiet during the election campaigns, so that it could be put into practice afterwards. This is in part why the electoral results varied – according to the promises made by both new and old parties, which were more or less reformed; but also according to what was the most urgent or important for the population in facing the uncertainty of the market: punishing the former corrupt leaders, the desire for radical change, or rather the fear that the perceived changes would be a threat.

For the majority of the population, markets and privatisations were at the beginning orientations given by economists, often less discredited than the political parties. And there was the idea that – against the former political choices made by the apparatus – economic choices were matters of 'scientific knowledge' and 'law' and were therefore outside of democracy. This facilitated the socio-political and ideological swing of a large number of former leaders from the single party system towards privatisations, at different paces and under different labels. Privatisations were presented as 'norms'. The form, the speed and the scope they took were without historical precedent.

'Direct privatisation' without capital input[404]

It is necessary to establish the major distinction between 'small privatisation' (which generally meant the creation of small new businesses) and 'large privatisation' (which concerned big enterprises; that is those that were essential to employment and production in these industrialised countries).[405]

Small privatisation was generally the driving force behind growth in the countries of Central and Eastern Europe, notably in Poland. It was often promoted as the privileged route to systemic transformation. It clearly did contribute to the creation of flexibility of response to certain needs in the sector of services (refurbishment, repairs, telephony, computing, commerce, restaurants etc.). It introduced a competitive mechanism, with genuine owners and a more or less rapid transfer of finances to the new private firms (start ups). Initial tax breaks for the new businesses generally made this process more favourable. But the small businesses were often fragile and their growth quickly reached its limits. So the issue at stake in the ownership transformation, and its main aspect was dealing with the large privatisation concerning big factories. Who could buy them, with what capital? Overall, privatisation by real sale did not, for the most part, find any other buyers apart from those with foreign capital. The non-capitalist nature of the former society (of the Soviet type) was associated with the absence of financial market and of private banks, the fact that money in the planned sector could not be used to buy and sell the means of production, but only for accounting. All that meant the general lack of national accumulated financial capital.

For those countries who wanted to gain their independence and their sovereignty by detaching themselves from the hegemony of the USSR, the decision to sell the best factories to foreign capital was hardly a popular one. And the aspiring national bourgeoisie did not want to be reduced to a 'comprador bourgeoisie', using their knowledge of the internal cogs for the service of foreign capital. In practice, only Hungary and Estonia opted for privatisation by foreign sales at the start of their transition.

The privatisations have been called mass 'direct privatisations' by the Polish sociologist Maria Jarosz, who used this term to describe the privatisations that operated without money, through a legal change in ownership. This would make it possible to change the socio-economic behaviour and the status of workers under the pressure of market competition, which was the goal of capitalist market privatisations.

However, this aim could not be explicit, in as much as it was necessary in the first years of systemic transformation to legitimise the process as 'democratic' in the eyes of the populations concerned and their workers which were, as we have stressed, according to the ideology and constitutions of the former systems, the official 'social owners' of the means of production. This was a kind of recognition of their 'official' role in the production and legal ownership of all these national assets – provided a part of them was put aside for 'restitution' to those who were private owners of the lands or firms when they were nationalised after the war. So, the workers have been in general given a 'choice' between different kinds of 'privatisations': selling to 'outsiders' (external actors from the factory) state property or (quasi) 'free' distribution to the workers or people of the major parts of shares of the transformed enterprises (the state becoming owner of the rest). Those two variants constitute, in essence, what was called 'direct privatisations' (without capital) at the start of the transition in the majority of countries concerned: either the state became the owner, or 'mass privatisations' occurred where insiders (employers and managers of the former enterprise) became dominant shareholders – with a rapid concentration of shares in the hand of the managers.

The paradoxical notion of 'direct privatisations' concealed a change in the socio-economic role of the state behind apparent continuities. For the population it was difficult to distinguish between the state of the past, managing means of production and distribution, and the new state mutated into the instrument of mass privatisation. This perception was even more confuse when the very same persons were still in power. But in reality, from this point on, the state was no longer ruling 'on behalf of the workers' (even at their expense) and without the attributes of a 'true' owner (able to use genuine management powers, bankruptcy, sale and transfer). This past reality was to be eradicated according to neoliberal criteria. Through direct privatisations, the purpose was to establish the power of 'real owners' – even if (in a paradoxical way for 'liberals') those were the state, allowing both a change in the status of the workers and the restructuring of firms under market constraints, before their subsequent sale. It was this that was known in Poland as the 'commercialisation' of public firms, and it was accompanied by the suppression of all traces of workers' councils.

The deepest source of ambiguity in these *refolutions* was there. The radical nature of these changes in ownership (in social status and in the relationship of production and distribution), which were introduced by the state, doubtless went unseen by the people they concerned. When the state became the major player in these businesses, it was often seen as continuity with the former state, which certainly had ruled as a dictator, but also as a social protector.

This popular illusion of continuity in social protection was also expressed rapidly in free elections by the vote in favour of those among former Communists who kept as new labels some kind of socialist or social democrat epithets. This was the case in Poland, fewer than three years after the neoliberal shock therapies. Nevertheless, once these social democrat ex-Communists had returned to power by way of the ballot box, in Poland and elsewhere, they generally made the decision to be zealous supporters of NATO and ultra-liberal transformations, a decision that was not free from corruption. They are paying for it today through the fact that it is the nationalist and xenophobic right that has put forward the issue of social protection against the 'left', winning elections on this very basis.

Conflicting dynamics were often at work behind the ambiguity of these 'mass privatisations'. From the workers' point of view, the pragmatic choice of this form of privatisation was to protect their jobs, and allow them to keep at least part of the social advantages that were allocated to them in big enterprises (flats, restaurants, childcares, hospitals, some products distributed by internal shops), compared with the re-structuring imposed by private individuals/outsiders. However, from the point of view of those who managed the reforms, it was a question of legitimising the privatisations in the eyes of the population, while at the same time this gave them the opportunity to 'prove' to the institutions of the on-going globalisation that 'privatisation' had occurred, that a radical break with the previous system was taking place. This was the precondition for loans and for negotiations to become candidate members to the European Union (EU). In this context, a new process of genuine social polarisation and concentration of ownership and financial montages took place behind the fragmented popular shareholding that brought to workers neither income nor power apart that of slowing down re-structuring. The 'privatised' state used its rights of property either with the clientelist approach or with the aim of selling the firms to 'real' private investors, foreign or national.

Behind the mass privatisations which occurred at the beginning of the systemic transformation[406], there was the emptying of the productive substance of big enterprises, but avoiding immediate bankruptcy and massive unemployment of the workers. The lack of credit available for these firms contrasted with the comparative financial support received by the sector that was truly 'privatised'. Although liberal 'experts' criticised the lack of restructuring linked with mass privatisation, they also eventually highlighted, from their point of view, the beneficial nature of this first period, because it permitted radical transformation of ownership. Inasmuch as 'insiders' were partially protected, it lessened the risk of social explosions, while destroying the former system.

'Transition to democracy'? The German symbol: what about 'Ostalgia'?

Because the East German mobilisations have become the symbol of the 'democratic revolution', the concrete scenario is worth examining. Few people know what is behind the 'Ostalgia', a neologism invented to describe the nostalgia rapidly felt by East Germans. Nostalgia of what? Certainly not the former political order based on the repressive Stasi. Was it, then a feeling due to some 'difficulty' in adapting to the new 'modernity' of capitalism that they had at first wanted so much? On 8 November 2009, the *Guardian* published an article 'East Germans lost much' written by Bruni De La Motte:

> Once the border was open the government decided to set up a trusteeship to ensure that 'publicly owned enterprises' (the majority of businesses) would be transferred to the citizens who'd created the wealth. However, a few months before unification, the then newly elected conservative government handed over the trusteeship to west German appointees, many representing big business interests. The idea of 'publicly owned' assets being transferred to citizens was quietly dropped. Instead all assets were privatised at breakneck speed. More then 85 per cent were bought by West Germans and many were closed soon after. In the countryside, 1.7 million hectares of agricultural and forest land were sold off and 80 per cent of agricultural workers lost their job.[407]

In the GDR, single mothers enjoyed free childcares. As a result, the share of professionally active women was 90 per cent. After 1989, this share dropped to 40 per cent, this fall being the highest contributor to unemployment. Childcare centres were closed, while rights and means for free contraception and abortion were suppressed (to keep their jobs or find them many young women above 30 years old resorted to sterilisation). Could this be called a 'democratic revolution'? No debate, no elected assembly and no bilateral procedure occurred to establish a new unified Germany. The GDR was simply absorbed: the East German population was not asked what they wanted to keep or not. And they felt profoundly humiliated, like second-class citizens.

A counter-revolution?

The social shock imposed on East Germans and on East European populations in general would probably be better characterised as a counter-revolution. But one is confronted here with several analytical difficulties, with symmetrical ambiguities: were there real 'revolutions' after the Second World War in those countries?

The occupation and division of Germany by foreign troops were foreseen by the Yalta agreements between antifascists allies before the defeat of the Nazis. The Potsdam agreement (August 1945) organised Germany's division into zones between the Allies supposedly under collective responsibility but in fact affected increasingly by Cold War tensions. Stalin would have preferred to keep access to the rich Ruhr than to divide Germany into two separate states: the richest western part was eligible for aid under the Marshal plan (introduced in 1947) while Stalin submitted the poorest eastern part under his control to radical pillage, considered as reparations for the huge destructions and the millions of Soviet citizens killed in the war. The decision to establish the GDR (October 1949) was an answer to the establishment of the Federal Republic in the Western Allies' occupied zones on 23 May of the same year.

Over the continent, a whole range of scenario occurred, from a genuine revolution in Yugoslavia – according to both criteria of mass mobilisations and radical changes – to the Moscow-led *refolution* establishing the GDR or Romania, through real popular mass mobilisation and welcoming of the Red army in Czechoslovakia. All the scenarios were the result of World War II, civil wars, intense class conflicts and political polarisations. With different scenarios, the populations of Eastern Europe have been confronted with and divided by the combined wars: civil and world wars, where different kinds of anti-fascist resistances (with or against Communists) led also to different attitudes towards the Red Army's invasion (from radical hostility to enthusiasm). But, even when the Soviet Union's intervention played the decisive role in the structural changes the national single Communist parties in power broaden their social basis by introducing radical 'reforms' against private ownership and market domination: extremely rapid vertical social promotion occurred for peasants and workers in comparison to their situation in pre-war peripheral capitalist societies – combined with repressive regimes claiming socialist goals. 1989 was the undoing of the post-1945 period.

The *refolutions* imposed by the CP apparatus were dominated by the Kremlin. But the socialist goals proclaimed could win popular support and a trend to reduce the gap between them and the existing regime did exist. In the GDR, Rosa Luxemburg or Karl Liebknecht enjoyed prestige, like the theatre of Berthold Brecht. But left-wing anti-Stalinist intellectuals or artists were repressed or were drastically separated from the workers by Stasi repression. In 1989 an embryonic 'Red and Green republic'[408] was discussed among those circles who had much sympathy with the 'Western' radical left led by Rudi Dutschke in the 1960s and with the Prague Spring. They did want the end of the Stasi and of Honecker's regime but certainly not its dissolution within the existing West Germany.

A 'systemic crisis' (linked with the dismantling of the system) occurred in all countries at the beginning of the 1990s, which the World Bank reports compared to the 1929 crisis in a different context: it was a drop of 30 to 50 per cent in production in all branches. After 1993, growth started again first in Poland – helped by the cancellation of the debt decided by the US without publicity – then in other Central and Eastern European countries. This has been called a 'catching up' but without noting two facts: first, the indicator used to measure the growth and catching up (GDP or equivalent) does not reflect the well-being of populations: it does not say how the production is done and distributed, which means that it is compatible with increasing poverty; and second, it was necessary to 'catch-up' first of all with the 1989 level of production. That occurred within more or less a decade, with a sharp structural transformation behind the figures. With the new millennium this growth was still accompanied by deepening unemployment and inequality – because the re-structuring of big enterprises and of agriculture only had begun and financial resources were concentrated in certain productive sectors.

Overall, both the starting points, and the different paths of systemic transformation have been varied. Nevertheless, behind these differences, the same outcome can be stated for all the former countries of the USSR and of Eastern Europe, expressed after the first decade of 'transition' by the World Bank: 'poverty has become more widespread and has increased at a greater speed than anywhere else in the world' while 'inequality has increased in all of the transition economies and amongst certain of them this has been dramatic'.[409] This happened even when 'the countries of this region have started their transition with levels of inequality that were amongst some of the weakest in the world'. For sure, the reports have been more positive during the period 2000-2007: impressive rates of growth (for instance more than 7 per cent or even 10 per cent in some Baltic States) leading to many comments about a 'success story' of the 'transition'. Unfortunately, the specific feature of that whole transformation has been the extremely unbalanced growth, and high dependence upon foreign capital and banks with dramatic side effects such as those seen in 2008 with the second sharp crisis and social shock, under the effect both of the world crisis and of international features of the systemic transformations.

As we have stressed, financial markets and private banks did not exist in the former system. As the dogmatic priority has been placed on being attractive to private (that is foreign) capital, the introduction of a private banking system has meant an absolute domination of the banking system by West European banks: in 2008 from 65 per cent of banks being foreign-owned in Latvia to nearly 100 per cent in Slovakia and more than 90 per cent in all other New Member States (NMS) except Slovenia (35 per cent, in 2008).[410] Their logic has been short-term profit and the highest possible return on loans. Concretely this meant a lack of credit for industry, and speculative borrowing to meet the demands for household credit for consumption (mainly flats and cars) through financial operations based on foreign currency borrowing (especially in Swiss Francs when the rate of exchange was attractive). So the very high growth, mentioned above, in the recent period (specially in the Baltic countries), and the so-called 'catching up', were based on a huge disequilibrium of external balance and debt in societies with high level of poverty and inequalities.[411] The *Financial Times* comments the last 'hard-hitting report' for 2009 published by the EBRD: 'Central and Eastern Europe must get rid of an 'addiction to foreign currency debt'.[412] The report recognises that the global recession plunged the region into crisis – the IMF was called to the rescue by Hungary, Latvia, Poland, Romania, Serbia, Ukraine, Bosnia-Herzegovina – but the social situation was not its real concern: the only concern of the Bank was whether there was any reversal trend of the 'transition'. And the answer was: no, for the moment. That was considered a success: the 'growth model for the region remains intact', in spite of fragilities, the state must be stronger, and accept IMF austerity policies. As long as social unrest is not too explosive there will be no systemic change.

The repressed 'third way'

The Slovenian philosopher Slavoj Žižek produced in November 2009 an article tribune under the title 'Behind the Wall, people did not dream of capitalism'.[413] There is certainly no direct possibility to check such a judgement, but it is possible to find some indications in what was expressed in the most important democratic movements within/against the past regimes and compare that to the main features of 1989. The Polish Solidarność in 1980-1 and the Prague upsurge of 1968 are surely the most impressive indications of 'third ways'. One cannot 'demonstrate' that they could be generalised, but one should at least respect – that is make known – what they expressed, and put questions on the way those alternative were 'closed' or condemned to oblivion.

'In Poland the transition [from communism to democracy] lasted ten years, in Hungary ten months, in Czechoslovakia ten days' states a significant presentation of the 1989 Velvet Revolution.[414] But fundamental questions arise from such descriptions: how far was the end of those regimes in 1989-91 imposed by massive democratic mobilisations defining the content and purposes of those 'revolutions' (as we have so far discussed)? Is there continuity between Solidarność in 1980 and in 1990? And what about the Prague upsurge in 1968 or the Hungarian and Polish anti-bureaucratic upsurges of 1956? In the above quotation, the Polish Solidarność is supposed to be part of the 'transition to democracy' ('10 years' in Poland and '10 days' for the Velvet Revolution) – meaning that the 1989 socio-economic changes have been made within that western oriented democracy. My thesis is, on the contrary, that Solidarność in 1980 in its dominant expectations, as expressed in documents adopted by the movement, was closer to the 1968 and 1956 mass movements than to the post-1989 shock therapy. I will try to explicit explain the reasons through the examination of the democratic demands put forward by these huge social mobilisations.

A systematic study of the different presentations of those past events is still to be made and would be a highly useful peace of historical research. Both the Kremlin and the West described the 1956 upsurges in Hungary and that of 1968 in Czechoslovakia as 'anti-communist'; for the Kremlin, that description served to 'justify' the Warsaw Pact military intervention and in western propaganda. The Stalinised Soviet Union 'the country of the big lie' (like wrote the Croatian Communist Ante Ciliga wrote in the 1930s) was in the continuity with the first 'justification' of the 1948 'excommunication' of the Yugoslav Communists because of their supposedly 'pro-capitalist' orientations.[415] The same logics prevailed in 1968: even if it was more difficult, the Soviet Union could not but 'justify' the sending of tanks in Czechoslovakia by speaking of a 'danger for socialism'. It is therefore quite 'normal' to find in western broadcasts or papers about 1956 or 1968 similar presentations to that during the beginning of 'the end of communism' and of the 'return' to democracy occurring in 1989. Elements of continuity do exist if the only criterion considered is the call for freedoms, without describing of their content. It is also true that the Polish events can appear closer to 1989 than the Prague Spring, because of the strength and expression of religious feelings, explicit anti-communist positions of the Church and of a certain number of strike leaders and advisers as opposed to the 1968's reforms introduced from within the Communist party itself, and the explicit call for 'a socialism with human face'.

So we will focus on the kind of democracy and rights which were put forward, and stress those demands that capitalism would not accept: workers councils, or workers self-management as a fundamental right to control the organisation and aim of economic system, the statute of workers and product of labour.

From Solidarność in 1980-1981 to the Balcerowicz's plan in 1989: continuity or antipodes?

When considering the scenario of the Polish strike movement in August 1980, which led to the establishment of the first (officially accepted) independent trade union within the former 'communist' bloc, one sees that its congress in September 1981 was much closer to a democratic revolution than any other events in Eastern Europe. After a decision taken by the regime to increase prices, a general movement of strikes occurred with a high level of self-organisation and coordination. Nearly all the state-owned factories of the country — that is the whole industrial sector — were involved. The movement rapidly took on political features. Horizontal links were established, and an inter-factory strike committee with a mandate to negotiate (the electrician Lech Walesa being chosen as delegate). In an earlier wave of strikes back in 1976, in solidarity with the striking workers, intellectuals had organised a committee, the KOR, rapidly transformed into a body of 'advisers'. Now, the Inter-Factory Committee (MSK) established a list of 'twenty-one demands'.[416]

A first group of demands could be expressed, and could in a certain context be accepted in a capitalist society. They indicated a very high level of social expectations of the population which would be, and has been, quite in conflict with the dominant liberal trends in the post-1989 kind of capitalism: wages protected from inflation and full payment of the days on strike, reduction in the retirement age (to 50 for women); pensions to reflect working life; universal healthcare; an increase in the number of school and nursery places for the children of working mothers; three year's paid maternity leave; increased help for those forced to travel far to work.

A second group of requests demands were was for benefits recognised in western democracies but not in all capitalist societies. In general these have been refused in the post-1989 European countries in the factories owned by foreign capital: the possibility to build free trade unions and to have the right to strike. These requests demands were, of course, also in conflict with the rules of the former 'socialist' regime's rules; but were not generally in conflict with socialist ideas. Both in Yugoslavia in the 1960s and in Czechoslovakia in 1968, trade unions tended to win autonomy — which was later repressed by the party in power like all autonomous movements when they became a danger for the political monopoly of power. In Poland, the Communist regime had to accept in September 1980 the demand for a free trade union: the preparation and meeting of its congress in two phases in September 1981 was legal. A third group of demands were linked with the specificities of the regime: the demand that factory management be selected on the basis of competence and not of Party membership; an end to privileges for the police and party apparatchiks; and an end to 'voluntary' Saturday working. A fourth group of demands could be put forward in a capitalist society, but were are rarely accepted: the demand for access to the mass media for all; the publication of the strikers' demands in the mass media; freedom of access to information about the economy.

But the main demands would be in essence very much in conflict with a capitalist logics: they asked for the involvement of the whole population in the debate on the economic situation and the reforms to answer to the crisis. This last demand was underlined once again in the program programme adopted at the congress organised one year later. Obviously different currents and conflicting views were expressed, which reflects a normal democratic and massive movement that took on the dynamics of a quasi-political 'constituent assembly'. What kind of society did it want to establish?

The simple presentation of the twenty-one demands stresses the sharp contrasts between on one hand the social expectations for social protection and of social gains and democratic control on economic decisions of those millions of workers in strike in 1980, and on the other hand the content of the 1989's shock therapy and privatisations. The fact that the twenty-one demands did not ask for privatisations but the opposite is rarely mentioned. Yet this was not a marginal issue: first the workers won legal recognition and therefore could really organise the congress democratically and not underground. As international observers could see, a dual social and political power within the whole society was already functioning.[417] A political and social programme for the whole society was elaborated during several days in the two sessions of September 1981 by several hundreds delegates under the control of 80 per cent of the organised Polish labour force: direct socially managed TV broadcasting made it possible to watch the debates of the congress within the factories in the whole of Poland, while the rank and file workers were democratically controlling their delegates.

But what was adopted by that significant democratic congress? How is it related to 1989? Let us look at Wikipedia's article on Solidarity in English,[418] for instance. It presents the whole Polish events as led by 'anti-Soviet' currents and the Church, and as the beginning of 'anti-communist revolutions' in

1989, and concludes: 'Solidarity's influence led to the intensification and spread of anti-communist ideals and movements throughout the countries of the Eastern Bloc, weakening their communist governments'. The defeat of the 'communist' candidates in 1989 elections in Poland 'sparked off a succession of peaceful anti-communist revolutions in Central and Eastern Europe known as the Revolutions of 1989 (Jesień Ludów).' Is this not that the dominant presentation still made of Solidarność? And this without a single quotation from those supposed 'anti-communist ideals'. Nothing about the twenty-one demands. Nothing about the programme of the congress.

In France all these documents have been produced and a broad movement of solidarity and direct links was developed among left-wing trade-unionists in the 1980s. That is probably why the Wikipedia article in French on the same topic, is quite different, because it quotes the documents adopted by Solidarity's congress in September 1981 and says the project was to establish 'a self managed Republic', adding that 'the congress demands a democratic and self-managed reform at whole levels of decision making, a new social and economic order which will articulate plan and self management with market'. The article comments that this was 'a deepening of the positions elaborate since autumn 1980 by the inter-factory strike committee', proclaiming that 'we are for a worker, progressive socialism, an egalitarian and harmonious development of Poland, collectively determined by the whole of the labour force's world (...) a social order which would be authentically worker and socialist'.[419]

The threat of a Soviet intervention was central at that time. On 13 December 1981, General Wojciech Jaruzelski, backed by the 'Military Council for National Salvation', declared that Poland was under martial law. Mobilising the army and security services, he took control of the TV and radio, and unleashed the hated internal police and motorised riot police to break up unauthorised meetings. Military tribunals sentenced thousands of trade unionists for up to three years in prison.

But the repression gave a different influence to those among the intellectual advisers who wanted to use the strength of the social movement to get rid of the system, suppress all dynamics of self management and reduce Solidarność to a classical trade union in a market economy. After such repression by a 'Communist' party, the ideological strength of the Church and of real anti-communist projects increased with the demobilisation (in spite of some strikes and anger). After the amnesty law, the second half of the 1980s opened the road towards a compromise with the ruling party which was losing members and any capacity to rule – it was looking to protect some political power and the links with the Gorbachev's Soviet Union. The high level of self-organisation and democratic revolution had been broken. Under Gorbachev's pressure, a 'round table' was organised with legalisation of a much weaker Solidarność; and the ruling party was defeated in the first free elections.

Huge 'financial' pressures and negotiations were at stakes behind the scene. The national debt in various foreign banks and governments reached in 1989 the sum of US $42.3 billion (64,8 per cent of GDP). The 'Balcerowicz plan' – also called shock therapy was adopted at the end of 1989. In late December, the plan was approved by the International Monetary Fund (IMF). The IMF granted Poland a stabilisation fund of US $1 billion and an additional stand-by credit of US $720 million. Following this, the World Bank granted Poland additional credits for modernisation of exports of Polish goods and food products. Western governments followed then and paid off about 50 per cent of the sum of debt capital and all cumulated interest rates to 2001.

One can compare programs and procedures. 1989 appears much more like a social 'liberal' counter-*refolution* than the continuation of the initial Solidarność congress.

In 1981, more than 80 per cent of the workforce was unionised and Solidarność had about ten million members. In 2008, those who were in trade unions made up no more than 11 per cent of the workers, according to official figures provided by trade union organisations. During the process of privatisation trade union leaders were often introduced – on an individual level – into the boards, where they were linked with the employers.[420] This corruption and integration into the processes of privatisation undermined the trade unions. The loss of resources and the bankruptcy of big enterprises produced huge unemployment (when Poland became member of the UE in 2004 the unemployment rate was nearly 18 per cent), the difficulties of daily life and the absence of trade unions in businesses run by foreign capital did the rest. Therefore the social discontinuities between 1980-1 and 1989 are closely linked with the totally different dynamic of 'reforms'[421].

From the Prague Autumn of workers councils (1968) to the Velvet Revolution (1989): continuity or antipodes?

The scenario is slightly different for Czechoslovakia, but the essence of the issues at stake and conflicting interpretations are the same. The economic and political reforms proposed in 1965-8 in Czechoslovakia by the reformist leader Dubček and the economist Ota Šik,[422] supported by a whole wing of the Communist party was very similar to the one implemented in Hungary at that time: the purpose of the reform was to introduce a stimulant to increase the efficiency of production (quality and productivity). But the proposed means were mainly based on a partial extension of market economy and on increasing the responsibility of managers (and increasing their income according to market results) as an alternative to the too vertical and authoritarian form of Soviet planning. Such reforms did not introduce workers rights for self-management.

That is why, up to the Prague Spring, the Czechoslovak workers had not felt great enthusiasm for the Ota Šik and Dubček's economic reforms: their effect would be to increase inequalities (through more market competition) and social insecurity (through the power and material incentive given to directors to push them to reduce production costs including labour cost). The ideology of socialism recognises the workers as the creative source of wealth, not as a commodity whose price is a 'cost' to be reduced. They were supposed to be the 'owners' of the factories – which would mean a responsible actor involved in the democratic and pluralistic elaboration of criteria of economic efficiency and mechanisms aimed at reducing waste and material costs. That was exactly the demands that the Polish workers expressed in 1980.

In the process of debate of the reforms in Prague just before 1968, some Communists and trade unionists have proposed a new law increasing workers rights of establishing organs of self-management of the factories, elect directors, and decide on the organisation of the productive process and distribution of the production. But that was pushed aside – or slightly reduced – by the Ota Šik reforms. And the liberalisation from above had in turn stimulated unexpected movements and demands from below in the whole society: in all sister countries ruling parties were afraid of contagion. The Prague Spring was also an immense international gathering in favour of 'socialism with a human face'. The Soviet intervention aimed to stop all that.

But it produced the opposite effect. And this is never said in TV broadcasts and dominant analysis on those events. The reality, is that during the autumn of 1968, in nearly 200 factories, more than 800,000 workers reacted to the Warsaw Pact's invasion and Soviet propaganda (which claimed that the Red Army was sent to Czechoslovakia to defend socialism) by establishing workers councils,[423] encouraged by a broad part of the Communists and trade-unionists in favour of a self managed socialism.

The movement spread and organised its first national conference in January 1969 – six months after the arrival of the tanks! In March there were 500 councils. It had become a massive political movement by its own coordination and through the support received by youth and intellectuals, many of whom were members of the Czechoslovak Communist Party (CCP) itself. Workers councils were often supported or even launched by factory cells of the CCP and of the trade union body (ROH), which at that time emancipated itself from the bureaucratic apparatus of the state. Their leaders were often elected to head the councils. A new bill was elaborated and presented to the government, still led by the reformist leader Alexander Dubček. Such proposals were backed by hundreds of occupied factories and by the part of the CCP resisting the occupation and organising clandestine meetings.

But that bill on factories would have given too much power to workers councils, and certainly frightened the Dubček wing, looking for compromises with the Kremlin. The bill was taken in account – which indicates how much it was still difficult simply to censor it – but the government introduced changes and reduced the rights given to the workers, to become closer to the Ota Šik and Hungarian sort of reforms. After some months the dynamic of the workers councils had been broken by pressures and direct repression.

Nearly twenty years after the Velvet Revolution of 1989, the debate about the Prague Spring began to reappear in the Czech Republic. It was relaunched in particularly relaunched by the republication[424] at the end of 2007 of two contradictory standpoints expressed immediately after the Soviet intervention, in December 1968, by Milan Kundera and by Vaclav Havel. Both these prestigious and well-known writers had challenged the former regime's censorship before 1968. The first one acted out of his Communist convictions while the second did it as a liberal anti-Communist. Vaclav Havel kept his anti-Communist and democratic standpoint through his involvement in the resistance to the Soviet occupation within the 'Charter 77' (initiated in 1977 to resist the Soviet 'normalisation', a front where Communists and anti-Communist democrats could join the fight for human rights), and became the first President of the new Czechoslovakia and then of the Czech Republic. In the meantime, Milan Kundera lost the Marxist convictions he had in 1968. But it this is not important here, because the standpoints he expressed at that time are quoted and still supported in the present period and debated by other Communists – Jaroslav Šabata is one of them. In 1968, he was leading the left current within the Communist party which gave radical support to self-managed socialist democracy and workers councils.

In presenting the present renewal of the controversy, Jacques Rupnik[425] writes that for Vaclav Havel, the Spring 1968 achievements (abolition of censorship, individual freedoms) 'only re-established what existed thirty years before and what is still the basis of democratic countries in general'. This point of view can also lead to consider the Velvet Revolution as a successful variant of the Prague Spring democratic movement (repressed by the Communist regime, whereas the Velvet Revolution was able to get rid of it). But Vaclav Havel's position today is closer to a second trend: to deny any significant consistency to the 1968 events because of their socialist aims. The repression is then stressed as the only possible issue: there is no possible third way.

Milan's Kundera's view, on the contrary, stresses that – as Jacques Rupnik summarises 'despite having been a defeat, the Prague Spring retains its universal significance as a first attempt at finding a route between the eastern and western models, a way of reconciling socialism and democracy'. The (still) Communist intellectual Jaroslav Šabata quoted recently and shared the former Kundera's judgment in a more radical way: 'The Czechoslovak Autumn is probably much more important than the Czechoslovak Spring. [...] Socialism, the logic of which is to identify itself with freedom and democracy, cannot but create a kind of freedom and democracy that the world has never known.'[426]

Such a movement and self-organisation was a danger for all ruling CPs wanting to keep the monopoly of political power, even if they opposed the Soviet domination.[427] The workers' council movement could embrace all demands against censorship, and for individual and collective freedoms. But it also stressed the contradictions or limits of all those who support the slogan 'socialism with human face' but 'forget' the fundamental socialist aims: the suppression of relations of domination within the economy permitting a radical subordination of economic choices, as all key human choices, to a democratic system to be invented. This stand contradicted both systems of the Cold-War camps.

The struggles for the commons in the Balkans*

The Balkan Forum Commons Working Group

In this paper we first offer a brief theoretical introduction to the concept of the commons, advancing a critical political approach to its understanding. In the second part of the paper we relate the concept of the commons to an outline of key features of the political economy of post-socialism in the Balkans, while in the third part we present some existing social movements and examples of popular resistance in the region that could be related to the concept of the commons. We conclude by suggesting ways in which the commons could be advanced as a political project for the Left in the Balkans.

Concepts, history and evolution

The commons is becoming a key theoretical concept used by the Left as many authors recognise its unifying potential for many on-going struggles that challenge the current political and economic system. The term 'commons' has historically been used to denote natural commons like land and pastures that were used in common. This was the case in England until around the 16th century when the process of enclosure started. Linked to Marx's concept of primitive accumulation, enclosure was fundamental in the formation of capitalist relations because it concomitantly secured the landless labour class and the initial accumulation of capital. However, Harvey (2003) argues that this process of enclosure happens continuously in capitalism, describing it as 'accumulation by dispossession,' essentially capturing an on-going process in

---

*   This paper was published for the 2nd Balkan Forum that took place on May 12-14, 2013 in Zagreb. It is online at <http://www.criticatac.ro/lefteast/the-struggle-for-the-commons-in-the-balkans/>. The paper was prepared by the Forum's Commons Working Group which was composed of Danijela Majstorović, Georgi Medarov, Dubravka Sekulić, Vladimir Simović, Tomislav Tomašević and Danijela Dolenec (coordinator).
It is reproduced here with the agreement of Igor Stiks who coordinated the Forum as a space for social movements in the region to discuss common strategies of resistance and alternatives.

which the logic of capital extends to ever new domains of society. This can take the form of land grabs and enclosures of previously community owned resources or privatization of formerly public services such as healthcare and education.

In the Balkans, as a European periphery, it may be argued that accumulation by dispossession has been the driving force of expanding capitalist relations, pushing struggles for the commons to the centre of political mobilisation. The current politics of austerity and the accompanying drive for privatization and commodification are jeopardizing public governance both of natural resources such as water and land, and of publicly managed services such as education, healthcare, or the media. Today, across the Balkans many social spheres are exposed to demands for privatization and pressured into demonstrating their short-term economic value, while private ownership is invariably presented as a superior solution. It is against these circumstances that various social movements have emerged across the region, and it is in this context that we aim to develop the commons movement as a political force which questions the fundamentals of current economic relations and proposes progressive alternatives to the status quo.

The concept of commons was introduced to mainstream social science by Elinor Ostrom. From the early 1970s she studied hundreds of cases where local communities managed natural common pool resources, like forests and fisheries, without the interference of either market or state. She wanted to contest Hardin's (1968) infamous concept of the 'tragedy of the commons,' which claimed that the only way to avoid the destruction of natural commons was through government regulation or privatisation. Ostrom (1990) showed that there were many cases where communities succeeded in sustainably managing commons without state regulation or private property regimes. However, her work only entered the mainstream when she was awarded the Nobel Prize in Economic Sciences in 2009, for challenging 'the conventional wisdom that common property is poorly managed and should be either regulated by central authorities or privatised' (Nobel Prize Committee, 2009). More recently, she expanded her theory from natural to social commons, like knowledge, providing social movements with new arguments that oppose privatisation and experiment with social innovations.

Notwithstanding this, it needs to be noted that Ostrom envisioned the commons as complementary to the existence of markets and states, and that she did not take on a structural critique of capitalist relations. She relied on rational choice institutionalism, analysing individual agency and the successful overcoming of dilemmas of collective action, which is an approach incapable of recognising macro-structural drivers like accumulation by dispossession, which systematically encroach on the commons all over the world. In that sense, we need to build on the legacy of Ostrom's work, but in a direction that will affirm the values of radical democracy, material sustainability and egalitarianism without forgetting to critically examine capitalism as a site of exploitation and domination. We propose to develop the theory of the commons by securing its link with the Marxian insistence that capitalism be analysed as a mode of production (Dolenec and Žitko, 2013).

The commons have been defined in many ways, but for us it is important to define them as a political concept. Following Harvey (2013), the commons are 'about how we develop a common purpose.' Contemporary debates have found it useful to distinguish between the environmental commons, i.e. the natural physical wealth that humans inherited, and the social commons, i.e. the knowledge, culture and other immaterial wealth that humans created (Ostrom i Hess 2007, Hardt 2012, Harvey 2012 and others). While the struggles around the natural commons are based in a deep awareness of material constraints to human life on this planet, the digital commons movement tends to disregard these constraints, and is often less critical of the underlying structural fundamentals of capitalist relations. Similarly, Hardt (2012) notices the different logic between social movements that fight for environmental and those that fight for social justice. Anti-capitalist movements for social justice, which put forward claims that do not have scarcity constraints are as a result more autonomist and longer-term oriented towards radically changing the system. Conversely, environmental movements are engaged in commons which are limited, which makes them more state-oriented in order to regulate their use and more short-term oriented because of urgency of environmental threats like climate change.

A commonality among all these movements is that they oppose property relations, since both material and immaterial commons are destroyed by capitalist property relations. The potential for uniting these types of movements seem particularly fruitful in the Balkans, where currently both types of social movements are growing and there is a need to establish a common platform for action.

A minimal common denominator around current commons movements is that they are critical of neoliberal capitalism and representative democracy. Localising this to our region, new democracies in the Balkans were seen as inept and prejudiced, having 'remarkably few legal, political, and civic skills' and there was an almost 'evangelic belief' in imposing democracy from above (Knaus and Martin 2003), as a much needed 'noble experiment' (Denitch 1996: 60). In effect the political transformation was accompanied with the restoration of capitalist relations, which has not been subjected to serious criticism. No government to our knowledge has been held responsible for the toxic recipe of liberalisation and privatization that contributed to de-industrialisation, high unemployment rates and increasing poverty across the region. A thorough analysis of the political economy of post-communist societies in the Balkans must subject the economic policies of the last two decades to serious criticism, which is why this platform is all the more important.

A radical critical conception of the commons

Sometimes the commons are defined as a new sphere that will supplement market and state to buffer both market and state failures. Many initiatives in the commons movement look towards reducing the reach of markets into various social domains, but they are not proposing to transform the underlying logic of capitalism (Dolenec 2012). We propose to advance those strands in the commons movement that reject this conception of the commons as a kind of 'third way' (Mattei 2012, De Angelis 2012), refusing to blunt 'their revolutionary potential and legitimate claims for a radical egalitarian redistribution of resources' (Mattei 2012:42). Similarly, while sometimes commons are seen as leading to autonomist efforts far removed from the state, for us the transformation of the state is part of the solution; its power must be grasped to be used in the socialist project of expanding the commons.

It is in direct confrontation with the state that we transform public goods into commons. For Helfrich and Bollier (2012) the distinction between these concepts is not in the property regime, but in the fact of effective social control. According to them, public goods are those resources, which are effectively controlled by the state and not by the people, which means that they are usually for the benefit of state elites and not for the people. Harvey (2012) distinguishes between public goods and commons, similarly but differently, through the medium of political action. For example, public space is the space of political power exercised by the state and not necessarily accessible to all, like homeless people for example. It becomes a common space through political action that contests this space like in Varšavska Street in Zagreb, Picin Park in Banja Luka, Peti Park in Belgrade, or Syntagma Square. For Harvey, the commons are inherently political and they are always contested.

De Angelis (2012) warns that capitalism can use the 'commons fix' for its further growth, focusing our attention on the need to use the commons to create a social basis for alternative ways of articulating social production. Commons are, in this conception, a vehicle for claiming ownership over conditions needed for life (social and biological) and its reproduction. Therefore, we have two tasks: to defend commons from new enclosures and to create new commons as they become a crucial terrain of struggle. According to De Angelis, 'whether the avenue ahead is one of commons co-optation or emancipation is not a given.' Therefore, one should always take a critical position towards the commons and not romanticise them. Communities as commons can be non-democratic and oppressive so we should not use the commons universally as normative, but rather as an analytical, critical and political concept. Harvey (2012), for example, warns how sometimes enclosure of commons by the state could be in common interest, like in the cases of enclosure of Amazonian rainforest by the state to protect it. It is always the question of who will benefit from the commons. We should examine commons critically, on a case-by-case basis and use it as concept for uniting common struggles but not as a panacea.

Balkans as the European periphery

The post-socialist Balkan states share a common trajectory from socialist to capitalist societies on the European periphery. In the late 1980s socialist countries began the transformation to capitalism and, unlike the on-going attack on the public sector in Western European countries, in our region capital started to spread to all spheres of society, permeating at the same time both the productive and the public service sector.

The last decade of the 20th century in the Balkans was marked by the dismantling of the socialist heritage, privatisation, and implementation of market reforms. The immediate effects have been a dramatic fall in production, rise of unemployment, rapid impoverishment of a large part of the population and the enormous enrichment of a small privileged elite. After a steep decline, the level of GDP Slovenia was the first to reach a level of GDP achieved in 1989 (in 1998). However, some countries such as Serbia and Macedonia are still way below the 1989 level and there is no indication that they will be able to reach this level in near future. Slovenia's more favourable position is influenced by stronger trade unions, gradual privatization and slower deindustrialization in comparison to other post-socialist countries – banks, public service sector and some parts of infrastructure in this country were not privatised and a low rate of local currency allowed competitiveness of domestic goods in the international market. In the period between 1991 and 2004 Slovenia was not in a better position in comparison to the other post-socialist countries because of its skills in adopting to capitalism but because it had preserved some socialist elements (Krašovec 2013).

The process of restoration of capitalism was almost always followed by lower taxes, such as taxes on corporate profits, or the introduction of a flat tax rate, under the pretext of liberalizing the economy and attracting foreign investors. But even when investors came, it was often because of cheap labour, low taxes and low environmental standards, as well as subsidies that post-socialist countries offered to these foreign investors. Foreign direct investment almost never enabled serious development of the real sector; usually investments were oriented towards services, agriculture, light industry, production of semi-finished goods, or assembly lines.

The devastation of local industry during last two decades further burdened state budgets. As productivity was falling, unemployment and the proportion of socially vulnerable people was rising. This tendency means both lower budget revenues from taxation of wages and the increasing pressure on social welfare systems, which are on the verge of collapse. The transformation from a socialist to a capitalist mode of production means that the profit stands as the centre of the economy and the measure of economic success is GDP growth. However, neither of these two measures tells us much about the wellbeing of the population – a high percentage of GDP growth can be accompanied with an increase in inequality, unemployment, and the degradation of social and environmental standards. Similarly, high profitability can come at the expense of a drastic reduction in wages and taxes and thus an erosion of social services.

In a situation where industry is almost destroyed, the public sector is still relatively large and the credit debt constantly grows, neoliberal-oriented governments are again turning to privatization in order to reduce budget deficits. Different natural resources such as mines, forests, water springs or parts of urban areas are being put up for sale. Exploitation of natural resources often lacks appropriate ecological standards. That is why the costs of remediation of environmental damage may exceed budget revenue. At the same time, in the context of the dominance of neoliberal ideology, the public sector is under constant pressure. It is usually emphasized that this sector of the economy is parasitic in the sense that it only spends budget money. The solution proposed is that the public services should be exposed to market relations in order to be more efficient. The state is, therefore, withdrawing from its role as provider of goods and services and, guided by neoliberal instructions, it appears only as a framework for the establishment of 'a favourable economic climate,' in which the market would decide on production and distribution.

Apart from privatization of public service utilities, we are also witnessing the commodification of non-privatized goods. Here it is useful to recall

Marx's emphasis according to which commodity production can never be production for human needs. In other words, the whole logic on which our societies are based today prevents a truly socially oriented production. Through the imperative of economic efficiency ever-new segments of the public sector are being commodified and exposed to market exchange. The fact that companies which remain state-owned – both those engaged in the production of services and those engaged in the production of goods – are often misused by political parties further complicates the problem. This form of exploitation of public property is not rare, but is, in a manner of self-imposed orientalism, usually attributed to some variant of Balkan backwardness. Actually it is capitalism that legitimates greed and creates 'institutionalised cynicism' (Streeck 2010) whereby we are all disposed to apply, avoid or circumvent rules for individual benefit. This is why capitalist relations are blind to ideas of the public good or the public interest, and why the claim that further advancement of market relations will reduce corruption is a fable and a myth.

In the Balkans, natural commons were dispossessed mostly through physical space in cities and in attractive real-estate locations where financial capital was invested to maintain the profit rate acquired from primitive accumulation. Cities became the physical space both for the accumulation of new capital and its rent, and for the materialisation of surplus capital in the real-estate market. The global financial crisis hit hard on this region that was deindustrialised and dependant on financial services and real-estate markets. There is strong pressure for further privatisation of public services like health, education, social services, water supply, waste disposal, and even some conventional core state services like defence and police. These measures are intended to reduce budgetary deficits and since monetary policy is impotent, economic growth can be only be assured by new dispossession, mostly through lowering of workers' wages and through the destruction and privatisation of natural commons which are now under unprecedented pressure. Harvey (2011) explains how capitalism in crisis needs a 'spatial fix' so surplus capital can finally be invested in physical space where it can secure a satisfying profit rate so surplus labour (the unemployed) can be put back in the production process. These structural problems cannot be solved from the European periphery. Nevertheless, we can still contest austerity measures, which are a self-destructing social mechanism. We can advocate redistribution from rich to poor, demand change in monetary policy, progressive taxation, economic regionalisation, socialisation of rents from natural resources and Green-Keynesian industrialisation together with democratic economies that are labour-intensive, capital-saving, create big social value and reduce ecological footprints.

A common struggle in the Balkans is possible if we focus on the *common ground* in existing struggles. It is necessary to connect struggles in the region that oppose privatisation of the commons and public goods like water, forests, agricultural land, factories, healthcare, education, urban public spaces, public transportation and other infrastructure.

Existing commons struggles in the Balkans[428]

Since 2006 social movements for free higher education have appeared in several countries in the Balkans: from Slovenia and Croatia to Serbia. Initiatives like the protest movement 'Independent Student Initiative' that emerged in Zagreb in 2008 had an impact not only in Croatia but in the region more broadly. In Fraser's (2003) terms, the movement did not focus narrowly on furthering particular interests and rights, but advanced a transformative approach, offering a scourging critique both of the capitalist economy and of the limits of representative democracy (Dolenec and Doolan 2012). Though this movement did not explicitly couch itself in the language of the commons, it initiated a radical critique of the political economy of capitalism, and affirmed principles of direct democracy, participation and solidarity that lie at the heart of commons struggles.

In Serbia the largest mobilizations on the topic of the commons happened at Belgrade University. Insufficient budgetary funds and the exposure of faculties to market competition caused a drastic increase in tuition fees that prevented members of poorer strata of society from accessing higher education. However, the problem is not only in direct charges for education, but also in the whole process of commodification in which knowledge is standardized and directed towards the needs of the market. In this situation education loses emancipatory potential and is used only to create an army of qualified and highly adaptive labour power i.e. for producing a highly qualified workforce that is fully subordinated to the demands of capital (Stojanović, Vesić and Simović 2013). Unfortunately, the student movement in Serbia predominantly questioned high tuition fees and demanded reform framed within the Bologna process. What was often left unremarked upon in these students' struggles was, on the one hand, the structure that determines the commodification of education and, on the other, that this process is not an isolated phenomenon, but a rule which is being implemented at all levels of society. In the fall of 2011, for the first time after a long period of internal conflicts, major trade unions in Serbia gathered in a protest where workers demanded the withdrawal of two legislative proposals concerning public utilities and the introduction of public-private partnership. Though these proposals were soon adopted by the Serbian Parliament, tens of thousands of protesting workers indicate an awareness about the negative effects of these laws.

The 'Right to the City' Initiative in Zagreb, which started in mid-2006, was an important engine of civic resistance in the city for over 5 years. Its activities were directed against the usurpation of public space by private interests, most notably in the fight for Varšavska Street in downtown Zagreb. Though that particular struggle was lost to the cosy liaison between Zagreb's mayor and a private investor, this protest movement has successfully advanced the agenda of the urban commons in Croatia. It introduced several critical issues into the public agenda such as citizen participation in urban planning and sustainable urbanisation, while at the same time exposing narrow economic interests and crony deals that jeopardize the public interest. A similar initiative centred around defending the urban commons emerged in Belgrade, called the 'Initiative for the Protection of Peti Park'. It emerged in the summer of 2005 after citizens of a Belgrade neighbourhood organised to resist a development project that would have replaced a city park with a multi-storey building. This resistance lasted for three years and it was successful in forcing the city government to protect the city park.

Furthermore, while the most obvious connection between recent struggles for the hill Srđ (in Dubrovnik, Croatia) and the space of the 'Beko' factory (Belgrade, Serbia) are the architects doing the development projects, closer inspection unfolds not only more similarities, but focuses analysis on ways in which urban struggles for commons take place in the region. Beko (Belgrade Confection) used to be the largest textile factory in Belgrade, with one of the production complexes situated in the historical centre of the city at the foot of Kalemegdan fortress. Since the mid-1960s it was planned for the factory to be removed and for the park to be extended. The project aimed at connecting the foot of the fortress and the bank of the river Danube. However, the factory stayed where it was, and after the 2000s it went into bankruptcy after which the property of the factory in the city centre was sold to a Greek developer in 2007. The Greek developer started changing the urban plan in order to build a closed mix-use complex consisting of a hotel, shopping mall, housing and sport facilities. It was only in 2011 that this transformation reached the media, thanks to a group of, mostly retired, professionals who protested mainly on the grounds of the height allowed by the new plan and the fact that it would ruin the landmark view of Belgrade fortress. The initiative also stressed that the proposed location should be a park as it was planned and that planning of such an important site should be done in a more participatory manner. Although this issue had the potential to unite a broader coalition of actors that would address issues related to the future of the city and public/common space, little had actually happened. In the next step, one of the most famous architecture bureaus in the world – Zaha Hadid Architects – was hired to design a new master plan. The plan was approved by the City, but it also successfully diverted the public debate from questions of spatial justice and the program planned for the site to questions concerning the aesthetics of the proposed project. The public debate showed the inability of both officials, but also of society to define the public interest for the site, and the future development of the City more broadly. An even more controversial Emirati-funded development project called 'Belgrade Waterfront', that would completely alter the urban landscape of the Sava riverbank has been aggressively promoted by the Serbian government.

Srđ is a plateau on a hill above Dubrovnik, overlooking the Old Town, and it became the focus of a civic initiative 'Srđ is Ours.' While not entirely owned by the city, the plateau in question is almost the only free space where Dubrovnik can spread and build much-needed public amenities. Regardless of that, the city has been, not so quietly, supporting plans for a Golf Resort that would enclose most of Srđ. Golf is here, following common practices in the world, just an excuse for extensive real-estate development – in this specific case of luxurious residential villas. Although the County had rejected the master plan for development in 2010, support for the project by the political strata has been increasing, often stressing the fact that this project will open many possibilities for employment for the local population, while undermining the investment the city needs to make in order to extend the infrastructure to the sites in question. Like in the case of *Beko*, in order to try to divert attention from the nature of this investment to aesthetics, Zaha Hadid Architects were hired to design concept villas for the resort. However, the project never managed to stir discussion away from the true nature of this project – the enclosure of the potential commons for Dubrovnik. The well-organized initiative 'Srđ is Ours', supported by a national alliance of other activist networks, successfully communicated what a golf course on Srđ would do to the city and the importance of getting involved, even managing to secure a local referendum. While the vast majority of people voted against the project, the problematic Croatian Law on Referendum does not make the vote binding for the Municipality. Although it seemed that the battle for Srđ had been lost, the transformation of a part of the activist initiative 'Srđ is Ours' into an independent list 'Srđ is the City' for the local elections in 2013 shows how it is possible to build a political platform by using the concept of the commons.

The actors that produce and reproduce the urban built environment are the most likely agents for social change today. The circumstances surrounding Srđ, and struggles focused on social and spatial justice more generally show the possibility of the struggle for the commons to become a platform for larger political articulation. In order for that to happen, it was necessary for those involved to use the commons paradigm as a critical tool in order to understand both national and transnational forces driving the privatization of Srđ and to position their struggle into a broader narrative. The Platform 'Srđ is Ours' built its strength upon the work and articulations developed in the Right to the City initiative in Zagreb, and more specifically on issues surrounding Cvjetni trg and Varšavska street, and pushed the struggle against the enclosure of the commons, not only for Dubrovnik, but also for the whole of Croatia a step further into the political sphere.

A larger coalition in which the struggles against privatization of the public/common goods are connected to unions on the one side, and environmental struggles on the other – thus forming a broad network of allies – in the longer run has the potential to redefine the political scene in Croatia. Unfortunately, in Serbia such tendencies are still weak. While the scale of the land grab, especially in Belgrade, had been disclosed by media on various occasions, this has not produced strong public reactions. Activism is isolated to issues of labour addressing the dispossession of workers due to the privatizations and deindustrialization that followed. The struggle against the enclosure of public space, such as the various struggles for public green open spaces (Peti Park and Zvezdara Forest in Belgrade, Aerodrom in Kragujevac) did not address the political arena beyond their particular demands, but only on the grounds of reclaiming the space to its immediate users. A true understanding of the deep connections among the various anti-privatization struggles still needs to happen.

When discussing the potential of the commons, the case of Bosnia and Herzegovina is particularly perplexing since it is a de facto divided society where ethno-nationalist politics, assisted by fear, uncertainty and neo-colonial international community politics (Majstorović 2007, 2013), have resulted in little consensus over who did what in the past to maintain a state of negative peace (Galtung 1996). The country lives in a kind of perpetual transition and state of emergency (Agamben 2005, Pandolfi 2010) while the lack of commonality and understanding of the commons in the aforementioned sense have greatly impeded the processes of anti-capitalist struggle and similar movements in the region. However, non-traditional models such as informal classrooms, like The Public Classroom-The Commons in June 2012, organized by the non-governmental organization 'Centar Grad' in Tuzla, and the series of lectures organized by the Language,

Ideology and Power group of intellectuals, students and activists at the Banja Luka University (Majstorović 2013) offer hope. These initiatives became a way of regionally and transnationally connecting intellectuals, students and activists protecting the commons by insisting on a politics of memory, antifascism, commonality and solidarity under galloping capitalism. The protests that erupted across Bosnia-Herzegovina in February 2014, as well as the establishment of the plenums, citizens' assemblies, in many cities show the huge political potential of struggles centred around questions of social justice and solidarity.

Direct democracy and the creation of social resistance on the street by grassroots citizens' associations or no-leadership movements in the last year in major Bosnian and Herzegovinian cities has also given way to expressing the political in non-traditional ways, going beyond nationalist options on offer by parliamentary parties in the country. Citizens' protest walks in Banja Luka under the slogan '(the?) Park is ours' between May and September 2012 became the first act of collective will against the authorities triggered by the destruction of Picin Park, a favourite hangout for Banjalukans, after the developer Milo Radišić received permits to demolish it in order to build a complex containing businesses and residences without public notice. At the first demonstration, in late May, a thousand people marched and although the number of 'walkers' dissipated in the following months, it was the largest protest to take place in Banja Luka after the 1992-1995 war. Activists from a dozen local organizations gathered 6,000 signatures on a petition against the construction project asking for evidence about the procedure that led to the sale of the parkland, and for documentation of the official decision-making process that led to it and delivered them to the city government. In July 2012, once again proving the links between repressive state apparatuses and capital, police brutally reacted against Željko Vulić who was beaten for protecting his own property against the planned development. In July 2013, the construction company ordered the destruction of a part of the road that Vulić family uses as the only access to their home and he practically lost the battle against the President of the Republika Srpska entity, Milorad Dodik, his oligarchy and family-friends' network. The city authorities did nothing to help his case while state owned media either barely reported on it or constantly held the official side, claiming its apparent legality.

Finally, triggered by the death of the three-month old Belmina Ibrišević from Gračanica, a baby that needed to travel abroad for urgent medical treatment, but couldn't leave the state because she was not allocated an ID number and could therefore not get a passport, showed that citizens protests in front of state institutions of BiH in Sarajevo were more than the sum of its parts. Starting as protests demanding that the Parliament immediately adopt the law on citizen IDs on the national level, it became an act of collective criticism of the dysfunctional nature of the Dayton peace accords and the ethnic-based violence it legitimated. All of these struggles, and especially mass protests in the Winter and Spring of 2014 linked up in the struggle for the common good, are good examples of debunking and openly challenging the power of dominant political elites in the country and their accumulated wealth and a good sign that, almost twenty years after the war, the situation in Bosnia and Herzegovina is changing.

In Bulgaria, the first serious resistance against commodification of the commons happened in 2007, when the so-called Socialist Party introduced principles of new public management into the public high school system. Teachers and schools were forced to compete with each other. There was a massive strike against the reform that lasted over a month, but in the end was not successful. Currently, these reforms are being deepened through new legislative amendments that enable the redistribution of public money to private schools, legitimated, once again, with the rhetoric of competition, efficiency, individual choice and 'money follows the student' arguments, as funding is made dependent on the number of pupils. At the same time, an identical regime is being introduced in the media sector where the government is designing ways of transferring funding from public to private media. Principles of new public management have also been imposed in the healthcare sector, pushing it into a serious crisis. All this has lead to the closing down of dozens of schools and hospitals in rural regions. Currently, there are attempts to privatize the public railroad company, but this was met with strong workers' resistance, leading to a wave of strikes in 2011. Similarly, there has been strong resistance against the commodification of the digital commons. Attempts to close down torrent sites and to limit file sharing were met with a series of protests. ACTA was opposed by thousands of people marching in the streets in early 2012, forcing the government to back down on its support for the trade agreement. In the protests of early 2013, tens of thousands of people marched around the country against high electricity bills and demanded the nationalization of utility companies. Over time, however, the protests became wider and rather ambivalent and the spontaneous movement against the political system did not bring tangible results.

In Bulgaria social mobilizations around the commons were strongest within the environmental movement. There have been a few attempts to liberalize genetically modified (GM) food production, but all were met with nation-wide resistance and mobilization, forcing the government to back down and effectively limiting the attempted commercialization of the genetic heritage of humanity. Mobilizations against the privatization of natural parks have also been on going since 2006 and have succeeded in protecting them as commons. Moreover, since 2012 these movements were not only maintaining a reactive stance against commodification, but articulating positive proposals and initiatives for new progressive management of the commons. This has taken the form of a new food cooperative movement, inspired by the ideas of community-supported agriculture and Via Campesina's concept of food sovereignty. After 1999 state land was transferred to municipalities, which in turn often engaged in lucrative sales to private investors. After 2005, regulations regarding the purchasing of land were liberalised, further incentivising enclosures of rural and urban space. Environmental groups mobilized against the destruction of protected land in 2007, and again more recently, in 2012, when demonstrations were organised against the Forestry Act. The legislation was amended in favour of a private investor who wanted to enclose parts of what used to be publicly accessible land in Pirin. As a result of the protests, the Act was vetoed and amended.

In conclusion, like elsewhere in the region, in Bulgaria processes of accumulation by dispossession in the 1990s were not met with serious opposition. Only after 2006 were there wider mobilizations. The ones that were more successful were against the enclosure of the digital commons, against GMOs, and against the privatization of natural parks. Effective workers' mobilizations proved to be more difficult to organize. The protests in early 2013 against high electricity bills were not able to articulate clear demands. A serious challenge faced by all of those movements is that they find it hard to articulate an adequate language for understanding the political economy of enclosures of the commons since 1989. Instead they often became caught up within liberal ideological clichés of fighting against corruption, against monopolies, for more transparency and so on.

Commoning the struggle

Anti-austerity protest in Sarajevo. The banner reads 'You've plundered for 20 years. Enough!' Today the public sector is probably the most important field of our struggle, through this struggle is not without contradictions. The public sector employs a large number of workers who can lose jobs if reforms driven by the logic of austerity measures continue. However, the capacity for mobilization is even greater, because privatization and the reduction of the public sector affects a much wider population. Bonding the interests of workers with those of beneficiaries of services seems to be a key to building a broader and more efficient movement for the defence of the public sector.

This potential movement should not forget that a political strategy based only on 'fighting cuts' risks giving the impression that it is simply the scale of state expenditure that is being contested, rendering invisible the underlying logic of commodification and the new reality that public services themselves have become a site of accumulation that is crucial for the continuing expansion of international capital (Huws 2012). Therefore we must extend our demand to the issue of how and by whom the public sector should be managed.

With all its flaws, the trade union movement in the public sector, student mobilizations, struggles for urban commons and natural resources like the ones we described should be seen as sparks that could trigger a broader struggle. Awareness of the need to protect the commons across the region is currently low, so any attempt of shaking these sleepy societies into action are more than welcome. However, the creation of a broader movement that will truly be able to shake the foundations of the dominant system is hard. In an impoverished society with high unemployment and rising poverty people are focused on short-term survival. Privatization and the creation of a 'favourable business climate' which attracts foreign capital as opposed to the reproduction of the current situation then, at best, seems as the lesser of two evils. Therefore the need for systemic change in society is probably the most important argument in which left-wing groups and individuals have to convince the wider part of the population.

The movement established on a line of defence and taking over of the commons could have considerable potential. It could encompass and articulate the issues that currently fail to initiate mobilizations, even though they attract public attention. Here we can include the issue of privatization of agriculture, mineral resources, forests and water, a range of environmental issues, as well as the privatization and commercialization of public services – from kindergartens to universities, from water supply systems to garbage and electricity. A true understanding of the deep connections among these various struggles for the commons still needs to happen in the region of the Balkans, which is where the political conception of the commons comes into play – as a demand for developing alternative ways of social production, taking effective social control over resources and conditions needed for life and human emancipation. Our political action should be directed at defending the commons from new enclosures and creating new commons, while always being reminded that they should foster human emancipation.

In building effective political alliances, it is important to link regional struggles with global struggles for global commons like the Internet, genetic resources, science, atmosphere, oceans, biodiversity and others. It is also tactically important to join forces with Keynesians and oppose austerity measures which are destroying the welfare state and social reproduction, and which could lead to authoritarian reversals. This includes policy advocacy that tries to stop current trends imposed by the state through legislation and policy making from health to education and urban planning. It is not wise to dogmatically give up on state power so social movements should when possible directly engage into or support democratic progressive and radical left political organisations that compete for state power. Also, it is important to be aware of neoliberal attempts to solve the current multiple crises with what had caused them in the first place, namely more market solutions. This happens for instance in proposing to impose carbon trading schemes as a policy for climate change mitigation, which effectively means privatizing the atmosphere to protect it from pollution.

We need to demonstrate how the Left is not just good at criticising structural forces but that it can offer proposals for an alternative political and economic system. We should directly encourage collective production and consumption on the local level through workers cooperatives, community gardens, communal energy production and consumption systems, consumer/food and agricultural cooperatives, digital and material tools and resources libraries. This social experimentation on the local level and in cyberspace should include experimentation with radical democratic practices that could be reproduced on a larger scale. Finally, the commons seem a more productive concept for common struggle in the Balkans than public goods. Public goods are a narrower concept than the commons and they rely on the state. The commons imply *real* social control over state-owned resources by the people rather than relying on representational democracy.

We need to engage both in an act of commoning between green and left movements, and across national borders. Common tactics as commons themselves should be diverse to be successful. Sometimes we have to construct new commons as autonomous zones of physical and social reproduction which will logistically strengthen our struggles. Sometimes we have to experiment and innovate commons in order to demonstrate alternatives to the current system. Sometimes we have to directly defend existing commons that are under threat of privatisation and commodification because it will be difficult to recommunise them later. Sometimes we have to expand existing commons in order to enlarge the commons sphere towards the state and market. Sometimes we have to transform current public goods into commons through expanding social control to ensure that they are for the benefit of people. Sometimes we have to lobby the state to support new and existing commons practices through policy and legal changes. Sometimes we have to engage in a battle for state power to make at least part of the political sphere a commons. In other words, what we need are diverse and innovative tactics by social movements that are coordinated within a common platform.

Bibliography

Agamben, G., *The State of Exception*, Chicago, University of Chicago Press, 2005.
Bollier, D. and Helfrich, S. (eds.), *The Wealth of the Commons: A World Beyond Market and State*, Amherst MA, The Commons Strategies Group, 2012.
De Angelis, M., 'Crisis, Capitalism and Cooperation: Does Capital Need a Commons Fix?', in D. Bollier and S. Helfrich, (eds.) The Wealth of the Commons: A World Beyond Market and State, Amherst MA, The Commons Strategies Group, 2012.
Denitsch, B., *Ethnic Nationalism: The Tragic Death of Yugoslavia* (revised ed), Minneapolis, University of Minnesota Press, 1996.
Dolenec, D., 'The Commons as a Radical Democratic Project', paper presented at the MAMA conference 'Economy of Crisis Capitalism and Economy of the Commons', 22-24 November 2012, Zagreb.
Dolenec, D. and Doolan, K., 'Reclaiming the Role of Higher Education in Croatia: Dominant and Oppositional Framings', in Zgaga, Treichler and Brennan (eds.) *The Globalisation Challenge for European Higher Education*, Frankfurt am Main, Peter Lang Publishing, 2013.
Dolenec, D. and Žitko, M., 'Ostrom and Horvat: Identifying Principles of a Socialist Governmentality', Group 22 Working Paper, 2013, (available at <http://www.grupa22.hr/wp-content/uploads/2013/07/ Dolenec-Zitko-Working-Paper-2013.pdf>).
Fraser, N., 'Social Justice in the Age of Identity Politics: Redistribution, Recognition and Participation'. In: N. Fraser, A. Honneth (eds.), *Redistribution or Recognition: A Political- Philosophical Exchange*. London, Verso, 2003.
Galtung, J., *Peaceful Means: Peace and Conflict, Development and Civilization*, London, Sage, 1996.
Hardin, G., 'The Tragedy of the Commons', *Science*, vol. 162 Hardt, M. (2012). 'Dva lica apokalipse: Pismo iz Copenhagena', *Up & Underground: critical theory dossier*, 21/22 Bijeli Val, Zagreb, 1968.
Harvey, D., *The New Imperialism*. Oxford, Oxford University Press, 2003.
Harvey, D., *Rebel Cities: From the Right to the City to the Urban Revolution*, London, Verso, 2012.
Harvey, D., 'An Interview with David Harvey: Practice of Commoning', 2013, (available at <http://tanpelin.blogspot.fr/2013/03/an-interview- with-david-harvey-practice.html>).
Huws, U.,'Kriza kao kapitalistička prilika: Nova akumulacija kroz komodifikaciju javnih usluga'. In: Darko Vesić et al. eds. *U borbi za javno dobro: analize, strategije i perspektive*. Beograd, Centar za politike emancipacije, str. 23-59, 2013, (available at <http:// pe.org.rs/wp-content/ uploads/2013/01/U-borbi-za-javno-dobro-CPE-2012.pdf>).
Knaus, G. and Martin, F., 'Lessons from Bosnia and Herzegovina: Travails of the European Raj'. *Journal of Democracy*, Vol. 14 (3), 3 July 2003.
Krašovec, P. (2013). 'Intervju: Zaglavljeni na periferiji', in *Vreme*, 7. 3. 2013, pp.

18-20, (available at <http://www.vreme.com/cms/ view. php?id=1102238>).
Majstorović, D., *Diskurs, moć i međunarodna zajednica*, Banja Luka, Filozofski Fakultet, 2007.
Majstorović, D., *Diskursi periferije*, Beograd: Biblioteka XX Vek, 2013.
Mattei, U., 'First Thoughts for a Phenomenology of the Commons' in D. Bollier and S. Helfrich (eds.) *The Wealth of the Commons: A World Beyond Market and State*, Amherst MA, The Commons Strategies Group, 2012.
Ostrom, E., *Governing the Commons: The Evolution of Institutions for Collective Action*, Cambridge, Cambridge University Press, 1990.
Ostrom, E. and Hess, C., 'Introduction: An Overview of the Knowledge Commons', in Ostrom, E, Hess, C (eds.) *Understanding Knowledge as a Commons: From Theory to Practice*, Cambridge MA, The MIT Press, 2007.
Pandolfi, M., 'From Paradox to Paradigm: The Permanent State of Emergency in the Balkans,' in Didier Fassin and Mariella Pandolfi, eds., *Contemporary States of Emergency: The Politics of Military and Humanitarian Interventions*, Cambridge, MA, MIT Press, Zone books, 2010.
Stanojević, A, Vesić, D. i Simović, V., 'Kome je odgovorno naše društveno odgovorno visoko obrazovanje?' In: Maja Solar et al. eds. *Stvar: časopis za teorijske prakse*, Novi Sad, KSF Gerusija, 2013, (available at <http://gerusija.com/downloads/STVAR_4. Pdf>).

Feminism and the politics of the Commons*

Silvia Federici

Our perspective is that of the planet's commoners: human beings with bodies, needs, desires, whose most essential tradition is of cooperation in the making and maintenance of life; and yet have had to do so under conditions of suffering and separation from one another, from nature and from the common wealth we have created through generations. The way in which women's subsistence work and the contribution of the commons to the concrete survival of local people are both made invisible through the idealizing of them are not only similar but have common roots…In a way, women are treated like commons and commons are treated like women.[429]

Reproduction precedes social production. Touch the women, touch the rock.[430]

Introduction: why commons?

At least since the Zapatistas took over the *zócalo* in San Cristobal de las Casas on 31 December 1993 to protest legislation dissolving the *ejidal* lands of Mexico, the concept of 'the commons' has been gaining popularity among the radical left, internationally and in the USA, appearing as a basis for convergence among anarchists, Marxists, socialists, ecologists, and eco-feminists.[431]

There are important reasons why this apparently archaic idea has come to the centre of political discussion in contemporary social movements. Two in particular stand out. On one side is the demise of the statist model of revolution that for decades had sapped the efforts of radical movements to build an alternative to capitalism. On the other, the neo-liberal attempt to

---

* This article was first published online at *The Commoner* in January 2011, <http://www.commoner.org.uk/?p=113>, and was published in *Revolution at Point Zero: Housework, Reproduction and Feminist Struggle,* Oakland: PM Press, 2012. It is reproduced here with the kind permission of Silvia Federici.

subordinate every form of life and knowledge to the logic of the market has heightened our awareness of the danger of living in a world in which we no longer have access to seas, trees, animals, and our fellow beings except through the cash-nexus. The 'new enclosures' have also made visible a world of communal properties and relations that many had believed to be extinct or had not valued until threatened with privatization.[432] Ironically, the new enclosures have demonstrated that not only the common has not vanished, but also new forms of social cooperation are constantly being produced, including in areas of life where none previously existed like, for example, the Internet.

The idea of the common/s, in this context, has offered a logical and historical alternative to both State and Private Property, the State and the Market, enabling us to reject the fiction that they are mutually exclusive and exhaustive of our political possibilities. It has also served an ideological function as a unifying concept prefiguring the cooperative society that the radical left is striving to create. Nevertheless, ambiguities as well as significant differences remain in the interpretations of this concept, which we need to clarify if we want the principle of the commons to translate into a coherent political project.[433]

What, for example, constitutes a common? We have land, water, air commons, digital commons; our acquired entitlements (e.g., social security pensions) are often described as commons, and so are languages, libraries, and the collective products of past cultures. But are all these commons equivalent from the viewpoint of their political potential? Are they all compatible? And how can we ensure that they do not project a unity that remains to be constructed? Finally, should we speak of 'commons' in the plural, or 'the common' as Autonomist Marxists propose we do, this concept designating in their view the social relations characteristic of the dominant form of production in the post-Fordist era?

With these questions in mind, in this essay, I look at the politics of the commons from a feminist perspective where 'feminist' refers to a standpoint shaped by the struggle against sexual discrimination and over reproductive work, which, to paraphrase Linebaugh's comment above, is the rock upon which society is built and by which every model of social organization must be tested. This intervention is necessary, in my view, to better define this politics and clarify the conditions under which the principle of the common/s can become the foundation of an anti-capitalist program. Two concerns make these tasks especially important.

Global commons, World Bank commons

First, since at least the early 1990s, the language of the commons has been appropriated by the World Bank and the United Nations and put at the service of privatization. Under the guise of protecting biodiversity and conserving the global commons, the Bank has turned rain forests into ecological reserves, has expelled the populations that for centuries had drawn their sustenance from them, while ensuring access to those who can pay, for instance, through eco-tourism.[434] For its part, the United Nations has revised the international law governing access to the oceans in ways that enables governments to concentrate the use of seawaters in fewer hands, again in the name of preserving the common heritage of mankind.[435]

The World Bank and the UN are not alone in their adaptation of the idea of the commons to market interests. Responding to different motivations, a re-valorisation of the commons has become trendy among mainstream economists and capitalist planners; witness the growing academic literature on the subject and its cognates: social capital, gift economies, altruism. Witness also the official recognition of this trend through the conferral of the Nobel Prize for Economics in 2009 to the leading voice in this field, the political scientist Elinor Ostrom.[436]

Development planners and policymakers have discovered that, under proper conditions, a collective management of natural resources can be more efficient and less prone to conflict than privatization, and that commons can be made to produce very well for the market.[437] They have also recognized that, carried to the extreme, the commodification of social relations has self-defeating consequences. The extension of the commodity form to every corner of the social factory, which neo-liberalism has promoted, is an ideal limit for capitalist ideologues, but it is a project not only unrealizable but undesirable from the viewpoint of long-term reproduction of the capitalist system. Capitalist accumulation is structurally dependent on the free appropriation of immense quantities of labour and resources that must appear as externalities to the market, like the unpaid domestic work that women have provided, upon which employers have relied for the reproduction of the workforce.

It is no accident, then, that long before the Wall Street meltdown, a variety of economists and social theorists warned that the marketization of all spheres of life is detrimental to the market's well-functioning, for markets too, the argument goes, depend on the existence of non-monetary relations like confidence, trust, and gift giving.[438] In brief, capital is learning about the virtues of the common good. Even the *Economist*, the organ of capitalist free-market economics for more than 150 years, in its 31 July 2008 issue, cautiously joined the chorus.

The economics of the 'new commons' – the journal wrote – is still in its infancy. It is too soon to be confident about its hypotheses. But it may yet prove a useful way of thinking about problems, such as managing the Internet, intellectual property or international pollution, on which policymakers need all the help they can get.

We must be very careful, then, not to craft the discourse on the commons in such a way as to allow a crisis-ridden capitalist class to revive itself, posturing, for instance, as the environmental guardian of the planet.

What commons?

A second concern is that, while international institutions have learned to make commons functional to the market, how commons can become the foundation of a non-capitalist economy is a question still unanswered. From Peter Linebaugh's work, especially *The Magna Carta Manifesto* (2008), we have learned that commons have been the thread that has connected the history of the class struggle into our time, and indeed the fight for the commons is all around us. Maine are fighting to preserve access to their fisheries, under attack by corporate fleets; residents of Appalachia are organizing to save their mountains threatened by strip mining; open source and free software movements are opposing the commodification of knowledge and opening new spaces for communications and cooperation. We also have the many invisible, commoning activities and communities that people are creating in North America, which Chris Carlsson has described in his *Nowtopia* (2007). As Carlsson shows, much creativity is invested in the production of 'virtual commons' and forms of sociality that thrive under the radar of the money/market economy.

Most important has been the creation of urban gardens, which have spread, in the 1980s and 1990s, across the country, thanks mostly to the initiatives of immigrant communities from Africa, the Caribbean or the South of the United States. Their significance cannot be overestimated. Urban gardens have opened the way to a 'rurbanisation' process that is indispensable if we are to regain control over our food production, regenerate our environment and provide for our subsistence. The gardens are far more than a source of food security: they are centres of sociality, knowledge production, and cultural and intergenerational exchange. As Margarita Fernandez (2003) writes of urban gardens in New York, they 'strengthen community cohesion' as places where people come together not just to work the land, but to play cards, hold weddings, and have baby showers or birthday parties.[439] Some have partner relationships with local schools whereby they give children environmental education after school. Not least, gardens are 'a medium for the transport and encounter of diverse cultural practices' so that African vegetables and farming practices, for example, mix with those of the Caribbean (ibid.).

Still, the most significant feature of urban gardens is that they produce for neighbourhood consumption, rather than for commercial purposes. This distinguishes them from other reproductive commons that either produce for the market, like the fisheries of Maine's 'Lobster Coast,'[440] or are bought on the market, like the land trusts that preserve open spaces. The problem, however, is that urban gardens have remained a spontaneous grassroots initiative and there have been few attempts by movements in the USA to expand their presence and to make access to land a key terrain of struggle. More generally, the left has not posed the question of how to bring together the many proliferating commons that are being defended, developed, and fought for, so that they can form a cohesive whole and provide a foundation for a new mode of production.

An exception is the theory proposed by Antonio Negri and Michael Hardt in *Empire* (2000), *Multitude* (2004), and recently *Commonwealth* (2009*)*, which argues that a society built on the principle of 'the common' is *already evolving* from the informatisation and 'cognitivisation' of production. According to this theory, as production presumably becomes production of knowledge, culture, and subjectivity, organized through the internet, a common space and common wealth are created that escape the problem of defining rules of inclusion or exclusion. For access and use multiply the resources available on the net, rather than subtracting from them, thus signifying the possibility of a society built on abundance – the only remaining hurdle confronting the 'multitude' being how to prevent the capitalist 'capture' of the wealth produced.

The appeal of this theory is that it does not separate the formation of 'the common' from the organization of work and production but sees it immanent to it. Its limit is that its picture of the common absolutises the work of a minority possessing skills not available to most of the world population. It also ignores that this work produces commodities for the market, and it overlooks the fact that online communication/production depends on economic activities – mining, microchip and rare earth production–that, as presently organized, are extremely destructive, socially and ecologically.[441] Moreover, with its emphasis on knowledge and information, this theory skirts the question of the reproduction of everyday life. This, however, is true of the discourse on the commons as a whole, which is mostly concerned with the formal preconditions for the existence of commons and less with the material requirements for the construction of a commons-based economy enabling us to resist dependence on wage labour and subordination to capitalist relations. It is in this context that a feminist perspective on the commons is important. It begins with the realization that, as the primary subjects of reproductive work, historically and in our time, women have depended on access to communal natural resources more than men and have been most penalized by their privatization and most committed to their defence. As I wrote in *Caliban and the Witch* (2004), in the first phase of capitalist development, women were at the forefront of the struggle against land enclosures both in England and in the 'New World' and they were the staunchest defenders of the communal cultures that European colonization attempted to destroy. In Peru, when the Spanish *conquistadores* took control of their villages, women fled to the high mountains where they recreated forms of collective life that have survived to this day. Not surprisingly, the sixteenth and seventeenth centuries saw the most violent attack on women in the history of the world: the persecution of women as witches. Today, in the face of a new process of Primitive Accumulation, women are the main social force standing in the way of a complete commercialization of nature, supporting a non-capitalist use of land and a subsistence-oriented agriculture. Women are the subsistence farmers of the world. In Africa, they produce 80% of the food people consume, despite the attempts made by the World Bank and other agencies to convince them to divert their activities to cash-cropping. In the 1990s, in many African towns, in the face of rising food prices, they have appropriated plots in public lands and planted corn, beans, cassava 'along roadsides...in parks, along rail-lines..' changing the urban landscape of African cities and breaking down the separation between town and country in the process.[442] In India, the Philippines, and across Latin America, women have replanted trees in degraded forests, joined hands to chase away loggers, made blockades against mining operations and the construction of dams, and led the revolt against the privatization of water.[443]

The other side of women's struggle for direct access to means of reproduction has been the formation across the Third World, from Cambodia to Senegal, of credit associations that function as money commons (Podlashuc, 2009). Differently named, the *tontines* (as they are called in parts of Africa) are autonomous, self-managed, women-made banking systems that provide cash to individuals or groups that have no access to banks, working purely on a basis of trust. In this, they are completely different from the microcredit systems promoted by the World Bank, which function on a basis of mutual policing and shame, reaching the extreme (e.g., in Niger) of posting in public places pictures of the women who fail to repay the loans, so that some women have been driven to suicide.[444]

Women have also led the effort to collectivize reproductive labour both as a means to economize the cost of reproduction and to protect each other from poverty, state violence, and the violence of individual men. An outstanding example is that of the *ollas communes* (common cooking pots) that women in Chile and Peru set up in the 1980s when, due to stiff inflation, they could no longer afford to shop alone.[445] Like land reclamations, or the formation of *tontines*, these practices are the expression of a world where communal bonds are still strong. But it would be a mistake to consider them something pre-political, 'natural', or simply a product of 'tradition.'

After repeated phases of colonization, nature and customs no longer exist in any part of the world, except where people have struggled to preserve them and reinvent them. As Leo Podlashuc has noted in 'Saving Women: Saving the Commons,' grassroots women's communalism today leads to the production of a new reality, it shapes a collective identity, it constitutes a counter-power in the home and the community, and opens a process of self-valorisation and self-determination from which there is much that we can learn.

The first lesson we can gain from these struggles is that the 'commoning' of the material means of reproduction is the primary mechanism by which a collective interest and mutual bonds are created. It is also the first line of resistance to a life of enslavement and the condition for the construction of autonomous spaces undermining from within the hold that capitalism has on our lives. Undoubtedly the experiences I described are models that cannot be transplanted. For us, in North America, the reclamation and commoning of the means of reproduction must necessarily take different forms. But here too, by pooling our resources and re-appropriating the wealth that we have produced, we can begin to de-link our reproduction from the commodity flows that, through the world market, are responsible for the dispossession of millions across the world. We can begin to disentangle our livelihood not only from the world market but also from the war machine and prison system on which the US economy now depends. Not last we can move beyond the abstract solidarity that so often characterizes relations in the movement, which limits our commitment, our capacity to endure, and the risks we are willing to take.

In a country where private property is defended by the largest arsenal of weaponry in the world, and where three centuries of slavery have produced profound divisions in the social body, the recreation of the common/s appears as a formidable task that could only be accomplished through a long-term process of experimentation, coalition building and reparations. But though this task may now seem more difficult than passing through the eye of a needle, it is also the only possibility we have for widening the space of our autonomy, and refusing to accept that our reproduction occurs at the expense of the world's other commoners and commons.

Feminist reconstructions

What this task entails is powerfully expressed by Maria Mies when she points out that the production of commons requires first a profound transformation in our everyday life, in order to recombine what the social division of labour in capitalism has separated. For the distancing of production from reproduction and consumption leads us to ignore the conditions under which what we eat, wear, or work with have been produced, their social and environmental cost, and the fate of the population on whom the waste we produce is unloaded (Mies 1999:141ff.). In other words, we need to overcome the state of irresponsibility concerning the consequences of our actions that results from the destructive ways in which the social division of labour is organized in capitalism; short of that, the production of our life inevitably becomes a production of death for others. As Mies points out, globalization has worsened this crisis, widening the distances between what is produced and what is consumed, thereby intensifying, despite the appearance of an increased global interconnectedness, our blindness to the blood in the food we eat, the petroleum we use, the clothes we wear, and the computers we communicate with (ibid.).

Overcoming this state of oblivion is where a feminist perspective teaches us to start in our reconstruction of the commons. No common is possible unless we refuse to base our life and our reproduction on the suffering of others, unless we refuse to see ourselves as separate from them. Indeed, if commoning has any meaning, it must be the production of ourselves as a common subject. This is how we must understand the slogan 'no commons without community.' But 'community' has to be intended not as a gated reality, a grouping of people joined by exclusive interests separating them from others, as with communities formed on the basis of religion or ethnicity, but rather as a quality of relations, a principle of cooperation and of responsibility to each other and to the earth, the forests, the seas, the animals.

Certainly, the achievement of such community, like the collectivization of our everyday work of reproduction, can only be a beginning. It is no substitute for broader anti-privatization campaigns and the reclamation of our common wealth. But it is an essential part of our education to collective government and our recognition of history as a collective project, which is perhaps the main casualty of the neo-liberal era of capitalism.

On this account, we too must include in our political agenda the communalization of housework, reviving that rich feminist tradition that in the USA stretches from the utopian socialist experiments of the mid-nineteenth century to the attempts that 'materialist feminists' made from the late nineteenth century to the early twentieth century to reorganize and socialize domestic work and thereby the home and the neighbourhood, through collective housekeeping – attempts that continued until the 1920s when the Red Scare put an end to them (Hayden 1981 and 1986). These practices and, most importantly, the ability of past feminists to look at reproductive labour as an important sphere of human activity not to be negated but to be revolutionized, must be revisited and revalorized.

One crucial reason for creating collective forms of living is that the reproduction of human beings is the most labour-intensive work on earth and, to a very large extent, it is work that is irreducible to mechanization. We cannot mechanize childcare, care for the ill, or the psychological work necessary to reintegrate our physical and emotional balance. Despite the efforts that futuristic industrialists are making, we cannot robotize care except at a terrible cost for the people involved. No one will accept nursebots as caregivers, especially for children and the ill. Shared responsibility and cooperative work, not given at the cost of the health of the providers, are the only guarantees of proper care. For centuries, the reproduction of human beings has been a collective process. It has been the work of extended families and communities on which people could rely, especially in proletarian neighbourhoods, even when they lived alone so that old age was not accompanied by the desolate loneliness and dependence on which so many of our elderly live. It is only with the advent of capitalism that reproduction has been completely privatised, a process that is now carried to a degree that it destroys our lives. This trend must be reversed, and the present time is propitious for such a project.

As the capitalist crisis destroys the basic elements of reproduction for millions of people across the world, including the United States, the reconstruction of our everyday life is a possibility and a necessity. Like strikes, social/economic crises break the discipline of wage work, forcing new forms of sociality upon us. This is what occurred during the Great Depression, which produced a movement of hobos who turned the freight trains into their commons seeking freedom in mobility and nomadism (Caffentzis 2006). At the intersections of railroad lines, they organized *hobo jungles*, pre-figurations, with their self-governance rules and solidarity, of the communist world in which many of the hobos believed.[446] However, but for a few Boxcar Berthas,[447] this was predominantly a masculine world, a fraternity of men, and in the long term it could not be sustained. Once the economic crisis and the war came to an end, the hobos were domesticated by the two great engines of labour power fixation: the family and the house. Mindful of the threat of working class recomposition during the Depression, American capital excelled in its application of the principle that has characterized the organization of economic life: cooperation at the point of production, separation and atomization at the point of reproduction. The atomized, serialized family house that Levittown provided, compounded by its umbilical appendix, the car, not only sedentarised the worker but put an end to the type of autonomous workers' commons that hobo jungles had represented (Hayden 1986). Today, as millions of Americans' houses and cars are being repossessed, as foreclosures, evictions, and massive loss of employment are again breaking down the pillars of the capitalist discipline of work, new common grounds are again taking shape, like the tent cities that are sprawling from coast to coast. This time, however, it is women who must build the new commons so that they do not remain transient spaces, temporary autonomous zones, but become the foundation of new forms of social reproduction.

If the house is the *oikos* on which the economy is built, then it is women, historically the house workers and house prisoners, who must take the initiative to reclaim the house as a centre of collective life, one traversed by multiple people and forms of cooperation, providing safety without isolation and fixation, allowing for the sharing and circulation of community possessions, and, above all, providing the foundation for collective forms of reproduction. As has already been suggested, we can draw inspiration for this project from the programs of the nineteenth century materialist feminists who, convinced that the home was an important 'spatial component of the oppression of women,' organized communal kitchens, cooperative households calling for workers' control of reproduction (Hayden 1981).

These objectives are crucial at present. Breaking down the isolation of life in the home is not only a precondition for meeting our most basic needs and increasing our power with regard to employers and the state. As Massimo de Angelis has reminded us, it is also a protection from ecological disaster. For there can be no doubt about the destructive consequences of the 'un-economic' multiplication of reproductive assets and self-enclosed dwellings that we now call our homes, dissipating warmth into the atmosphere during the winter, exposing us to unmitigated heat in the summer. Most importantly, we cannot build an alternative society and a strong self-reproducing movement unless we redefine our reproduction in a more cooperative way and put an end to the separation between the personal and the political, and between political activism and the reproduction of everyday life.

It remains to be clarified that assigning women this task of commoning/collectivizing reproduction is not to concede to a naturalistic conception of femininity. Understandably, many feminists view this possibility as a fate worse than death. It is deeply sculpted in our collective consciousness that women have been designated as men's common, a natural source of wealth and services to be as freely appropriated by them as the capitalists have appropriated the wealth of nature. But to paraphrase Dolores Hayden, the reorganization of reproductive work, and therefore the reorganization of housing and public space, is not a question of identity; it is a question of labour and, we can add, a question of power and safety (Hayden 1986:230). I am reminded here of the experience of the women members of the Landless People's Movement of Brazil [the MST] who, after their communities won the right to maintain the land that they had occupied, insisted that the new houses be built to form one compound so that they could continue to communalize their housework, wash together, cook together, take turns with men as they had done in the course of the struggle, and be ready to run to give each other support when abused by men. Arguing that women should take the lead in the collectivization of reproductive work and housing is not to naturalize housework as a female vocation. It is refusing to obliterate the collective experiences, the knowledge and the struggles that women have accumulated concerning reproductive work, whose history has been an essential part of our resistance to capitalism. Reconnecting with this history is a crucial step for women and men today both to undo the gendered architecture of our lives and to reconstruct our homes and lives as commons.

EPILOGUE

Decolonial communism: Analytical, political and democratic dimensions*

Catherine Samary

Decolonial Communism, Democracy and Commons is rooted in the anniversaries of three historical 'events/periods': the Russian Revolution in the context of the First World War; the Tito/Stalin split of 1948, which is linked to the Yugoslav Revolution during the Second World War and which led to the introduction of the self-management system; and finally, the anniversary of the international 'years of 1968', which were a climax of radicalisation around the world against relations of domination. All these events/periods were linked to a global structural 'systemic' crisis and to the search for an anticapitalist alternative, based on the mobilisation of subaltern classes. This alternative is being revisited in 2018 – another period of structural intertwined crises of the globalised capitalist system. It is in such a specific historical conjuncture that the redefinition of a radical, democratic decolonial communism could be enriched by the experiences of emancipatory movements that are facing immense dangers. This process of redefinition could in turn contribute to the urgent theoretical and political necessity for these movements 'to think big'[448] together.

From the commons to communism

'The concept of commons has been gaining popularity', as Sylvia Federici[449] has stressed, at least 'since the Zapatistas took over the zócalo in San Cristobal de las Casas on 31 December 1993'. It appeared 'as a basis for convergence among anarchists, Marxists, socialists, ecologists, and eco-feminists', and seemed to allow for an alternative which transcended the 'market' or the 'state'. But, as she points out, this needed clarification. We have established links between the Yugoslav self-management experiences and those of the 'commons', which have been revisited in light of the complex strategic issues that have arisen since the 1990s, as the Balkans Forum or Sylvia Federici

---

*   This Epilogue was edited by Bill McKeith.

remind us.⁴⁵⁰ Our conviction is that these experiences can and should be embedded within broader theoretical and political issues associated with the 'communist' concept, which has to be updated.

Putting the emphasis on the democratic process of 'commonising' goods highlights a fundamental distinction between goals – which have to be explicit – and practical results of the process (tools and methods collectively adopted and implemented). For communism as well, reducing the gap between aims and results is the concrete and democratic way (and not a dogmatic approach) which leads to possible corrections and rejections of what appear to be inefficient 'tools' for the given aim.

Communism is retained here not as a 'model of society' – far from that – but as a 'concrete utopia' as Ernst Bloch would say. It is associated to current aspirations for a not yet existing but possible other world without relations of exploitation and domination. This implies self-organised movements for the satisfaction of 'basic needs' which can trigger mobilisations because they are felt to be 'legitimate'. Who decides what are the basic needs to be satisfied for all? The people concerned, in each given context. How should they be satisfied (i.e. under what conditions of production and distribution)? This also should be analysed by the 'commoners' in the given context and territorial 'political space' of their action.

There is no 'precondition' or any pre-defined 'level of development of the productive forces' for the development of struggles for legitimate demands. Conflicting choices and alternative solutions confront concrete obstacles: free access to education, transport, child care, health services, and other basic needs could be, and has been, more developed in a 'poor' country such as socialist Yugoslavia than in post-socialist states integrated into global capitalism with its 'free market'. Contrary to the 'classical' Marxist assumption, a socialist/communist future should also fully integrate ecological concerns in its choices by rejecting the hypothesis of abundance. It will still have ongoing but transformed conflicts, as it will have to consider and make choices with new forms of 'political' institutions under democratic control. The real issue associated with the communist ends-and-means dialectics is therefore the invention of a 'revolutionary democracy' adapted to diverse contexts – as it is called by the Indian Marxist and feminist historian Soma Marik.⁴⁵¹

It is because of its dual dimension – satisfaction of needs and democracy – that a 'communist process' has to develop its choices in a 'realm' where direct judgments on use values (ecological included) and egalitarian human relationships dominate. Fundamental distinctions, which Ernest Mandel stressed, should be retained between using 'market indicators' (money, prices) while resisting 'market relations' (first, when they cover relations of domination and exploitation, but also more broadly) and rejecting the market as a 'regulator'.[452] As Marx and Polanyi stressed, capitalism is the only historical society where the free market is generalised. It is neither an efficient nor a 'neutral' mechanism, and it hides the class criteria which de facto 'evaluate' what is 'costly' and 'necessary. As Michael Lebowitz notes, 'Marx's *Political Economy of the Working Class* has not been written'.[453] But one can 'read' it in all the struggles against the so-called rules of the free market, and for different criteria to evaluate 'efficiency', for different ways of financing fundamental needs, and for different rights – refusing discriminations in access to health care, education, housing or even basic goods according to your class, wealth, gender or skin-colour. In another 'realm' where market and profit no longer dominate, the markets for labour and capital would be suppressed while the market for goods would be 'socialised', as Diane Elson argues,[454] which could then be used to monitor and complement a 'socialised' planning system.[455]

Darko Suvin[456] supports a similar concept of communism as a concrete utopia and a 'radical plebeian democracy'. Calling it C1, he distinguishes it from concrete and historical party/state-led communist revolutions and experiences (C2) claiming a socialist/communist ideal. He introduces a stimulating dialectical approach that does not deny the real presence of an emancipatory concept (C1) in the party-led and institutional communism of the C2 kind. But he critically analyses it on the basis of the experience of bureaucratisation and capitalist restoration. His concrete balance sheet of the Yugoslav case is open to democratic pluralist appreciations with possible nuances or differences. He proposes to understand the 'splendour, misery, and possibilities' of the Yugoslav socialist experience with 'a central hypothesis':

> that the party/state government was a *two-headed Janus*, at least from 1945 to 1971. It was not only a factor of alienation, but also the initiator and lever of real liberation – up to a certain limit (the liberation is important and the limit is important!).

He points out that

> very soon, the party became a centaur: the head part was a state-party, the main rump were idealist or careerist followers. Yet there permanently smouldered within it the tension between the horizons of liberation and domination. Insofar as it was an emancipatory backbone, the party was a possible feedback instrument for plebeian class interests from below. But

since there was no democracy inside it, such pressures were inchoate, leading in practice to an eager or unwilling execution of decisions from the leadership.[457]

Darko Suvin, like us, considers the repression of the June 1968 student movement in Belgrade as a turning point.[458] We can introduce a nuance in the analysis: the links between the party leaders and the intellectuals were certainly broken. But it is probably not so clear for the links between Tito, Kardelj and the workers who saw their self-management rights increased with the constitutional amendments and the Law on Associated Labour of 1974-76. Certainly, the new constitution of Yugoslavia incorporated contradictory logics, on the one hand favouring planned agreements between 'basic organs of associated labour' and dismantling the autonomous banking system, while on the other hand supressing any federal control on foreign trade. Therefore it did not offer any consistent and democratic system of socialist self-management. The repressive trend prevented a socialist way out of the crisis by consolidating self-management rights at the federal level against the transformation of the nationalist bureaucracies into pro-capitalist forces. In addition, before that final phase, as Darko Suvin also stresses, the composition of the party had changed and the regime 'lived with three major denials, marginalisations or Freudian repressions: of the peasantry, the women, and eventually the not fully employed workers'. This important issue has been highlighted in Susan Woodward's major study on *Socialist Unemployment*.[459] There will be no communist alternative with similar 'Freudian repressions'.

Darko Suvin's analysis breaks in general with the false dichotomy of emancipation 'from below' as opposed to 'from above', or of spontaneous movements as opposed to organised parties. It is the political consciousness of the existence of a bureaucracy within parties and 'workers states' that could stop this false dilemma. By posing direct democracy and self-organisation as the basic condition for emancipation, the usefulness for pluralist choices of any institution (e.g. party, state) can be judged by the 'commoners' themselves as their role and functioning are changed under such rules. The transformation of the Communist Party into a League of Communists of Yugoslavia and the democratisation of the system, reflected by, amongst other things, the existence of the *Praxis* current, was an embryonic illustration of that logic. But it was stopped at the end of the 1960s when a more repressive trend occurred, which brought Yugoslavia closer to the 'brother' regimes and weakened its capacity to resist capitalist transformation.

Darko Suvin also supports the notion of conflictual 'transitional societies' between capitalism and socialism/communism (without specific 'stages'), as we have argued in this book. This allows an updating of several controversial dimensions of Marxist/communist concepts. Against a linear approach to revolutions, it stresses in particular that struggles within/against the capitalist system are confronted by dominant forces and privileges which will defend themselves by all means before and after a possible revolutionary break, including by corrupting those who lead resistances and revolutions. Neo-colonial 'coups' using a variety of 'tools' can prevent the establishment of any project of self-managed democracy. The analysis of experiences shows that counter-revolutions (like revolutions) articulate internal and international issues, and that the strongest element of resistance to the huge international forces is the internal strength of the popular mobilisation for 'legitimate' goals – including against neo-colonialism. Elements of the dual reality of the 'Janus' kind of party, analysed in Yugoslavia by Darko Suvin, can certainly be recognised with variants in all phases of struggles and revolutions, in particular today in Cuba[460] and Latin America.[461]

What 'decolonial studies'?

'Decolonial' has been added to 'communism' in the title of this book to indicate the need to revisit the October Revolution and the other revolutions of the 'short 20th century', and because it is still at present a strategic issue. The first dividing line among the early Marxists who were breaking from the Second International was the understanding that the world capitalist crisis and wars were organically linked to the internal contradictions and conflicts of an imperialist system. The building of the Comintern, which adopted in 1920 its '21 Conditions of Admission', in particular the 8th anti-colonialist one, was a clear indication of that dividing line. Analytical and political issues were involved with long-term implications both at national and international level, in the core imperialist countries and in those 'at the margins'. Trotsky's theses of the 'uneven and combined development' and 'permanent revolution'[462] as well as the experience in Yugoslavia, a peripheral European country, are to be appropriated by 'decolonial studies'. A similar appropriation of Lenin's struggle against Great-Russian policies and behaviour, including within the Bolshevik party, is greatly aided by Matthieu Renault's recent major researches.[463] Finally, how can we understand 'non-aligned' decolonial struggles without Tito's struggles on several fronts on the basis of a real socialist/communist project?

The concept of 'decolonisation' is extended here outside the dominant fields of current studies on these issues.[464] But, as already stressed, it expresses the same criteria that the decolonial currents put forward: the need to analyse and fight against any lasting form or trace of (neo)colonialism within former or present dependent or/and dominant countries and in their international relations. We defend the hypothesis that a decolonial orientation can and should be integrated into a 'communist' orientation, defined as being opposed to all forms of domination and exploitation. But that is in conflict with any reductionist Marxist or non-Marxist approach, which sets 'hierarchical' concepts of oppressions, whether they are 'workerist' (e.g. ignoring gender,[465] race or 'non historical people'[466]), or ignore class and race, as do some mainstream feminist currents. The defence of national self-determination combined with democratic and social struggle is – as Michael Löwy reminds us – to be distinguished from 'nationalisms', and supposedly 'national liberation' at the expense of other people. Such nationalisms have destroyed both the gains of the Yugoslav Revolution and the *Praxis* current,[467] and opened up the space for an international counterrevolutionary trend.

How to 'exist politically'?[468] Globalised analytical and political issues

We are now in a 'contradictory political conjuncture', as was stressed in May 2017 by the new radical journal *Catalyst*[469] following sharp discussions between Marxist and post-colonial studies. Robert Brenner also argues that we are in a 'moment of the greatest promise for the working class and popular forces since the 1960s, but also one of significant danger'.[470] At a commemoration of Gramsci's death in February 2017, Gilbert Achcar expressed a similar view about polarisations and dangers:

> …we have entered again into a situation where the old is 'already' dying and the new can 'not yet' be born. The hitherto weakness and fragility of the forces of progressive change have meant that the accelerating crisis of global capitalism's socio-economic and political conditions has until now mostly benefitted the rise of the far right around the globe. It is hence on the far right of the political spectrum that we are witnessing at present the most spectacular 'morbid symptoms' produced by the degeneration of capitalist politics.[471]

In such a context, starting from Samuel Huntington's 'clash of civilisations', Gilbert Achcar has opposed his analysis of a 'clash of barbarisms'[472] against the racist and Islamophobic discourse which developed in the aftermath of 11 September 2001. Achcar went on to denounce the way the notion of 'barbarian' has been used to describe as 'non human' people who do not qualify for 'human rights'. Dominant forces are 'selecting' those whom they consider to be 'Islamic terrorists' (treated as 'barbarians') according to evolving criteria of '*realpolitik*', alliances or conflicting interests. We are confronted with increasingly numerous narratives associated with neoliberalism about 'the Islamic invasion' or other supposed 'immigrant invasion'.

While finalising this book, I attended an important event linked to the context and issues raised in this book. It was organised in a Paris suburb by intellectuals, activists and organisations with whom I have been working for a decade against 'state racism'[473] and islamophobia.[474] The title of this event was 'Bandung of the North – Towards a Decolonial International'.[475] It was held at a moment when *Catalyst* argued that 'our focus is ... to develop a theory and strategy with capitalism as its target – both in the North and in the Global South'. 'Time to think big' should mean transforming polemics between those who should be together into real 'conversations' and possible common political action.

For all political currents, this begins with updating analyses of imperialism and dependence theories since we now confront a radically new international context, as the Argentinian Marxist Claudio Katz has stressed.[476] The theoretical and strategic renewal of critical analysis of globalised capitalism and its transformations should also integrate Nancy Fraser's feminist and Marxist approaches, with gender dimensions. Fraser's updating of Rosa Luxemburg's analyses of imperialism[477] in non-capitalist or pre-capitalist systems highlights new forms of 'dispossession', something which is also stressed by David Harvey.[478] A major fact is that a 'North' is developing within the former 'Global South' while a 'South' is growing in the North. This development is based on all subaltern classes and in particular coloured ones who are made 'scapegoats' to turn the white 'working poor' and the unemployed against 'immigrants'. This analysis could also be in 'conversation' with the Canadian First Nation scholar Glen Sean Coulthard,[479] who has been revisiting Franz Fanon's *Black Skin, White Face* and Marx's 'primitive accumulation'.

All these theories confront different, and often contradictory, 'politics of recognition' with or without rejection of the capitalist system and its social relations of exploitation. This is the real analytical and political choice between what Nancy Fraser calls 'affirmative action' and 'transformative action'. The former leads to adaptation to the system while producing class polarisations (including among racialised populations), while the later 'transformational' approach rejects the existing order and is looking for another 'civilisation', that arises from the local and moves on to the global, and which takes lessons from the gains and failures of all past attempt to change the world.

That is what this book wishes to contribute to.

About the authors

The Balkan Forum Commons Working Group was established for the 2nd Balkan Forum that took place on May 12-14, 2013 in Zagreb. The members of the group were Danijela Majstorović, Georgi Medarov, Dubravka Sekulić, Vladimir Simović, Tomislav Tomašević and Danijela Dolenec (coordinator).

Samuel Farber was born in Cuba where he was active in the Cuban high school student movement against Fulgencio Batista in the 1950s. He is a political science professor at Brooklyn College, NY. Samuel Farber has written extensively on Cuba including *Cuba since the revolution of 1959* and *The Politics of Che Guevara: Theory and Practice* (both by Haymarket Books).

Silvia Federici is a feminist writer, teacher, and militant. In 1972, she was cofounder of the International Feminist Collective, which launched the Wages for Housework campaign, and has written several books on that subject. She is a Professor at Hofstra, NY. Silvia Federici has been researching and organizing recently on the struggle against capitalist globalization and for a feminist reconstruction of the commons.

Franck Gaudichaud is a PhD in Political Science, lecturer and researcher in Latin-American studies at the Grenoble Alpes University, France. He is the author of several books on Latin America, including *Chilean popular unity 1970-73 – One thousand days that shook the World* (Brill/Haymarket Books, forthcoming). He is Co-President of the solidarity organisation *France Amérique Latine*, and a member of the editorial committees of *Contretemps* and of the website <www.rebelion.org>. Frank Gaudichaud is also a member of the *Nouveau Parti Anticapitaliste* (NPA) in France. Email: franck.gaudichaud@univ-grenoble-alpes.fr

Ernest Mandel was an activist, journalist and author of 30 books, including *Late Capitalism* and *Trotsky as Alternative*. He was arrested for the resistance activities during World War 2 in Belgium, and joined the leadership of the Fourth International from 1946. He was barred for a while from West Germany, the United States, France, Switzerland, and Australia. Ernest Mandel was co-founder of the International Institute for Research and Education. Ernest Mandel died in 1995. The Ernest Mandel Internet Archives can be viewed at <www.ernestmandel.org/en>.

Goran Marković is an associate professor of the Constitutional Law at the Faculty of Law, University of East Sarajevo (Bosnia and Herzegovina). He is also the editor-in chief of the web magazine *Novi Plamen* (The New Flame). He published two books in Serbo-Croatian, and one textbook as a co-author. His scientific research is centred around the issues of the constitutional system of Bosnia and Herzegovina, direct, and workers' self-management. Email: goran.markovic@pravni.ues.rs.ba.

Zagorka Pešić-Golubović is a philosopher, anthropologist and sociologist. She was part of the group called the 'Belgrade 8', of eight university professors, members of the Praxis group, who were expelled in January 1975 from the Belgrade University Faculty of Philosophy because of their influence on the student movement in June 1968. Since then, she has continued her academic work in Belgrade, keeping her distance with Serb nationalism and maintaining her social concern. She was born in 1930.

Catherine Samary is an economist, specialising in the Balkans and Eastern Europe, and is the author of several books on this subject, including *Yugoslavia Dismembered* (Monthly Review Press, 1995). Catherine Samary writes about socialism and the experience of 'socialist countries', their contradictions and transformation within capitalist globalisation and European integration. She was a lecturer in economics at Paris universities, and is a visiting lecturer at the International Institute of Research and Education (Amsterdam). She has collaborated since the 1990s with *Le Monde Diplomatique*, is a co-founder of the Espace Marx (Paris), and a member of the scientific council of ATTAC-France. Catherine Samary has been a member of the Fourth International and of the French radical left since 1963, and she is actively involved in anti-racist and feminist associations. Website: <csamary.free.fr>; Email: samarycatherine@yahoo.fr.

Svetozar Stojanović was a philosopher, political scientist and an academic at the Belgrade University. He was involved in the Praxis group (founded in Croatia), helped organise the Korčula summer school and was part of its anti-Stalinist humanist Marxist current. He was one of the 'Belgrade 8' professors who encouraged the independent socialist student movement in June 1968, and as a consequence were all expelled from the University in 1975. From

1987 to 1990, he edited *Praxis International*, which was published abroad but longer reflected the anti-nationalist stance of the original Praxis group. Svetozar Stojanović shared the Serb nationalism of the author Dobrica Ćosić, who became president of the third Yugoslavia (Serbia and Montenegro) in 1992-1993 when Slobodan Milošević was president of Serbia. Born in 1931, he died in 2010 in Belgrade.

Raquel Varela is a historian, researcher and professor at the New University of Lisbon/IHC, where she coordinates the study group on Global Labour History. She is international visiting professor at the Fluminense Federal University and an honorary fellow of the International Institute for Social History. She is Vice-Coordinator of the Portuguese Network for the Study of Labour, Labour Movements and Social Movements. She coordinated the labour network of the European Social Science History Conference in 2012-2014 – ESSHC. In 2013 she was awarded the Santander Prize for Internationalization of Scientific Production. Raquel Varela is the author of 23 books on labour and revolution, including *The Peoples History of the Portuguese Revolution* (Pluto Press, 2018). Email: raquel_cardeira_varela@yahoo.co.uk.

Notes

Introduction

1. Interview with David Harvey <https://www.jacobinmag.com/2016/07/david-harvey-neoliberalism-capitalism-labor-crisis-resistance>. See also David Harvey, *A brief history of neoliberalism,* Oxford: Oxford University Press, 2007.
2. This is the title of Moshe Lewin's book, *The Soviet Century,* London: Verso Books, 2016. But whereas this book concentrates on the different phases of the history of the USSR, I use this formula as a temporality inside of which the impact of the transformations of the USSR is grasped at the international level, notably in its relation to the other countries of 'actually existing socialism'. I combine Lewin's formula with the best known of Eric Hobsbawm (the 'short 20th century') which effectively covers the same period, from the First World War to the end of the USSR. Eric Hobsbawn, *The Age of Extremes: The Short Twentieth Century, 1914–1991,* London: Michael Joseph/Penguin, 1994.
3. I was only able to follow it through by being directly in contact with these youth and the *Praxis* current.
4. We leave to those who were more enthused by the Cultural Revolution the task of reviewing it critically. In contrast with the regimentation of Chinese youth in the Cultural Revolution, the student movement in June 1968 in Yugoslavia was independent from the regime, under the influence of the Yugoslav Marxist intellectuals producing the review *Praxis* and its international conferences. We reproduce from that review some texts analysing the crisis and contradictions of the Yugoslav system as well as the student movement of June 1968. More can be found on the site <https://www.marxists.org/subject/praxis/index.htm>. We also reproduce in this book, the critical balance sheet by Goran Marković who is involved in the Marxist review *Novi Plamen* publishged in Croatia.
5. We present these debates in this book, by updating them in the light of the Yugoslav case. And we also reproduce in relation to the Cuban debate the analysis by Samuel Farber, the exiled Cuban intellectual, and that of Ernest Mandel who was a protagonist in this debate with Che Guevara and Charles Bettelheim.
6. We can recall notably the 'Open Letter' to the Polish Workers Party by Jacek Kuron and Karol Modzelevski in 1966 <http://www.unz.org/Pub/NewPolitics-1966q2-00005>; Rudolf Bahro, *The Alternative in Eastern Europe,* London: Verso, 2017; Miklos Haraszti, *A Worker in a Worker-State. Piece-Rates in Hungary,* London: Pelican Books/Penguin, 1977; or on Czechoslovakia, Peter Uhl, *Le Socialisme Emprisonné,* Paris: Stock/La Brèche, 1980.
7. See Zbigniew Kowalevski, *Rendez nous nos usines: Solidarność dans le combat pour l'autogestion ouvrière,* Paris: La Brèche, 1985.
8. The chapter 'Eastern Europe: revisiting the ambiguous revolutions of 1989' in this book returns to the ambiguity of 1989 and the opacity of forms of privatisation. Capitalist restoration is also evoked to clarify the presentation of the old system. But this is not the subject of this book. Read on this subject Catherine Samary, 'The social stakes of the great transformation in Eastern Europe', *Debatte: Journal of Contemporary Central and Eastern Europe,* Volume 17, 2009 – Issue 1, <http://www.tandfonline.com/doi/abs/10.1080/09651560902778345?mobileUi=0&journalCode=cdeb19 then on the crisis of 2008/9>; Catherine Samary, 'Eastern Europe Faced with the crises of the

system', CADTM, 7 April 2011, <http://www.cadtm.org/IMG/pdf/EEcrisis.pdf>; or Catherine Samary, 'From the short Soviet century to Putin's Russia, *International Viewpoint*, 29 February 2015, <http://www.internationalviewpoint.org/spip.php?article3855>.

9   Contrary to the management of the commons, or to self-management, 'workers' control' in pre-revolutionary crises as in Russia supposes the non-responsibility of workers in management, combined with the radicalisation of conflicts which often made 'workers' control' evolve towards real powers of management. In order to illustrate these types of conflicts, we have published in this book 'Chile and Portugal in the 1970s: the left, nationalisations and 'workers' control' in the revolutionary processes' by Franck Gaudichaud and Raquel Varela. In that chapter is examined the contradictory logics, radical or reformist, notably that of the CPs under the influence of Soviet statism, and a radicalisation of 'workers' control' which could lead to the demand for nationalisation.

10 It is in sharing their approach that we reproduce in the final part of the book two articles about the commons: one from Silvia Federici, 'Feminism and the politics of the commons', and the text 'The Struggles for the Commons in the Balkans' produced for the Zagreb Balkans Forum in 2013.

11 David Harvey, 'The future of the Commons', *Radical History Review*, issue 109, winter 2011.

12 Extremely diverse experiences must be discussed on that point of view. Read for instance *Patterns of Commoning*, David Bollier and Silke Helfrich (eds), Amherst, Mass.: Levellers Press, 2015; David Bollier and Silke Helfrich, *Wealth of the Commons: A World Beyond Market and State,* Amherst, Mass.: Levellers Press, 2012. David Bollier and Silke Helfrich are from the Commons Strategies Group, <www.commonsstrategies.org>. The website <https://www.stirtoaction.com/issues/issue-21> also reflects a dynamics which has to be concretely explored to judge the possible alternative logics that we mentioned about on-going processes of 'commonising'.

13 John Holloway, *Change the World Without Taking Power: The Meaning of Revolution Today*, London: Pluto Press, 2010.

14 John Holloway, *Crack Capitalism*, London: Pluto Press, 2010.

15 David Harvey, *Rebel Cities*, London:Verso, 2012, or <http://abahlali.org/files/Harvey_Rebel_cities.pdf>.

16 Murray Bookchin, *The Third Revolution: Popular Movements in the Revolutionary Era,* London and New York: Cassell and Bloomsbury, 1996-2005. On the evolution of Bookchin, see <https://theanarchistlibrary.org/library/janet-biehl-bookchin-breaks-with-anarchism#fn_back92> and Murray Bookchin, *Social Ecology and Communalism*, Chico, California: AK Press, 2004.

17 In order to illustrate such process and strategic stakes, we have reproduced in this book the text by Frank Gaudichaud 'Latin America: state, popular power and class struggle'.

18 See notably Trebor Scholz, 'Platform cooperativism: Challenging the corporate sharing economy' <http://www.rosalux-nyc.org/wp-content/files_mf/scholz_platformcoop_5.9.2016.pdf>, New York: Rosa Luxemburg Stiftung, 2016.

19 <https://viacampesina.org/en/who-are-we/>.

20 See the contributions of Ramón Grosfoguel and of the different research collectives, in particular in Latin America, on 'modernity/coloniality' relations, for example Hurtado López Fátima, 'Universalisme ou pluriversalisme? Les apports de la philosophie latino-américaine', in *Tumultes*, 2017/1 (no. 48), pp. 39-50, <https://www.cairn.info/revue-

tumultes-2017-1-page-39.htm>. Well-known along such lines are also contributions by the Palestinian American theorist Edward Saïd on the 'Orientalism', notably cultural, which precedes and accompanies colonisation in the Middle East. See also of course the writings of Frantz Fanon.

21 Words are important, and the notion of 'post-colonialism' can lend to the idea that the date of independence ends any form and trace of colonisation – that is why 'decolonial' approaches are important. But in the Marxist tradition, we can continue to use against any simplifications the notion of 'neo-colonialism': it permits to distinguish a 'post-colonial' phase without neglecting the analysis of the forms of domination of formally independent states.

22 It is not in our competence or our task to present the richness of 'decolonial' and 'post-colonial' studies and their debates. Neither can we deal here with the conflicts which have arisen in France on the colonial past, the 'coloniality' or (neo)colonialism of France. They aptly accompany the caricatures and ignorance of post-colonial and decolonial studies. Read in relation to this Capucine Boidin, Études décoloniales et postcoloniales dans les débats français', *Cahiers des Amériques Latine*, no.62, 2009, pp. 129-140, <http://journals.openedition.org/cal/1620#ftn1>.

23 Glen Sean Coulthard, *Red Skin, White Masks: Rejecting the Colonial Politics of Recognition*, Mineapolis MN:University of Minnesota Press, 2018.

24 Kevin B. Anderson, *Marx at the Margins, on nationalism, ethnicity and non-Western Societies*, Chicago: University of Chicago Press, 2010, <http://abahlali.org/files/Anderson%20-%20Marx%20at%20the%20Margins.pdf>.

25 For a presentation of the different Marxist approaches to imperialism and their theoretical and political controversies, see the Argentine economist Claudio Katz, *Bajo el Imperio del Capital,* Buenos Aires: Ed. Luxemburg, 2011. See the extract published in French in *Contretemps*, November 2017, <http://www.contretemps.eu/theorie-imperialisme/>.

26 It is at this level the major contribution of Ernest Mandel who contests, for this reason, the notion of the 'Kondratieff cycle' and substitutes for it that of 'Long waves of capitalism' integrating fully therein the political conflicts and wars of uncertain outcomes in Ernest Mandel, *Long waves of capitalist development, a Marxist interpretation*, London: Verso, 1995.

27 Linked to this issue, read Matthieu Renault, *L'Empire de la Révolution: Lénine et les musulmans de l'empire russe*, Paris: Syllepse, 2017.

28 Evoked by Saïd Bouamama in his work on the Tricontinental, as one of the milestones of the colonial revolutions of this century and preparing what would become the Tricontinental.

29 I borrow this notion of 'capitalist world system' in a sense which can be appreciably different from that given to it by Immanuel Wallerstein (2009). See more in the Epilogue of this book. I retain from his approach the analysis (common to Marxist theses on imperialism) of a capitalist system articulated and marked in the 19th century by relations of domination between the countries of the 'centre' and (neo)colonial '(semi)peripheries'; but I explicitly insert here, contrary to Wallerstein, the Marxist approach of relations of production and crises of capitalism at the root of imperialist globalisation, exploiting the assets of the previous colonisation. In omitting to do so, Wallerstein 'extends' the notion of 'capitalism' in an unconvincing fashion – which is criticised by Robert Brenner (1981) in relation to the emergence of capitalism; but this critique applies, in my view, to Wallerstein's failure to take into account another, non-

capitalist (and largely autarkic) 'world system' which emerged from the revolutions of the 'Soviet century' over a third of the planet – also favouring anti-colonial resistance movements. External trade is not sufficient to 'determine' internal choices.

30 See Catherine Samary, 'Europe: No 'LEXIT' without 'Another Europe Possible' – based on struggles in/outside/against the EU', Liege: CADTM, 22 September 2016, <http://www.cadtm.org/Europe-No-LEXIT-without-Another>.

31 Peter Worsley, 'One or three: A critique of the world-system of Immanuel Wallertein', *Socialist Register*, 1980, <http://www.socialistregister.com/index.php/srv/article/view/5456>.

32 Read Darko Suvin, *Splendour, Misery and Possibilities. An X-Ray of Socialist Yugoslavia*, Leiden: Brill, 2015.

October 1917-2017: From a decolonial communism to the democracy of the commons

33 Moshe Lewin, *The Soviet century*, London: Verso, 2016.

34 I cannot deal with the question here, but I have tried to interpret it from the perspective of the strategic issues in 'Essor et crises du mouvement altermondialiste', in *'En quête d'alternatives. L'état du monde 2018'*, Paris: La Decouverte, 2017.

35 Michel Husson, *Un pur capitalisme*, Lausanne: Cahiers libres/Editions Page deux, 2008.

36 The Communist International established by the Bolsheviks could not yet be 'post' colonial but certainly began to be 'decolonial'. Franz Fanon argues in *The Wretched of the Earth* that 'Marxist analysis should always be slightly stretched every time we have to do with the colonial problem'. On 'post-colonial' communism see notably <http://revueperiode.net/provincialiser-le-sujet-occidental-pour-un-communisme-postcolonial>. See also Benjamin Bürbaumer (2014) and K.B. Anderson (2010).

37 See I. Wallerstein's concepts of 'World-systems' mentioned in note 29.

38 See R. Galissot (2005); S. Bouamama (2016)

39 Following Moshe Lewin, we should distinguish a specifically totalitarian phase – which Trotsky himself compared in many of its traits to Nazism – and other periods of the USSR before and after, with continuities and discontinuities. After the 20th congress, the regime attempted to stabilise itself by other methods and specific relations of production without socialist democratic transformation: this amounted then to a semi-rupture with Stalinism. See notably Lewin's texts as gathered and presented by Denis Paillard, *Russie/URSS/Russie (1917-1991)*, Paris: Sylepse 2017. Lewin does not analyse the international dimensions of the Soviet century.

40 Formula borrowed from Henri Maler (2000). Solidarność.

41 Daniel Bensaïd, 'Puissances du communisme', *Contretemps*, 2010.

42 We will explain below the context and contributions of these movements which took up the propositions of the Yugoslav Marxists seeking to challenge alienation by both statism and commodity relations.

43 This is the title of Zbigniew Kowalewski's book (1985) on Solidarność's fight.

44 Ali, Z. and Dayan-Herzbrun, S. (ed.), 'Un pluriversalisme décolonial', *Tumultes* no. 48, 2017.

45 This contribution is situated within the problematic of 'common goods' explained by Silvia Federici (2011) or David Harvey (2011), Jean-Marie Harribey (2013), Pierre Dardot and Christian Laval (2014), Benjamin Coriat (2015). Whatever differences in

other dimensions of their analysis, it implies a critical approach to debates on 'common goods' which 'would define' their management on the basis of their 'nature', or which do not analyse in which dynamic the experiences of management of the commons is registered. It is about stressing the choices established between human beings (or a given population), deciding the 'putting in common' of various goods or/and territories and determining together the criteria and terms of their management.

46 Except that in this text the cleavage is expressed on the question of a parliamentary democracy versus soviet powers. There is in fact a superposition and mixing up of several debates: Rosa Luxemburg supported the global approach of the Bolsheviks on October and the soviets as component of the world socialist revolution, but that did not stop her from contesting their approach to the democratic issues, including the Constituent Assembly. We will come back to this point.

47 The Russian Marxists, organised at the beginning of the century in the RSDLP (Russian Social Democratic Labour Party) became divided into two current on various organisational and strategic issues – the 'Bolsheviks', with Lenin at their head (from the Russian term for 'majority') and the 'Mensheviks' (minority). Trotsky initially criticised Lenin on the organisational questions but had at the same time supported the thesis of an anti-capitalist dynamic of the Russian Revolution in its world context (see below on the 'permanent revolution'), a thesis which Lenin expresses explicitly in April 1917. After the October revolution, the Bolsheviks took the name of Communist Party, establishing the Communist International/CI or Comintern. The Mensheviks remained linked to the Second International along with the 'social democrats', an appellation which then took on the meaning of a 'reformism' inside capitalism, associated with the rejection of the October revolution.

48 Kevin B. Anderson, *Marx at the Margins, on nationalism, ethnicity and non-Western Societies*, Chicago: University Press Chicago, 2010.

49 See Jean-Jacques-Marie, *Lénine, La révolution permanente*, (2011).

50 On 'the classical analyses of imperialism', see Claudio Katz (2014).

51 See also, on Marx and the Russian peasantry, Teodor Shanin, Late Marx and the Russian Road: Marx and the 'Peripheries' of Capitalism, 1983.

52 Rosa Luxemburg, *The Russian revolution* (1918).

53 On the actuality of the permanent revolution see Michaël Löwy (2000); see also the debates on 'combined and uneven development', Benjamin Bürbaumer (2014).

54 At the heart of this dynamic, Marc Ferro (1997) stresses the radicalism of class antagonisms; but above all it is necessary to measure the complex dialectic between spontaneous actions and political orientations which worked in various senses, notably highlighted, notably by Alexander Rabinowitch (2016) or David Mandel (2016).

55 See the organisation by the CI of the Congress of the Peoples of the East in Baku in 1920 (texts, published by Maspero in 1971, republished in 2017 by Editions Radar and La Brèche). See the presentation <https://npa2009.org/idees/culture/1920-le-premier-congres-des-peuples-dorient>.

56 On 'The Marxists and the national question' see Georges Haupt, Michaël Löwy and Claudie Weill (1979); and the critique by Roman Rosdolsky of the positions of Engels on peoples 'without history' <https://www.marxists.org/francais/rosdolsky/works/1948/00/rosdolsky-engels-table.htm>. More specifically on the Ukrainian question, K. Kowalewski (1989, 2015); see also N.G. Varela (2014).

57 See note 56. NB: even the defence of the right of self-determination of dominated peoples and thus the distinction between dominated and dominant nations (on which Lenin insisted as conditions of proletarian unity) did not imply any clear programmatic viewpoint on the interwoven national, social, political and indeed religious questions: see the emergence of a Communist Bund or of Muslim Communist currents, like the Tartar Bolshevik Mirsaid Sultan Galaiev. On this subject see Renault Matthieu <http://www.europe-solidaire.org/spip.php?article41639>.

58 See Samuel Joshua 'Ils ont osé! L'expérience de l'école soviétique des années 1920' (2017).

59 See in relation to this notably the presentation by Jean-Michel Kay (2005), *L'Epreuve du pouvoir, Russie 1917,* Collectif Smolny, 2005. See also D. Mandel and A. Rabinowitch, op. cit. note 23. Also, on the general problems of lack of preparation, from libertarian as well as Marxist viewpoints, see the introductory remarks of the 'Platform' of 1926 of the Russian anarchist group abroad, Bielo Trouda, on the site dedicated to Nesto Makhno <http://www.nestormakhno.info/index.htm>.

60 Jean-Jacques Marie, Lénine, *La révolution permanente*, (2011).

61 Written in August-September 1917, and published in May 1918.

62 See also on this subject Antoine Artous (1999) or Henri Maler (1995, 2016), or Isaac Johsua (2012) and his controversy over 'Marxism in question' with Pierre Khalfa in the review *Contretemps* (2012).

63 See on the 'Left Communists' and the review *Kommounist*, L. Shapiro (1997) who evokes the various oppositions, whether inside the Bolshevik party or outside it – libertarian, socialist revolutionary, Menshevik; Maurice Brinton (1970), Michel Olivier (2012) who criticise Shapiro's ending his study in 1922, as if there was no internal opposition in a position to express itself after that date.

64 Which did not prevent many of them from participating some months later in the United Opposition, with Trotsky, Zinoviev, Kamenev formed in the spring of 1926. See also Broué (1963).

65 Alexandra Kollontaï (1921) drew up its platform.

66 According to Michel Olivier (2012), there were three positions inside the Bolsheviks on trade unions. That of the Workers' Opposition, invoked above; that of Trotsky, who wanted an integration of the unions in the state apparatus, with the function of increasing the productivity of labour in a militarised fashion; and that of Lenin, for the maintenance of unions independent of the state and without responsibility for management, with the function of defence of the workers against the 'workers' state' (whose bureaucratisation he perceived).

67 Lebowitz, M., Beyond Capital: Marx's Political Economy of Workers, 2003.

68 Charles Bettelheim (1971) in his texts of the early 1960s, before his tilt towards the Chinese Proletarian Cultural Revolution, thus characterised this type of society as marked by a 'non-correspondence' between productive forces and relations of production.

69 Pierre Broué, *Trotski* (1988).

70 Paul Avrich, *Kronstadt 1921* (1970).

71 See Broué, 'La crise de la revolution', in *Trotski* (1988).

72 See in the first part of his text: <http://alencontre.org/societe/histoire/trente-ans-apres-la-revolution-russe-i.html>.

73 See the second part of his text, concerning the errors, at <http://alencontre.org/societe/histoire/trente-ans-apres-la-revolution-russe-ii.html>.
74 See Boukharine, N., Preobrajensky, E., Trotski, L., *Le débat soviétique sur la loi de la valeur*, (1972).
75 It is also common to Ernest Mandel or to Charles Bettelheim, whose divergences are of the same nature as those between Preobrazhensky and Bukharin. But the ideological Stalinisation of Mao's China would produce a caricatural variant of the analyses of conflicts assimilated to a class struggle.
76 Victor Serge, 'Thirty years after the Russian revolution', in *Russia, Twenty Years After* (1996).
77 Rosa Luxemburg, *The Russian revolution* (1918).
78 See Marc Ferro (1997), Alexander Rabinowitch (2016), Pierre Broué (1963) on the Bolshevik party and (1988) on Trotsky, or Jean-Jacques Marie, op. cit., on Lenin.
79 On the politics of the Russian anarchists, see Victor Serge (1920). See also the archive site in several languages: <http://www.nestormakhno.info/index.htm> and notably the Platform of the Dielo Truda group of Russian anarchists abroad (Makhno, Mett, Archinov, Valevski, Linski) criticised by others like Voline for being 'Bolshevised'. See also the reportage for *Médiapart* of July 17, 2017 by Jean-Arnaud Dérens and Laurent Geslin, 'Octobre 17. 'Nestor Makhno, le 'batko' anarchiste d'Ukraine' <https://www.mediapart.fr/journal/culture-idees/190717/octobre-17-nestor-makhno-le-batko-anarchiste-dukraine?onglet=full>. It does not seem that the libertarians had a homogeneous position on the national questions and in particular the independence of the Ukraine.
80 I cannot discuss here the other criticisms she formulates, which are far from being convincing, and which I do not share, against the slogans 'the land to those who work it' (which Lenin had taken from the S-R) and the 'right of self-determination' of peoples who want it.
81 Spartacus editions have reproduced Kautsky's texts and Lenin's replies in a collection introduced by Jean-Michel Kay, *L'Epreuve du pouvoir, Russie 1917* (2005). The convergences between Kautsky and Rosa Luxemburg on this democratic question did not imply, as has been stressed, that the latter shared Kautsky's hostility to the Russian revolution.
82 See Trotsky, *The New Course*, (1923) and Pierre Broué on 'The crisis of the revolution' <https://www.marxists.org/francais/broue/works/1963/00/broue_pbolch_8.htm#sdfootnote207anc>, and Trotsky (1923) 'The New Course and Letter to a Party Meeting': <https://www.marxists.org/francais/trotsky/livres/coursnouveau/cn6.html>.
83 I cannot discuss the causes here. Yet the impact of October would be broadly felt throughout Europe. The role of social democracy, the leftist orientations and repression are combined in the necessary interpretation.
84 Moshe Lewin, *Lenin's last struggle*, (2005).
85 In his essay *On Bureaucracy*, Ernest Mandel (1978) distinguishes the critique of 'substitutionism' of the party at work from the 1920s, which facilitated the Stalinist bureaucratic crystallisation, and the latter itself. He synthesises simultaneously the significant stages of becoming conscious of the bureaucratic evil, notably inside the workers' movement, and the means of consciously fighting it. Moshe Lewin has written of *Lenin's last struggle* notably against Stalin's Great Russian tendencies and

the bureaucratisation of the workers' state. On the debates and struggles inside the Bolshevik party against bureaucratism in the 1920s, read notably Eric Toussaint (2017).

86 This debate is especially necessary with the anarchist currents, attached to principles of self-management, with a necessary review of both the Titoist past and the phase of 'mass privatisation' (by popular shareholding) after 1989. See my contribution to the centenary of the CNT in Barcelona (Samary 2010). My site <http://csamary.free.fr> contains texts on the different dimensions and phases of this experience.

87 This conference brought together forces mobilised against imperialism and colonialism on three continents (Africa, Asia and Latin America) in the presence of delegations from the USSR, China and numerous other countries. See on this subject R. Galissot (2005), S. Bouamaman (2016).

88 Robert J.C. Young, 'Postcolonialism: From Bandung to the Tricontinental', *Historein* Vol 5, 2005.

89 These are the terms of the resolution adopted by the Fourth International (FI)/ See *Quatrième Internationale* (QI/FI) which can be found in its digitalised archives (QI/FI, 1963).

90 A special number of the review *Contretemps* (2008), *Mai 2008 – 1968: un monde en révolte* stresses this international context. It includes, notably, an article on the Prague Spring of 1968 and the autumn of the workers councils under the occupation of the Soviet tanks, and another on June 1968 in Belgrade and the impasses of Titoism.

91 Karl Polanyi, *The great transformation*, (1945).

92 Charles Bettelheim has – correctly – insisted on the need to distinguish juridical relations of property and real relations – in other words the gap between the proclamation of 'socialism' and the reality. But this sensible method has been applied by all Marxists and other analysts who did not follow an apologetic and ideological approach to 'actually existing socialism' – notably Ernest Mandel. It in no way implies the use of concepts of capital outside of a capitalist system. On the modalities of the new 'great capitalist transformation' in Eastern Europe, see Samary (2008b).

93 Gerard Roland, *Economie politique du système soviétique*, (1989).

94 The non-market character of international exchanges between the countries of 'actually existing socialism' is organically linked to similar traits at the national level. Read on this subject Marie Lavigne (1990). These realities of a non-capitalist 'system of production' without commodity regulator were expressed in the growing importance (in the USSR) of the non-monetary 'social wage' (housing, crèches, health services and free shops, associated with the work place) rendering employment more rigid, well analysed by David Mandel (1997); but also through the 'passive role' of the money(not orienting investment choices) analysed by Wladimir Brus (1968, 1975) or, again, by the 'absence of strong budgetary constraint' weighing on the enterprises, to take up the well-known formulations of Janos Kornaï (1971). See also Gérard Roland (1989), on the dominant role of use values.

95 But the currents using this concept are eclectic, like the criteria underlying it – encompassing Stalino-Maoists and currents identifying with anarcho-communism as well as variants of Trotskyism (see Tony Cliff, *State Capitalism in Russia*, (1974). This is also true of the other concepts – analysing the bureaucracy as new class – or preferring the approach in terms of caste and bureaucratised workers' states. With the same concepts totally polar positions could be taken in relation to major events (revolutions and uprisings). Conversely, with different concepts, common positions

– indeed a durable presence in the same International (the United Secretariat of the Fourth International) were possible – and desirable.

96 I will return below to the failures of this conceptualisation (notably the absence of real autonomisation of this 'new class' in relation to the workers' movement both at the social and international political levels. But the basic aspects of these approaches – the crystallisation of specific social interests, antagonistic to those of the workers under a non-capitalist form – can be fully integrated with more convincing approaches of the bureaucracy as 'caste' or intermediary quasi-class oscillating between the fundamental classes according to context.

97 It is necessary to study each scenario, which does not involve any 'economic' automatism: the contradictions and impasses of the said societies of 'actually existing socialism' imposed no fatality of capitalist restoration inasmuch as the dominant apparatuses had not decided on it. While preserving a solid control of the party-state (contrary to what was the case in Russia), China has shifted towards a true bureaucratic state capitalism (see Au Long Yu, 2012) – I don't know enough about the Vietnamese scenario, which has also clearly shifted towards capitalism. For the scenarios of Russia and the comprador bourgeoisies of Eastern Europe, see Samary (2008b, 2015); Myant M. and Drahokoupil J. (2011), *Transition Economies: Political Economy in Russia, Eastern Europe, and Central Asia*. See also the works coordinated by Wladimir Andreff (notably 1990, 2006, 2007). For the specific situation of Cuba, see Samuel Farber (2016), Brana et al. (2002)

98 Michael Lebowitz, *Beyond Capital: Marx's Political Economy of Workers*, 2003.

99 With certain traits of the epoch of Lenin.

100 This is what I have tried to do, in the context of Soviet planning or reforms, with or without self-management. See Samary (1988, 2008b) – and the articles on this subject on my site <http://csamary.free.fr>.

101 See notably Cornélius Castodiaris (1973).

102 This is a very concrete element of the social relations of ownership, at work in planning and which has always been completely absent from Bettelheim's analyses on the 'market' character of the links between enterprises.

103 Hence the dialogue of the deaf on the 'political revolution' although the notion had the function of describing the resumption of the 'permanent revolution' in the sense of a phase opened by October – which would be closed in 1989/91.

104 Her letter to the FI was published with the United Secretariat's reply in the dossier *Controverses, D'Octobre 1917 à l'effondrement de l'URSS* of the Forum pour la Gauche Communiste Internationale: <http://www.leftcommunism.org/IMG/pdf/CT-1.pdf>.

105 Milovan Djilas, *Wartime: With Tito and the Partisans*, (1980).

106 Vladimir Dedijer, *The Battle Stalin Lost; Memoirs of Yugoslavia 1948-1953*, New York: Viking, 1970.

107 Che Guevara, *Socialism and Man in Cuba*, (1965).

108 Ernest Mandel, *'Du nouveau sur la question de la nature de l'URSS: lutte entre la 'loi de la valeur' et la logique du plan'*, (1970).

109 Charles Bettelheim, *Calcul économique et formes de propriété*, (1970).

110 Edvard Kardelj, *Contradictions of Social Property in a Socialist Society*, (1981).

111 This was the case with Ernest Mandel and the major part of the Fourth International of which he was one of the leaders in the late 1960s. This allowed a reunification with the 'Pabloite' currents favourable to self-management.
112 See on this subject Che Guevara (1965), Samuel Farber (2017), Mesa-Lago C., (1971); E. Germain (1963), Ernest Mandel (1987), C. Bettelheim (1971); the collection edited by Michael Löwy, *Man and Socialism in Cuba; The Great Debate*, edited by Bertram Silverman (1971); *Ernesto Che Guevara: Ecrits d'un révolutionnaire*, edited by Michael Löwy with texts by Charles Bettelheim and Ernest Mandel, (1987).
113 Charless Bettelheim, 'On socialist planning and the level of the development of the productive forces', *Man and Socialism in Cuba: The Great Debate,* (1971).
114 Ernest Germain/Mandel, 'The Law of Value in Relation to Self-Management and Investment in the Economy of the Workers' States', 1963. < https://www.marxists.org/archive/mandel/1963/xx/value-self-man.html>.
115 <https://www.ernestmandel.org/en/works/txt/1963/law_of_value.htm>. Mandel's viewpoint here was explained in numerous articles, notably in the debate with Alec Nove.
116 Samuel Farber, 'Building Socialism in Cuba', *The Jacobin*, October 2016.
117 Michaël Löwy (1970), supporting Che and Mandel, criticised in 'L'humanisme historiciste de Marx – ou relire le Capital', the Althusserian viewpoint distinguishing an 'abstract' humanism of the 'young Marx' from the 'true' Marx of *Capital*, after an 'epistemological rupture'.
118 Samuel Farber, 'Building Socialism in Cuba', *The Jacobin*, October 2016.
119 See Samary, 1988, 2010.
120 In the first phase of self-management, the 'surplus income' (what remained after payment of incomes and costs linked to the replacement cost of means of production) – allowing an 'enlarged reproduction', that is new investment, was centralised in para-state investment funds. The 1965 reform dismantled these funds in favour of self-managed organisations in the enterprises and the new banking system.
121 It is interesting to find on a site of archives of the anarchist press in 2013 a text reproduced from *Communist Anarchist Tribune*, number 2 (winter 1969), entitled 'L'autogestion et la Yougoslavie' <http://www.la-presse-anarchiste.net/spip.php?article3616> which asks their comrades to seriously consider the self-managing reformism of the Yugoslav CP, ending thus: 'We understand that many comrades find it hard to fully acknowledge this development of Yugoslavia and its Communist party. It amounts in fact to a true reformism inside a socialist state. It is then worth envisaging the role of the revolutionary organisation in a new way according to generalised self-management. But it seems to us legitimate to consider Yugoslavia as part of a general approach to self-management and that it occupies here perhaps the most significant position, in any event at the current time. This article will undoubtedly be considered by some as an apologetic schema. We would reply that it is only an attempt to locate the problem and that in these perspectives we are ready to criticise Yugoslavia and its self-management, but in these perspectives, to allow this critique to be fruitful and not chaotic.'
122 It is notably on this point that I discuss the application of the analyses of Michael Lebowitz to the Yugoslav context.
123 This 'moment of Yugoslav socialism', in the broadest sense of a phase of crisis at the crossroads, was analysed by the editorial of the review *Praxis*, number 3-4 published in 1971. See also Rudi Supek (dir.) 1973. The archives for 1965-1973 are on the site:

<https://www.marxists.org/subject/praxis/>. See notably 'Dissolutionary process in the system of self-management of Mladen Caldarovic' (1965/4) and the articles of the 1970s, notably by Zagorka Golubović, Mladen Čaldarovič, Svetozar Stojanovič. On the pressures of the regime against *Praxis* see J.M. Palmier, (1973).

124 Except that it was true this time (contrary to what he had analysed in Soviet planning) that the introduction of 'market socialism' allowed the pressures of the law of value in the relations between self-managed enterprises. But these pressures were negative and not efficacious. Bettelheim (1968) could moreover show (as did the Yugoslav Marxists) how it did not allow a 'socialisation' of self-management of the means of production. But was it necessary to conclude from this that the market reforms were destructive – contrary to his position in the Cuban debate – and orient towards a third path absent in the Cuban debate and defended by the Yugoslav Marxists?

125 See the Second Congress of Self-Managers of Yugoslavia (1972) where we find the official speeches by Tito and Kardelj, the analysis of the destructive conflicts and tendencies created by the market reforms and the logic of the constitutional amendments which would be made concrete in 1974.

126 The publication of *Praxis* was blocked from 1975 onwards. The *Praxis* academics were forbidden from teaching, but could continue their research.

127 See Michael Hardt and Antonio Negri, *Commonwealth,* (2009).

128 John Holloway, *Change the World Without Taking Power: The Meaning of Revolution Today*, London: Pluto Press, 2010.

129 Hardin, G., 'The Tragedy of the Commons', *Science,* vol. 162, no. 3859, Washington DC, 1968.

130 David Harvey, 'The future of the Commons', *Radical History Review,* issue 109, Winter 2011.

131 Elinor Ostrom, *Governing the Commons: The Evolution of Institutions for Collective Action*, Cambridge: Cambridge University Press, 1990.

132 Sebastien Broca, 'Les Communs, un projet ambigu', *Monde Diplomatique, December 2016.*

133 John Holloway, *Change the world without taking power,* 2003. See the discussion on this subject in *Contretemps* (2003), 'Changer le monde sans prendre le pouvoir?' with in particular a discussion of John Holloway by Daniel Bensaïd.

134 John Holloway, *Crack Capitalism,* (2010).

135 Catherine Samary, 'Essor et crises du mouvement altermondialiste', *'En quête d'alternatives. L'état du monde 2018',* 2017.

136 P. Dardot and C. Laval, *Commun. Essai sur la révolution au XXIè siècle,* (2014).

137 See Antoine. Artous et al., *'Marx et l'appropriation sociale', (Les) Cahiers de Critiques Communistes,* 2003.

138 Benjamin Coriat, (ed.), *Le Retour des communs. La crise de l'idéologie propriétaire*, Paris: Les Liens Qui Libèrent, 2015.

139 David Harvey, 'The future of the Commons', *Radical History Review,* issue 109, Winter 2011.

140 Naomi Klein, *This Changes Everything: Capitalism vs. the Climate,* (2015).

141 David Harvey, *Rebel Cities, From the Right to the City to the Urban Revolution*, not without confrontation with the projects of finance and the market exploitation of urbanity: 'Cities in the Hands of Global Finance', lecture at Centre de Cultura Contemporània

de Barcelona by Raquel Rolnik, June 2017 < http://www.cccb.org/en/activities/file/cities-in-the-hands-of-global-finance/226015>.
142 See the manifesto 'La ville que nous voulons' drawn up in Barcelona <http://www.somosmuitas.com.br/index.html>.
143 <https://www.mediapart.fr/journal/international/130617/le-plaidoyer-du-maire-de-valparaiso-en-faveur-du-municipalisme>.
144 'Comité pour l'abolition des dettes du tiers monde' (CADTM), which became the 'Comité pour l'abolition des dettes illégitimes' (The Committee for the abolition of illegitimate debts) <www.cadtm.org>, extending its network on the international scale – a component of the global justice movement.
145 <http://www.autogestion.asso.fr/?p=6491>.
146 <http://aitec.reseau-ipam.org/spip.php?article1628>.
147 <https://france.attac.org/mot/grand-marche-transatlantique>, Attac (2017). On the strategic issues of the global justice movement see also G. Massiah (2011). See also the contributions of Thomas Coutrot, including *Jalons vers un monde possible: redonner des racines à la démocratie*, 2010.
148 <http://www.confederationpaysanne.fr/rp_article.php?id=6081> and <http://www.alainet.org/fr/articulo/186917?#>.
149 <http://intercoll.net/IMG/pdf/bulletin_intercoll_-_mai_2017.pdf> and on the continental experiences, F. Gaudichaud (2015).

Yugoslav self-management: a balance sheet

150 They began, notably in Slovenia, during an international conference in October 2007, in resistance to the new official interpretations of history, criminalising the anti-fascist resistance during the Second World War and rehabilitating as 'patriots' the fascist and anti-communist forces. See <http://uneventment.blogspot.com/>.
151 I have contributed to this debate in various ways in the articles which can be found on ESSF <www.europe-solidaire.org> and on <http://csamary.free.fr> (under alternatives).
152 There were more than a million deaths in the Yugoslav area during the Second World War. These were the victims of the war against the German and Italian occupying powers and of the civil wars intertwined with this struggle which were against the internal reactionary forces advocating nation-state projects based on inter-ethnic hatreds.
153 Tito was responsible for sending the International Brigades to Spain to fight Francoism – and this fight marked and educated numerous Yugoslav communist cadres. Stalin knew what he was doing when he wanted to dissolve this party. To protect himself, Tito avoided certain trips to Moscow and supported a mode of functioning for the Yugoslav CP which was clandestine and independent, including of Soviet financing.
154 Milovan Djilas, *Wartime: With Tito and the Partisans,* London: Martin Secker & Warburg, 1977 and *Conversations with Stalin*, London: Penguin, 1969; Vladimir Dedijer, *Le défi de Tito*, Paris: Gallimard, 1970; François Fejtö, *A History of the People's Democracies*, London: Pelican, 1974.
155 See Pierre Maurer, *La réconciliation soviéto-yougoslave 1954-1958 – Illusions et désillusions de Tito*, Fribourg: DelVal, 1991.
156 Edvard Kardelj, *Les Contradictions de la propriété sociale dans le système socialiste,* Editions Anthropos, 1976.

157 On the various phases and mechanisms of the Yugoslav reforms see Catherine Samary, *Le marché contre l'autogestion, l'expérience yougoslave*, Paris: Publisud/LaBrèche, 1988; and with comparative aspects in other countries of Eastern Europe, Catherine Samary, *Plan, Market and Democracy*, Amsterdam: IIRE, 1988; on the period of crisis, see Catherine Samary, *Yugoslavia Dismembered*, New York: Monthly Review Press, 1995; on the final phase of dismantling of the system, Catherine Samary, *Yougoslavie: de la décomposition aux enjeux européens*, Paris: Ed. du Cygne, 2008.

158 Michel Roux, *Le Kosovo*, Paris: La Découverte, 1999.

159 The 1980s saw a restrictive policy of external adjustment and a stagnation of social income. The result was growing political tensions and the rise of nationalisms, and finally the break-up of Yugoslavia.

160 On the big transformations in Eastern Europe see <http://semimarx.free.fr/>.

161 Susan L. Woodward, *Balkan tragedy: chaos and dissolution after the Cold War*, Washington: Brookings Institution, 1995.

162 The neologism used at the time by Timothy Garton Ash (1993) to describe the transformations in Eastern Europe and by Predrag Matvejevitć, a Croatian-Yugoslav author who has written notably *Le monde 'ex' – Confessions*, Paris: Fayard, 1996.

163 O.L Kubli, *Du nationalisme yougoslave aux nationalismes post-yougoslaves*, Paris: L'Harmattan, 1998; 'Yougoslavie: logiques de l'exclusion', special issue of *Peuples méditerranéens*, no. 61, ed. M. Morokvasić, October-December, 1992; D. Masson, *L'utilisation de la guerre dans la construction des systèmes politiques en Serbie et en Croatie, 1989-1995*, Paris: l'Harmattan, 2002

164 The Serbs of Bosnia-Herzegovina rejected this Republic, becoming independent, and the Croats who lived there demanded that 'Herzeg-Bosna' be attached to Croatia. See X. Bougarel, *Bosnie. Anatomie d'un conflit*, Paris: La Découverte, 1996; J-A Dérens & C. Samary, *Les conflits yougoslaves de A à Z*, Ivry: Ed. De l'Atelier, 2000; D. Masson, *L'utilisation de la guerre dans la construction des systèmes politiques en Serbie et en Croatie, 1989-1995*, Paris: l'Harmattan, 2002; M. Glamocak, *La transition guerrière yougoslave*, Paris: l'Harmattan, 2002.

165 Y. Rizopoulos (ed.), *Les transformations économiques dans la péninsule des Balkans*, Revue d'études comparatives Est-Ouest, vol. 30, no.4, Paris: CNRS, 1999, <http://www.persee.fr/issue/receo_0338-0599_1999_num_30_4>; Yann Richard & André-Louis Sanguin (ed.), *L'Europe de l'Est quinze ans après la chute du Mur. Des pays baltes à l'ex-Yougoslavie*, Paris: l'Harmattan, 2004; Mirjana Morokvasić & Nebojsa Vukadinović (ed.), *Sortir de la transition bloquée: Serbie-Monténégro*, Revue d'études comparatives Est-Ouest, vol. 35, no.1-2, 2004; Catherine Samary, 'Réinsérer la Serbie dans l'analyse de la transition: rapports de propriété, Etat et salariat', *Sortir de la transition bloquée : Serbie-Monténégro*, 2004, <http://www.europe-solidaire.org/spip.php?article7526>; Z. Papiic, *International Support Policies to Southeast European Countries: Lessons (not) Learned in Bosnia-Herzogovina*, Sarajevo: Müller, 2001.

166 N. Vukadinović, 'Slovénie', Études du CERI, Paris (several years since 1999) Fondation nationale des sciences politiques; see also, M. De Felice, 'Slovénie: des atouts mis à profit', in *L'Europe centrale et orientale. Dix ans de transformations (1989-1999)*, Les études de la Documentation Française, Paris: CEDUCEE, 2000.

Socialism and humanism

167 K. Marx, 'A Contribution to the Critique of Hegel's Philosophy of Law', in K. Marx, F. Engels: *Werke*, Band 1, p. 378.

168 This made it possible for long-term humanistic principles to change in Stalinist practice into their opposites, because such practice was based on a limited theory, moving only within the framework of what was given and what was most immediate (changing the idea of the withering-away of the state into the theory of the strengthening of the state; ignoring Marx's idea of the free association of workers in favour of strengthening bureaucratic and technocratic organisation; changing the theory of the liberation of man into the theory of the liberation of the mass, from which follows the subordination of personal to social interests, etc.).

169 The system of workers' self-management does not in itself provide a solution of the comprehensive problem of the alienation of work, but offers only a basis on which a more thorough revaluation of work can be more completely achieved. This will be dealt with in greater detail later on.

170 The thesis of the primary importance of meeting material needs which, when satisfied, would automatically produce needs of a higher level and of a non-material character, has not been confirmed either in modem capitalist countries or in developed socialist ones. On the contrary, the modern world has shown that material needs can develop and reproduce themselves infinitely, becoming an obsession which limits and hampers the development of other and higher human needs. Socialist theory must draw consequences from this.

171 *Programme of the League of Yugoslav Communists,* published by Jugoslavia, Belgrade 1958, pp. 143 and 144.

172 *Ibid.,* p. 157.

173 *Yugoslav Constitution*, published by Sluzbeni list, 1963, p. 32.

174 There is an institution called the Institute for the Productivity of Labour which ought to study this problem more seriously, enlisting the co-operation of experts who could become engaged in this sphere. At present the Institute makes exclusive use of other people's experiences and often translates works dealing with work organisation which are extremely unsuited to our conditions.

The June student movement and social revolution in Yugoslavia

175 Report of the Inspectorate of Labour of the Federal Secretariat for Labour submitted to the Federal Assembly, 1964.

176 As far as I know, only Kenneth Boulding (in *The Meaning of the 20th Century,* Harper & Row, 1964) used, and only incidentally, the concept of entropy to explain social phenomena. However, he only refers to the entropy of social institutions and social systems, and not to the entropy of revolutions.

177 See *Praxis international edition*, no.1/2, 1969, p. 4, Zagreb, <https://www.marxists.org/subject/praxis/praxis-international/Praxis,%20international%20edition,%201969,%20no.%201-2.pdf>.

178 Leon Trotsky dreamed of communism this way: 'Man will become immeasurably stronger, wiser and subtler; his body will become more harmonized, his movements more rhythmic, his voice more musical. The forms of life will become dynamically

dramatics.' See his *Literature and Revolution,* Ann Arbor: University of Michigan Press, 1960, p. 256.
179 In the book *Kritik und Zukunft des Sozialisinus*, Munchen: Carl Hauser Verlag, 1970.
180 It is interesting that for Maoists it is the Twentieth Congress of the Soviet Communist Party, which initiated a certain de-Stalinisation, that represents the beginning of an alleged restoration of capitalism in the USSR.
181 Two months after the demonstrative strike of university students and teachers in June 1968, several articles about it were published in the journal *Delo,* but this issue was suppressed. Recently the journal *Gledišta,* no. 5/6, 1969, printed the transcript of a rather interesting discussion about the student movement in the world and in Yugoslavia.

From post-revolutionary dictatorship to socialist democracy

182 The English translation is published by the Oxford University Press,1973.
183 In Slovenia, for example, a group of twenty-five representatives-communists was checked and fiercely attacked for wanting to add another *of their own choice* to the list of candidates for the Presidium of Yugoslavia. It made no difference that they proposed another highly placed and 'reliable' political functionary, and that their action was in complete accord with the law which had been previously passed by the Slovenian Parliament. Their action was, nevertheless, seen as violating the principles of self-government in politics!
184 This concept should include those who create material as well as those who create spiritual values and live exclusively from their own labour.
185 There is another factor which reinforces this legitimization: the fear of risk involved in the radical reforms of the existing system, especially when it is combined with a sense of external threat to the achievements of de-Stalinisation in Yugoslavia.

Workers' councils in Yugoslavia: successes and failures

186 *Istorija Saveza komunista Jugoslavije,* Izdavački centar 'Komunist' – Narodna knjiga – Rad, Beograd, 1985, p.309.
187 *Samoupravljanje u Jugoslaviji 1950-1980* (dokumenti razvoja), Privredni pregled, Beograd, 1980, p. 434.
188 This was also stressed in the 'Theses' prepared for the First Congress of Workers' Councils, which took place in 1957: 'Yugoslavia's working class is too young; it suffers from insufficient general, professional and economic education, as well as other knowledge necessary for the successful management of enterprises.'
189 'Maybe someone thinks that the law is premature, that workers will not be able to acquire complicated techniques of managing factories and other enterprises.... It [self-management], therefore, is not premature but has been introduced with certain delay...' (Tito, Speech in People's Assembly on occasion of announcement of Basic Law on Management of State Enterprises and Higher Economic Associations by Work Collectives, in *Samoupravljanje u Jugoslaviji 1950-1980*, p.68).
190 Branislav Gligorijević, 'Uvođenje radničkih saveta (1950-1953), Užice nekad i sad <www.graduzice.org/userfiles/files uvodenjeradnickihsavetaod1950do1953.pdf>
191 The text of the Basic Law can be found in *Samoupravljanje u Jugoslaviji, 1950-1980,* pp.59-66. The reasons for creating workers' councils were defined in 'Theses' for the

First Congress of Workers' Councils in 1957: 'to enable the working class to realize its historic right of practicing direct management of the economy; to enable the working class to realize its social role and extend its rights won during the socialist revolution; to remove dangers rooted in administrative management of the economy; to secure better conditions for the development and unimpeded operation of productive forces; to make the material and moral interests of the workers the essential moving factor of socialism under the conditions of the system of social ownership....'

192 According to daily *Borba*, in 1956 there were 208,000 members of workers' councils (*The Impending First Workers' Councils Congress in Yugoslavia*, RFE News and Information Service 1957, Open Society Archives, <www.osaarchivum.org/files/holdings/300/8/3/pdf/72-3-181.pdf>

193 See George A. Potts, The Development of the System of Representation in Yugoslavia with Special Reference to the Period Since 1974, Lanham, MD: University Press of America, 1996, pp.319-34.

194 'Delegates act according to guidelines of workers or a workers' council of a BOAL which elected them and are responsible to them for their action' (Art. 101/4 of 1974 Constitution).

195 Duško Sekulić, 'Društveno-ekonomske reforme u jugoslovenskom društvu s osvrtom na društva 'realnog socijalizma,"in: *Teorija i praksa 'realnog socijalizma'* (*Theory and practice of 'really existing socialism'*), Beograd, 1987, p.97.

196 [*Ed. Note:* 'republican' refers throughout to the six constituent republics that formerly made up the Federal Republic of Yugoslavia.]

197 'In order to encourage creativity of self-managers and to introduce a more efficient system, it was necessary to liberate them from the state's vice, for which introduction of the market was necessary' (*Teorija i praksa 'realnog socijalizma,'* p.99).

198 Teorija i praksa 'realnog socijalizma', p.213.

199 In one extreme case, 7,000 workers voted in a referendum for a decision. In just one participating BOAL, the result was 31 to 29 against the decision. This 2-vote margin within a single BOAL blocked the verdict of 7,000 (ibid., p.214).

200 'The feeling that the administration can manipulate decisions led to rapid disillusionment with the system. Revolutionary change, where workers would be real masters of labor and its results, was promised, but the administration remained the main decision-maker, at least in practice' (ibid., pp.212-13).

201 While in 1952 there were 105,018 members of workers' councils, this number rose to 484,784 in 1983 (Potts, *Development of the System of Representation in Yugoslavia*, p.341). In 1969 30% of workers participated in different organs of self-management in enterprises. 70.5% of members of workers' councils and 55.5% of members of management boards were workers (Drago Gorupić, 'Razvoj samoupravne organizacije preduzeća,' in *Teorija i praksa samoupravljanja u Jugoslaviji*, Radnièka ¹tampa, Beograd, 1972, p.695).

202 Istorija Saveza komunista Jugoslavije, p.395.

203 'The autonomy of an enterprise is determined by the right of its organs of management to independently enact its economic plan and dispose of its income after it pays its obligations to the state...' Gorupić, 'Razvoj samoupravne organizacije preduzeća' (note 16), p.682.

204 Workers' strikes were rare in Yugoslavia until the 1980s. The first one was organized in the Slovenian mine center Trbovlje in 1958 when 4,000 workers struck. However, it was perceived that strike as a means of workers' struggle was inappropriate in a society

where workers had institutional possibilities for their predominance. The fact that workers organized strikes against management and that workers' council members also took part in them showed that workers' councils were not dominant decision-makers (see also: Josip Obradović, 'Sociology of Organization in Yugoslavia,' *Acta Sociologica*, Vol. 19 No. 1/1976, p.31).

205 According to Janja Beč's research, between 77 and 80% of workers thought that self-management was the best and the fairest method of development for Yugoslav society; between 95 and 98% thought that workers have to control the results of their work, while at the same time around 60% (in some cases even 84%) thought that self-management did not mean much in practice (Potts, *Development of the System of Representation in Yugoslavia*, p.356).

206 Overall social product in Yugoslavia grew faster than the world average in the period between 1950 and 1980 (indexes 636 and 396 respectively). Average annual growth rate globally was 4.7%, while in Yugoslavia it was 6.4%. Agricultural population decreased to 29% in 1981 (*12. kongres Saveza komunista Jugoslavije*, Izdavački centar Komunist, Beograd, 1982, pp.20-21).

207 Studies of the impact of workers' participation in management on economic efficiency showed a positive correlation (see Aleksandra Kanjuo-Mrčela, *Lastništvo in ekonomska demokracija*, Fakulteta za družtvene vede, Ljubljana, 1999, p.182, p.197).

208 'A mission of the International Labor Organization to Yugoslavia in 1960 concluded that 'while self-managerial machinery reduced the former power of superintendents, it seemed that it did not diminish their authority... It doubtless strengthened the position of the work collective in relation to management, but it did not undermine work discipline'' (Branko Horvat, *Politička ekonomija socijalizma*, Globus, Zagreb, 1984, p.144). Horvat made the same point regarding self-management in Chile.

209 'Attempts to introduce workers' management were met with three usual objections. It had been said that self-management would undermine discipline; workers' councils would be incompetent to work as boards of CEOs and that workers would distribute all profits as personal income, thus depleting developmental potential of the economy. None of these prophecies were accurate' (ibid., p.209).

210 According to a report at the Second Congress of Self-Managers (Sarajevo 1971), in the big Varteks textile factory in Varaždin (Croatia) an economic crisis occurred in 1966 as a result of bad economic policy of management and its disrespect for self-management. As a consequence, the enterprise was left without necessary resources. Workers' assemblies and workers' councils then decided to rehire the previous CEO, allow him to name a new management team, renounce one month's wages, take a wage-cut of 20%, etc. (Stanislav Grozdanić, 'Novije tendencije i pojavu praksi radničkog samoupravljanja,' in *Teorija i praksa samoupravljanja u Jugoslaviji* [note 16], pp.726-27).

211 According to Ivan Grdešić, in 1977 81.6% of those questioned said that they always attended workers' assemblies and other meetings in the BOAL although only 42% of them regarded themselves as having any influence (Potts, *Development of the System of Representation in Yugoslavia*, pp.358-59).

212 'Since CEOs are better educated than workers (at the present time) and better informed about business administration than anyone else, they will have more power than some other groups' (Horvat, *Politička ekonomija socijalizma*, p.214).

213 Karen Wendling, 'Unavoidable Inequalities: Some Implications for Participatory Democratic Theory,' *Social Theory and Practice*, Vol. 23, No. 2, Summer 1997, p.165.

214 According to a 1971 analysis by Workers' University in Mostar (Bosnia and Herzegovina), only 26% of workers knew what the productivity of labor was, 26% of them knew what indirect organs of self-management were, while none of them knew what direct organs of self-management were (Grozdanić, 'Novije tendencije' [note 25], p.731).

215 This was especially the case when a CEO had better connections with political centers of power and at the same time was less educated (Horvat, *Politička ekonomija socijalizma*, p.214).

216 According to Anton Vratuša, enterprises by 1968 controlled only up to 6% of social production, 'with a tendency toward a further decrease' (Anton Vratuša, 'Yugoslavia, 1971,' *Foreign Affairs*, Vol. 50, No. 1, October 1971, p.154).

217 Cliques in particular enterprises had a lot of experience in imposing their proposals without much open pressure. For example, their members could try to postpone discussion of an issue. If they didn't succeed in this, they would purposely fail to provide necessary material and information. Another measure could be to raise an issue at the end of a meeting, so that exhausted self-managers would not have enough patience to discuss it carefully. These maneuvers of informal groups could be neutralized only by experienced and conscious self-managers

218 According to Vladimir Arzenšek's research, workers' councils had less power than CEOs. It is interesting that officials of the League of Communists had less power than workers' councils in 1969, 1970, 1971 and 1974, but more in 1981 (Potts, *Development of the System of Representation in Yugoslavia*, p.354). This research showed two important conclusions: first, the influence of the ruling party at the enterprise level was not as big as one might surmise given the party's role in society as a whole; second, workers lost the power struggle against managerial strataat the micro level.

219 Laslo Sekelj, *Jugoslavija – struktura raspadanja*, Rad, Beograd, 1990, p.57.

220 For example, the difference between Kosovo and Slovenia grew from 1:3.9 in 1952 to 1:7.9 in 1989 (Dejan Jović, *Jugoslavija – država koja je odumrla*, Prometej, Zagreb, 2003, p.218).

221 Before 1965 the state controlled 73% of gross income and 2/3 of accumulation (Sekelj, *Jugoslavija*, p.18).

222 'Our system represents a mixture of self-management at the base and a pretty tough etatist structure above' (Svetozar Stojanović, 'Diskusija o predavanju Predraga Vranickog,' *Praxis*, No. 5-6/1967)

Plan, Market and Democracy: the experience of the so-called socialist countries

223 Branko Horvat defined five factors which were necessary for successful development of workers' self-management. These were: long industrial tradition (because skilled workers showed much more positive predisposition for self-management than unskilled ones), long tradition of political democracy, high personal incomes of workers, short working day, high level of education (*Politička ekonomija socijalizma*, p.218). None of these existed at the time workers' councils were introduced in Yugoslavia, while some of them did not exist there at any time.

224 There is no unanimity, even among Marxists, on the complex way in which this hierarchy operates, combines with national realities and has evolved in the course of

the 20th century. The notion of uneven and combined development and the different theories on the uneven development of capitalism on a world scale are essential to an understanding of the Yugoslav case. We state this even though we do not agree with all the 'centre and periphery' analyses, a debate which would take us beyond the confines of this study.

225 Lenin, 'Left-Wing Childishness and the Petty Bourgeois Mentality,' *Collected Works,* Volume 26, p. 335.

226 David Mandel (1983), has shown the extent to which the idea of a socialist transformation of the economy only became widespread in 1918, as a defence against sabotage and factory closures. Among the workers, as well as in the Bolshevik program, the first demand was for the imposition of controls on firms which remained under capitalist management. For the evolution of the Bolshevik position, see among others, Ernest Mandel, 'Stages of the Soviet Economy,' in *Marxist Economic Theory* (1982), Bettelheim, 'First period: 1917-1923', *Class Struggles in the USSR* (1976) and Trotsky, *History of the Russian Revolution* (1980).

227 Stalinist slanders have propagated a caricature of the theory of permanent revolution: at a time when the Soviet people was exhausted, Trotsky allegedly advocated 'more' revolution, not just in the USSR but internationally, 'since' the building of socialism in the USSR was impossible. The truth is quite different. Trotsky's theory included three facets: In the countries of the capitalist periphery in the era of imperialism, industrialisation 'was subordinated to foreign capital and the national bourgeoisie could not experience the same organic growth as it did in old Europe or the United States. Revolutions broke out in a context of 'uneven and combined' development of archaic forms and recent industrialisation. It was therefore incumbent upon the proletariat to play a leading strategic role in the revolution of these countries.

The second aspect stressed that a class-struggle dynamic would set in, and take the revolution beyond its initial goals. The revolution would combine the tasks of the bourgeois and proletarian revolutions. The seizure of political power by the proletariat would be only the first link in a chain of social transformations.

In continuity with the classical Marxist approach, the third facet emphasised that communism could only be achieved as a mode of production superior to capitalism if it drew on productive forces at least as developed and internationalised as capitalism. The socialist revolution began on the national arena but could only be completed on the international plane. This did not dictate a policy of artificially 'exporting' revolution. Victories in this field would depend above all on national conditions. But the 'building of socialism in one country' was a utopia.

Socialism required not only worldwide productive forces, but a high level of cultural and economic development in each country. The legacy at the outset was a handicap. The social transformations made possible by the seizure of power would take time to materialise. The 'permanent revolution' emphasised the need for a permanent transformation of social relations, of the cultural and material level of development, in order to build the foundations of really socialist relations, free of oppression and exploitation. See Trotsky, 'Socialism in One Country', *The Third International after Lenin* (1929)

228 Translated from the French – M. Djilas, *Sur les voix nouvelles du socialisme* (1950), p.8.
229 Mandel (1974 and 1977).
230 Bettelheim (1968 and 1975).

231 Horvat (1969).
232 Kardelj (1976).
233 Mandel (1977, p. 8)
234 Here, Ernest Mandel uses the concept of 'mode of production' in an analytical sense, to designate a structured and coherent system with stabilised laws of reproduction. According to this approach, a transitional society therefore has 'relations of production,' as every society does, but not a coherent 'mode of production'.
235 Idem, p. 9.
236 In addition to Bettelheim (1968 and 1970), Kardelj (1976) and Horvat (1969), see among others: Brus (1975), Kowalewski (1985), Maksimovic (1976), Djurdjevac (1978) and Markovic (1973).
237 Brus (1975).
238 Trans, from the French: Karl Marx, *L'ideologie allemande,* Paris, Pleïade, p. 1121.
239 Marx is not the only one to claim this. Paradoxically, the free-enterprise School of Property Rights has adopted a similar problematic, combined with an apologetic view of capitalist private property rights. See Henri Lepage, one of the main French spokesperson for this school in *L'Utopie capitalistes* and *Capitalismes et autogestion*.
240 Nove (1983).
241 See M. Lavigne, 'La difficile adaptation de la 'perestroika' aux Economies d'Europe de l'Est,' *Le Monde Diplomatique*, January 1988.
242 Brus (1968).
243 Bakaric (1971, p. 102).
244 Bakaric (1975, p. 81).
245 Typewritten document.
246 Brus (1975).
247 Horvat (1969)
248 Translated from the French, 'La révolte des étudiants en juin a Belgrade', *Quatrième Internationale*, no.34, November 1968, p. 38.
249 Translated from the French, 'Le mécontentement des ouvriers yougoslaves,' *Quatrième Internationale*, no.38, juillet 1969, p. 32.
250 See selected works on the Soviet 1920s debates in the bibliography.
251 'A New Revelation on the Soviet Economy or How to Sink the Worker-Peasant Bloc,' first published in *Bolshevik,* Moscow, December 10, 1924.
252 Ibid, p. 186.
253 Ibid.
254 Translated from the French, Preobrajensky, *From NEP to Socialism,* p. 328.
255 Ibid., p.332-333.
256 Lewin, *The Making of the Soviet System.*
257 Bukharin quoted in Brus, W., *Problèmes généraux du fonctionnement de l'économie socialiste,* p. 75.
258 Preobrazhensky, 'Preface,' *The New Economics* (Translated from the French, 1966, pp. 59 and 68).
259 Ibid, p. 70.
260 Preobrazhensky, 1966, p. 184.
261 Ibid, p. 70.
262 Translated from the French, 'Perspectives de la NEP', *Critiques de l'économie politique,* p.116.

263 Preobrazhensky, 'Preface,' *The New Economics*, p. 78.
264 Translated from the French, 'Utilité de l'étude théorique de l'economie soviétique', *Bolshevik* no. 15-16, August 1926, in *Critiques de l'économie politique,* p. 108.
265 Preobrazhensky, 'Preface,' *The New Economics* p. 92.
266 Ibid., p. 107.
267 We would add today (2018), the full consciousness of environmental goals – CS.
268 Ota Sik, 'Pillars of a Democratic and Socialist System', document produced for the international symposium on The lessons of the Prague Spring, in Paris 1981.
269 Ibid., p. 16.
270 Ibid., pp. 18-19.
271 For a discussion of optimum growth and socialism see Lavigne (1978), Despres (1978) Tartarin (1978), Duchêne (1978), Ellman (1978) Godelier (1978) Markovic (1981).
272 Sik, Ota, 'Pillars of a Democratic and Socialist Economic System', p.13, 1981.
273 See Mihailovic (1982) and Bensaid (1976).
274 See in particular Benassy et al. (1979).
275 Ernest Mandel, 'Du nouveau sur la question de la nature de l'URSS', (1970).
276 Rosdolsky draws attention to this in (1972).
277 Engels's letter to C. Schmidt (Vm-1890) about a debate in the *Volkstribune,* quoted by Rosdolsky (1972, p. 23).
278 Che Guevara, 'Socialism and Man', (1987), pp. 250-251.
279 Bettelheim (1970), *Economic Calculation and Forms of Property,* New York: Monthly Review, 1975 pp. 19-22.
280 In the same vein, Bettelheim emphasised that 'the solution of this problem requires ... a sufficient degree of transformation of the transitional social formations' (1970, p. 3). But he did not pursue his critique of existing social relations further. He later described his earlier position as 'economism' ('Introduction', 1974).
281 On these issues of the status of labour in the transitional period, see Bettelheim (1946, 1968 and 1970), Bonceur (1981), Horvat (1964), Preobrazhensky (1966), Bukharin (1976) and Ernest Mandel ('Du nouveau sur la question de la nature de l'URSS', 1970).
282 Bettelheim (1946).
283 Nove (1983).
284 In his article on new forms of democracy and socialism (1981), Markovic gives a general statement of this approach: he believes that federalism is the optimal form of representation of diverse communities in an overall socialist society; Houses of representatives of the citizens, the nationalities and the producers would make it possible for the various views to be compared and proceed to osmosis. Negotiation and consensus should be the most favoured form of decision-making.
285 Kolm (1984).

The law of value in relation to self-management and investment in the economy of the workers states

286 'Planned economy in the transitional period, while founded on the law of value, violates it nevertheless at every step and establishes relations among the different economic branches, and between industry and agriculture in the first place, on the basis of equal exchange. The state budget plays the role of a lever for forced accumulation and planned distribution. This role must be increased in accordance with the latest economic progress.

Credit financing dominates relations between the coercive accumulation of the budget and the fluctuations of the market, insofar as the latter enter in ... If the domestic Soviet market is 'freed' and the monopoly of foreign trade suppressed – exchange between the city and countryside will become much more equal, the accumulation of the village (I refer to the capitalist accumulation of the farmer, the 'kulak') will follow its course, and it will soon be seen that Marx's formulas likewise apply to agriculture. Once on this road, Russia would rapidly become a colony that would serve as the base for the industrial development of other countries.' (Leon Trotsky: 'Stalin Theoretician' available in French in *Ecrits 1928–40*, Tome I, p. 106, available in English in different translations as 'Stalin as a Theoretician' in *Militant*, 15 September–11 December 1930 and 'Stalin as a Theoretician' in *International Socialist Review*, Fall 1956 & Winter 1957.

287 Among others, Novochilov, Kantorovitch and Menchinov. This question underlies the famous debate on the possible use of profit as the sole criterion in carrying out the plan. In reality, these economists are the spokesmen of the economic bureaucracy, who demand *increased rights for the directors of enterprises* – particularly the right to freely dispose of a part of the 'invisible funds' (fixed equipment).

288 From 1924 to 1927, the Stalinist faction violently accused the Left Opposition – Preobrazhensky in particular – with wanting 'to increase the prices of industrial products.' Preobrazhensky had simply proposed that industrial products could be sold 'above their value' to the village, which could have been tied in perfectly with a progressive lowering of the sales price in view of the rapid growth of the productivity of labour. But when the Stalinist faction made the turn to accelerated industrialization, it increased the prices of industrial consumers goods through extremely high indirect taxes. While in 1928, the tax on turnover was not above 17.9% of the real turnover of retail trade, it rose to 78.1% in 1932, and in 1936, the nominal turnover of this trade was 107 billion rubles, of which taxes accounted for 66 billion rubles and the real turnover only 41 billion! (L.H. Hubbard: *Trade and Distribution in the Soviet Union*).

289 Thus Milentiji Popovic, in an article entitled *Self-management and Planning*:
On the other hand, in the sector of expanded social reproduction, in perfecting the system of investment on the basis of the new relations, our results are less conclusive, although the first steps have been taken in this direction. The establishment of non-administrative relations, of economic relations, in this sphere, reverts quite simply to the establishment of credit-interest (!) relations, and to taking them as the basis ...
One must first of all counteract the contradiction which arises from the fact that the resources servicing social reproduction are deducted exclusively through administrative measures (taxes, duties, contributions) thus leaving free the organization of labour without the latter on the other hand becoming the 'proprietor;' the organization of labour evolves, in fact, into a unique system of credit in which these resources are at one and the same time 'theirs' and 'common' (article 11) ...
It is possible to avoid, on the other hand, having subjective and political considerations as the only ones to be taken into consideration at the time of the adoption of the decisions concerning investments. It goes without saying that this method cannot and must not ever be pushed to its final conclusion. But a system can be constructed in which the political decisions will bear on the general orientation of the political economy while the distribution of the means destined for investment is carried out in accordance with the credit mechanism, according to financial and material (!) criteria fixed with more or less precision. In operating in this way the process of expanded reproduction is likewise

'depoliticalised.' This 'depoliticalisation' is not absolute. It must be carried out to the degree that *bureaucratism must be deprived of its base in this sphere as in the others.*' (My emphasis – E.M.). – *Current Questions of Socialism*, No. 70, July–Sept. 1963, pp. 67–68.

290 This obviously does not apply to cases where raw materials, equipment, goods and sometimes even means of consumption are centrally distributed, becoming veritable hotbeds for germinating corrupted bureaucrats.

291 'Only the co-ordination of three elements, state planning, the market and Soviet democracy, can assure correct guidance of the economy of the epoch of transition and assure, not the removal of the imbalances in a few years (this is utopian), but their diminution and by that the simplification of the bases of the dictatorship the proletariat until the time when new victories of the revolution will widen the arena of socialist planning and reconstruct its system.' (Leon Trotsky: *The Soviet Economy in Danger.* Available in French in Tome I of *Ecrits 1928–1940*, p. 127, in English, in a different translation, see The Soviet Economy in Danger', *Militant*, 12 November 1932–7 January 1933.)

292 Certain Yugoslav authors take quite correct positions in this respect. See, for example, Dr. Radivoj Uvalic: 'While the open market can be widely utilized, it cannot be the sole or even the principle regulator of the socio-economic relations of a socialist country.' And again: 'The importance of the planned guidance of economic development under the conditions of socialism lies first of all in the possibility that is offered of considering profitability from the point of view of the economy as a whole and not from the point of view of each particular unit of the economy ... This is the case in all branches of high concentration of capital (?), such as the production of the means of production and raw materials, which could be never developed sufficiently on the basis of the accidental play of the market, with the rate of profit as the sole stimulate.' (In: *Socialist Thought and Practice,* No. 6, pp. 47 and 55).

Chile and Portugal in the 1970s: the left, nationalisations and 'workers' control' in the revolutionary processes

293 Salvador Allende, *Obras Escogidas (1970-1973)*, Barcelona: Editorial Crítica, 1989, p. 219. Also at <https://historiadeamericalatina.files.wordpress.com/2010/08/clase17_salvador-allende.pdf>.

294 Nacionalização da Banca – Grande Vitória do Povo', As Comissões Concelhias da Póvoa do Varzim e Vila do Conde do PCP, 14 March 1975, Documents of the Portuguese Communist Party at the Centro Documentação 25 de Abril.

295 The CUT was the only trade union federation in Chile in 1970.

296 Encarnación Lemua, *En Hamelin...La Transición Española más allá de la Fronte,* Oviedo: Septem Editores, 2011.

297 Fernando Rosas, *Pensamento e Acção Política. Portugal Século XX (1890-1976),* Lisboa: Editorial Notícias, 2004.

298 Philip Schmitter, *Corporatism and Public Policy in Authoritarian Portugal,* London: Sage Publications, 1975.

299 José da Silva Lopes, *A Economia Portuguesa desde 1960*, Lisboa: Gradiva, 1999.

300 Maurice Brinton, *The Bolsheviks and Workers' Control. The State and Counter-Revolution,* London: Solidarity, 1970.

301 Maurice Brinton, *The Bolsheviks and Workers' Control. The State and Counter-Revolution*, op. cit.
302 Ernest Mandel, *Workers' Control and Workers' Councils* (Spring 1973). In <www.marxists.org/archive/mandel/1973/xx/wcwc.html>
303 John Hammond, 'Worker Control in Portugal: The Revolution and Today'. In *Economic and Industrial Democracy*, London: Sage Publications, 1981, p. 415.
304 Maria de Lurdes Santos, Marinús Pires de Lima, Vítor Matias Ferreira, *O 25 de Abril e as Lutas Sociais nas Empresa,* Porto: Afrontamento, 1976, 3 volumes, pp. 49-50.
305 See the numerous documents of files and texts available on line: www.archivochile.com and Víctor Farias, *La izquierda chilena (1969-1973): documentos para el estudio de su línea estratégica*, Berlin: CEP, 6 tomos, 2000-2001.
306 *Programa de la Unidad Popular*, 17 de diciembre de 1969, Santiago (published online at <http://www.abacq.net/imagineria/frame5.htm>).
307 Hugo Cancino, *La problemática del poder popular en el proceso de la vía chilena al socialismo 1970-73*, Aarhus: Aarhus Universitet Press, 1988, p.135-132.
308 Maurice Brinton, *The Bolsheviks and Workers' Control. The State and Counter-Revolution*, op. cit.
309 Karl Marx, *The Civil War in France* (1871). In <www.marxists.org/archive/marx/works/1871/civil-war-france/index.htm>.
310 V. I. Lenin, On Worker's Control and the Nationalization of Industry, NL, Fredonia Books, 2002.
311 António Gramsci, 'Controle Operário', L'Ordine Nuovo de 10 de fevereiro de 1921. In <www.marxists.org/portugues/gramsci/1921/02/10.htm>.
312 Korsch cited in Luciano Martorano, *Conselhos e Democracia. Em busca da participação e da socialização*, São Paulo: Expressão Popular, 2011, p. 32.
313 Leon Trotsky, 'Workers Control of Production', letter to a group of German Left Oppositionists, August 1931.In <www.marxists.org/archive/trotsky/germany/1931/310820.htm>.
314 Anton Pannekoek, *Workers' Councils,* Oakland: AK Press, 2003.
315 See Adler regarding the work of synthesis of workers' control theory resented by Luciano Martorano, *Conselhos e Democracia. Em busca da participação e da socialização*, São Paulo: Expressão Popular, 2011.
316 Marx, *The Civil War in France* (1871), in <www.marxists.org/archive/marx/works/1871/civil-war-france/index.htm>.
317 António Gramsci, 'Controle Operário', *L'Ordine Nuovo*, Op. Cit.
318 Leon Trotsky, 'Workers Control of Production', Op. Cit.
319 V. I. Lenin, *On Worker's Control and the Nationalization of Industry*, NL, Fredonia Books, 2002.
320 Anton Pannekoek, *Workers' Councils*, Op Cit.
321 Korsch, cited in Luciano Martorano, *Conselhos e Democracia. Em busca da participação e da socialização*, Op. Cit., p. 32.
322 The concrete case of the participation in the social security system is for example mentioned.
323 *Programa de la Unidad Popular*, 17 de diciembre de 1969, Op. Cit.
324 Fernando Castillo, Jorge Larrain, Rafael Echeverría, 'Las masas, el Estado y el problema del poder en Chile', *Cuadernos de le Realidad Nacional*, Santiago, 1973, pp. 3-70.

325 J. G. Espinoza, A. S. Zimbalist, *Economic Democracy: workers' participation in Chilean industry 1970-1973*, London: Academic Press, 1978.
326 *Punto Final*, Santiago, 12 octobre 1971.
327 Peter Kornbluth, *Los EEUU y el derrocamiento de Allende: Una historia desclasificada*, Barcelona: Ediciones B Chile, 2003.
Consult also the website of the University of Washington: <www.gwu.edu/~nsarchiv/latin_america/chile.htm>, which displays the whole of the declassified files of the Department of State of the US about this issue.
328 Allende could took into office with only 36.3% of the votes, partly thanks to the division of the opposition between the Christian-Democratic center and the Right (National Renewal): we find here the division, called the 'three thirds', that marks the Chilean political system up to 1973 (M. N. Sarget, *Histoire du Chili de la conquête à nos jours*, Paris, Harmattan, 1996).
329 J. G. Espinoza, A. S. Zimbalist, *Economic Democracy: workers' participation in Chilean industry 1970-1973*, Op. Cit.
330 Eduardo Novoa, 'L'utilisation de la loi sous le gouvernement Allende' in Jorge Maghasich, *Chili, un pays laboratoire*, Bruxelles: Maison de l'Amérique Latine, 1998, pp. 11-24.
331 Fernando Mires, 'Les contradictions de l'Unité populaire' in José Del Pozo and André Jacob (ed.), *La Chili de 1970 à 1990. De l'Unité populaire à l'après Pinochet,* Montréal: VLB éditeur, 1994, pp. 31-48.
332 Héctor Vega Tapia, 'L'économie du populisme et le projet de passage au socialisme proposé par l'Unité populaire', Université Aix-Marseille II, Thèse d'Etat en économie, 1981.
333 Patricio Guzmán, *The Battle of Chile*, Chile-Cuba, El Equipo Tercer Año/ICAIC, 1975–9, 315 mins.
334 Mariana Ferreira Gomes Stelko, *Entreprises sous la responsabilité de l'Etat au Chili 1970-1973: un regard sur la participation des travailleurs*, Paris: Mémoire de recherche, CNAM, 2010.
335 The '*Contraloria*' is officially charged of controlling the accounts of the State, but also the functionaries and the legality of the measures of the Executive. During all the period, it acted as a stronghold of the opposition, and, moreover, systematically hindered the government's reforms that touched the private property of the means of production.
336 Manuel Castells, *La lucha de clases en Chile*, Buenos Aires: Siglo 21 Editores, 1974; Augusto Samaniego, 'Los limites de la Estrategia de la Unidad Popular y el Área de propiedad Social', *Contribuciones Científicas y Tecnológicas*, Santiago, no. 109, 1995, p. 21-35.
337 In 1981, the name was changed to *Empresa Pública das Águas Livres* (Public Free Waters Company) and in 1991, to *Empresa Portuguesa das Águas Livres* (Portuguese Free Waters Company) which it bears to this day.
338 José de Medeiros Ferreira, *Portugal em Transe (1974-1985)*. In José Mattoso (ed.), *História de Portugal,* Lisboa: Círculo de Leitores, 1993, p. 114.
339 Journal *Diário Popular*, 15 de março de 1975, pp. 9 e 11.
340 José da Silva Lopes, *A Economia Portuguesa desde 1960*, Lisboa: Gradiva, 1999, p. 310.
341 Ibid., pp. 314-315.
342 José de Medeiros Ferreira, *Portugal em Transe (1974-1985),* Op. Cit., p. 116.
343 José da Silva Lopes, *A Economia Portuguesa desde 1960*, Op. Cit., p. 316.

344 José de Medeiros Ferreira, *Portugal em Transe (1974-1985),* Op. Cit.
345 Martha Harnecker, Faride Zeran, 'Empresa de Trabajadores: un análisis de fondo', *Chile Hoy,* nos. 1 & 2, 1972, Santiago.
346 Document approved on 7 December, 1971: *Normas básicas de participación de los trabajadores en la dirección del área social y mixta,* Santiago: Publicación del Dpto. Educación y Cultura de la CUT, 1972.
347 See our book of oral history: Franck Gaudichaud, *Poder popular y cordones industriales, Testimonios sobre el Movimiento Popular Urbano, 1970-1973,* Santiago: Lom Ediciones, 2004.
348 Peter Winn, *Weavers of revolution, the YARUR workers and chile's road to socialism,* New York/Oxford: Oxford University Press, 1986.
349 See the survey by Michel Raptis, carried out in 1971-1972: *Quel socialisme au Chili – Etatisme ou autogestion – dossier de la participation des travailleurs au processus révolutionnaire du pays,* Paris: Antropos, 1973.
350 Salvador Allende, 'Párrafos del discurso en el 1 de mayo', *Central Única,* Santiago, June, 1971.
351 ODEPLAN, *Informe económico anual 1971,* Santiago, Ed. Universitaria, 1972, p. 77.
352 Luis Figueroa was one of the main trade-union leaders of the CP and was president of the CUT from 1965 to 1973. He was Labour Minister under Allende from November 1972 to July 1973.
353 Luis Figueroa, 'La renta nacional tanto aquí como en la URSS se aumenta en base a una mayor producción', *Central Única,* Santiago, 2 (1971).
354 Luis Figueroa, 'Producir y estudiar', *Central Única,* Santiago, 4, 1971.
355 Luis Barria, 'La participación de los trabajadores', *Principios,* Santiago, 1972, pp. 87-88.
356 The newspaper of the MIR, *El Rebelde,* returned regularly to this issue.
357 Henry Lefebvre, *De L'Etat. Le mode de production étatique,* Paris, Collection 10/18, 1977, tome 3, p. 333.
358 Franck Gaudichaud, 'Chile. A broken collective memory in Memory and Popular culture', *Latin American Perspectives,* no.36, vol. 5, 2006, Riverside CA.
359 For a detailed analysis of this process we refer to our Ph.D thesis (under the guidance of M. Löwy): 'Étude sur la dynamique du mouvement social urbain chilien' Pouvoir populaire' et cordons industriels durant le gouvernement de Salvador Allende (1970-1973)', Paris: Paris 8, Thèse en Science Politique, 2005. Translation and publishing in English: *Chilean popular unity 1970-73. One thousand days that shook the world,* Leiden: Brill, forthcoming.
360 Luis Cruz Salas, 'Estado, partidos y movimiento obrero'. In Luis Vitale (ed.), *Para recuperar la memoria histórica. Frei, Allende, Pinochet,* Santiago: Ed. ChileAmerica – CESOC, 1999, pp. 411-412.
361 Sydney Tarrow, *Power in Movement. Social Movements, Collective Action and Politics,* Cambridge: Cambridge University Press, 1994.
362 E.P Thompson, *The Making of the English Working Class,* London: Harmondsworth/ Penguin, 1968.
363 Franck Gaudichaud, '¿Construyendo poder popular? El movimiento sindical chileno en el periodo de la Unidad Popular'. In Julio Pinto (ed.), *Y hicimos historia. La historia de la Unidad Popular,* Santiago: Lom Ediciones, 2005, pp. 81-106.
364 See the statement of the Cordon Vicuña Mackenna in *Tarea Urgente,* Santiago: 1, 1973.
365 Luis Corvalán, *El Gobierno de Salvador Allende,* Santiago: Lom Edciones, 2003.

366 Fátima Patriarca, 'Controlo Operário em Portugal (I)', *Análise Social*, Lisboa, ICS, Vol. XII (3), no. 47, 1976, pp.1056-1057.
367 Fátima Patriarca, 'Controlo Operário em Portugal (I)', *Análise Social*, Op. Cit., pp. 765-816.
368 Raquel Varela, *A História do CPP na Revolução dos Cravos*, Lisboa: Bertrand, 2011.
369 Comissão Coordenadora das Empresas em Autogestão, *A Realidade da Autogestão em Portugal*, Lisboa: Perspectivas e Realidades, s/d.
370 Eugénio Rosa, *A Economia Portuguesa em Números*, Lisboa: Moraes Editora, 1975.
371 *Avante!*, Serie VII, 22 de maio de 1975, p. 4.
372 *Avante!*, Serie VII, 22 de maio de 1975, p. 1.
373 *Avante!*, Serie VII, 22 de maio de 1975, p. 6.
374 *Avante!*, Serie VII, 19 de junho de 1975, p. 6.
375 Eugénio Rosa, *A Economia Portuguesa em Números*, Lisboa: Moraes Editora, 1975.
376 *Avante!*, Serie VII, 3 de julho de 1975, p. 4.
377 *Diário de Lisboa*, 12 de maio de 1975, pp. 1 and 20.
378 *Avante!*, Serie VII, 26 de junho de 1975, p. 9.
379 Speech by Vasco Gonçalves on May Day 1975, <www1.ci.uc.pt/cd25a/wikka.-hp?wakka=poderpol01>.

Latin America: state, popular power and class struggle

380 See bibliography at the end of the chapter for this and other similar references in the text.
381 See dossier 'Changer le monde sans prendre le pouvoir ? Nouveaux libertaires, nouveaux communistes', *ContreTemps,* February 2003.
382 Antoine Artous, *Marx, l'État et la politique*, Paris: Syllepse, 1999.
383 Michael Löwy, Écosocialisme: L'alternative radicale à la catastrophe écologique capitaliste, Paris: Mille et Une Nuits, 2011.

Eastern Europe: revisiting the ambiguous revolutions of 1989

384 Timothy Garton Ash, *The Guardian*, 4 November 2009, '1989 changed the world. But where now for Europe?' <https://www.theguardian.com/commentisfree/2009/nov/04/1989-changed-the-world-europe>.
385 Timothy Garton Ash, *We the People*, London: Penguin, 1993.
386 '1989: year of revolutions', *The Guardian*, November 2009, <http://www.guardian.co.uk/commentisfree/series/1989-year-of-revolutions>
387 The gap between that historical experience and the socialist goals have led to three kinds of concepts: the characterisation of the bureaucracy of the state-party as a bourgeoisie leading a 'state capitalist' society as a new class in a system not foreseen by Marx; or as an impure 'caste' having kept historical links with the workers movements and anti-capitalist revolutions, but blocking the socialist evolution of the regimes from which they were taking their privileges. I feel closer to that third approach. I have contributed to those debates elsewhere. Read for instance my presentation of Ernest Mandel's analysis of Socialism and of Soviet Union in opposition with 'state capitalist' kind of approaches, or my comparative analysis of the process of capitalist restoration in the Serbian 'transition' on my website <http://csamary.free.fr>.

388 I have developed such analysis in 'The social stake of the Great transformation in the East', *Debatte*, Journal of contemporary Central and Eastern Europe, vol. 17, April 2009, pp 1-39.
389 Leon Trotsky, *The Revolution Betrayed – What is the Soviet Union and where is it going*, New York: Doubleday, Doran & Co., 1937.
390 Examples of rich and complex analysis have been Jean-Marie Chauvier *URSS: Une société en mouvement*, Paris: Editions De l'Aube, 1988; or the thesis of Myriam Désert, *Le contremaître soviétique sur le front du travail, aspects organisationnels, idéologiques et sociaux*, 1986, on the specific position of the foreman within social relationships in the factories; or the different analysis produced or directed by Sandrine Kott, e.g. *Le communisme au quotidien. Les entreprises d'Etat dans la société est-allemande (1949-1989)*, Paris/Berlin, Collection socio-histoire, 2001.
391 Very interesting studies begin to appear about these conflicts of memories and of interpretations of '1989'. Read Jérôme Heurtaux & Cédric Pellen, *1989 à l'Est de l'Europe, une mémoire controversée*, Paris: Editions De L'Aube, 2009.
392 Articles have commented on the content of the newly opened archives about Gorbatchev's view and conversations with Margaret Thatcher on the Berlin Wall and her opposition to the German unification. Read for instance Michael Binyon, 'Thatcher told Gorbachev Britain did not want German unification', *The Times*, 11 September 2009, < https://www.margaretthatcher.org/document/112006>. Comments on Anatoli Tchernaieev's diary about his conversations with Gorbatchev, Mitterand's position and the 'Paris Charter' are also presented in <http://www.horizons-et-debats.ch/index.php?id=684>
393 One can find analyses I wrote about the Yugoslav crisis, NATO's intervention in Kosovo, and the world order and especially Balkan instability on my website <http//:csamary.free.fr>.
394 Yugoslavia was supposed to become again a kingdom, while the Serbian Monarchy found refuge in Great Britain and was supported by the Serbian nationalist (and anti-Communist) Chetnik resistance. The Yugoslav Communists (who had been repressed and prohibited under the first Serbian kingdom which ruled the first Yugoslavia between the two world wars) succeeded in gaining a deep legitimacy in the resistance both to fascism and to nationalist projects, while recognizing all nations in the federal project they build in the war. The meeting, during the war and against any future Kingdom, of the Assembly of delegates of National Liberation Committees from all nations (AVNOJ) in 1943 gave the real democratic legitimacy to a new Republican and federal project. The 'excommunication' of the new Yugoslav regime by Stalin in 1948 was essentially because it escaped the Kremlin's control and was popular in the whole region. Read the articles on Yugoslavia in note 10.
395 *Le Figaro*, 30 October 2009 – interview with Vaclav Havel [my translation – CS].
396 Anna Spysz, *Panic! on the Streets of Prague*, <http://www.prague-life.com/prague/velvet-revolution>.
397 On the role of the former elites in the capitalist transformation, read, Eyal G., Szelenyi I. & Townsley E. *Making Capitalism without Capitalists – The New Ruling Elites in Eastern Europe*, London/New York: Verso, 1998. Read also Georges Mink & Jean-Charles Szurek *Démocratie et capitalisme, le rôle des anciennes élites dans la transformation post-capitaliste*, Diogène, 2001-2, n°194, Paris, PUF.

398 *Die Linke* was founded in 2007 as the merger of the Party of Democratic Socialism (PDS) and the Electoral Alternative for Labour and Social Justice (WASG). The party won 8.6% of the vote in the 2013 federal elections with an initial particular support coming from pensioners and unemployed in Eastern Länder. Later on, it increased its influence in Western Länder, and is divided by important debates (about social issues , refugees and alliances, reflected in shifts in its implantation.

399 See note 2.

400 Jarosz Maria, *Ten years of direct privatisation*, Warsaw: Institute of political studies, 2000.

401 Jacques Sapir, *Les économistes contre la démocratie − Pouvoir, mondialisation et démocratie*, Paris: Albin Michel, 2002.

402 Szalai E., *Post-socialism and Globalization*, Budapest: Istvan Nemeth, 1999; Gorzelak G., Ehrlich E., Faltan L. & Illner M. (eds._, *Central Europe in Transition: Towards EU Membership*, Regional Studies Association, Polish Section, Warsaw: Scholar, 2001; Drweski B., 'Du Parti 'ouvrier' à la 'gauche démocratique' − Les métamorphoses d'un parti de pouvoir polonais (1989-2001)', in J.-M. de Waele, éd., *Partis politiques et démocratie en Europe centrale et orientale*, pp. 71-83, Université de Bruxelles, 2002, coll. 'Sociologie politique'.

403 These differences have been eroded under the pressure of international and European institutions (especially after its integration in the EU in 2004), but also because of different scandals of clientelism and corruption, in the process of privatisation, like elsewhere.

404 See note 14, Eyal et al. Read also Kornai J., *La transformation économique postsocialiste − dilemmes et decisions*, B. Chavance et M. Vahabi (eds.), Paris: Éditions de la Maison des Sciences de l'Homme, 2001.

405 The dominant weight of agriculture in China is a major difference with Eastern Europe and the USSR, where it was between 10 per cent and 30 per cent of GDP at the end of the 1970s. But as far as the industrial privatisation is concerned, the crucial difference has been that China was not under the pressure neither of IMF nor of European institutions to make its choices, without dismantling public credits and central control on currency to implement its own (capitalist) state priorities in favour of Chinese public firms. Our study here is mainly based on Eastern Europe.

406 What we call the first phase of the systemic transformation corresponds to the initial 'systemic crisis' with sharp falls in all branches. It was absolutely generalised after 1989 and lasted several years. But its end (or the beginning of a growth incorrectly called 'recovery) was slightly different from one country (or set of countries in a similar position) to another. This recovery began in general in the mid-1990s for the countries of Central and Eastern Europe which became EU's 'New Member States' in 2004, and later for others (see further on that point).

407 Bruni de la Motte, 'East Germans lost much in 1989', *The Guardian*, 8 November 2009, <http://www.guardian.co.uk/commentisfree/2009/nov/08/1989-berlin-wall/print>.

408 For such alternative view of those events read the interview the former East German opponent to the Honecker regime Bernd Gehrke: <http://www.europe-solidaire.org/spip.php?article15475>.

409 World Bank, Regional Overview, Challenges, 2002, <http://Inweb18.worldbank.org> and the report: *Transition − the First Ten Years, Analysis and Lessons for Eastern Europe and the Former Soviet Union*, Washington DC, The World Bank, 2002.

410 From the European Bank of Reconstruction and Development statistics

411 Read Catherine Samary, 'Towards a social and banking tsunami in East/West Europe', April 2009, <http://www.europe-solidaire.org/spip.php?article13710>. The financial dimension of such a tsunami has been avoided by the 'Vienna Intiative' involving in 2009 all international, European and dominant national financial institutions. A 'Vienna Initiative 2' was needed in 2011, and a 'Steering Committee' is still functioning. See <http://vienna-initiative.com/>

412 *Financial Times*, 2 November 2009, 'EBRD – European Bank for Reconstruction and Development – cautions on currency debt'.

413 *Le Monde*, 7 November 2009, 'Derrière le Mur, les peuples ne rêvaient pas de capitalisme'. An English version was published by the *New York Times* on 9 November 2009.

414 <http://www.prague-life.com/prague/velvet-revolution>. One can read on that website descriptions of those events.

415 About the conflicts between the Yugoslav Revolution and then the Titoist regime and Stalin, one must read Milovan Djilas books or Vladimir Dedijer 's biography of Tito. The polemics with Moscow and documents of the Yugoslav CP congress in 1948 have been published in *Le Livre Yougoslave*, Paris, 1949. On the Khrushchev's excuses about the excommunication, read *La réconciliation soviéto-yougoslave 1954-1958 – Illusions et désillusions de Tito*, Pierre Maurer, Fribourg: Editions DelVal, 1991.

416 The documents of the Gdansk strikes in August 1980 have been published in a special issue of *L'Aternative*, Paris: Maspero, 1980. The whole programme of the Gdansk Congress in September 1981 was printed in 1982: *Le programme de Solidarność au congrès de Gdansk en 1981*, Lille: Presse Universitaire de Lille, 1982.

417 I was myself sent as an observer for my trade union – the Snesup (National trade union of lecturers in higher education).

418 Wikipedia the Free Encyclopedia – Solidarity Polish trade union (last edited on 28 December 2017, at 09:18.)

419 <http://fr.wikipedia.org/wiki/Solidarność>

420 Information about the struggles and the Polish trade unions can be found in the article by Cyril Smuga, *Inprecor,* 518.6 (2006), which is available in its entirety in the online archives of this journal, <http://inprecor.fr>.

421 In an interview published in *Contretemps* in 2008 for the anniversary of 1968 <http://www.contretemps.eu/wp-content/uploads/Contretemps%2022.pdf>, Karol Modzelevski stressed the discontinuities between Balcerowicz plan of privatisation in 1989 and Solidarność's demands for a 'self-managed Republic' with workers fundamental rights in 1980-1981: as an 'expert' involved in that movement and in continuity with the *Open letter to the Party* he co-wrote in 1964 with Y. Kuron, he stressed (my translation-CS) that after Jaruzelski coup and repression there was no more in 1989 'the pressure of equalitarian and collective currents defining the first Solidarność, which was broadly a child of socialism'.

422 Ota Šik was the economist whose projects of reforms had been backed by the Dubček wing in the CPC. The main difference between those reforms (like the Hungarian one under the Kadar regime in the 1960s) and those referring to 'self-management' was the rights of management given to the workers. I compared the different Yugoslav and East European reforms of the 1950s and 1960s in *Plan, market and democracy – the experience of the so-called socialist countries*, Notebook no. 7/8, 1992, IIRE, Amsterdam.

423 Read Vladimir-Claude Fišera, professor of contemporary history, who wrote with Jean-Pierre Faye *Prague. La révolution des conseils ouvriers 1968-1969*, Paris: Robert Laffon, 1978. Read also his article '1968: le printemps et l'automne autogestionnaires de Prague', *Self-management in the Prague's Spring and Autumn,* <http///www.alternativelibertaire. org>.
424 *Literarny Noviny*, no. 52/1, 27 December 2007, Milan Kundera 'Česky udel' (the Czech destiny) and Vaclav Havel, same title but with a question mark: 'The Czech destiny?'
425 Jacques Rupnik, *Les deux printemps de 1968*, [The two Springs of 1968], Paris: Etudes du CERI, Sciences-Po, 2008.
426 Jaroslav Šabata died in 2012. Milan Kundera's views were produced in *Listy* N°6, December 2007, and quoted by Vladimir Claude Fišera in '1968, the self-managed spring and autumn in Prague', <http//:alternativelibertaire.org>.
427 The positions taken by the different CPs was either to condemn the Soviet intervention (the Yugoslav, Albanian, or Romanian CPs – but then supporting in fact at best, the kind of Dubček reforms and realism') or to be involved in the Warsaw troops. But no one did popularise and support the workers councils: only Trotskyist or anarchist currents did, which were marginal forces at that time. The Titoist regime was at that very same moment repressing its own left Marxist current and youth organisations for going 'too far' in self-organisation. I wrote in the review *Contretemps*, May 2008, an analysis of the specific conflicts occurring in 1968 within a system where self-management was officially introduced in 1950 after the break with Stalin, and several times reformed to channel tensions.

The struggles for the commons in the Balkans

428 After this text was published, new struggles erupted which are analysed by Igor Stiks and Srecko Horvat (<https://www.opendemocracy.net/can-europe-make-it/igor-%C5%A1tiks-sre%C4%87ko-horvat/new-balkan-revolts-from-protests-to-plenums-and-beyond>). Read also *Radical politics in then Desert of Transition,* by Igor Stiks and Srecko Horvat, London: Verso, 2015. The political and social situation has deteriorated since then, producing a massive exodus, in particular of young, qualified and politicised citizen. Without transnational (European) links and the building of an alternative European strategy, many struggles for the Commons in the Balkans encounter major difficulties (read Catherine Samary <http://www.cadtm.org/Europe-No-LEXIT-without-Another>). These struggles should be supported and extended in a collective and internationalist way: that is the message of this text.

Feminism and the politics of the Commons

429 Marie Mies and Veronika Bennholdt-Thomsen, *The Subsistence Perspective: Beyond the Globalized Economy*, London: Zed Books, 1999.
430 Peter Linebaugh, *The Magna Carta Manifesto*, Oakland: University of California Press, 2008.
431 A key source on the politics of the commons and its theoretical foundations is the UK-based electronic journal *The Commoner*, now entering its fourteenth year of publication <www. commoner. org.uk>.
432 A case in point is the struggle that is taking place in many communities in Maine against Nestle's appropriation of Maine's waters to bottle Portland Spring. Nestlé's theft has

made people aware of the vital importance of these waters and the supporting aquifers and has truly reconstituted them as a common (*Food and Water Watch Fact Sheet*, July 2009). Food and Water Watch is a (self-described) 'non-profit organization that works to ensure clean water and safe food in the United States and around the world.'

433   An excellent site for current debates on the commons is the recently published issue of the UK based movement journal *Turbulence. Ideas For Movement,* 5 December 2009, <www.turbulence.org.uk>.

434   For more on this subject, see the important article 'Who Pays for the Kyoto Protocol?' by Ana Isla, in which the author describes how the conservation of biodiversity has provided the World Bank and other international agencies with the pretext to enclose rain forests on the ground that they represent 'carbon sinks' and 'oxygen generators.' In Salleh, 2009.

435   The United Nations Convention on the Law of the Sea, adopted in November 1994, establishes a 200-mile offshore limit, defining an Exclusive Economic Zone in which nations can exploit, manage, and protect the resources it contains, from fisheries to natural gas. It also regulates deep-sea mining and the use of the resulting revenues. On the development of the concept of the 'common heritage of mankind' in United Nations debate see Susan J. Buck, *The Global Commons. An Introduction,* Washington DC: Island Press1998.

436   As described by Wikipedia, Ostrom's work focuses on common pool resources and 'emphasizes how humans interact with ecosystems to maintain long-term sustainable resource yields.' *Wikipedia,* 9 January 2010, p.1.

437   For more on this topic, see Calestous Juma and J.B. Ojwang eds., *In Land We Trust,* London, Zed Books, 1996, an early treatise on the effectiveness of communal property relations in the context of capitalist development and efforts.

438   David Bollier, *Silent Theft: The Private Plunder of Our Common Wealth.* New York/ London: Routledge, 2002: 36-39.

439   See Margarita Fernandez, 'Cultivating Community, Food and Empowerment,' project course paper, unpublished manuscript, 2003:23-6. An early, important work on urban gardens is Bill Weinberg and Peter Lamborn Wilson eds., *Avant Gardening: Ecological Struggle in the City & the World,* Brooklyn NY: Autonomedia, 1999.

440   The fishing commons of Maine are presently threatened with a new privatization policy justified in the name of preservation and ironically labelled 'catch shares.' This is a system, already applied in Canada and Alaska, whereby local governments set limits on the amount or fish that can be caught by allocating individual shares on the basis of the amount of fishing that boats have done in the past. This system has proven to be disastrous for small, independent fishermen who are soon forced to sell their share to the highest bidders. Protest against its implementation is now mounting in the fishing communities of Maine. See 'Cash Shares or Share-Croppers?' *Fishermen's Voice,* Vol. 14, No.12, December 2009.

441   It has been calculated, for example, that 33,000 litres of water and 15-19 tons of material are required just to produce a personal computer. (See Saral Sarkar, *Eco- Socialism or Eco- Capitalism?: A Critical Analysis of Humanity's Fundamental Choices,* London, Zed Books, 1999:126). Also see Elizabeth Dias, 'First Blood Diamonds, Now Blood Computers?' July 24, 2009. Dias cites claims made by Global Witness – an organization campaigning to prevent resource related conflicts – to the effect that the trade in the minerals at

the heart of the electronic industry feeds the civil war in the Democratic Republic of Congo.
442 Donald B. Freeman, 'Survival Strategy or Business Training Ground? The Significance of Urban Agriculture For the Advancement of Women in African Cities.' *African Studies Review,* Vol.36, N.3 (December 1993), pp. 1-22. Federici 2008a.
443 Shiva 1989, 1991:102-117, 274.
444 I owe this information to Ousseina Alidou, Director of the Center for African Studies at Rutgers University (NJ).
445 Fisher 1993, Andreas 1985.
446 Anderson 1998, Depastino 2003, Caffentzis 2006.
447 Boxcar Bertha (1972) is Martin Scorsese's adaptation of Ben Reitman's *Sister of the Road*, 'the fictionalized autobiography of radical and transient Bertha Thompson.' (Wikipedia).

Decolonial communism: Analytical, political and democratic dimensions

448 *Catalyst,* <https://catalyst-journal.com/about>.
449 'Feminism and the politics of the commons', reproduced in this book in the section 'Summing up and further debates' of this book.
450 See contributions in the section 'Summing up and further debates'.
451 Soma Marik, *Revolutionary Democracy: Emancipation in Classical Marxism*, Chicago: Haymarket Books, 2018.
452 We have stressed the theoretical and practical distinctions and the possible updating of debates on this issue, both in the section 'General outlook' of this book, and in the chapter on 'Plan, market and democracy: The experience of so-called socialist countries'.
453 Michael A. Lebowitz, *Beyond Capital: Marx's Political Economy of the Working Class*, London: Palgrave Macmillan, revised edition, 2003.
454 These issues have been discussed in the debate opposing Alec Nove, who argued for a 'market socialism' as the only 'feasible' one, and Ernest Mandel, who defended democratic planning. This discussion was held in several issues of the *New Left Review* in 1987 and 1988. Read also Diane Elson, <https://newleftreview.org/I/172/diane-elson-market-socialism-or-socialization-of-the-market>; Michael Lebowitz, 'What is Socialism for the 21st Century', *Monthly Review*, October 2016: <https://monthlyreview.org/2016/10/01/what-is-socialism-for-the-twenty-first-century>.
455 Read also Darko Suvin's text on Boris Kidrič (Yugoslav minister of cconomics at the beginning of the 1950s), who was close to such concepts combined with self-management: <https://darkosuvin.com/tag/boris-kidric/>.
456 Darko Suvin describes himself as a 'Yugoslav' epistemologist. He has a deep interest in science fiction literature, and is a Marxist whose approach is close to that of Ernst Bloch and Bertolt Brecht. Born in 1930, he joined the Communist Youth at the end of the war at the age of 15. During the Titoist period he studied and then taught literature at Zagreb University. In the mid-1960s he won a grant to pursue his studies in the USA, and later became a professor at McGill University in Canada. See his blog <https://darkosuvin.com/> and download his papers at <https://independent.academia.edu/DarkoSuvin/Papers>.

457 Darko Suvin, *Splendour, Misery, and Possibilities: An X-ray of Socialist Yugoslavia*, Chicago: Haymarket Books, 2018. Read my review of his book 'A utopian in the Balkans', *New Left Review*, Nov/Dec 2018. Quotations here are from his theses, which can be read at <https://www.academia.edu/34695145/BERLIN_THESES_ON_S.F.R._YUGOSLAVIA_2014-16_10_100_words_.pdf>.

458 The Titoist leaders considered that the *Praxis* 'Belgrade 8' professors influenced the independent student movement in June 1968, and they were forbidden to teach. We reproduce, in the section 'The Yugoslav experience' of this book, texts which give an idea of what they wrote about the Yugoslav self-management crisis at the time. In the same period, the nationalist dimension of the 'Croatian Spring' in 1971 was criticised by the Croatian *Praxis* scholars. The Titoist leaders considered them less dangerous then the nationalist current, which is why they were not expelled from Zagreb University. Nevertheless, the review *Praxis* and the summer school were de facto banned in 1974. The later evolution of Praxis has been analysed in <https://www.jacobinmag.com/2018/06/yugoslavia-praxis-journal-tito-marxism-socialism>.

459 Susan Woodward, *Socialist Unemployment: The Political Economy of Yugoslavia, 1945-1990*, Princeton NJ: Princeton University Press, 1995.

460 See 'Cuba in 1968' by Samuel Farber, *The Jacobin*, <https://www.jacobinmag.com/2018/04/cuba-1968-fidel-castro-revolution-repression>.

461 These conflicting dialectics, between social movements and diverse left political parties in various contexts, are illustrated in the chapters in this book by Samuel Farber, Raquel Varela and Frank Gaudichaud.

462 Read Michael Löwy, *The Politics of Combined and Uneven Development: The Permanent Revolution*, Chicago: Haymarket, 2010.

463 Read 'Revolution decentered: Two studies on Lenin', in *ViewPoint Magazine*, 1 February 2018. <https://www.viewpointmag.com/2018/02/01/revolution-decent>.

464 The (retrospective) extension I give here to 'decolonial' theories and political orientation does not come from 'within' decolonial studies (in particular those led by Ramon Grosfoguel in Latin America). Neither is it directly linked to the debate between British Marxists and postcolonial studies around 'deprovincialising Europe'. It would not be my competence and aim to present here those studies and debates – in particular within the French context (see Capucine Boidin's presentation https://journals.openedition.org/cal/1620). But my approach and knowledge of these debates comes from my political and practical commitment within internationalist currents and 'political anti-racism' de facto linked to these stakes.

465 Read Cinzia Arruzza, *Dangerous Liaisons: The Marriages and Divorces of Marxism and Feminism*, London: Resistance Books and Merlin Press, 2013, and the last part published as a reworked article in October 2016 <https://www.contretemps.eu/union-queer-marxisme-feminisme/#_ftnref1>.

466 Read in particular in *New Left Review* I/96, March-April 1976, <https://newleftreview.org/I/96/michael-lowy-marxists-and-the-national-question>.

467 During the Titoist phase, debates about the national question were avoided. Within the crisis, the Croatian *Praxis* philosophers maintained a radical opposition to Croatian nationalism, while a broad part of the *Praxis* Serbian component turned towards a reinterpretation of the past and present Yugoslavia against Titoist concepts and defended a new centralised Serb-dominated Yugoslavia close to the first one. An evaluation of the *Praxis* orientation and crisis can be read on <https://jacobinmag.com/2018/06/

yugoslavia-praxis-journal-tito-marxism-socialism>. One can read my interpretation of the different responsibilities in that crisis on <http://www.internationalviewpoint.org/spip.php?article1093>.

468 'Existing is existing politically' used to say the Algerian sociologist Abdelmalek Sayad, *The Suffering of the Immigrant*, Oxford: First Polity Press, 2004.
469 *Catalyst*, <https://catalyst-journal.com/about>.
470 *Catalyst,* <https://catalyst-journal.com/vol1/no1/editorial-robert-brenner>.
471 His contribution, 'Morbid symptoms: What did Gramsci mean and how does it apply to our time?', was published in *International Socialist Review.* <https://isreview.org/issue/108/morbid-symptoms>.
472 Gilbert Achcar, *The Clash of Barbarisms: The Making of the New World Disorder* (2nd augmented edition) London: Saqi Books, 2006.
473 The notion 'state racism' referred in France to police violence and post-colonial laws or official discourses. It is to be distinguished from the notion of a 'racist state' where discrimination is legalised.
474 One of the most active organisations in this field has been the PIR (Parti des Indigènes de la République), with its leading figure Houria Bouteldja, which was involved in the preparation of the 'North Bandung'.
475 Its 'Declaration' can be read at <http://bandungdunord.webflow.io/en>.
476 Read <https://katz.lahaine.org/imperialism-and-dependency-similarities-and-differences/>.
477 One can listen to Nancy Fraser analysing this at <https://socialistproject.ca/leftstreamed-video/feminism-marxism/>. Read also Nancy Fraser <https://newleftreview.org/II/56/nancy-fraser-feminism-capitalism-and-the-cunninof-history>.
478 <https://socialistregister.com/index.php/srv/article/view/5811/2707>.
479 Glen Sean Coulthard, *Red Skin, White Masks: Rejecting the Colonial Politics of Recognition,* Minneapolis MN: University of Minnesota, 2014. I discovered this book at the Bandung of the North Conference bookshop.

About Resistance Books and the IIRE

Resistance Books

Resistance Books is the publishing arm of Socialist Resistance. We publish books independently, and also jointly with Merlin Press (London) and the International Institute for Research and Education (Amsterdam). Further information about Resistance Books, including a full list of titles available and how to order them, can be obtained at www.resistancebooks.org.
To contact Resistance Books:
Email: info@resistancebooks.org;
Website: www.resistancebooks.org;
Post: Resistance Books, PO Box 62732, London, SW2 9GQ.

Socialist Resistance is a revolutionary Marxist, internationalist, ecosocialist and feminist political network. Analysis and news from Socialist Resistance can be read online at www.socialistresistance.org.
To contact Socialist Resistance:
Email contact@socialistresistance.org;
Website: www.socialistresistance.org;
Post: Socialist Resistance, PO Box 62732, London, SW2 9GQ.

Socialist Resistance collaborates with the Fourth International, whose online magazine, *International Viewpoint*, can be viewed at www.internationalviewpoint.org.

The International Institute for Research and Education

The IIRE is a centre for the development of critical thought and the exchange of experiences and ideas between people engaged in their struggles. Since 1982, when the Institute opened in Amsterdam, its main activity has been the organisation of courses for progressive forces around the world. The seminars, courses and study groups deal with all subjects related to the emancipation of the oppressed and exploited around the world. It has welcomed participants from across the world, most of them from developing countries. The IIRE provides activists and academics opportunities for research and education in three locations: Amsterdam, Islamabad and Manila.

The IIRE publishes *Notebooks for Study and Research,* which focus on contemporary political debates, as well as themes of historical and theoretical importance. The *Notebooks* have appeared in several languages besides English and French. All the *Notebooks* are available by going to http://iire.org/en/resources/notebooks-for-study-and-research.html. Other publications and audio files of the events held at the IIRE are available in several languages and can be freely downloaded from www.iire.org.

To contact the International Institute for Research and Education:
Email: iire@iire.org;
Website: www.iire.org;
Phone: 00 31 20 671 7263;
Post: International Institute for Research and Education,
Lombokstraat 40, Amsterdam, 1094 AL, The Netherlands